It's a Crime

Women and Justice

It's a Crime
Women and Justice

Roslyn Muraskin
Long Island University

Ted Alleman
Pennsylvania State University

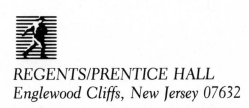

REGENTS/PRENTICE HALL
Englewood Cliffs, New Jersey 07632

Library of Congress Cataloging-in-Publication Data

It's a crime : women and justice / [Editors], Roslyn Muraskin, Ted
  Alleman.
      p.   cm.
  Includes bibliographical references.
    1. Female offenders—United States.   2. Women criminal justice personnel—
United States.   I. Muraskin, Roslyn.   II. Alleman, Ted.
HV6046.I86   1993   92-38141
364.3′74′0973—dc20   CIP

Acquisitions editor: Robin Baliszewski
Editorial/production supervision and interior design: WordCrafters
    Editorial Services, Inc.
Cover design: Marianne Franso
Prepress buyer: Ilene Levy
Manufacturing buyer: Ed O'Dougherty

Cover: "Undertow," 1986, by Richard Hull. Oil/wax on linen, 48″x36″
Courtesy Phyllis Kind Gallery, New York/Chicago

1993 by REGENTS/PRENTICE HALL
A Division of Simon & Schuster
Englewood Cliffs, New Jersey 07632

Printed in the United States of America

10 9 8 7 6 5 4 3 2 1

ISBN 0-13-962051-6

Prentice-Hall International (UK) Limited, *London*
Prentice-Hall of Australia Pty. Limited, *Sydney*
Prentice-Hall Canada Inc., *Toronto*
Prentice-Hall Hispanoamericana, S.A., *Mexico*
Prentice-Hall of India Private Limited, *New Delhi*
Prentice-Hall of Japan, Inc., *Tokyo*
Simon & Schuster Asia Pte. ltd., *Singapore*
Editora Prentice-Hall do Brasil, Ltda., *Rio de Janeiro*

To Our Parents
who gave us life,
and to our children,
who can bring about change.

Contents

Foreword

The era of modern scholarship may be assumed to coincide with the existence of universities. The first of these was the University of Bologna, a daughter of the Renaissance, founded in 1119. Eight hundred and seventy-three years have passed since then, and, during most of these years, scholarship produced no insight whatsoever on any aspect of the role of women in crime and justice. It was less than a century ago that the first scholarly book on female offenders appeared: Cesare Lombroso's *La Donna Delinquente* (1893). The following half-century produced only three additional works on the topic: W.I. Thomas's *Unadjusted Girl* (1923), Sheldon and Eleanor Glueck's *Five Hundred Delinquent Women* (1934), and Otto Pollack's *Criminality of Women* (1952). By contrast, over the last twenty years we have witnessed a flowering of interest, of concern, and of dedicated scholarship, focused on women as offenders, as victims, as justice officials, and as change agents. The books, essays, and dissertations on this topic, in many languages, and for many cultures, number in the thousands.

Rita Simon and I did not anticipate this avalanche of interest and response when, in 1975, we independently sought to make a contribution to criminological scholarship focused on what we perceived to be a subject that was consciously or unconsciously suppressed. Since then, the subject of women in crime and justice has undergone a rapid and significant metamorphosis. Initially, much of what was written on women in crime—and, later, in criminal justice—was viewed by some as subjective. Indeed, it had to be anticipated that the abuses and discrimination uncovered by scholars in the field would cause the disapproval and condemnation of those who learned of them. Thus, the literature of the 1970s reflected a fervor born out of frustration over apparent or perceived biases and neglect in the system. In this sense, all scholars are conditioned by the *Zeitgeist* of their era. Indeed, was not Lombroso a captive of the prejudices of his time, as much as he wanted to escape them by addressing a subject that had been taboo until then?

It was not until the decade of the 1980s that the subject of women and justice became a recognized area of concern in the increasing body of empirical research dealing with contemporary problems. Questions for researchers rose faster than they could be answered. How does current female criminality relate to historical stereotypes, to the present criminal justice system, and to future patterns of behavior? What are the effects of economic marginalization? How does the criminal justice system discriminate against women offenders, victims, and functionaries? What accounts for the differential treatment of male and female delinquents? Empirical research flourished. So, also, did feminist theoretical explanations.

At the American Society of Criminology meeting in 1975 (Toronto, Canada), one lone panel represented women and justice. Through the 1980s the number of papers presented grew above all expectation. At major scientific meetings convened in all parts of the world, women's issues were debated—and manuscripts began to make their way into major journals. That is not to say that the subject has fully "arrived." But it is well on its way.

The scholarly essays in this volume demonstrate my point. They reflect the broad range of contemporary issues that have captured the attention of criminologists as the body of knowledge on this relatively new subject matures. The new focus is on motherhood (voluntary or enforced), termination of pregnancy, fetal abuse, AIDS, spouse abuse, and a host of issues on which criminal justice was at best ambivalent and at worst discriminatorily punitive. Heretofore hidden issues surface in this volume's contributions on female imprisonment, the acceptance of women in policing and corrections, and the fear of crime among elderly women. After twenty years of scholarship, the field has also become ripe for inquiries into theory. And, three hundred years after the events, one of the essays investigates the penal scapegoating of women in New England, a forerunner of the marginalization of especially vulnerable women, an issue with which many of the other essays are also concerned.

Indeed, Roslyn Muraskin and Ted Allemen have developed a volume on women in crime and justice that is entirely novel, challenging, and scholarly. It comes at a time when nearly every university or college offers, or even mandates, courses on women's issues, including those on crime and justice. This volume brings into the classroom an exciting, new-era assembly of contributions by some of the country's most respected researchers in the field. I anticipate that the readers will derive as much pleasure and insight from the twenty-three creative contributions as I have. This book is bound to find an honored place in the scholarly literature on the role of women in crime and criminal justice. As for the students reading this book, may they carry its message into the twenty-first century.

Freda Adler
Distinguished Professor
Rutgers University

Preface

It's a Crime: Women and Justice is a comprehensive text with readings
on the subject of women and their involvement in the criminal justice
system. The book also addresses the experience of women as offenders
and working professionals in criminal justice.

The book is written to provide a means of studying and integrating the diversity of perspectives that exist in this very contemporary and provocative field of study. Section 1, "Varieties of
Feminist Thought and Their Application to the Study of Crime and
Criminal Justice," provides an overview of the variety of perspectives
on women's issues which students of the subject need to understand
today. Contained in this volume is a very useful descriptive typology
that emphasizes the diversity of feminist thought and serves to break
down common stereotypes of feminists as being of only one kind or
type.

The focus of the work is gender-based differences related to law
and justice. The book's themes center on a range of contemporary
issues. Section 2 deals with the historical development of women's
issues; Section 3 investigates the issues of women, drugs and AIDS;
Section 4 looks at women and policing; Section 5 studies women and
prisons; Section 6 examines the issues of abortion; Section 7 talks
about women as victims of violence; and Section 8 looks at the family.
Provocative subject overviews introduce each section and discussion
questions appear at the end of every section, enhancing the presentation of the individual chapters and aiding in effective study of the
material.

It's a Crime is written by scholars and practitioners in the field. This text deals with issues pertaining to women as well as those basic human rights that are fundamental to us all. We have done our utmost to provide relevant material concerning the gender-based problems in society. It is now up to you, the reader, to take this material and add your own personal concerns and perspectives. We anticipate that a combination of the issues and outlooks contained in this text combined with the concerns and perspectives of faculty and students alike will surely result in more meaningful and thought-provoking dialogue concerning the important problems of women and justice. We provide the raw material. It is now up to you to make it come alive.

Roslyn Muraskin and Ted Alleman

Acknowledgments

We wish to thank all of our contributors who wrote articles for this work of love. Each of our authors has presented a work which is provocative, original, and written from varying perspectives which emphasizes the struggles that women endure.

Tremendous thanks to Freda Adler for her Foreword as she looks back at the history of women from the days of the 1960s and the issues then and now. We also wish to extend our thanks to Elaine Congress from Fordham University; Elizabeth Grossi, a doctoral candidate at Indiana University of Pennsylvania; Linda Brenner Lengyel from Trenton State College; Susan Ross, a doctoral candidate in Speech Communcation at Penn State University; and Dora Schiro, Correctional Superintendent in St. Louis, Missouri, for their contributions and statements on women. Additional thanks to Tom Bernard, Rosemary Gido, and Sam Richards, all of Penn State University, for their comments and ideas.

Special thanks is extended to Tom Klevan of Penn State University, who painstakingly edited the manuscript for Chapter 1 and provided valuable source material for that chapter, "Varieties of Feminist Thought."

We extend our thanks to both the administration of the C.W. Post Campus of Long Island University and of the Penn State University for their continuous encouragement to work on projects such as this.

A big thanks also to Robin Baliszewski of Prentice-Hall, a very resourceful and talented editor who offered useful encouragement and advice throughout the life of this publishing project. Her many valuable contributions are much appreciated.

And, of course, to our familes, who have endured many long hours of our being away from them in order to complete this text, we say THANK YOU.

Roslyn Muraskin and Ted Alleman

Introduction

Justice means fairness. This is a book about women and the issues of justice facing them over a period of time. The book is divided into eight sections. Each chapter is written by an individual or individuals who bring to the reader a clear understanding of the issues that impact women today.

The book introduces us to the issue of equality, or lack of it, between the sexes. Men and women are not the same. But the theme that runs throughout this work is that both sexes are entitled to equal justice under the law. Both deserve equal protection of the law as well as an enjoyment and protection of their constitutional rights.

Each section of the book is introduced in such a way as to generate thought and spark debate. Although women's issues infuse every aspect of social and political thought, in this book we have focused on the areas of crime and criminal justice because our basic human rights in society are inextricably linked to our treatment by and our participation in the criminal justice system.

Historically, women have not enjoyed equal protection under the law as afforded by the Fourteenth Amendment. Nor have they enjoyed many of those rights fully enunciated in the Bill of Rights. As we approach the twenty-first century, women have yet to enjoy the full protection of the Constitution as men do. There is no way to automatically allow both sexes to enjoy equal protection under the law unless there is a commitment to the elimination of all sexual discrimination. As pointed out by Justice Brennan in *Frontiero* v. *Richardson* (411 U.S. 677, [1973]):

Traditionally, [sex] discrimination was rationalized by an attitude of romantic paternalism which in practical effect put women not on a pedestal, but in a cage.

Women have yet to achieve all they want. They still struggle. They are still victims of the justice system. They are still discriminated against, and they are still harassed.

Theoretically, the law has attempted to end discrimination. What has not ended is the practice of discrimination. Discrepancy of treatment based on sex is what is under discussion in this text. The criminal justice system is a microcosm of the turbulence in society as a whole. Thus, a study of women's issues as they operate in the criminal justice system can provide a solid basis from which to explore ourselves and the society of which we are a part.

Roslyn Muraskin and Ted Alleman

Section 1

Varieties of Feminist Thought and Their Application to Crime and Criminal Justice

Feminism is a way of seeing the world—it is not strictly a sexual orientation. To be a feminist is to combine a female mental perspective with a sensitivity for those social issues that influence primarily women. For those who "become feminists," and, in the process, adopt a feminist perspective as a basic component of their personal identities, feminism and self-image merge. Today, the questioning or criticism of feminist thought may be construed as personal attack. Since gender is as basic a component of personality as is family, race, or nationality, a criticism of feminism, for some, constitutes defamation of character.

A part of present-day feminism is an intolerance for sexist language and attitude. For feminists and women in general, the public denigration of women is no longer socially acceptable. As feminism takes hold in Western society, public discourse and even the very language we speak has taken on a new sensitivity and awareness of the position and status of women. Sexist language and jokes must now retreat to all-male enclaves of gender bigotry and ignorance.

A study of feminist issues as they operate in the criminal justice system can provide a solid basis from which to explore ourselves and the society of which we are a part. This is what this text purports to do.

1

Varieties of Feminist Thought and Their Application to Crime and Criminal Justice

Ted Alleman

Any serious discussion pertaining to women and their treatment in society leads one inevitably to a discussion of feminism. Feminism can be many things to many people. But one thing it is not is a narrow, radical view of the opinions of a relatively small group of women in society. Mainstream as well as radical perspectives are contained within the scope of feminism. Feminism is defined in a broad sense as those varying perspectives which place women and the concerns of women at their center. As we shall see, feminist thought is, in actuality, quite broad and diverse.

When addressing issues of gender, a woman's perspective can be deprecated, ignored, or adopted. Those who choose to resist the inroads of the modern women's movement and who refuse to accept the ideal of social equality between men and women can be classified as antifeminist in their thinking. Those who see the world entirely from a man's perspective and are simply blind to the existence and influence of women are said to be androcentric in their thinking. And for all of those who remain, feminism views the world from a woman's perspective and focuses in on issues of concern to women. Since much of the traditional literature in criminal justice either plays down or ignores entirely the role of women, this first section introduces varieties of feminist thought and the ways in which feminist perspectives add to our knowledge of crime and criminal justice.

This section begins with a presentation of a typology of the major schools of feminist thought. The typology provides a useful overview that can be used to compare and contrast each of these perspectives. Following this overview is a presentation of each of the four major schools of feminist thought and how each applies to issues of crime and criminal justice. You are now invited to enter the world of female crime through a study of feminism and the many important issues pertaining to women and their treatment by the criminal justice system.

Introduction to Feminist Issues

Men as well as women can be feminists. Feminism is a way of seeing the world; it is not strictly a sexual orientation. To be a feminist is to combine a female mental perspective with a sensitivity for those social issues which primarily influence women. Feminism involves a fresh outlook on human affairs. Due to the historical and pan-cultural dominance of patriarchal society, taking on a feminist perspective is akin to seeing the world anew. Even if the avowed purpose of becoming a feminist is simply to sensitize oneself to a woman's view of the world, gender, as a human variable, is quickly appreciated as a potent and pervasive social force. Particularly in the social sciences, feminism represents a new, vibrant paradigm with which to observe, study, research and explain that complex whole we know as human society.

But such an introduction to feminism does little justice to the emotional and, for some, almost fanatical allegiance the term evinces. For those who "become feminists," and, in the process, adopt a feminist perspective as a basic component of their personal identities, feminism and self-image merge. Today, the questioning or criticism of feminist thought may be construed as personal attack. Since gender is as basic a component of personality as is family, race, or nationality, a criticism of feminism, for some, constitutes defamation of character. A part of present day feminism is an intolerance for sexist language and attitude. For feminists and women in general, the public denigration of women is no longer socially acceptable. As feminism takes hold in Western society, public discourse and even the very language we speak has taken on a new sensitivity and awareness of the position and status of women. Sexist language and jokes must now retreat to all-male enclaves of gender bigotry and ignorance.

Feminism has induced new perspectives for feminists and non-feminists alike. Those men, and women, who unquestionably accept patriarchy and male social dominance as the "natural order of things" are as profoundly affected by the feminist movement as are avowed feminists. For those who benefit from the way things are, any transformation of the status quo generates a degree of strain, resistance, and struggle. Challenges to male authority can be as emotion-provoking for the male chauvinist as challenges to womanhood are for the feminist. It is, in fact, through the heated dialectic of social discourse that new positions, either refuting or espousing feminist perspectives, emerge and give feminisn its vibrant, energizing, and transforming qualities. The vitality of the feminist movement and its life as a social movement depend as much on its alienating and threatening features as on the belief that feminism is a positive, constructive force.

All of this, of course, is of interest to the student of women and women's issues. Why are *you* interested in the study of women? Do feminist ideas inspire you and instill in you visions of a better world? Or, do feminist ideas bother and alienate you? What is your gut reaction? Answers to these questions—your personal answers—provide insight into where you stand with respect to feminist thought. If used for purposes of self-reflection and personal insight, these answers also serve as an indicator of the role that gender plays in your self-identification. Your individual position is a blend of personal and social variables. As such, it will, in part, determine your acceptance or rejection of feminist ideas, your support or non-support of feminist initiatives. Why do you feel the way you do? A study of men, women, and the human society of which we are all a part can be as revealing of self as it is of human social affairs.

Varieties of Feminist Thought

Feminist thought emanates from a variety of sources and perspectives. Although feminists share an emphasis on placing women at the center of their analysis, it is important to differentiate the ways in which feminists approach their subject. As with all scholarship, theory and research are the intellectual products of highly skilled practitioners who themselves have been socialized into accepting and rejecting ideas in accordance with particular schools of thought. Scholars in all fields of knowledge are influenced, to some degree, by who they are personally, how and where they have been trained, who they choose as role models, and what valued ends or purposes they associate with their work. As such, to understand any piece of scholarship, it is always informative to understand a bit about the person(s) who produced the work and the values they hold, as well as the school of thought with which they identify.

Four major perspectives are presented. These four perspectives are commonly accepted as the major divisions of feminist thought. The purpose of this particular system of classification is to identify the major assumptions and orientations that constitute what we understand today as representing mainstream feminist thought.

Although eclectic approaches to the study of women's issues can be taken where ideas are drawn from more than one perspective, it is more often the case that scholars choose particular ideological perspectives and apply those perspectives to much of their writing and research. Having a working knowledge of each of the major feminist perspectives is therefore invaluable for analyzing the work of others. Also, surveying the entire range of feminist perspectives helps you to better understand the perspectives with which you are most comfortable and which of these value orientations you share with others.

Analyzing Feminist Perspectives

As in all intellectual endeavors, a range of perspectives exists. To understand how these perspectives differ from one another, it is important to identify the main dimensions of each. Scholars do not start out fresh when they begin to build a critical view of society. Like all other forms of intellectual enterprise, feminist thought has a history. Feminist thought, in being essentially a critical view of society, shares many fundamental ideas and concerns with scholarship in related fields and disciplines. To understand the stance taken by each of the major feminist perspectives, it is important to understand what each perspective defines fundamental problems to be, the causes of these problems, and suggestions for eliminating or ameliorating these problems. These points are all covered in the following chart.

An additional consideration to pay attention to is the degree of social change the various feminist perspectives advocate. Take a minute to note in the chart which perspectives see the gender issue as being systemic and which do not. The distinction is important. A systemic social problem is one that exists at the very heart of society and can be eliminated only through a radical reorganization of society itself. Systemic problems infer more radical solutions.

To help clarify this point, liberal feminists believe that the passage and enforcement of laws against sex discrimination will go a long way toward eliminating the unequal treatment of women in American society. For liberal feminists, the structure of society is not the problem; sexism is the problem, and sexism can be eliminated or reduced sufficiently by passing new, tough legislation barring sexual discrimination. Liberal feminists, therefore, do not see gender problems as being systemic since they are willing to work within the present economic, political, and social systems of society to advance their cause. Marxist, Socialist, and Radical Feminists disagree adamantly with this liberal approach; for them, simply passing new laws to stop sexism is like applying a band-aid to a bleeding artery. The targets of this latter group of feminists are patriarchy, capitalism,

Varieties of Feminist Thought

THEORETICAL DIMENSIONS	LIBERAL FEMINIST	MARXIST FEMINIST	SOCIALIST FEMINIST	RADICAL FEMINIST
Primary Problem	Discrimination	Capitalism and class relations	Class and patriarchy	Patriarchy and the nature of man
Manifestation of the Problem	Gender inequality	Class relations and private property as basis of male inheritance	Social oppression	Subordination and sexual exploitation of women
Causes of Gender Inequality	Societal inhibitions to female opportunities and participation	Capitalist class relations	Gender and class relations in which sexuality and labor are linked	Man's biological need to control and exploit women
Process of Gender Formation	Socialization into gender roles and sex types	Master/slave relations applied to husband/wife	Power relations that grow out of human reproduction	Gender power relations based on male heterosexuality
Gender Problem Systemic	No	Yes	Yes	Yes
Program for Change	Affirmative action; ERA; Equal opportunity laws and policies	Bring women fully into economic production; socialize housework and child care; eliminate male-dominated inheritance system	Construct a new social order based on equality of class and gender	Create women-centered and all-women social institutiones that are void of power relations

Varieties of Feminist Thought *Continued*

THEORETICAL DIMENSIONS	LIBERAL FEMINIST	MARXIST FEMINIST	SOCIALIST FEMINIST	RADICAL FEMINIST
Primary Criminal Justice Concerns	Social repression and discrimination of women and female offenders; the criminalization of women	Curb the harsh treatment of working class offenders, and curb the violence against women due to inequality	Identify the societal causes and abuses that result in the double oppression of women in the home and workplace	Heterosexual rape; pornography and exploitation of women for male perverse pleasure and economic exploitation

TYPOLOGY PARTIALLY ADAPTED FROM THE FOLLOWING SOURCES:
"Feminism And Criminology." By Kathleen Daly and Meda Chesney-Lind, *Justice Quarterly*, Vol. 5, No. 4, December, 1988.
"Feminist Theory, Crime, And Justice." By Sally S. Simpson, Vol. 27, No. 4, November, 1989.
"From Marx to Bonger: Socialist Writings on Women, Gender, and Crime." By James W. Messerschmidt, *Sociological Inquiry*, Vol. 58, No. 4, Fall, 1988.

and class society itself. Therefore, whether feminists see gender to be systemic or not is an important element of feminist thought.

The last dimension to be considered in the chart is the kind of criminal justice concerns that typify each of the varying feminist perspectives. Although feminist views on any particular criminal justice subject such as rape or prostitution do share a common concern for the rights and dignity of women, each of the four schools of thought listed in the chart interpret criminal justice issues from their own individual perspective. It is for this reason in our study of women's issues in crime and criminal justice that we should first have a firm understanding of each of the four schools of feminist thought before proceeding to examine how each assesses various criminal justice issues.

As you proceed through the discussion of each of the feminist schools of thought presented in the next section, you are encouraged to refer back to the chart. The learning objectives of this introductory chapter include being able to: (1) identify the variey of feminist perspectives that currently exist; (2) explain how the various perspectives differ one from another in their logic and orientation to women's issues; and (3) apply the teachings of each perspective to matters of concern in the fields of crime and criminal justice. If you are successful at grasping the point of view of each of the feminist perspectives presented in this chapter, you will have taken a big step toward understanding feminism as a whole and, more importantly, you will have gained an appreciation of why gender and "women's perspectives" are becoming central variables in the study of crime and criminal justice. With these objectives in mind, we now turn to a discussion of each of the four schools of feminist thought.

Overview of Liberal Feminist Thought

Liberal feminist thought lies at the heart of feminism. To the extent that women are excluded from full and equal participation in society, liberal feminism will continue to be a dominant force in the women's movement.

Liberal feminist thought is an extension and application of the philosophical doctrine of liberalism. For this reason, a knowledge of liberalism is invaluable for understanding a liberal feminist perspective. Liberal feminism is often termed "mainstream" because it adheres to predominant democratic principles. Liberal feminism is also mainstream because liberal feminists choose to work within the established political and legal structure of society to accomplish their goals and objectives.

As will be discussed, liberal feminists not only aspire to full equality and participation in society; they also want to be equal partners with men. The goal of attaining equality with men is what makes liberal feminism appealing to so many women while, concurrently, posing problems for feminists who seek more radical, women-centered approaches. Liberal feminism, therefore, serves as a centerpiece which helps to explain the general appeal of feminism as well as providing a standard against which more extreme feminist perspectives can be measured. This is why a knowledge of the underlying principles of liberal feminism is essential for understanding feminism itself.

Section 1—Equal Rights Amendment

> Equality of rights under the law shall not be denied or abridged
> by the United States or by any State on account of sex.

Such a simple, direct statement. Isn't the essence of the idea underlying this proposed constitutional amendment fully compatible with the philosophy of a country characterized by honesty, justice, and freedom for all? Wouldn't fair-minded people everywhere agree that discrimination, sexual or otherwise, has no place in a free society? Is such an amendment to the Constitution really all that controversial?

The history of the struggles that various groups of people have had to endure to gain equality and equal rights in a country that proclaims itself to be free and egalitarian epitomizes the rapacity and hyprocrisy that underlies much of human affairs. Not only are women not free; in many ways women are treated as if they are subservient and inferior. It took a constitutional amendment in 1920 just to give women the right to vote. Sexual discrimination abounds in society and affects almost every sphere of social life (Henslin, 1990). The Equal Rights Amendment, which simply gives women the same rights as men, was first drafted in 1923 and as of this date is still not part of the law of the land. The great disparity between the ideals and the reality of social life is one of the primary reasons why liberal feminism continues to form the bedrock of the women's movement.

To understand the direction and thrust of liberal social reform, and in particular to understand liberal positions pertaining to issues about crime and criminal justice, it is beneficial to have a working knowledge of liberalism as a social doctrine. Put differently, if you want to understand the actions of liberals and the kinds of programs liberals advocate, it is important to understand how liberals think. Although we need not embark on an in-depth study of liberalism, it is important to emphasize a few of the ideas central to liberal thought.

In general, contemporary liberalism is a system of thought that values the free expression of individual personality and cherishes a form of government in which individual freedom is fostered and protected. Liberals favor an equal disposition of liberty that is founded on rational principles and provides all people the opportunity to freely compete and fulfill their life's ambitions to the best of their individual abilities. Liberals also favor the expansion of opportunity and believe it to be the duty of the state to actively intervene when opportunities are not open to all people. Liberals believe in a strong educational system which helps to make citizens responsible and actively participating members of society. Liberalism lies at the heart of democracy and has served as the guiding philosophical force behind many social and civil rights struggles.

As a general course of action, liberalism can be viewed as a doctrine that accepts the basic form and process of democratic government but objects when specific groups of people are denied access to and full participation in society. Liberal feminism, by drawing much of its focus and energy from liberal perspectives: (1) sees the roots of women's oppression as lying in women's lack of equal civil rights and educational opportunities; (2) objects to government intrusion into the private lives of women, particularly in terms of their sexuality and control over their own reproductive processes; and (3) resents sex roles that are not of their own making and make women subservient to men (Humm, 1989). Each of these general "roots of oppression" translates into many of the issues and concerns which affect women and their status in the criminal justice system. With the perspective of liberalism in mind, we turn to its application to topics of interest in criminology and criminal justice.

The Criminalization of Women

Criminalization is a process of socialization in which individuals who have committed initial acts of deviance are caught up by the criminal justice system and as a result of being defined, processed, and stigmatized as criminals become further alienated and removed from law-abiding behavior. The effect of criminalization is particularly profound when it involves young people.

Normally when we think of juvenile delinquency we conjure up images of violent and dangerous youth who have committed serious crimes such as assault, robbery, and homicide. And of course this can be the case. But in fact the vast majority of youth who are processed by the criminal justice system are arrested for committing what are termed "status offenses." Status offenses are behaviors that are violations of law not because they are serious offenses but because they have been performed by young people who are often detached in some ways from the control of their parents. Kids who take to the streets can be arrested for a variety of status offenses such as using alcohol, skipping class, petty theft, or simply having no place to stay.

Meda Chesney-Lind, a researcher who has studied the differences between male and female delinquents, points out that girls far more frequently than boys are arrested for a wide range of behaviors that are actually violations of parental authority. Charges such as "running away from home," "being a person in need of supervision," "being incorrigible," and "being beyond control" are typical. In addition, she documents the unusual extent to which evidence of sexual affairs enter into defining girls as delinquent, whereas the sexual behavior of boys is virtually ignored. The evidence she provides regarding the traditional concern the justice system has paid to the sexual misconduct of girls is illuminating.

> In Honolulu, during the period 1929–30, over half of the girls referred to court were charged with "immorality," which meant evidence of sexual intercourse. In addition, another 30% were charged with "waywardness." Evidence of immorality was vigorously pursued by both arresting officers and social workers through lengthy questioning of the girl and, if possible, males with whom she was suspected of having sex. Other evidence of "exposure" was provided by gynecological examinations that were routinely ordered in virtually all girls' cases. Doctors . . . would routinely note the condition of the hymen: "admits intercourse hymen rupture," "no laceration," "hymen ruptured" are typical of the notations on the forms. . . . Obsessed with precocious female sexuality, the institutions set about to isolate the females from all contact with males while housing them in bucolic settings. The intention was to hold the girls until marriageable age and to occupy them in domestic pursuits during their sometimes lengthy incarceration. . . . The links between these attitudes and those of juvenile courts some decades later are, of course, arguable; but an examination of the record of the court does not inspire confidence. . . . For more evidence of official concern with adolescent sexual misconduct, consider Linda Hancock's (1981) content analysis of police referrals in Australia. She noted that 40% of the referrals of girls to court made specific mention of sexual and moral conduct compared to only 5% of the referrals of boys. These sorts of results suggest that all youthful female misbehavior has traditionally been subject to surveillance for evidence of sexual misconduct. (Chesney-Lind, 1989)

Let us try to put this information into its proper perspective. Consider the following scenario. It's about midnight on a hot July night in the big city. Two officers in a squad car stop for a routine talk with some juveniles hanging out on the corner. One of the girls who appears to be about sixteen years old is unfamiliar to the officers. Upon questioning her they determine that she is from out of town and cannot give them a local address where she is staying. They say that they must take her in "for her own protection." She begins to cry. She pleads that she cannot go home and that she would just like to be left alone. The officers take her to juvenile hall and charge her with vagrancy. The authorities determine the girl's identity and contact her parents, who come to pick her up. The parents claim that the girl is a real problem for them and that they appreciate being contacted. The officers tell the girl that the next time she is found on the street she will be charged with a more serious crime and could possibly be institutionalized. How does this fictitious scenario compare with real cases?

According to the research of Chesney-Lind, cases such as this are typical. But what has been left out of the description of this incident and overlooked by the police officers as well as by the juvenile authorities is that a young girl such as the one described is most probably being sexually and/or physically abused at home. According to statistics, girls are much more likely than boys to be victims of child sexual abuse. Research cited by Chesney-Lind indicates that roughly 70% of the victims of sexual abuse are girls. Girls' sexual abuse tends to start earlier than boys' and they are most likely to be assaulted by a family member. The abuse is, of course, traumatic and often results in the girl running away from home, having difficulties in school, being a truant, or, perhaps, getting married at an early age. Also of relevance is the finding that a predominance of the backgrounds of adult women in prison includes being sexually abused as youngsters and running away from home at an early age (Chesney-Lind, 1989).

Of particular note is the fact that boys who leave home and take to the streets are more frequently perceived as being tough "street kids" who are capable of taking care of themselves. Girls who are runaways are perceived as needing the protection provided by home and family, and are often forced to return to these abusive environments. Research indicates that female runaways who were sexually abused do tend to engage in delinquent or criminal activities such as substance abuse, petty theft, and prostitution in order to survive (Chesney-Lind, 1989). According to Chesney-Lind, the reaction of the criminal justice system to these young women in need is to "sexualize" their delinquent behavior and "criminalize" their survival strategies. By punishing their transgressions and forcing them back into a home environment, the criminal justice system in effect is reinforcing the obedience of young women to the demands of patriarchal authority no matter how abusive and arbitrary it may be.

Women's Liberation, Crime, and Criminal Justice

One of the important outcomes of the modern women's movement has been the impact feminist perspectives have had on the study of crime and criminal justice. Beginning in the 1960s, significant numbers of women throughout the industrialized world took on a new consciousness concerning themselves and their place in society. As millions of women made the transition from home to business, the day-to-day social roles of these women changed. New female self-images and lifestyles accompanied the social movement. Many envisioned the emergence of a new kind of woman—one who was free and independent and capable of charting her own course in life. As social opportunities for women opened up, it appeared that women could now be anything they wanted to be: doctor, lawyer, artist, merchant-chief, and, yes, even beggarman and thief. It was pertaining to the social impact of these latter options, of course, that was of most interest to criminologists.

Two criminologists who made a strong impact on the study of female crime were Freda Adler and Rita Simon. With the publication in 1975 of *Sisters in Crime: The Rise of the New Female Criminal* by Adler and *Women and Crime* by Simon, a new era in the study of women and crime had begun. The central theme of both books pertained to the impact the new, emerging social roles of women had on the rates and types of female crime occurring in society. With Adler's emphasis on the changing nature of female self-images and Simon's emphasis on the changing structure of society, the liberation thesis of female criminality was born.

The liberation thesis asserts that the women's liberation movement has had a significant impact on female crime. In terms of cause and effect, the women's movement is seen as an independent variable that causes an increase in female crime because of the changing social roles and employment patterns of women taking place in society. Although both Adler and Simon agree that women's liberation has had a significant impact on female crime, their explanations do vary as to how the process works.

Adler's position is that, as the result of moving from traditional homebound social roles into positions of power and influence, women—like men—become more competitive and aggressive. According to Adler, women have the same basic motivations as men and, apart from obvious natural differences and the arbitrary differences imposed through the process of socialization, men and women are very much the same. The importance of the women's movement, for Adler, is that women for the very first time are able to express their true nature—a nature that is as pugnacious, assertive, and goal-oriented as necessary to fulfill any of the new social roles women may find themselves a part of. For Adler, all of society is opening up for women, and women are quite capable of proving themselves worthy no matter what the occupation or the demands of the job. Notice in

Adler's dialog how similar women are assumed to be to men as they enter legitimate as well as illegitimate all-male social roles.

> Women are no longer indentured to the kitchens, baby carriages, or bedrooms of America.... Allowed their freedom for the first time, women—by the tens of thousands—have chosen to desert those kitchens and plunge exuberantly into the formerly all-male quarters of the working world.
>
> There are now female admirals, longshorewomen, stevedores, and seagoing sailors (tattoos and all); there are police women patrolling in one-person cars, women FBI agents, and female sky marshals. Women can now be found clinging to telephone poles as installers and line workers; peering from behind acetylene welding torches and seated behind the wheels of over-the-road tractor-trailer trucks. They can be found at work as forklift drivers and crane operators, pipe fitters and carpenters, mail carriers and morticians, commercial airline pilots and jet-engine mechanics. Women now serve as Congressional pages. They have run for, and won, a substantial number of powerful positions throughout the American political system; and ever-increasing numbers of women continue to become judges, lawyers, and high-level executives in industry and government.
>
> In the same way that women are demanding equal opportunity in fields of legitimate endeavor, a similar number of determined women are forcing their way into the world of major crimes.... Like her sisters in legitimate fields, the female criminal is fighting for her niche in the hierarchy.... The mob, like other successful organizations, reacts to competition and accomplishment. They are not likely to ignore the increasing numbers of women who are using guns, knives, and wits to establish themselves as full human beings, as capable of violence and aggression as any man. (Adler, 1975)

Implicit in Adler's thesis is that women have made it. Not only does Adler assume that in 1975, the publication date of her book, equal opportunity for women has arrived; she also assumes that the nature of women has been transformed to match their new roles and status. Adler sees women as being no different from men, and in the world of crime women are depicted as no longer being satisfied to engage in second-rate kinds of criminal activity. In Adler's own words, "It (the new feminism) describes the women who have concluded that prostitution and shoplifting are not their style: embezzlement, robbery, and assault are more congenial to their self-image.... In summary, what we have described is a gradual but accelerating social revolution in which women are closing many of the gaps, social and criminal, that have separated them from men. The closer they get, the more alike they look and act." (Adler, 1975).

Two important points concerning Adler's thesis need to be emphasized. First, men and women are assumed to be basically the same, and it is the process of socialization and the social roles they play that make men and women different. Second, it is assumed that qualities such as assertiveness, aggressiveness, and pugnacity (all qualities that are traditionally associated with masculinity) are inherent to positions of leadership and power and that as women take on such positions in society they will, in turn, act as men act. It is because of this latter point that Adler's theory is termed the masculinity thesis of women's liberation. The masculinity thesis states that as women take on the social roles traditionally performed by men, women will become more masculine in their thoughts and actions. Therefore, with respect to crime and criminal activity, the masculinity thesis predicts that as women's liberation takes place women who engage in crime become more daring and more violent in their criminal acts.

Rita Simon's explanation of how the women's movement affects female crime is different from Adler's masculinity thesis. Simon's view is that as women move out of the domestic sphere and into upper levels of employment they will have opportunities to commit crimes that previously were not available to them. For Simon, the reasons men and women commit crime are really no different—it is the differential opportunities, skills, and social networks of men versus women that make a difference. So, according to Simon, as women move into the same social and occupational spheres as men, they will increasingly commit the same kinds of crime as men because they are being accorded the same opportunities to commit crime. For this reason, Simon's theory is called the opportunity thesis of female crime. The opportunity thesis suggests that criminals must have access to other people's goods and money before a crime can be committed; as women enter the workforce and take on jobs involving expert knowledge and skills, they will commit the types of crimes characteristic of men. (Simon & Landis, 1991)

Although both the masculinity and the opportunity theses predict increases in female crime as a result of the women's movement, an important difference between the two theses is how women's liberation affects rates of violent crime. The masculinity thesis assumes that the nature of women change as they take on new social roles; the opportunity thesis makes no such assumption. The masculinity thesis—by assuming that women become more aggressive and pugnacious as they take on previously all-male social roles—predicts that women, like men, will increasingly commit crimes of violence. The opportunity thesis predicts the opposite.

The opportunity thesis states that as they raise their social status and move into positions of prestige and authority, women increas-

---

The Liberation Thesis

The Women's Movement as a Cause of Female Crime

Adler's Masculinity Thesis

Changing   The Masculination of   Increased
Sex Roles   →   Female Behavior   →   Female Crime

Simon's Opportunity Thesis

Changing   Increased Opportunity   Increased
Employment →   to Commit Crime   →   Female Crime
Patterns

---

ingly fulfill themselves as human beings. They become more independent and, as a result, women are less dependent on men. Simon in her formulation of the opportunity thesis implies that women commit violence only as a last resort—only as a result of frustration and desperation. So as they gain self-esteem, confidence, and economic self-sufficiency, women are seen as increasingly moving away from the role of victim and thereby extricating themselves from situations that are likely to result in violent acts (Simon & Landis, 1991). In other words, according to the opportunity thesis, increased opportunity invites property and white-collar-related criminal activity among women while concurrently reducing the frustrations and situationally related variables that cause women to resort to violence. An important difference, therefore, between the two theories is that the masculinity thesis predicts increases in violent crimes committed by women, whereas the opportunity thesis predicts decreases in violent crimes committed by women.

Our primary purpose in reviewing the masculinity and the opportunity theories of female crime is not to assess whether these theories are right or wrong, but to provide two prominant examples of liberal feminist thought.[1] By comparing the reasoning employed

---

[1]The question of whether or not "women's liberation" has resulted in a rise in female crime is still unanswered. One prominant researcher, Darrell Steffensmeier,

by these theories with the general tenets of liberalism, it is clear that both theories fit well within the liberal purview. Both theories, for example, assume the women's movement to be of social significance and to have precipitated substantial changes in the rates and types of female criminality. Both theories downplay biological or physical differences between the sexes by assuming socialization and social participation to be predominant social processes that cause women to act and behave like men as women take on the social roles traditionally held by men. And both theories also focus on the importance of the roles women play in the public sector as they are "emancipated" from the domestic sphere. But, while both theories celebrate the presumed liberation of women, from a feminist perspective these theories also raise some interesting questions and issues.

One obvious feminist issue generated by the liberation thesis is that women's emancipation causes increased rates of female crime. By linking crime with liberation, it is difficult not to conclude that women's liberation constitutes a serious social problem. Ironically, the data generated by the liberation thesis serves as fodder for anti-feminist arguments that women should stay in the home where they are said to belong. Is it really true that as women occupy the same social environment as men they will, in turn, act in the same manner as men?

Additionally, as is the case with the masculinity thesis, many feminists are reluctant to accept the idea that as women take on traditional all-male roles they become more like men. Much of the idological thrust of feminism with its drive for freedom and emancipation is certainly not compatible with the thought that the end result of liberation is simply women committing male-like forms of violence and destruction. Is it true that, as women are shaped and molded by the new social roles in which they find themselves, the vital force of woman will become essentially the animus of man?

And finally, as the liberation thesis emphasizes the importance of gaining equality of the sexes in the public sphere, it deemphasizes, although perhaps not intentionally so, the problems and issues regarding the inequality of women in the home or domestic sphere. By not conceptualizing the traditional patriarchal relations of men and

---

has provided much empirical evidence that shows the liberation movement to have had little, if any, impact on the rates of female crime (see Steffensmeier, 1978). Others, employing equally impressive empirical presentations, show female crime to be undergoing significant change (see Austin, 1982). But if, in fact, female criminality is increasing, the prominant explanations for this phenomenon remain those of Rita Simon and Freda Adler.

women as a fundamental problem and by accepting the political, economic, and social systems of society as legitimate and fair, the liberal emphasis on equality of participation and opportunity in the public sphere tends to ignore feminist problems stemming from the private, interpersonal relationships between women and men. Is it really true that equal opportunity in the public sphere will yield satisfactory solutions for women in the domestic sphere?

By analyzing the implications of a particular theory or perspective and by questioning its major suppositions and conclusions, we are better able to predict its relevance and practicality. When liberal as well as other feminist perspectives are recognized as alternative ways of viewing the world rather than ideologies to live by, we, as students of social affairs, are able to step back and more realistically weight the pros and cons of each perspective. All social perspectives are limiting in that, as they emphasize some chosen aspect of social reality, others are simultaneously deemphasized or even ignored. As an element of ideology, for example, equality becomes a central canon of liberal thought and sexual discrimination in any of its multitudinous forms serves as the objectification of evil. As such, instances of inequality or differential treatment of men and women are sought out and, in the name of the liberal cause, eradicated. But is it always in the best interests of women that women be treated the same as men?

This word of caution applies to the treatment women receive by the criminal justice system. A "chivalry thesis," for example, can be found to exist in the criminal justice literature that documents instances of women traditionally being accorded more lenient treatment by the criminal justice system (Simon & Landis, 1991). If women are, in fact, not being treated as harshly by the criminal justice system, should liberal feminists in the name of equality campaign against such "discriminatory" treatment? Is it true that a difference in treatment always implies discriminatory treatment? Even if it is evident that judges or the police are according women differential treatment due to paternalistic values—the intent of which is to restore women to "their proper place" as mothers and wives—are these situations against which feminists should take a stand? These are tough issues that deserve careful consideration.

Overview of Socialist and Marxist Thought

Both socialist and Marxist feminism use a conflict perspective to attack the social conditions that oppress women. By adopting a critical view of the structure of capitalist society, socialist-feminism and

Marxist-feminism share a common emphasis. But although Marxist and socialist-feminists adhere to the same school of thought, they do differ in the way they apply Marxist principles.

The discussion of socialist and Marxist-feminism begins with the critical perspective that is common to both schools of thought. In the beginning sections that introduce this critical view of society, the terms socialism and Marxism are used interchangeably. But, as the inquiry into feminism develops, some clear distinctions are made between the approach of socialists and Marxists to the study of women and women's issues.

As will be emphasized, Marxist-feminists discuss feminist issues from a traditional Marxist perspective as originally formulated by Karl Marx and Frederich Engels. Marxist-feminists are first and foremost Marxists. Marxist-feminists stipulate that the oppression of women is no different than the oppression experienced by other groups in capitalist society. For Marxists-feminists, the root cause of the oppression of women is class society. Socialist-feminists provide a different theoretical emphasis.

Socialist-feminists are first and foremost feminists. Socialist-feminists adhere to traditional Marxism and its critical view of society; but when it comes to explaining the root cause of female oppression, socialists emphasize that sex class is just as fundamental as economic class as an explanatory variable. Whereas Marxist-feminists *apply* Marxism to the problems of women, socialist-feminists *extend* Marxism to accommodate within its intellectual purview a feminist perspective. A primary learning objective of this section is to understand the differences between these two approaches to the study of women and women's issues.

Socialist and Marxist-Feminist Thought

Socialist and Marxist feminism can best be understood by comparing and contrasting these two approaches to the problems of women in society. In many ways socialism and Marxism share what is termed a "conflict" view of society. As such, socialist and Marxist scholars hold in common some very fundamental perspectives concerning the nature and resolution of social problems. But while it is important to understand the similarities of these two schools of thought, it is also necessary to understand their differences. In this section, we consider socialism and Marxism together in order to more clearly see their combined and separate contributions to feminist theory.

To many Americans, socialism and Marxism are dirty words. Images of totalitarian regimes, repressive political systems, and gulags filled with political prisoners are commonly associated with these terms. In part, these negative perceptions are a natural by-product of a cold war that has dominated the better part of the lives of three generations of Americans. Whether in school, at home, or in the workplace, "loyal" Americans express their love of democracy and their dislike for communism. But as is true in any ideological war, images of the enemy are often tainted with hate, exemplified by fear, and reinforced by ignorance. Socialism and Marxism are, in fact, respectable bodies of knowledge that offer much in terms of their critical view of the world, and both have contributed considerably to our understanding of society and the process of social change. As intellectual disciplines, socialism and Marxism, along with liberalism and conservatism, form the bedrock of our sociology of knowledge. It is imperative, therefore, that we wipe our mental slate clean of negative stereotypes and false impressions in order to take a fresh look at the socialist and Marxist perspectives to see what they have to offer to our understanding of feminist issues.

To see the world from a socialist perspective is to see the world from the bottom looking up. The principles of socialism appeal to the underclass of society primarily because those principles give that class a perspective that reflects its views of the world. From a socialist perspective, to be impoverished is not necessarily a sign of failure but, rather, evidence of an unjust political and economic system, From a socialist perspective, capitalism, as an economic system, has certainly proven successful at generating vast quantities of wealth. As a social system, however, capitalism has failed by creating vast pockets of misery alongside this wealth. While Wall Street aptly stands as an appropriate symbol of capitalist enterprise, so, too, does the sprawling, poverty-stricken urban ghetto.

It is important to recognize that ghettos of the mind and spirit exist in capitalistic society as well as in ghettos of poverty. In the ghetto, the capitalistic ideology of winning is offset by an aura of despair. Intrinsic to the capitalistic spirit is the ethos of the game. To participate, to struggle, and to win ostensibly proves one's superiority, one's vitality and spirit. But winning also implies losing. Success and dominance go hand in hand. Viewed from above, life in capitalistic society is a competitive struggle out of which emerge those who are most worthy and powerful. Viewed from below, from a socialist perspective, life is an accommodation to a set of conditions and circumstances that are beyond comprehension and control. The image makers in western society have done well at showing us what it is like to be successful and live the good life. Let us now take a close look at life at the bottom of society where failure and despair are a part of every waking moment.

A Critical Look at Capitalist Society

Poverty pervades all aspects of life at the bottom of capitalist society. Poverty, as the term is used here, means much more than simply not being able to obtain the essentials of life such as food, clothing, and shelter. Poverty also means not having sufficient power, resources, or self-sufficiency to make one's life better. The conscious awareness of not being able to fulfill life ambitions, not being able to adequately provide for loved ones, and not being able to maintain self-respect is an integral part of what it means to be poor. Life at the bottom of capitalist society includes a poverty of spirit as well as pocketbook.

The Marxist vision of capitalist society is critical. It perceives the spirit of capitalism as an invidious spirit by which all relationships, economic as well as human, become reduced to mere monetary value. In capitalist society everything has a price, everything can be bought and sold, everything has cash value. The value of one's life translates into how much money one makes, how much property one owns, and how much wealth one accumulates. The Marxist view of society is also critical because it sees wealth, and the power and control that come with it, as being concentrated in the hands of a few. From the Marxist perspective, naked self-interest and a callous disregard for others are characteristic of capitalist society. While the vast resources of capitalist society are concentrated in the hands of the very rich, the very poor live a life of misery surrounded by affluence. Economic misery quickly translates into psychological misery as it becomes painfully clear to the underclass that their poverty, their misery, their fate is not shared by all. To be set aside, to be left out, to not be able to participate is to be isolated, and when isolation is combined with a sense of powerlessness, meaninglessness, and self-estrangement, alienation results.

Traditional Marxian theory points to the economic "means of production" in society as being the basic causal factor that determines how societies are organized. Marxists maintain that those who control the material means by which the essential resources of society are produced and distributed also control the political, educational, and military institutions of society. This social fact translates into raw power—power which is used by the elite to rule society in their own name and to their own benefit. Marxism views social relationships in a capitalist society as unnatural since the elite who rule society come to perceive themselves and come to be perceived by others as somehow deserving of their power and their ability to oppress others. Thus, to Marxists, the political structure of capitalist society exists for basically one purpose: to allow those in power to maintain the power and control they hold over others.

We have begun our discussion of socialist and Marxist thought by emphasizing the relationship between power and economics primarily because much of modern conflict theory posits economic power as ultimately being the basis of all exploitative and oppressive relationships in society. According to traditional Marxian theory, ownership of the mode of production is the primary social fact that divides members of society into haves and have-nots, oppressors and oppressed. Those who control society are those who own the means by which the material basis of life is sustained. Understanding the concepts and logic of Marx's explanation of social life is of primary importance because: (1) to a great degree Marx's original theory is still influential and is accepted by many critical theorists as being an accurate depiction of social organization and change; and (2) when Marx's critique of society is applied to specific issues and problems—many of which did not exist in Marx's day—contemporary critical theorists are often careful to thoughtfully reproduce the logic of Marx's theory as he himself might have done if he were still alive.

Marx made clear his "discovery" that economics is the chief element of change and social organization in society. Marx was living at a time when the Industrial Revolution was clearly responsible for much of the social change that was taking place. As the factory was revolutionizing the workplace and transforming an agrarian world into an industrial world, Marx maintained that the corresponding changes taking place in the social sphere were a direct outgrowth of the material forces of production. It was Marx's thesis, in fact, that all components of society—the social, political, ideational—were by-products of the economic organization of society. Those who owned the means of production, which in Marx's day meant those who owned the factories and other forms of industrial capital, according to his logic, also controlled and influenced all the other segments of society. Oppression (the institutionalized and coercive control of one group by another), as conceptualized by Marx, becomes a prerogative of the economic elite to use and manipulate at will the institutions of society to keep the economic underclass of society down and in their place. The oppression of capitalist society is depicted visually on the next page.

Although Marx clearly identified economics as the chief agent of social control, he was not principally an economist, but a social philosopher. As emphatic as Marx was that economics was the major force in human history, he engaged in economic analysis primarily to demonstrate the source of power in society. In his intellectual pursuit to explain the foundation and progression of social history, Marx found the ownership of property to be the lever that permitted one class of people to control, manipulate and exploit other classes of people. According to traditional Marxist theory, power, in its most raw and potent forms, resides with those who own the tools, equip-

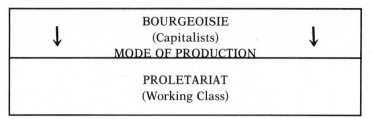

Traditional Marxist Image of Class Society—Class
Oppression Based on Economic Exploitation

ment, and raw material needed to sustain life. In Marx's day these
brokers were the capitalists.

Socialist and Marxist Thought as Applied to Women's Issues: Social Conflict and the Oppression of Women

The previous section provides an overview of some of the relevant
aspects of a socialist/Marxist critique of capitalist society. This review
has been necessary because socialist and Marxist feminists adhere
closely to Marxist principles in their analysis and critique of women's
issues. According to Sally Simpson, a contemporary feminist scholar,
both socialists and Marxists accept capitalism as a necessary and/or
sufficient cause of female oppression. Whether one is a socialist-feminist or a Marxist-feminist is simply a reflection of the weight given
to class oppression as a casual variable (Simpson, 1989). What is now
necessary is to determine just how patriarchy and the oppression of
women fit within a Marxian theoretical framework that emphasizes
class and economic production as the driving forces of social history.

The Marxist-Feminist Perspective

Karl Marx and Friedrich Engels, the authors of traditional Marxism,
emphasized a materialistic conception of society because they believed that before all else people must organize to satisfy their most
basic needs. For this reason, Marx and Engels claimed that: (1) their
theory was grounded in empirical reality; (2) economics was the
prime mover in society and all else (social institutions of all kinds)
derived from economic forces; and (3) associated with the productive
forces of society (the relation between people and their work) are
productive relations (the relations between people themselves) which
determine whether society, socially, is cooperative or exploitative
(Hunt, 1971). Hence, according to Marxism, the degree of patriarchy
(the dominance of men in society) and the relative position of women
is ultimately determined by the relations of production and economic
class.

These ideas, in summary form, are relevant to our discussion primarily because a difference between Marxist-feminism and socialist-feminism is the degree to which traditional Marxist theory is adhered to in the analysis of gender and issues of concern to women. A Marxist-feminist approach sees topics of concern to women as being another field of study to which Marxist theory applies. The Marxist-feminist, more than the socialist-feminist, accepts Marxism as providing the best means of integrating women's issues into an overall conception of society. Such an approach has the advantage of analyzing feminist issues, along with all the other problems generated in capitalistic societies, in a consistent, logical manner. Therefore it is necessary in our discussion of the Marxist-feminist perspective to start first with traditional Marxist theory and then advance toward the object of our study—the analysis of women and their concerns in modern society.

Although many theorists, past as well as present, are drawing criticism today from feminists because of their failure to recognize gender as a causal variable, the claim of "gender blindness" cannot be unequivocally leveled against Marxism. James Messerschmidt, a prominent feminist scholar, points out that Marx and Engels did recognize reproduction (the production of human life through procreation, socialization, and daily maintenance) in their social analysis. As documented by Messerschmidt (1988), Engels provided the following comments concerning the importance of both production and reproduction for understanding a materialistic conception of human society.

> According to the materialistic conception, the determining factor in history is, in the final instance, the production and reproduction of immediate life. This, again, is of a two-fold character: on the one side, the production of the means of existence, of food, clothing and shelter and the tools necessary for that production; on the other side, the production of human beings themselves, the propagation of the species. The social organization under which the people of a particular historical epoch and a particular country live is determined by both kinds of production; by the stage of development of labour on the one hand and of the family on the other. (Engels, 1884)

The important distinction to be made from these comments concerning the application of Marxism to issues of female concern is not that Marx and Engels failed to recognize gender as a variable, but that they considered reproduction and the family to be secondary to the economy and production as causal variables. In the words of Messerschmidt, "Gender relations are made subordinate to class relations and the oppression of women becomes for Marx and Engels simply a reflection of the more important and fundamental class oppression" (Messerschmidt, 1988; Eisenstein, 1979).

One reason Marx and Engels may not have chosen to treat production and reproduction equally as codeterminants of social organization was their view of history. The Marxist conception of the origins of social life was one of a primitive communism in which all members of society, men and women alike, shared equally in the production and distribution of material goods. Everyone had their place and everyone contributed and consumed according to their respective abilities and needs. The division of labor between the sexes in such a communal society was not arbitrary or coercive, but rather reflected the unique sexual and biological nature of women and men to contribute to life in society. Men "naturally" organized their efforts around a "public sphere" of endeavor which gave them a broader range of activity as they brought essential goods into the community and arranged for their distribution, while women "naturally" dominated a "domestic sphere" of productive activity which was based around the home and included the care and nurturing of the young. Such a system was both communal and egalitarian and, of course, predated the deleterious social conditions associated with the coming industrial revolution.

As societies began to evolve and horticultural and pastoral societies emerged, the forces of production began to create an economic surplus which resulted in new forms of social relations. As Engels argued, since these economic developments took place in the "public sphere," the affairs of men grew in importance. Like any other class system in which self-interest and egoism grow out of ownership and control (Bonger, 1905), men changed the communal nature of society to a patrilineal, private property system which permitted them to not only accumulate wealth but also to pass it on to their children (Messerschmidt, 1988). As a result of these economic and social changes in society, women lost out. Women not only found themselves to be subservient to men, but their world—the domestic sphere— was vastly diminished in importance. The communal nature of society was replaced by a class-based system that caused women to be but minor parts of the organizational makeup of society.

With this understanding, we are now in a position to see just how Marxist-feminist scholars approach their study of women and women's issues. With the development of a class-based economy that increased both the importance of the public sphere and the involvement of men, not women, in the organizational activity of society, we see the unique oppression of women in capitalist society. The primary cause of female oppression, according to the Marxist-feminist perspective, is the class-based system. Both men and women— especially those of the underclass in capitalist society—are oppressed socially and economically by a system that serves only the interests of the dominant economic class. The majority of people in capitalist society face poverty and economic marginality, but women are doubly oppressed through their tie to a domestic sphere that is inconsequential in terms of its power and influence. While both men and women in the family unit must work cooperatively to survive the poverty imposed by class society, women bear the additional oppression of men who strip them of any form of decision-making and power relating to the dominant sphere of activity—the public sphere. Add to this the expectation that domestic labor (the care and maintenance of the home and the nurturing of all its members) is performed without wages, and the case is made that women are enslaved by men as well as by their class-based economic oppression.

A summary of the social conditions that serve to place women in an oppressive position in society is provided in the following diagram. Notice how the division of labor, patriarchy, and the dominance of men in the public sphere all serve to oppress women and drive them to the bottom of society. The essence of the Marxist-feminist position, therefore, is that women, like men, are oppressed economically but, unlike men, women are once again enslaved by their domesticity.

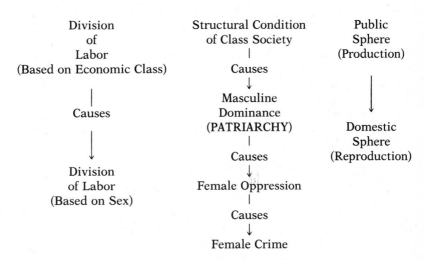

**A Marxist-Feminist Conception of
the Causal Nexus of Female Oppression**

Application of Marxist-Feminism to the Problems of Crime and Criminal Justice

By applying a Marxist view of the oppression of women, the nature of female criminality and the treatment of women by the criminal justice system are seen as reflecting the oppressed condition of women in a capitalist economic system. Women commit less crime than men basically because of their isolation from the means of production and their lack of participation in the public sphere. Given their isolation in the home, when women do commit crime, their crimes are individualistic and generally reflect the powerlessness and economic marginality resulting from their unique place as women in a capitalist, patriarchial system. Petty theft and shoplifting, therefore, are found to be typical examples of female property crime. Violent crimes are also committed by women, but such crimes are reflective of conditions of female alienation and frustration rather than being acts of aggression and domination. Rather than their conduct being overtly aggressive, violence by women reflects their domestic position, arising mostly from marital or family disputes and employing weapons common to the home and kitchen. And when caught up by the bourgeois criminal justice system, women are not generally perceived as dangerous and sociopathic, but rather simply displaced from their "proper" role in capitalistic society. Thus they must be "rehabilitated" to their supportive positions in the home and workplace.

In addition to documenting how capitalism produces female crime, Marxist-feminists also concentrate their study on the kinds of victimization typically experienced by women. Since violence against women, like female crime, is reflective of the oppressive nature of capitalist society, Marxist-feminists study the degree to which economic and gender inequality produce or intensify violence against women (Schwendinger and Schwendinger, 1983). A common thesis among Marxist-feminists is that rape and other forms of sexual violence occur more frequently in societies where greater inequality between the sexes exists (Beirne and Messerschmidt, 1991).

The value of the Marxist-feminist approach lies in its analytic ability to tie the behaviors toward and of women to the larger social structure of modern society. By adopting traditional Marxism as its theoretical framework, Marxist feminism constitutes a substantial contribution to and expansion of critical Marxist thought. But although Marxist-feminists draw on the strengths of Marxism as a theoretical and explanatory scheme, the perspective is weakened since, by definition, it makes women's issues subordinate to what are purportedly more overriding issues of class and political economy. Through Marxism, women are offered the hope that by participating in the struggle to bring about more equitable economic and social conditions, they and all other oppressed peoples will benefit.

In the next section, socialist-feminists take the logic of Marxism a step further by arguing that partriarchy is equally as oppressive as capitalism in the struggle for women's rights.

The Socialist-Feminist Perspective

As depicted in the previous section, by arguing that gender oppression is the result of class oppression, the oppression of women becomes of secondary concern in traditional Marxism since women are seen as merely another class who would benefit from a socialist transformation of society. This, of course, presents substantial problems for those feminists who see sexual exploitation as being every bit as fundamental and important as economic exploitation. A problem of substantial theoretical significance for socialist-feminists, therefore, is how to place women and their concerns at the center of a Marxist framework. The solution to this problem is to take a critical look at both Marxism and the social organization of patriarchy as they apply to capitalist society.

When analyzing the traditional Marxist literature from a broader socialist perspective it is clear that: (1) Marx and Engels as theorists, like anyone else, were products of their environment and cannot have been expected to totally transcend their time and place in history (Messerschmidt, 1988); and (2) the essence of Marxism is really its analytic method and not the attitudes of Marx and Engels concerning women and their social condition (Firestone, 1970). Therefore, while adhering to the principles of dialectic materialism, socialist-feminists reformulate and rethink traditional Marxism and some of its most basic assumptions.

The first assumption of a feminist approach to socialist thought is that sex class is just as fundamental as economic class as an analytic concept. Also, it is clear that if production (the creation of material goods) as a social process can be traced back to the origins of society, reproduction (the creation of human beings) too has to be just as basic and materialistic a process. According to one feminist's analysis of sex class, the biological family is characterized by these fundamental—if not immutable—facts:

1. Women throughout history before the advent of birth control were at the continual mercy of their biology—menstruation, menopause, "female ills," constant painful childbirth, wetnursing and care of infants—all of which made them dependent on males (whether brother, father, husband, lover, or clan, government, community-at-large) for physical survival.

2. Human infants take an even longer time to grow up than animals, and thus are helpless and, for some short period at least, dependent on adults for physical survival.

3. A basic mother/child interdependency has existed in some form

in every society, past or present, and thus has shaped the psychology of every mature female and every infant.

4. The natural reproductive difference between the sexes led directly to the first division of labor based on sex, which is at the origins of all further division into economic and cultural classes and is possibly even at the root of all caste. (Firestone, 1970)

By fitting the above biological facts into a socialist conception of dialectical materialism, we arrive at a depiction of the nature of female oppression that emphasizes not the ownership of tools and equipment but the ownership of women's bodies. Notice in the diagram that follows how the oppression of women by men parallels that depicted previously of the oppression of the working class by capitalists. In this way, the logic of Marxism is extended from economic class to sex class by substituting the ownership of the means of production with the ownership of the means of reproduction. This conceptualization is essential for understanding how the logic of traditional Marxism becomes directly applicable to contemporary problems associated with the oppression of women.

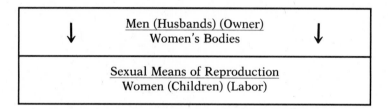

Socialist-Feminist Image of Female Oppression: Sex-Class

Oppression Based on Sexual Exploitation. (Chart adapted from *The Dialectic of Sex: The Case for Feminist Revolution*, by Shulamith Firestone. New York; William Morrow & Co., Inc., 1970)

The socialist-feminist reconstruction of the dialectic process based on sex class, like the traditional economic class analysis of Marx and Engels, has revolutionary implications.

1. The socialist-feminist image of female oppression places its emphasis squarely on the problem—the male ownership and control of women's bodies.

2. By equating reproduction with production, the socialist-feminist reformulation of female oppression observes the fundamental rules of class conflict and the dialectic process: a materialistic, class-based dichotomy that forms the basis of social organization and change in society.

3. By identifying the root of the problem for women (the lack of control and ownership of their bodies and the reproductive process), the means by which women can take control of their own lives and thereby change the oppressive arrangements within which they live is made clear. The key to a truly egalitarian society becomes a sex war in which women take over control of thier own bodies through the seizure and control of reproductive technology.

The socialist-feminist reformulation puts gender and sex class at the center of the dialectic. With such a reconceptualization of the fundamental importance of sex class, socialist-feminists must no longer limit their analysis to the politics of economics. Gender oppression becomes more than a simple extension or byproduct of class society. Gender oppression is not just a manifestation of a social condition that emanates solely from the public sphere; women are shown to be oppressed in the home as well as in the workplace. It is clear that with the socialist reformulation of classic Marxist thought, partriarchy and capitalism become codeterminants of female oppression.

Application of Socialist-Feminism to the Problems of Crime and Criminal Justice

By identifying the essence of female oppression to be the control men have over female sexuality, crimes of and against women come more clearly into focus. Marx, for example, saw prostitution as merely another example of the "universal prostitution of the worker" (cited in Messerschmidt, 1988; Jagger, 1983). By not seeing women as an oppressed class in their own right, Marx, and the Marxists who uncritically followed his lead, found no reason to pay special attention to women and crime. However, with a new sensitivity to the importance of gender as a causal variable, socialists are now able to trace the origin of crimes such as prostitution (male pimps manipulating and controlling the bodies of women) back to the rape and sexual abuse experienced in childhood by many prostitutes. The entire history and scope of male domination over women and the lack of control women have over their own lives takes on new meaning as sex and economics become causally linked.

With the awareness that oppressive conditions in the domestic as well as the public sphere exist and are central to understanding women's place in society, crimes such as acquaintance rape and woman battering take on new meaning. To the extent that men perceive themselves as owning, or at least controlling, women and their sexuality, beatings and sexual abuse can be seen as a means by which male power is asserted and reinforced. Without control over the decision of when and if they are to be pregnant, women's biological condition continues to bind them to their historical role as dependent and subservient creatures. Even the ideology that serves to justify and perpetrate women's place in the domestic sphere becomes a subject of analysis since inquiries into the predominating ethic of home life become, essentially, studies of the predominating rationale for patriarchy.

Without an understanding of the relations between men and women, there simply cannot exist an understanding of the differences in male and female criminality (Messerschmidt, 1988). In addition, unless gender relations and the power stemming from male-female relationships are taken into consideration, the prevalent methods for treating women accused and convicted of criminal activity in capitalistic, patriarchal societies cannot be properly assessed. The extent to which patriarchy and capitalism reinforce one another must be determined in order to properly address these kinds of relevant issues.

The socialist emphasis that sex class is just as important as economic class for understanding the unique condition of female oppression opens up the homes, lifestyles, and criminal activity of the rich and powerful as well as those of the working class since the dialectics of sex, unlike those of class, are certainly not limited solely by economic boundaries. Through the construction of a uniquely socialist perspective that is built upon, but substantially extends, the scope of traditional Marxism, a socialist-feminist perspective is emerging that promises to expand our knowledge of the structure, process, and change related to the oppression of all women in modern society. To the extent that women are oppressed in the domestic as well as the public spheres of activity, and to the extent that men continue to control female productive as well as reproductive labor, the socialist-feminist perspective, being in concert with the analytic power of the dialectic, provides a highly relevant theoretical base from which to view, analyze, and critique the condition of women in modern society.

Summary of Marxist and Socialist Feminist Thought

The Marxist and socialist perspectives emphasize the inclusion of a broad institutional setting that embodies the economic, political, and ideational aspects of society for analyzing issues of concern to women. Although differing with respect to the degree that capitalism is responsible for the oppressive condition of women, Marxists and socialists share a critical view of society that serves well the contemporary concerns of women. Through application of the Marxist-feminist and the socialist-feminist perspectives to problems of crime and criminal justice, the contribution of variables such as capitalism, class, gender, patriarchy, and ideology become clearer. To the extent that the eradication of gender oppression is possible, both the Marxist-feminist and the socialist-feminist perspectives point to the source(s) of the problem and thereby suggest its solution.

In the following section we look at yet another feminist perspective that arises when sex itself is considered to be problematic.

Overview of Radical Feminism

Radical feminism is a potent force in contemporary society. By unequivocally adopting a woman's view of the world, radical feminism is forcing a restructuring of the traditional male-female roles in society. Taken-for-granted assumptions about the world are being called into question as radical feminists attack nearly every aspect of social life. Particularly in the area of crime and criminal justice, radical feminists are successfully formulating into the law what were previously considered by many to be outlandish claims. Anyone who does not take radical feminism seriously does not understand the pervasive influence it has already had.

Because radical feminists make the boldest of statements and suggest the most radical kinds of changes, the views and programs of radical feminism have drawn much attention to it. If feminists as a group are stereotyped as "man-haters" or "lesbians," it is primarily because radical feminists have boldly identified men and the norm of heterosexuality as being the real basis for the subordination of women in society. By extricating themselves from their dependence on men, radical feminists have managed to expose the roots of female oppression. It is perhaps their questioning and scrutiny of male authority that makes radical feminism such a threat to men and the world men have constructed for themselves.

Analyzing radical feminist thought is essential for understanding the soul of the women's movement. Radical feminism is clearly on the cutting edge of change. Without the heat and fire generated by the radical perspective, feminism would surely die as a social movement. Learning what radical feminism is all about is essential for understanding much of the thrust and direction of the modern women's movement.

Radical Feminist Thought

Imagine waking up one day and finding that nothing fits. No, we are not referring here to clothes or garments, we are referring to you as a person. We are referring to you and the world of which you are a part.

Adjustment to the world around us is not as easy as many presume. "Fitting in" is far from being an automatic or effortless process. People differ from each other, and adjustment—in a social as well as a psychological sense—depends in part on how closely we as individuals match the social surroundings in which we live. All seems well and natural for those whose personal attributes and predilections conform to the way the world is structured. But it sometimes takes being blind before one fully realizes the extent to which the world is constructed for those who can see, being left-handed to uncover the ubiquitous skew of a right-handed environment, being homosexual to grasp the enormity and depth of a heterosexual world, and being female to comprehend the intricate web of reinforcing contingencies that prevail throughout a society that is made for and by men.

Some have embraced feminism as the result of alienating or frustrating life circumstances, others have always been feminists. Some have chosen feminism as a preferred way of seeing the world, others have always seen the world as feminists. Some have had their consciousness raised to the level of feminist awareness, others have always adopted a woman-centered perspective. However, to experience, perceive, or think feminism is not the same as living it. Radical feminism goes to the depths of the human soul. Radical feminism analyzes and inspects the world with a critical, penetrating, and microscopic focus. Radical feminism strips society, tearing away its patriarchal and androgenic facade to see its true shape and form.

Of all the schools of feminist thought, radical feminism asks the most penetrating of questions, pokes its inquisitive nose in the most private of places, and demands—not requests—that fundamental change take place. For those most content with and supportive of the status quo, radical feminism is the most irritating and abrasive form of feminism. For those who refuse to adjust and accommodate to a world that forces them outside and defines them as marginal and deviant, radical feminism is the most stimulating and encouraging of feminist perspectives. Let us inquire further into radical feminism to determine how this perspective concurrently has the power to alienate some while inspiriting others.

Fundamental Notions of Radical Feminism

The thoughts typically associated with the word 'feminist' are primarily the result of the actions and efforts of radical feminists. The position taken by radical feminists is the most extreme (men are the problem), and their program for change is the most revolutionary (the dominance of men must be eliminated from society). If taken to its logical extremes, radical feminism asserts that 1) men have established their position of dominance through the use of force, violence and sexual intimidation, 2) women do not need men and must sever all relationships that place women in submissive or dependent relationships vis-a-vis men, and 3) the ultimate solution to the oppressive condition of women is to either separate from men entirely, or at least to start anew by socializing all children to live in and prefer a gender-free world.

The "radical" in radical feminism derives from the fundamental reshaping of all social life that such a program for change entails. Imagine a society in which all the traditional relationships between men and women were suddenly abolished. Sex, marriage, masculine power and privilege, the sexual divisions of labor, as well as the many-faceted social relationships that stem from heterosexuality would all be erased from the social scene. What would be left, according to radical feminism, would be a gender-free society in which women, for the first time in history, would be able to interact and compete on an equal basis with men.

Once man is identified as the primary reason for the subordination of woman, men in general become the problem and the entire social world becomes problematic. All social practices, according to radical feminism, must be analyzed to determine their sexist and oppressive nature and then reformulated to exclude masculine power and privilege. Such an extreme reconstruction of social life forces an awareness of the depth to which our lives are shaped by the belief that men are superior to women, the assumption that heterosexuality is normal and natural, and the acceptance of the social practices that have grown out of such conceptions as being legitimate and inevitable.

The extent to which radical feminism defines men as "the enemy" cannot be overemphasized. In addition to separating themselves from the world of men, radical feminists also separate themselves from other feminist groups who shy away from going as far as they do in seeing "men" as the cause of female oppression. Some radical feminists define heterosexual women as collaborators (Tuttle, 1986), presumably since they sleep with the enemy. According to Sally Simpson, a feminist scholar, male domination—not class—is the fundamental origin of female subordination. She emphasises that "subordination" is a term favored by radical feminists because they identify the holder of power (men) as the culprit. Another prominent radical feminist, Catharine MacKinnon, advances the feminist anti-male sentiment still further by depicting the United States as, "a vast conspiracy of men to rape and terrorize women" (Strebeigh, 1991).

When one enters the world of radical feminism, one enters a revolutionary sphere in which the normal becomes abnormal and what has been should no longer be. Since male dominance permeates all of society—all of culture—the battleground becomes extensive. In their writings, by analogy and through example, radical feminists strike at men as hard as they can. What is of pride to men (their masculinity, their physical strength, their machismo), become objects of scorn. For radical feminists, male genitalia become a weapon and the symbol of male superiority (Brownmiller, 1975). All men—not merely the "patriarchy" or male-dominated institutions—are identified as the enemy because all men benefit from women's oppression (Tuttle, 1986). History itself becomes suspect since most historians have been men. Radical feminism, therefore, engages in a reinterpretation of "the history of man" to reveal the intimidation, fear, and subjugation allegedly used by men to control and dominate women. Illustrative of such a radical reconstruction of history are the writings of Susan Brownmiller on "the mass psychology of rape."

> Man's structural capacity to rape and woman's corresponding structural vulnerability are as basic to the physiology of both our sexes as the primal act of sex itself. Had it not been for this accident of biology, an accommodation requiring the locking together of two separate parts, penis into vagina, there would be neither copulation nor rape as we know it.
>
> . . . one of the earliest forms of male bonding must have been the gang rape of one woman by a band of marauding men. This accomplished, rape became not only a male prerogative, but man's basic weapon of force against woman, the principal agent of his will and her fear. His forcible entry into her body, despite her physical protestations and struggle, became the vehicle of his victorious conquest over her being, the ultimate test of his superior strength, the triumph of his manhood.
>
> Man's discovery that his genitalia could serve as a weapon to generate fear must rank as one of the most important discoveries of prehistoric times, along with the use of fire and the first crude stone axe. From prehistoric times to the present, I believe, rape has played a critical function. It is nothing more or less than a conscious process of intimidation by which all men keep all women in a state of fear.
>
> Female fear of an open season of rape, and not a natural inclination toward monogamy, motherhood or love, was probably the single causative factor in the original subjugation of woman by man, the most important key to her historic dependence, her domestication by protective mating. (Brownmiller, 1975)

As part of their quest to rip the foundation out from underneath patriarchy and other bastions of male dominance and control, radical feminists not only depict man as totally egotistical, violent, and animalistic, but the position is also advanced that women do not need nor want men. Radical feminism sees man's control of women's sexuality as being central to masculine dominance (MacKinnon, 1982). For many feminists, sexuality is a central issue that demands resolution if women are ever to free themselves from the control of men. Heterosexuality, therefore, is identified by many radical feminists as the cornerstone of women's oppression, thus taking the battle between men and women right into the bedroom. Radical feminists see heterosexuality not as a natural biological need but, rather, as a ploy used by men to keep women dependent on them. By rejecting heterosexuality as a biological need, women are able to extricate themselves from men while at the same time devaluing still another source of male pride. Consider the following radical feminist's debunking of the "myth" that vaginal penetration by a penis is necessary for female orgasm.

> The theory of vaginal orgasm was the concoction of a man, Freud, whose theories generally place women in an inhumane and exploited role. His theory of vaginal orgasm reaches the apex of these. This theory was inspired by his confrontations with women who were sick to death of the female role, and it adjusted women back into this female role by conning them that it was in a woman's interest, by her very nature (i.e., it is in the interest of her vagina), to be dehumanized and exploited. While Freud's theory is inconsistent with female anatomy, it is excellent evidence in support of the theory that the concept of sexual intercourse is a political construct, reified into an institution. (Atkinson, 1974)

Radical feminism is clearly confrontational in its approach. By attacking man directly and calling into question all relationships between men and women, public and private, the adversarial nature of radical feminism is evident. Besides confrontation, an additional dimension of radical feminism is the symbolic nature of its feminist discourse. Radical feminism does not assert that some men are sexist; it declares all men to be sexist. Radical feminism does not identify certain aspects of society as being patriarchal; it affirms society itself to be a bulwark of patriarchy. By focusing on such large-scale patterns that characterize society as a whole, radical feminism becomes a cultural war in which battles are fought over the use and meaning of symbols. The everyday language we use, our taken-for-granted assumptions about each other, the images portrayed by the media, as well as the cultural themes that abound in society, are for radical feminists the stuff out of which the subordination and oppression of women are made. By focusing on the success radical feminists have had in raising questions about fundamental ideas in society, we next address the impact of radical feminism on issues of crime and the criminal justice system.

Radical Feminism on Crime and the Criminal Justice System

Due to the identification of sexuality as a central element of masculine dominance, it should not be surprising that radical feminists have concentrated on sexual violence against women as a topic of prime concern. Rape, wife beating, incestuous assault, sexual harassment and pornography serve as common examples of criminal behaviors that are typically addressed by radical feminists (Beirne & Messerschmidt, 1991). By identifying the implicit assumptions held about the victims and motives of sexual assault, radical feminsts have been particularly successful at showing the law and its application to be male-dominated, male-centered, as well as male-serving. Changing such a sexist application of the law is fully compatible with the philosophy and political activism of radical feminism. A prime example of the impact of radical feminism in criminal justice is that of the crime of rape.

In the early 1970s rape came to be defined not as a sexual crime, as it had been traditionally envisioned, but as a violent crime (Greer, 1970). The influential book *Against Our Will*, published in 1975 by Susan Brownmiller, reinforced the image of rape as being a crime of violence and domination rather than a crime of passion. This change in perception altered in a fundamental way the perceived seriousness of the crime of rape as well as the way in which the offender-victim relationship was interpreted. As a sexual crime, rape is likely to be viewed as a natural outgrowth of courting behavior. Arguably, a sexual act is one in which the woman may be as culpable as the man. And, seated firmly within a male, heterosexual purview of the sex act, rape is at least partially understandable as simply an expression of normal sexual urges. According to MacKinnon, this traditional view of rape sees women as the rapist sees women (cited in Strebeigh, 1991). Such traditional notions of rape change in a radical way when "violence" replaces "sex" as the principal motivating factor for the crime.

Today the attitude of the criminal justice system, as well as research on the topic of rape, have changed considerably as a result of seeing rape as an act of violence (Groth, 1979). At last the full impact of the physical and psychological trauma associated with rape is being recognized. Instead of treating rape victims as "co-conspirators" in the act, women are now being treated as innocent victims. Rather than treating rapists as normal men with strong sexual urges, we are beginning to recognize the intentional terror and harm of rapists and process them as violent and dangerous criminals. And what constitutes a truly revolutionary change in our thinking about rape as a result of the influence of radical feminism is that we are now beginning to realize that boyfriends, relatives, and husbands can be rapists too. "Acquaintance rape" is a new category of rape that is a direct outgrowth of the efforts of radical feminists to redefine personal wrongs as criminal.

Another realm of behavior that radical feminists have impacted is that of pornography. In our heterosexually-dominated society, pornography (material designed to sexually arouse and excite) has become a $7-billion-a-year industry, with its products available at corner newsstands in cities throughout the country (Robertson, 1987). As traditionally viewed, pornography is merely another form of expression in a free society. Although pornography may not be good in and of itself, according to those who argue in its favor, it does minimal harm in that those who find it offensive do not have to read or purchase it. Indeed, the traditional view not only condones pornography, but at times argues in its favor as being a "safety valve" that allows for the private release of sexual fantasies (Henslin, 1990). Radical feminists, of course, attack such conceptions as being totally erroneous and fallacious.

Radical feminists not only view pornography as personally offensive and degrading: they argue that pornography causes violence against women. "Hard-core" pornography is that which typically depicts women as enjoying various kinds of sexual perversions and even inviting acts of sexual violence. According to Andrea Dworkin (1981), pornography shapes men's behavior toward women. The imagery of women being stripped, bound, assaulted, and tortured, combined with heterosexual lust, results in acts of sexual violence such as kidnapping, rape, mutilation, and even death. Masturbating to pornographic images is not viewed as a harmless outlet for sexual tension, but rather as part of a cycle of conditioning and reinforcement that eventually leads to sexual assault. Pornography, according to the radical feminist perspective, is nothing more than the graphic and sexually explicit subordination of women. Pornography does not view women as human beings, but as sexual objects who exist exclusively for male perverse pleasure. If the imagery conveyed through pornography is taken literally, women actually enjoy being raped and brutalized and penetrated by objects or animals. Nothing could be further from the truth. If radical feminism is correct in its assertions, pornography, as a powerful agent of socialization in society, is a disease that infects the minds and morals of all of those who are exposed to it. Hence, pornography is not harmless or passive entertainment. Pornography is, in fact, an active criminogenic force that must be eliminated from society.

Many find little argument with feminist efforts to reduce violent crimes against women or curb the distribution of "hard core" pornography. So, perhaps, the efforts of radical feminists to change all aspects of social life is better illustrated by the emergence of "sexual harassment" as a new form of deviance.

Not long ago, "sexual harassment" was not a part of our language. The first book on the subject, written by radical feminist Catharine MacKinnon, did not appear until 1979. The Supreme Court did not hear its first sexual harassment case until 1986 (Strebeigh, 1991). But now, primarily due to the national media coverage that focused on charges of sexual harassment brought against then-Supreme-Court-nominee Clarence Thomas, sexual harassment became an issue that will probably affect male-female relations far into the future.

Sexual harassment is defined as "the use of one's position to force unwanted sexual demands on someone" (MacKinnon, 1979). Due to the emerging social and legal sanctions accorded such behavior, the potential charge of sexual harassment is forcing a rethinking of the previously taken-for-granted male prerogative to use sex as a criteria for evaluating work performance and/or interacting with women personally. The crux of the problem lies in the fact that interaction between men and women that was previously viewed as "personal" or "natural" is now being interpreted as "harassment." Radical feminists charge that sexual harassment is really a variant of sexual discrimination and/or abuse. Here are a few examples of behavior or situations that previously were overlooked by women but now can evince charges of sexual harassment.

- A supervisor finds one of his secretaries to be sexually attractive. He asks her out on a date. She refuses. Thinking that persistence might pay off, he continues to ask her for dates discretely and privately. The employee formally charges her supervisor with sexual harassment.

- A female music teacher enters her classroom to find that an 18th Century work of art depicting a nude woman resting on a couch has been hung on the wall. The teacher files a claim of sexual harassment against the university because teaching in this room is part of her work assignment.

- A female government employee files sexual harassment charges against several coworkers because she overhears them telling "dirty" jokes during the lunch hour.

As illustrated by these examples, feminists are clearly moving women's issues into everyday life. Are these kinds of behavior private and natural, or are they a form of sexual discrimination? Are the secretary, the music teacher, and the government employee depicted above really victims of sexual abuse? Or are the men and the university in these examples victims of an overzealous female radicalism? The answers to these and a host of related questions are not clear because they have yet to be hammered out in the institutions, businesses, schools, homes, and courts of this country. But this is the point. The standards by which men and women judge each other are being redefined, primarily due to the impetus of radical feminism. To the extent that radical feminism is successful in making personal relations into political relations, the whole realm of social existence will be affected.

REFERENCES

Atkinson, Ti-Grace. *Radical Feminism and Love*. New York: Links Books, 1974.

Austin, Roy L. "Women's Liberation and Increases in Minor, Major, and Occupational Offenses," *Criminology*, Vol 20 (November), #3-4, 1982.

Bartol, Curt R. *Criminal Behavior, A Psychosocial Approach*. Englewood Cliffs, NJ: Prentice Hall, 1991.

Beirne, Piers and James Messerschmidt. *Criminology*. San Diego, CA: Harcourt Brace Jovanovich, 1991.

Blumer, Herbert. *Symbolic Interaction*. Englewood Cliffs, NJ: Prentice Hall, 1969.

Brownmiller, Susan. *Against Our Will: Men, Women, and Rape*. New York: Simon & Schuster, 1975.

Chesney-Lind, Media. "Girls' Crime and Woman's Place: Toward a Feminist Model of Female Delinquency." *Crime & Delinquency*, Vol. 35 No. 1, January 1989: 5–29.

Daly, Kathleen, and Meda Chesney-Lind. "Feminism and Criminology." *Justice Quarterly*, 5(4), 1988:101–143.

Del Giudice, Marguerite. "The Mobster Who Could Bring Down the Mob." *The New York Times Magazine*, June 2, 1991.

Firestone, Shulamith. *The Dialectic of Sex: The Case for Feminist Revolution*. New York: Bantam, 1970.

Gallese, Liz Roman. "Blue-Collar Women." *Wall Street Journal*, July 28, 1980.

Gibbons, Don C., and Marvin D. Krohn, *Delinquent Behavior*. Englewood Cliffs, NJ: Prentice Hall, 1991.

Gilligan, Carol. *In a Different Voice: Psychological Theory and Woman's Development*. Cambridge, MA: Harvard University Press, 1982.

Giordano, Peggy C., and Cernkovich, Stephen A. "On Complicating The Relationship Between Liberation And Delinquency." *Social Problems*. Vol 26, No 4, April, 1979.

Greer, Germaine. *The Female Eunuch*. New York: McGraw-Hill, 1970.

Hanmer, Jalna. "Violence and the Social Control of Women." *Feminist Issues*. 1, 1981:29–46.

Harris, Marvin. "Why Men Dominate Women." *New York Times Magazine*, Vol 46, Nov. 13, 1977.

Henslin, James M. *Social Problems.* Englewood Cliffs, NJ: Prentice Hall, 1990.

Humm, Maggie, (Ed.). *The Dictionary Of Feminist Theory.* New York: Harvester Wheatsheaf, 1989.

Jaggar, Alison M. *Feminist Politics and Human Nature.* Totowa, NJ: Rowman and Allanheld, 1983.

Jaggar, Allison M., and Paula Rothenberg, (Eds.). *Feminist Frameworks.* New York: McGraw-Hill, 1984.

Jeffery, C. Ray. *Criminology, An Interdisciplinary Approach.* Englewood Cliffs, NJ: Prentice Hall, 1990.

Leonard, Eileen B. *A Critique of Criminology Theory, Women, Crime and Society.* New York: Longman, Inc., 1982.

Maris, Ronald W. *Social Problems.* Belmont, CA: Wadsworth Publishing Company, 1988.

Marris, Anthony R. "Sex and Theories Of Deviance: Toward A Functional Theory of Deviant Type-Scripts." *American Sociological Review,* Vol 42 (February, 1977):3–16.

Messerschmidt, James W. *Capitalism, Patriarchy, and Crime: Toward a Socialist Feminist Criminology.* Totowa, NJ: Rowman and Littlefield, 1986.

Oakley, Ann. *Sex, Gender, and Society.* New York: Harper and Row, 1972.

Phillips, Anne, (Ed.). *Feminism and Equality.* Oxford: Basil Blackwell, 1987.

Rosenblum, Karen. "Female Deviance and the Female Sex Role: A Preliminary Investigation." *British Journal of Sociology,* 25(2), 1975:169–85.

Simon, Rita J. and Landis, Jean. *The Crimes Women Commit, The Punishments They Receive.* Lexington, MA: D. C. Heath and Company, 1991.

Simpson, Sally S. "Feminist Theory, Crime, and Justice." *Criminology,* Vol. 27, #4, 1989.

Smart, Carol. *Women, Crime and Criminology: A Feminist Critique.* London: Routledge & Kegan, 1976.

Steffensmeier, D., E. Allan, and C. Streifel, "Development and Female Crime: A Cross-National Test of Alternative Explanations." *Social Forces,* September, 68(1), 1989:262–83.

Steffensmeier, Darrell J. "Organization Properties and Sex-Segregation in the Underworld." *Social Forces,* Vol.61:4, June 1983.

Steffensmeier, Darrell J. "Crime and the Contemporary Woman: An Analysis of Changing Levels of Female Property Crime." *Social Forces,* 57(December), 1978: 566–583.

Theodorson, George A. and Achilles G. *A Modern Dictionary of Sociology.* New York: Barnes & Noble, 1979.

Section 2

Historical Development of Women's Issues

The study of history is important because it discloses the underlying pulse of existence. To demonstrate regularity in social affairs is to uncover the fundamental structure of society. The study of history and its treatment of women reveals a long chain of events that binds generation after generation of women to the control of men.

That women have historically been discriminated against by law is a fact. In the opening chapter in this section, Roslyn Muraskin traces the history of litigation and its connection to patriarchal control. She succinctly states that "women have historically been victimized by policies designed to protect them." A study of women's inequality before the law is of utmost importance because it is clear that in a democracy, without the force of law behind them, women have been and will continue to be civilly dead. Because changes in the criminal justice system are fundamental to the advancement of women in society, a clear understanding of the specific ways in which the criminal justice system has reinforced and intensified patriarchal control of women is of utmost importance.

In the concluding chapter of the section, Nanci Wilson, in her fascinating account of the witch hunts that occurred in Puritan Salem Village in the year 1692, demonstrates that casting out demons was not simply an anomaly of life that occurred in early America. As made clear by Wilson's insightful historical analysis, the need to tame women and nature is one of those persistent themes that ties the cosmos of Western culture to a system of male patriarchal control and that persists to this day. Casting out devils by the Puritan community, according to this account, is no different from today's efforts by the criminal justice system to criminalize drug use by pregnant mothers. Read this engaging account of how the motivation to destroy female witches is really an account of how men continue to act to preserve the privileged position they hold in what they define to be "the natural order of things."

2

Remember the Ladies

Roslyn Muraskin

Women have taken their case to court to argue for equality. The history of women's struggles teaches us that litigation is but a catalyst for change. A change in attitude is still needed. Discrimination still exists. This chapter highlights what women have sought since the early days of our country's history. Equality!

Controversy still abounds. Women of today, admittedly, are involved in professions where they were not allowed. The classification by sex evident in the early days is slowly being eroded. But sexual harassment still exists. The decision makers are mainly men. The women's movement is the most integrated and populist force in this country. Women have waited more than two hundred years for the equality promised by the Declaration of Independence. When both men and women can be defined as persons, *then equality will abound for all.*

The search by women for equality is not a recent phenomenon. In 1776, Abigail Adams admonished her husband, John, to "remember the ladies" in the drafting of the Constitution. She insisted that:

> we . . . will not hold ourselves bound by any laws in which we have no voice or representation.

The Declaration of Independence as signed in 1776 stated that all men are created equal and that governments derive their power from the consent of the governed. Women were not included in either concept. In fact, nowhere in either the Constitution or the Declaration of Independence is the word woman used. The only time the word sex is used is in the Nineteenth Amendment to the Constitution, signed in 1920, giving women the right to vote.

The original American Constitution of 1787 was founded on English law and did not recognize women as citizens or as individuals with legal rights. A woman was expected to obey her husband or nearest male kin—the power of the ballot was denied to her.

Women were not considered persons under the Fourteenth Amendment to the Constitution, which guaranteed that no state shall deny to "any person within its jurisdiction the equal protection of the laws." Women have historically been victimized by policies designed to protect them.

In 1848, a convention was held in Seneca Falls, New York to mark the beginning of the organized feminist movement of the nineteenth century. The convention, attended by some three hundred women, demonstrated a collective effort to achieve equal rights for women. Their focus was on property rights and suffrage. They went so far as to adopt their own Declaration of Independence:

> We hold these truths to be self-evident: that all men and women are created equal; that they are endowed by their creator with certain inalienable rights; that among these are life, liberty, and the pursuit of happiness; that to secure these rights governments are instituted, deriving their just powers from the consent of the governed.
>
> Whenever any form of government becomes destructive of these ends, it is the right of those who suffer from it to refuse allegiance to it, and to insist upon the institution of new government. . . . The history of mankind is a history of repeated injuries and usurpation on the part of men toward women, having in direct object the establishment of an absolute tyranny over her. To prove this, let the facts be submitted to a candid world.
>
> He has never permitted her to exercise her inalienable right to the elective franchise.
>
> He has compelled her to submit to laws in the formation of which she had no voice.
>
> He has withheld from her rights which are given to the most ignorant and degraded men—both natives and foreigners.
>
> Having deprived her of this first right of a citizen, the elective franchise, thereby leaving her without representation in the halls of legislation, he has oppressed her on all sides.
>
> He has made her, if married, in the eyes of the law, civilly dead.
>
> He has taken from her all rights in property, even to the wages she earns.
>
> He has made her, morally, an irresponsible being, as she can

commit crimes with impunity, provided they be done in the presence of her husband. In the covenant of marriage, she is compelled to promise obedience to her husband, he becoming, to all intents and purposes, her master—the law giving him power to deprive her of her liberty, and to administer chastisement.

He has so framed the laws of divorce, as to what shall be the proper cause, and in cases of separation, to whom the guardianship of the children shall be given, as to be wholly regardless of the happiness of women—the law, in all cases, going upon a false supposition of the supremacy of man, and giving all power into his hands.

After depriving her of all rights as a married woman, if single, and the owner of property, he has taxed her to support a government which recognizes her only when her property can be made profitable to it.

He has denied her the facilities for obtaining a thorough education, all colleges being closed against her.

He allows her in Church, as well as State, but in a subordinate position.

He has endeavored, in every way that he could, to destroy her confidence in her own powers, to lessen her self-respect, and make her willing to lead a dependent and abject life. (Schneir 1972, pp. 77–82)

And so three hundred women declared. They therefore resolved the following at Seneca Falls:

That all laws which prevent women from occupying such a station in society as her conscience shall dictate, or which place her in a position inferior to that of man, are contrary to the great precept of nature, and therefore of no force or authority.

That the women of this country ought to be enlightened in regard to laws under which they live, that they may no longer publish their degradation by declaring themselves satisfied with their present position. . . .

That the same amount of virtue, delicacy, and refinement of behavior that is required of women in the social state, should also be required of man, and the same transgressions should be visited with equal severity on both man and woman.

And that it be further resolved

That the speedy success of our cause depends upon the zealous and untiring efforts of both men and women, for the overthrow of the monopoly of the pulpit, and for the securing to woman an equal participation with men in the various trades, professions, and commerce. (Schneir 1972)

This was the year 1848.

A federal equal rights amendment was first introduced to Congress in 1923 and was submitted to the states continuously over a period of time for ratification until it finally failed in 1972. It simply stated:

> Section 1. Equality of rights under the law shall not be denied or abridged by the United States or by any other State on account of sex.
>
> Section 2. The Congress shall have the power to enforce, by appropriate legislation, the provisions of this Article.
>
> Section 3. This Amendment shall take effect two years after the date of ratification.

It never happened.

Oberlin College was the first college to admit women in 1833. Until 1841, women could take only a shortened literary course, on the theory that the education of women had a different purpose than for men. For many years women were not permitted to speak in class and were required to wait on male students. It was believed that women's high calling was to be the mothers of the race and that they should stay within that special sphere in order that future generations should not suffer from the want of devoted and undistracted mother care. If women were to enter the areas of law, religion, medicine, academics, government, or any sort of public character, the home would suffer from neglect. Washing men's clothes, caring for their rooms, serving the men at the tables, remaining respectfully silent in public assemblages, the Oberlin coeds were being prepared for motherhood and to serve their men.

Elizabeth Blackwell was the first woman to get a medical degree in 1849. She applied to twenty-nine medical schools until one finally accepted her.

In 1873, the Supreme Court upheld an Illinois state law prohibiting female lawyers from practicing in state courts (*Bradwell* v. *State of Illinois*, 83 U.S. 130 [1872]). The Court in its wisdom declared that:

> the civil war as well as nature herself, has always recognized a wide difference in the respective spheres and destinies of man and woman. Man is or should be woman's protector and defender. The natural and proper timidity and delicacy which belongs to the female sex evidently unfits it for many of the occupations of civil life. The constitution of the family organization, which is founded in the divine ordinance, as well as in the nature of things, indicates the domestic sphere as that which belongs to the domain and functions of womanhood. The harmony of interests and views which belong or should belong to the family institution, is repugnant to the idea of a woman adopting a distinct and independent career from that of her husband.

The court continued and stated that:

> The paramount destiny and mission of woman are to fulfill the noble and benign offices of wife and mother. This is the law of the Creator. And the rules of civil society must be adopted to the general constitution of things, and cannot be based upon exceptional cases.

Justice Miller summed it up when he stated:

> I am not prepared to say that it is one of her fundamental rights and privileges to be admitted into every office and position, including those which require highly special qualifications and demanding social responsibilities. In the nature of things it is not every citizen of every age, sex, and condition that is qualified for every calling and position.

It took until 1860 in New York to pass the Married Women's Property Act, an attempt to give to women property that she owned to be her sole and separate property. A married woman until this time was not entitled to own or keep property after marriage. This act stated "that which a woman married in this state owns at the time of her marriage, and the rents, issues and proceeds of all such property, shall notwithstanding her marriage, be and remain her sole and separate property."

The right to vote, which was not won until 1920, was a struggle for women. In the case of *Minor* v. *Happersett* (88 U.S. 162, 1874) the Supreme Court denied women the right to vote. The argument then was "that as a woman born or naturalized in the United States is a citizen of the United States and of the State in which she resides, she has therefore the right to vote." The Court stated that there is no doubt that women may be citizens. The direct question was therefore presented whether all citizens are necessarily voters. "The Constitution has not added the right of suffrage to the privileges and immunities of citizenship as they existed at the time it was adopted." In no one state constitution was suffrage conferred upon women. It took the Nineteenth Amendment to the Constitution to grant women the right to vote. Neither John Adams or those following him were willing to "remember the ladies."

> Federal and state legislation prohibiting sex discrimination in selected areas does not fill the absence of a constitutional prohibition of discrimination on the basis of sex. Under the federal constitution and most state constitutions, women have not yet been raised to the status of constitutional protection enjoyed by males. (Thomas 1991, p. 95).

Even the language of the law refers to such terms as a "reasonable man," "he," and "his." When a question about this is raised, the answer given is usually that the male terms used generically include females. Gender-neutral language does not solve the problem either.

Such gender-neutral language "serves only to reward the employers ingenious enough to cloak their acts of discrimination in a facially neutral guise, identical through the effects of [a facially neutral seniority] system may be to those of a facially discriminatory one" (Thomas 1991).

Struggles ensued with women bringing their case to court to serve on juries. In the case of *Hoyt* v. *Florida* (368 U.S. 57, 1961) Justice Harlan delivered the opinion of the Supreme Court. The issue was whether exclusion of women from jury service discriminated against a defendant's right to a fair trial. Justice Harlan stated:

> Manifestly Florida's [law] does not purport to exclude women from state jury service. Rather, the statute "gives to women the privilege to serve but does not impose service as a duty." It accords women an absolute exemption from jury service unless they expressly waive that privilege.

> It has given women an absolute exemption from jury duty based solely on their sex, no similar exemption obtaining as to men.

> Despite the enlightened emancipation of women from the restrictions and protection of bygone years, and their entry into many parts of community life formerly considered to be reserved to men, *woman is still regarded as the center of home and family life.* (emphasis added)

This was 1961.

In 1975, the *Taylor* case (*Taylor* v. *Louisiana*, 419 U.S. 522, 1975) a male criminal defendant challenged his conviction on the ground that his jury had not been drawn from a fair cross-section of the community. Women had been systematically excluded from jury lists. Using statistics to show that 54.2 percent of all women between eighteen and sixty-four years of age were in the labor force, that 45.7 percent of women with children under the age of eighteen were working, that 67.3 percent of mothers who were either widowed, divorced, or separated were in the work force, and that 51.2 percent of the mothers whose husbands were gainfully employed were also working, the court stated:

> if it was ever the case that women were unqualified to sit on juries or were so situated that none of them should be required to perform jury service that time has long since past.

The women won a victory.

A rational relationship test was developed indicating that a classification "must be reasonable, not arbitrary, and must rest upon some ground of difference having a fair and substantial relation to the object of the legislation, so that all persons similarly situated shall be treated alike" (*Reed* vs. *Reed*, 404 U.S. 71, 1971). There can exist today no discrimination against women unless it is shown that reasonable ground exists. Yet the Supreme Court has yet to make sex a *suspect classification,* meaning that the burden of proof is on the accused and not the accuser. The Court's failure to do so has had a great impact on women's rights. Women continue to sue and take their cases to court. Women have to fight the courts and legislatures in order for the government to justify discrimination on the grounds of it not being arbitrary and irrational.

Each case is decided on its own merits. Some progress has been demonstrated. For example, the changing roles of men and women have led to sex-neutral, functional family laws. The obligation of supporting a spouse is predicated on who can afford it and not simply who needs it.

Women are not inferior to men. Sex discrimination, nonetheless, remains, regardless of some progress and regardless of the prohibitions by the courts, the legislatures, and the Constitution. Women have yet to be raised to the status of full constitutional protections as enjoyed by all men.

"Remember the ladies," said Abigail Adams. We are constantly reminded of her statement as we are of the statement in *Glover* v. *Johnson* (478 F. Supp. 1075, 1975): "Keep it simple, they are only women."

REFERENCES

Schneir, Miriam (ed.), *Feminism: The Essential Historical Writings.* New York: Vintage Press, 1972.

Thomas, Claire Sherman, *Sex Discrimination.* St. Paul, Minn.: West Publishing, 1991.

3

Taming Women and Nature: The Criminal Justice System and the Creation of Crime in Salem Village

Nanci Koser Wilson

Female on female, violent crime is a rarity. Yet in 1692, in Puritan Salem Village, Massachusetts, hundreds of women were accused, and fourteen executed for violent crimes, many of whose victims were female. Contemporary Americans view witchcraft as an imaginary offense, so this episode has been seen by most scholars as an aberration, atypical of American criminal justice. But a careful examination of charges against these women reveals an offense that was not so imaginary after all— one for which women are still being brought to account. The Salem witches were persecuted because they were seen as wild women, in need of taming, just as was the rest of "nature." For the patriarchal mind, wild women and wild nature still pose a significant threat to orderly, male-controlled production and reproduction, and are still sometimes met with a criminal justice response.

American women, like most women, are infrequent criminal offenders, especially as against one another and especially in violent crime. The rarest criminal event is female on female violent crime. Yet in 1692, in Puritan Salem Village, Massachusetts, hundreds of women were accused, and fourteen executed for violent crimes, many of whose victims were female.

The Salem witch hysteria has been seen by most historians as an aberration, a bump in our history, completely atypical of American criminal justice. No longer believers in witchcraft, modern Americans are horrified that such an injustice could have occurred in relatively modern times. It is assumed that the witches were innocent of any crime, and (with the exception of Chadwick Hansen [1968]) scholars have sought explanations outside the phenomenon of witchcraft itself to account for the persecutions.

Yet if we examine carefully the charges against these women, we discover an offense that was not so imaginary after all, and one for which women are still being brought to account. The witches of Salem Village were thought to be disruptive of a natural hierarchy established by men at the behest of a male god. The image of divinely ordained masculine control of nature was captured for Puritans in the metaphor of the Great Chain of Being. This metaphor is still powerful today, with the exception that contemporary Americans have replaced the top rung in the hierarchy. Now, scientific technology reigns as God, and the only telos, or design, in nature is the continued unfolding of evolutionary process. The new divinity is as thoroughly masculinist as Yahweh, and is capable of directing evolution by itself. A masculinist science embodies, as completely as did the old God, the American Dream of conquering wilderness, in its vision of total control over nature. In this vision, what counts is not so much more and more productivity (though this is certainly important) but *human control* of natural productivity.

This is well illustrated in modern agricultural practices. Bovine growth hormone does not produce more milk per cow over the entire span of the cow's life. Similarly, chemical fertilizers do not make the soil more fertile in the long run. Nor do dams create water, nor does experimentally induced laboratory growth replicate natural growth. At the core of all these ways of growing and knowing is the farmer's and the scientist's total control over (what are deemed to be) relevant conditions. It is apparent that this control is desired more than fertility itself. In the 1990s, this can be seen clearly in plans to "develop" wetlands as farms and shopping malls. Though the necessity to the hydrological cycle of these wetlands is now recognized, legislators and environmental agencies in state after state are permitting the development of wetlands upon the agreement by developers to create man-made substitute wetlands as "replacement parts."

But as Lewis (1988, p. 449) has noted, control over nature is really "a power exercised by some men over other men with nature as its instrument." Many feminist scholars believe that control over women was exerted in order to exploit their labor, and was the first form of exploitation man invented, upon which he then modeled other forms of exploitation. Ecofeminists hold that the exploitation of nature and of woman developed coterminously, nourishing one another. And, many scholars have noted the centrality of conquest, especially the conquest of wilderness, to the development of the American character. (Turner 1920.)

In the Salem witchcraft hysteria we see the convergence of all of these themes, as the Puritan criminal justice system created in the Bay Colony a frightful specter to contain their fears of wild nature—both in human females and in the nonhuman nature around them. In tracing witch-beliefs within the context of Puritan theology and examining the evidence brought against the witches, we will see a strong device for social control of natural forces—as Lewis stated, the control of some men over other men (and all women), using nature as the tool. The relevance of Puritan cosmology and its use of criminal justice to achieve the ends of control and domination to contemporary gendered criminal justice will be seen as evidence for a consistent theme running through Western and American history.

Puritan Metaphysics

According to a contemporary witch (Starhawk 1989, p. 18) "witchcraft takes its teaching from nature." Further, witches understand nature as cyclical, spiral. "There is nothing to be saved *from*, no struggle of life *against* the universe, no God outside the world to be feared and obeyed; only the Goddess, the Mother, the turning spiral that whirls us in and out of existence, whose winking eye is the pulse of being" (Starhawk 1989, p. 29).

Whether any Salem women understood themselves to be practicing an ancient religion centered on the immanence of divinity in the natural world (as Murray [1921] asserted of the European witches), or whether any of the accused believed themselves to be malefic witches (as Hansen [1968] maintains), it is clear that at one time such religions were strong competitors for Christianity. In Europe, that part of earlier nature-centered religion which could not be absorbed effectively into Christianity was vigorously suppressed. The struggle with these heretics left a legacy of witch-beliefs among European Christians, which, imported to the American continent with the Puritans, formed the basis for the Salem female crime wave of 1692.

Puritan metaphysics (like all such patriarchal systems) presented a markedly different view of nature to that embodied in nature-centered religions. Puritan cosmology was strongly hierarchical, and, within its metaphysics, the ultimate source of life existed beyond it. Puritans saw the cosmos as a

> Vast chain of being! which from God began,
> Natures aethereal, human, angel, man,
> Beast, bird, fish, insect, what no eye can see,
> No glass can reach; from Infinite to thee,
> From thee to nothing. —On Superior pow'rs
> Were we to press, inferior might on ours;

Or in the full creation leave a void,
Where, one step broken, the great scale's destroy'd;
From Nature's chain whatever link you strike,
Tenth, or ten thousandth, breaks the chain alike.

(Pope 1733)

These lines from Pope, though written in the eighteenth century, reflect a "conception of the plan and structure of the world which, through the Middle Ages and down to the late 18th century, many philosophers, most men of science, and indeed, most educated men, were to accept without question" (Lovejoy 1936, p. 59). The universe was seen as a Great Chain of Being, "composed of an immense . . . number of links ranging in hierarchical order from the meagerest kind of existence, which barely escape non-existence, through 'every possible' grade up to . . . the Absolute Being."

For Puritans, each link in the chain fulfilled its nature and purpose partly by obeying the next highest link in the chain. Among human beings, a similar hierarchy had been ordained with "husbands superior to wives, parents to children, masters to servants, ministers to congregants, and magistrates to subjects. . . . In each of these relations, inferiors served God by serving their superiors. Men promised to ensure obedience in all their dependents, in return for God's promise of prosperity" (Karlsen 1987, p. 164).

Although the Puritan God existed prior to his creation, and Puritan theology embraced a diety whose transcendence outshone his immanence, their theology was also strongly incarnational. Elements of the natural world reflected and sometimes revealed to humans a supernatural plan, and, on occasion, a struggle between supernatural forces. Both God, and Satan his fallen angel, took an intense interest in the created world.

Created below God in the hierarchy, but above all other beings, angels were required to fulfill their place in the Chain through obedience. Satan's disobedience consisted precisely in his rebellion against his place. His desire to be "as God" included a struggle with the deity *within nature itself*. Satan not only attempted to seduce humans but also caused various natural disasters lower on the chain.

Long before Puritanism arose, European Christians had begun to undertand Genesis 1:28[1] as a mandate to exploit all of nature below man in the hierarchical chain (White 1967); and this exploitation, of course, required the taming of wild nature—both human and non-

---

[1]"And God said [to man], Be fruitful, and multiply, and replenish the earth, and subdue it: and have dominion over every living thing that moveth upon the earth."

human. Puritan theology thus fit neatly with the colonization of an uncivilized territory. The new immigrants found a land peopled by hunting and gathering groups who, for the most part, did not have established cities, agriculture, or a settled existence. Puritans viewed this land as a wilderness in need of taming, which would order it to God.

Part of this impulse was surely secular; but it had a sacred stamp and warrant. Strong strains in Judeo-Christian mythology emphasize the wilderness experience. The wilderness is a setting for man's struggle with his lower nature, a place of suffering and purification, from which he emerges dedicated completely to God and to His divine plan.

> ... the desert wilderness ... where the very existence of man is constantly threatened, is also the place specially chosen by God to manifest Himself in His "mighty acts" of mercy and salvation. Obedience to a divine call brings into this dreadful wilderness those whom God has chosen to form as His own people ... Failure to trust Yahweh in the wilderness is not simply an act of weakness: it is disobedience and idolatry.

> (Merton 1978, p. 190)

This theme of wilderness was "taken over in the theology of radical Protestantism in the seventeenth century and hence entered into the formation of the Christian ideal of North American culture that grew up out of the Puritan colonies of New England" (Merton 1978, p. 195).

The wilderness, once tamed, would become the orderly paradise the Puritan God commanded man to create. Importantly, a failure to conquer the wilderness was also a failure at individual salvation. If the Bay Colonists failed to establish the paradise of the "City on the Hill," this might be a sign that each Puritan was damned. Fearful for their own souls, frightened of wild nature both on its own terms and for the damnation which failure to tame it portended, Puritans attempted to contain their fears by sacrificing some of their middle-aged women. These women became the very emblem of their fears— of wilderness, of failure, and ultimately of eternal damnation.

The Witches as Wild Women

While it has been suggested that "a genuine coven was meeting in the woods of Salem before the trials" (Starhawk 1989, p. 21) evidence from the Salem trials does not support such a conclusion. What is more important are the witch-beliefs Puritans held which allowed for the persecutions.

Nature-focused religions had been of concern to the Judeo-Christian tradition since its inception. In the fifth century B.C., tempted to desert his patriarchal God during a time of great personal suffering, Job had proclaimed:

> If I beheld the sun when it shined, or the moon walking in brightness; and my heart hath been secretly enticed . . . this also were an iniquity to be punished by the judge; for I should have denied the God that is above.

(Job 31:27–28)

Steeped in a tradition that had shaped its theology in direct contrast to animistic, nature-centered rival religions, the Puritans inherited a linear, hierarchical monotheism. While ancient religions had long since ceased to pose a genuine threat to the newer, patriarchal religion, during time of stress, the fear of heresy arose with new vigor.

Christianity met the challenge in two ways. It absorbed prior religions by building churches on the old sacred sites and by changing names of festivals while keeping their dates. It directly challenged such religions by turning its gods and goddesses into the Christian devil (Adler 1986, p. 45). The witch persecutions were part of that transformation. What came to be called witchcraft included some elements of pagan belief systems, but "These survivals only became an organized system when the Church took the older beliefs and fragments and created an organized, systematic demonology, complete with new elements including the pact with the devil, the coven and the sabat" (Adler 1986, p. 53 and Trevor-Roper 1970).

But witch persecutions were useful beyond the purposes of the Church in validating the new patriarchal religion. As Trevor-Roper (1970) notes, in the sixteenth and seventeenth centuries this new demonology acquired momentum. These were the centuries during which modern science was born and the Western world-view became more and more human-control oriented. The massive witch persecutions of the period also validated an increasingly centralized secular and male hierarchy in medicine, politics, and agriculture. The specter of possible resistance to this project of taming all of nature produced intense witch fears culminating in the deaths of perhaps nine million persons (Daly 1978, p. 183).

The struggle against wild nature as seen in untamed women produced important tracts whose dissemination was aided by the invention of printing. In the *Malleus Malificarum* of Institoris and Sprenger (1948; o.d. 1486), readers would learn precisely what to fear from women presumed to be in league with the devil. In books such as this and in the teachings of the clergy, witchcraft was invented.

The *Malleus Maleficarum* (o.d. 1486) "explained and justified the

Church's view that most witches were women" (Karlsen 1987, p. 155). Women, the authors instructed, were more evil than men by nature, and because they were created inferior to men, were more susceptible to deception. Witches were also seen as dissatisfied with their place in the natural hierarchy. This made them angry and vengeful. Specific sorts of crimes were likely to be performed by witches, according to this tract. They were responsible for generative problems—they could cause men to be impotent, they could prevent conceptions and procure abortions in women. They also might kill newborns. They frequently attempted to dominate their husbands, which was a "natural vice" in women (Karlsen 1987).

The witch-beliefs that the Puritans imported thus were strongly marked by fears of disruption of the Chain of Being, particularly of rebellion among women and damage caused to domesticated nature. The fear was that of tamed nature "going wild."

Theologically and legally, the crime of witchcraft consisted in making a pact with the devil, whose supernatural power he lent to humans. With this power, a person could perform *maleficium;* that is, harm various parts of the natural order. She could cause disease, injury, or even death among humans and other animals. She could interfere with domestic processes like dairying, brewing beer, and making cloth. Witches were also thought capable of causing disturbances in weather patterns—they could create droughts and storms at sea, for instance. Meleficium could be performed by look, by touch, and, specifically, *by curse.*

Although invested with supernatural power, witches apparently refrained from certain kinds of harm, and specialized in others. They were not suspected of financial offenses such as theft, fraud, or embezzlement. In fact, they appeared unable to bring about good outcomes for themselves. It was not said that they increased the productivity of their own fields or domestic stocks; that they could weave superior fabrics or make finer butter, produce more food, or enhance the health of children, adults, or stock.

Rather, witches specifically engaged in actions which threatened to upset a natural hierarchy, to wreak havoc in domesticated nature—to unleash wild forces. The New England witch "was frequently suspected of causing illnesses or death, particularly to spouses or infants and young children." She also was likely to direct her malice toward domesticated animals—she could bewitch cows, horses, and swine—they would sicken and die, or simply wander off. She was often accused of "obstructing reproductive processes, either by preventing conceptions or by causing miscarriages, childbirth fatalities or 'monstrous' (deformed) births." She could procure abortions and cause impotence among men. She harmed domestic processes by spoiling beer in the brewing or making it disappear altogether. She could cause cows to stop giving milk and hens to lay fewer eggs. She could make spinning and weaving impossible (Karlsen 1987).

If the Salem hysteria can be explained by Puritan uneasiness and fears during a period of political upheaval, as some have suggested (see, for example, Erikson 1966), it is clear from the nature of the accusations that these fears were of a specific sort. And, if the high concentration of women among the accused can be explained in terms of misogyny and the desire to control women, as most feminist students of witchcraft have maintained (Ehrenreich and English 1973, Daly 1978, and Karlsen 1987), it is similarly clear from the nature of the accusations that women were thought to pose a particular kind of danger.

The Puritans had reserved an important and specific role for their women; and it is likely that female failure to fulfill their function was seen as extremely dangerous, in that one link in the Chain of Being broken, all else would disintegrate. Women were a part of wild nature that needed taming; once tamed, their role was to nurture. Men apparently realized that the creation of an inherently unfair and exploitative system carried within it the seeds of dissatisfaction and rebellion among the tamed. They expected women to rebel, and in their cosmology created an explanation for female dissatisfaction. Just as Eve had succumbed to the devil's wiles, so might other women. But Puritans did not fear self-aggrandizement on the part of the witches. Rather, they feared the vengeance of dissatisfied women. Insufficiently tamed women, it would appear, were the cause of fear. Untamed themselves, in league with the disruptive forces of wild nature, witches might unhook the carefully constructed Chain of Being.

Accusations against the Salem Witches[2]

The Salem hysteria began in the early months of 1692 when a number of young women were stricken with fits. Reverend Samuel Parris' household contained a prepubescent daughter and a household servant, Tituba, from the West Indies. Elizabeth Parris, age nine, a number of her preteen and teenage friends, and, often, three older women gossiped and chatted in the Parris kitchen. Tituba, who knew the

---

[2]Information on the specific charges leveled at the witches comes from *Woodward's Records of Salem Witchcraft*. Woodward collected and compiled material from preliminary hearings which includes testimony of witnesses, victims, and the accused. Woodward's records are incomplete but they provide us with a sample of forty-eight accused persons, thirteen men and thirty-five women. The tables in this section are based only on the women. Later, there is a separate discussion of the accused men.

witchcraft of her native island, helped the girls to forecast their futures, focusing on the occupations of their future husbands. Later, Jonathan Hale was to blame the entire event on these seemingly innocent actions. He maintained that the girls in their "vain curiosity" had "tampered with the devil's tools." (cited in Boyer and Nissenbaum 1974, p. 23)

The most immediate result of this tampering was that the young girls became possessed. Their symptoms ranged from feelings of being pinched, pricked, and choked, to full-scale seizures. Two of the "circle girls" were epileptics (Gemmill 1924, p. 48); the fits of the other girls were perhaps caused by ergot poisoning (Caporael 1976) or the power of suggestion (Caulfield 1943). Taken to the local doctor, they could neither be diagnosed nor cured by his arts, and he then declared the cause was outside his profession. The appropriate jurisdiction was theological and legal.

Witchcraft was more than crime, though it was that—it was treason and heresy as well. And, it was the most threatening offense in the Puritan world, because it was contagious. The authorities reacted promptly and predictably—they asked the girls to indicate who was bewitching them. Guided perhaps by the mother of one of the girls (Ann Putnam), who held grudges against some of her neighbors (Gemmill 1924, Boyer and Nissenbaum 1974), and by their own beliefs about just who a witch might be, the girls identified several local women—including, of course, Tituba, who immediately confessed. The hunt began.

In the pattern of the accusations, in the kinds of victims and offenders, and in the nature of the harm done, we begin to see what the Puritans feared. The power of maleficium was given by Satan himself, so Puritan officials were at pains to ascertain if the accused had actually made a pact with the devil. They looked for evidence of such a pact in confessions and in the testimony of witnesses that an accused had "signed the devil's book," had attended a witches' sabbat, or taken the devil's communion. Further, if a witness testified that an accused witch had urged them to engage in any of these actions, this testimony was evidence that the accused had attempted to seduce another human, drawing her, too, into the devil's snare, and therefore had obviously made a pact herself. Such evidence was produced for 77 percent of the accused women in our sample (see Table 1).

Entering upon such a pact with the devil meant that a Puritan was in league with profane forces, unsanctioned authority. As a being who himself had rebelled against established authority, Satan was wild. Satan's fight with God was a rebellion against authority which was carried out in the world—that is, within created nature. Thus, at the heart of the witches' crime was rebellion against hierarchical

TABLE 1   Evidence of Pact

	NUMBER	PERCENT
Confession	7	20%
Signing the Devil's Book	2	6%
Attending the Witch's Sabbath	13	37%
Taking the Devil's Communion	2	6%
Seducing Others	17	49%
Total*	27	77%

*In this and the following tables, totals will add to more than 100% because more than one form of evidence was brought for several of the witches.

TABLE 2   Evidence of Maleficium

	NUMBER	PERCENT
Harming Human Beings	34	97%
Assault upon Circle Girls	31	89%
Assault upon Others	20	57%
Murder	8	23%
Harming Domesticated Nature	9	26%
Damaging Domestic Production	1	3%
Stopping Domestic Production	3	8.5%
Damaging Domesticated Stock	9	26%
Possessing Supernatural Powers	18	51%
Flying through the Air	6	17%
Performing "Impossible" Physical Feats	1	3%
Predicting the Future	2	6%
Possessing Poppets	7	20%
Possessing Familiars	10	29%
Suckling Familiars, Having Witches Teats	5	14%

order and allegiance to an alternative force whose main purpose and power appeared to be the creation of chaos.

Maleficium directed at human beings was the most common charge in Salem, as it had been in England (Macfarlane 1970, p. 154 and Thomas 1971, p. 539, who estimates that 70 to 80 percent of the victims were other humans). In our sample, 97 percent of the women accused were charged with assaulting or murdering humans (see Table 2).

Evidence for human harm began with and most usually involved evidence that the circle girls had been tortured by the accused. These girls were present in court and frequently went into fits when an accused entered the room. Eighty-nine percent of the accused women were charged with tormenting these girls. Since the medical profession had not been able to find a natural cause, these fits were continually attributed to supernatural actions by witches. Obviously, for Salem Villagers, unexplained events were also uncontrollable events—and it was this lack of control which they feared. The first, and always the central, victims were the circle girls. They were the reliable indicators that an accused was actually a witch. In this regard, the age and sex of the victims and offenders is important.

There were ten circle girls; their ages ranged from nine to twenty, with a mean of 15.9 years (see Table 3). One of the oldest, Mary Warren, who was twenty, was later accused of witchcraft herself, as were two of the older women present (Sarah Biber and Goody Pope.) The accused were, for the most part, middle-aged women who were unmarried. Though the girls themselves could logically be accused, except for Warren (who confessed spontaneously, then later retracted her statements) they were not. Thus the pattern is that young, fertile, nulliparous women were assaulted by postfertile and/ or unmarried women. Women who were past the stage when their tamed fertility could be useful, apparently deliberately made fertile young women useless by making them wild.

The witches were thought to harm other humans as well, and 57 percent of them were accused of doing so, some (23 percent) to the point of death (see Table 2).

These middle-aged women were also accused of harming domesticated nature. They were thought to be able to damage domestic processes. As Table 2 shows, 3 percent of our sample was accused of doing so. Mary Bradbury, for example, caused butter to go bad. They were also thought to stop production altogether, as when Elizabeth How caused the Perley's cow to stop giving milk. Altogether, 8.5 percent of the sample were so accused. They could damage or bewitch domestic stock, as 26 percent of them did. Sometimes the cattle, pigs,

TABLE 3   The Circle Girls

	AGE
Elizabeth Parris	9
Abigail Williams	11
Ann Putnam	12
Mercy Lewis	17
Mary Walcott	17
Elizabeth Hubbard	17
Elizabeth Booth	18
Susan Sheldon	18
Mary Warren	20
Sarah Churchill	20

In addition, three older women were often present: Sarah Bibber, Goodwife Pope, and Mrs. Ann Putnam (Gemmill, 1924).

or draft animals sickened or died, and sometimes they went wild. One witch in our sample was accused of damaging an artifact—but, tellingly, one which kept tamed nature "inside"—she was accused of using supernatural means to break a fence.

Evidence of maleficium also frequently took the form of testimony that the accused possessed superhuman powers. As can be seen from Table 2, such evidence was brought for 51 percent of the accused women. These women were thought to raise storms at sea, thus casting away vessels, as was thought of Mary Bradbury. They were believed to make hogs chase men, as Mary Parker was accused of doing. They were thought to create a light in a field that caused human accidents. Some of them, it was thought, could perform seemingly impossible feats, such as walking through the rain without becoming wet. Or, they could fly through the air or ride airborne on a broom. They could predict the future.

Some of the witches were believed to have worked their evil through a medium. They were accused of possessing "poppets"—small rag dolls in the image of an enemy, which, when pricked with pins, would cause the victim himself to suffer pain. Thirty-five percent of the women were accused of possessing "familiars," or suckling them. Familiars were small animals (dogs, cats, birds) which the devil sent to witches to aid them in doing their evil work. The familiar was believed to suckle the witch from a preternatural teat located somewhere on her body. Thus, when a witch was accused, a jury of same-sex townspeople was appointed to conduct a physical examination in order to determine if the witch possessed such a teat. The Salem Villager who had a wart, mole, or hemorrhoid was in grave danger.

The role of the familiar was somewhat different from that of the poppet. Poppets were inert—the supernatural force somehow transferred itself from this image of the victim's body to the victim. Familiars had the added advantage that they could be sent on malefic missions—a small blue bird, a black puppy, or, usually, a cat—would suddenly appear in the victim's home to torment him.

The witch's possession and use of natural and supernatural forces was threatening because it was assumed to be evil. Puritans were able to conceive of nature as saturated with supernatural forces only when such forces were evil. Why was this so?

The Puritan God was not within nature. He had made it, and existed outside and above it. As created, it was chaos and could only fulfill its telos when ordered into a Great Chain of Being, tamed and controlled from above, by man. In this manner all being was ordered to the Supreme Being in hierarchical fashion, through many layers of command and obedience. For the Puritans, there was thus only one appropriate relation to nature—to tame wild nature, order it to God, and nurture it in its tamed state. They could not conceive of working with nature, respecting its boundaries and limits, its right to be *for* itself. A careful obervation of wild nature might allow one to predict its course. A respect for nature's own nature, for her limits and necessities, a capacity to "let grow and to make grow" (Meis 1986) might yield human good by creating a harmonious relationship. Instead, for the Puritans, all of nature was first, wild: uncontrollable, unpredictable, unyielding, profane. Unless it was controlled and tamed, it was not only unfruitful, it was dangerous.

In possessing supernatural powers, it was thought that the witch used life forces to pervert the Chain of Being. She did not work against nature to control it. Rather than working to tame animals, she worked with wild animals to do evil. Rather than staying in her place, she flew through the air. Rather than contenting herself to whatever fate God ordained for her, calmly waiting for it to unfold, she attempted to discern the future.

Susanna Martin's case[3] is quite typical. This seventy-two-year-old widow was accused by the circle girls, who ratified their accusation by falling into fits at her preliminary hearing. She did not help her case by laughing at their antics, and declaring a lack of sympathy for them.

Martin was charged with assaulting the circle girls, and she was accused of harming others as well. Bernard Peach testified that she (or her spectral shape) entered his bedroom one Sunday night, took hold of his feet and "drew my body into a whoope and lay upon me about an hour and one-half or two hours all of which time I could not stir or speak." He finally managed to bite three of her fingers. The next day he found her footprints and blood outside in the snow. She also apparently assaulted Elizabeth Brown who, when in her presence, experienced a sensation, "like birds pecking her leggs or picking her with the motion of their wings and . . . it would rise up into her stomach like a pricking payn as nayls and pinns . . . and it would rise up in her throat like a pullet's egg." She appeared in Jarvis Ring's bedchamber, lay upon him and bit his finger so hard that the mark "is still to be seen on the little finger of my right hand."

She was thought to not only have harmed humans, but to have harmed domesticated nature as well. In testimony against her, John Pressey claimed she had bewitched his milk cattle and was capable of directing supernatural forces against him. On one occasion, he had become lost after dark and kept sighting a strange light. Frightened, he tried to strike the light with his stick, but after he gave it about "forty smart blows," he fell into a deep pit yet "I do not know any

---

[3]Evidence on Susanna Martin's case comes from Woodward 1969, pp. 193 ff. and Gemmill 1924, pp. 114 ff.

such pit to be in the place where I was sliding into." Shortly there-
after, Susanna Martin appeared in exactly the place where the light
had been. A few years later, she reviled him and his wife, and claimed
that he should never prosper. Specifically, she told them they would
"never have but two cows" and "from that day to this we have never
exceeded that number for something or other has prevented it."

John Kimball testified that he and the Martins had had a quibble
about appropriate payment for a piece of land Kimball had bought
from him. Kimball had offered them their choice of two cows and
some other cattle but "did reserve two cows which I was not desirous
to part with they being the first I ever had." Susanna threatened him
in this way: "You had better [pay with those particular cows] for
those will never do you no good." Kimball testified, "And so it came
to pass that the next April following that very cow lay in the fair dry
yard with her head to her side but starc dead; and a little while after
another cow died and then an ox and then other cattle to the value
of thirty pounds." In the same year, Kimball desired to buy a puppy
from her, but she would not let him have his choice from the litter,
so he didn't agree to buy any. Upon hearing this, she said, "If I live,
I'll give him puppies enough." A few days later he stumbled unac-
countably upon some stumps in the woods. But soon he perceived
the source of his difficulty—he was being attacked by several dark
puppies, who were not hurt even when he cut them with his ax.

John Atkinson testified that Martin was angry with him because
her son had traded one of their cows to him. When he went to the
Martin place to receive the cow, she muttered and was unwilling that
he should have the cow. When he took possession of it "notwithstanding the homstringing and halting of her she was so mad that we could
scarce get her but she broke all ropes fastened to her and we put the
rope two or three times around a tree but she broke it and ran away
and when she came down to the ferry we were forced to run up to
our arms in water she was so fierce but after much adieu we got her
into the boat and she was so tame as any creature whatever."

On another occasion, William Osgood turned down the Martins
when they asked for a gift of beef. The next day one of his best cows
went wild. And when Joseph Knight encountered her in the woods,
his horses suddenly refused to cross a causeway—instead, they simply
ran wild.

Other testimony suggested that she was a woman who could fly,
walk in the rain without getting wet, and could change herself into
the shape of a hog or a cat. And clearly she had made a pact with
the devil because otherwise she would not possess such supernatural
powers, nor would she have urged Mercy Lewis to sign the devil's
book.

What did Puritans believe the motive for such damage was? The witches were asked repeatedly why they had bewitched the girls, but no satisfactory answer ever emerged. For other harms, a motive was sought and found. Usually, a witch who had harmed someone or someone's domestic production was seen to be displeased with that person. Just as Puritans believed that Satan was dissatisfied with his place, they believed some of their middle-aged women were similarly dissatisfied. Apparently, they were really frightened of this rebellion against authority and of the disruption in the Great Chain it signified.

This may explain why the officials were also interested in eliciting two other types of evidence. Table 4 shows that 34 percent of the women were accused of muttering after being refused some item for which they had begged, and 23 percent of possessing bad language or manners. Altogether, 43 percent of the women in the sample were accused of "unseemly behavior." Why were the Puritans interested in this type of evidence?

Muttering after begging might mean that the woman had actually placed a curse on the one who gave her offense. Some scholars have suggested that the real offense was not malefic witchcraft but abrasive behavior to the one who had refused following on the heels of the refusal of neighborly aid. Thomas (1971) argues that in the most common situation, "the victim had been guilty of a breach of charity or neighborliness, by turning away an old woman who had come to the door to beg or borrow some food or drink, or the loan of some household utensil." Witch-beliefs implied that a neighborly obligation left unfulfilled might result in malefic witchcraft directed against the unneighborly person. Thomas suggests that the high percentage of women is most "Plausibly explained by economic and social considerations, for it was the women who were the most dependent members of the community, and thus the most vulnerable to accusation" (Thomas 1971, p. 553).

Macfarlane's argument is similar, although he maintains that women predominated in the accusations because they were the most resistant to change, and their social position and power led to mounting hatred against them (Mcfarlane 1970).

These scholars refer to English witchcraft, but Boyer and Nissenbaum (1974) have made the same argument for Salem. They believe the accused were "on the move, socially and economically"; they were independent of the old social order. In their lack of will-

TABLE 4   Evidence of Unseemly Bahavior

	NUMBER	PERCENT
Muttering after Begging	12	34%
Bad Language/Ill Manners	8	23%
Total	15	43%

ingness to accept their given station in life, they were typical of the emergent personality of citizens in a capitalist economy. The accusers represented the old order. "The social order was being profoundly shaken by a superhuman force which had lured all too many into active complicity with it. We have chosen to construe this force as emergent mercantile capitalism. Mather and Salem Village called it witchcraft" (Boyer and Nissenbaum 1974, p. 209).

But this theory fails to explain why none of the men in our sample were accused of unseemly behavior and yet were accused of witchcraft. Nor does it explain why fewer than half of the accused female witches were accused of possessing bad manners, or why they were also accused of other depredations.

Rather, it seems the explanation may lie in the *meaning* of such behavior. Bad language or manners was evidence for rebellion against authority, the sign of a possible break in the Great Chain of Being. Six of the eight women accused of unmannerly behavior had been rude to a direct superior—a husband or a parent. The others were simply generally rude—but such testimony was always brought by a man.

The centrality of bad manners is demonstrated also by the evidence offered in *defense* of accused women. Testimony for Elizabeth How thus indicated that she was "neighborly," that she "carried it very well," that she never reviled anyone, that she had a courteous and peaceable disposition (Woodward 1969, p. 78).

Wild women were dangerous. Just by looking, touching, or cursing, just by being in the same room with domesticated pubescents, they were thought to be able to make tamed nature go wild.

The males in this sample are quite different from the women who were accused. For all thirteen, evidence was brought that they had afflicted the circle girls, and five of them were accused of harming other humans. But only one of them harmed domestic nature in any way, and none was accused of unseemly, unmannerly, or unruly behavior. The most striking thing about the male witches is their atypicality. Apart from George Burroughs, a former Puritan minister who was believed to be the Satanic priest officiating at the sabbats (where, of course, a priest was necessary) and a deputy sheriff (John Willard), who was accused probably because he was publicly sympathetic to those he was forced to jail, 72 percent (eight of eleven) of the accused men were relatives of accused female witches. They thus, as John Demos has suggested (1970, p. 1311) "belonged to a kind of derivative category."

The only truly typical witch among the men was Samuel Wardwell. About fifty-five years of age at the time of the hysteria, Wardwell owned a little farm and "for many years had been a fortune teller, strolling about, reading palms and solving life's mysteries from the broken tea leaves in the bottom of the cup" (Gemmill 1924, p. 185). His rather high success rate at this enterprise was part of his undoing. Accused and jailed, he promptly confessed. He claimed that he was able to control animal nature—he could banish wild creatures from his fields by "bidding the devil to take" them, and he could make domesticated stock "come round about and follow me." Wardwell later retracted his confession, whereupon he was tried, convicted, and hanged (Woodward 1969 and Gemmill 1924).

Reflection upon the patterns formed by the evidence brought against witches and by their age and sex leads us to select as symbol and metaphor of witch fears the unfortunate Sarah Biber. A middle-aged woman who gossiped in the Parris kitchen with the circle girls, perhaps participating in their fortune telling, Biber was never accused of maleficium, or indeed of having made a pact with the devil. She *was* accused of "often quarreling with her husband" during which quarrels she "would call him very bad names," and of behaving in an unnurturing manner toward her children. "She wished that when her child fell into the river she had never pulled it out." Three of the four men who testified against her cited her "unruly, turbulent spirit" (Woodward 1969, pp. 203–205). Apparently Sarah Biber's sole crime was her wildness.

Wilderness and Criminal Justice

At its birth, philosophers justified the modern criminal justice system as a device to tame the naturally wild instincts of human beings. Its necessity was recognized when men became "weary of living in a continual state of war," as Beccaria wrote (1963, p. 11), following Hobbes's (1947, p. 31) assumtion that all mankind possessed "A perpetual and restless desire for power after power, that ceaseth only in death."

Contemporary criminologists often retain this frightening vision of nature as wildly dangerous. Travis Hirschi (1969, p. 31) finds no need to search for motivations to crime because "we are all animals and thus all naturally capable of committing criminal acts."

Our modern criminal justice system is permeated with this view—that only when nature is controlled is it safe. Erickson says of it that we have inherited from the Puritans an assumption that "The convict's soul is permanently depraved and that sin is an inevitable part of his personal endowment." In light of this model of the convicted criminal as inherently wild, it "makes very little sense to . . . reform him . . . the best one can do for him is to contain his reprobate spirit, in much the same way that one tames the wilder instincts of animals . . . the object [of criminal justice] is not to improve his nature but to harness it so completely that it cannot assert itself" (Erikson 1966, p. 203).

What legacy then, did the witch hysteria of 1692 and the Puritan criminal justice system's handling of it bequeath to us? What did Puritans think their purpose was? How successful were they in achieving it? How successful is the contemporary criminal justice system in achieving this same purpose?

Puritans were intensely frightened by two kinds of wilderness—that in the forests surrounding them at the edges of their carefully cultivated fields and neat towns, and that which was within human nature (and especially female human nature). Both kinds of wilderness were evil precisely because they were wild.

"Seventeenth century writing is permeated with the idea of wild country as the environment of evil," Nash (1982, p. 36) tells us. "The new world wilderness was linked with a host of monsters, witches and similar supernatural beings" (p. 29). The wilderness was evil because it had not been ordered to the patriarchal God; it was seen not only as uncontrolled, but as the location of rival religion. A "dark wilderness cave" was believed to be the site of pagan rites, and the native Americans were "not merely heathens but active disciples of the devil" (pp. 33–36). For Puritans, "the untamed forests and the Indians that lurked in their shadows represented fallen nature inhabited by the powers of darkness" (Reuther 1983, p. 81). The wild evil of nature ouside the village and farm was echoed in human nature as well. The Puritan mission thus involved both "an inner battle over that 'desolate and outgrowne wildernesse of humain nature' and on the New England frontier it also meant conquering wild nature" (Nash 1982, p. 36). In the crime of witchcraft, these two wildernesses came together in wild women who used their evil power to make tamed nature wild, too. The Puritan "errand into the wilderness" (Miller 1956) was a mission that would bring Godly order out of a natural chaotic fecundity. Only through a project of taming could they bring fertility under control.

The criminal justice response to witchcraft focused on women apparently because it was precisely among women that the relationship to nature was wrong. Fearful of the wild in nature and in human beings, knowing no way to deal with these fears other than by creating an orderliness based upon hierarchical control, Puritan justice announced in the witch trials that which it absolutely would not tolerate. The idea of woman embodied, and some of their own middle-aged widows exemplified, what Puritans feared most. Where in the natural world there is harmony based upon each creature's capacity to be for-itself and simultaneously for-the-whole, the Puritan mind saw chaos. They sought to replace the "for-itself" and "for-the-whole" of nature with a system of nature-for-man, and man-for-God, ordered in hierarchical neatness through a Great Chain of (Patriarchal) Being.

In the witches, Puritans saw wild creatures independent of the Great Chain, immersed in untamed natural processes: pure chaos, pure evil. What they tried to kill in Puritan women, all Puritan women, when they hanged the witches, was a particular relationship to the created world and its fertility—a metaphysic and an epistemology diametrically opposed to their own. Were they successful?

As a boundary maintenance device (Erikson 1966), the witch trials were certainly successful. The Puritans sacrificed a few middle-aged widows, who were not particularly useful to them in any case. But the effect of trying, imprisoning, and hanging the witches was to send a message to all the Puritans, and especially to the women. Henceforward, gossiping in a group of women, having a close or familiar relationship with animals, and observing nature's ways in a respectful manner that would allow prediction of the future would be dangerous. Henceforth, fertility in women and in nature would be subjected to strict masculine design and control—and, where it went wild, it would be criminally punished.

Were the Puritans succesful in bequeathing to their descendants a metaphysic, an epistemology, and a criminal justice system that would continue to control unruly feminine nature?

Contemporary Witchcraft: The Criminal Justice System Response

> The . . . Great Chain of Being has been converted into a Becoming . . . [and] God himself is . . . identified with this Becoming. But the inversion . . . while it converts the Scale of Being into an abstract ideal schema, does not alter its essential character.
>
> (Lovejoy 1936, p. 326)

Americans no longer hunt witches in the fashion of their Puritan ancestors. But the fear of wild nature and the intense desire to tame it for man's benefit (the source of the hysteria in Salem) is still strong. Having lopped off the top of the Great Chain of Being, postmoderns have neither God nor telos to guide and restrain their interactions with nature. Instead, a "neutral," scientific technology informs our actions. Nature now tends toward no other end than to be molded by men in power to their current benefit. For, while the notion of the Great Chain of Being is now identified with evolution itself and inverted so that the tendency toward diversity and fullness is seen to arise from the bottom of the hierarchy, spontaneously rather than as a deliberate plan from the top; its danger to women and nature is not lessened, but perhaps increased. If there is a God in these waning years of the second millennium, He is science; now seen as capable of altering evolution itself, to the special benefit of those men currently in power.

For the patriarchal mind, wild women and wild nature still pose a significant threat to orderly, male-controlled production and reproduction. Sometimes this threat is met with a criminal justice system response, as it was in Salem Village.

Human reproduction was a significant concern of the Puritan witch hunters, who blamed female witches for abortions (both spontaneous and induced), "monstrous births," and untimely deaths from disease in young children. Exertion of male control over human reproduction is still a vital concern as evidenced by newly enacted abortion laws which require male consent, by strict hedges on surrogacy requiring contracts to protect the rights of fathers in their unborn children, denial of child custody to lesbian mothers (and to many heterosexual mothers where custody is challenged by fathers), restrictive laws on midwife-attended birthing, and the increasing criminalization of pregnancy, which prescribes a criminal justice system response of imprisonment for addicted mothers.

Concerns regarding domestic production plagued the Puritans as well. Witches were blamed for infertile fields, dairying problems, diseases among domesticated stock. Late twentieth-century Americans believe they have solved the problems of unruly nature through chemical control, vast water diversion projects, and an agriculture which has become agribusiness featuring vast monocultures. With agriculture almost completely under control of the patriarchal mind, contemporary Americans are satisfied that endless orderly production will prevail.

The newest wrinkles in control over nature with regard to domestic production are hormonal control of production and genetic engineering. Agricultural technologists invent methods to splice bean genes onto corn, frost-resistant genes onto strawberries. They feed BGH to dairy cattle to increase milk production, with the result that cows suffer mastitis and die untimely deaths after living what must be a very unpleasant existence.

While conservationists and animal rights activists deplore these devices and warn of impending disaster from soil depletion, deforestation, and a host of other possible ecocatastrophes, the desire to seek total control over natural processes and the belief that this is possible guide American policy in food production, as in human reproduction. The desire is total control—an orderly hierarchical arrangement of fecundity.

The Puritans sacrificed some of their middle-aged women to further their project of taming. Similarly, in the 1990s, the addicted women who give birth to crack babies are being sacrificed. Again, it is powerless women who are of very little use to the social system who are subjected to a criminal justice system response. And, again, the effect is boundary maintenance—a deterrence that affects all fertile women. Now all women are put on warning that what they ingest during pregnancy will be carefully monitored. Posters in liquor stores and labels on bottles warn us, as do a plethora of articles in women's magazines, that any misbehavior during pregnancy is dangerous not only to the fetus but also to the mother. Only a few women need be imprisoned for the most serious violations in order that all women receive the message. A chaotic fertility, a careless pregnancy, a selling of one's self "body and soul to the devil" (whether Satan or cocaine) will not meet with caring, with medical treatment—but with a punishment response.

Perhaps twentieth-century Americans have no more need than did our seventeenth-century ancestors to punish wild women for its immediate effect. Perhaps, now as then, the crucial effect of the criminal justice process is a boundary maintenance that tames all women, bringing their fertility under control, ordering it into a neat hierarchical Great Chain of (patriarchal) Being.

REFERENCES

Adler, Margot, *Drawing Down the Moon.* Boston: Beacon Press, 1986.

Beccaria, Cesare, *On Crimes and Punishment.* New York: Macmillan, 1963.

Boyer, P., and S. Nissenbaum, *Salem Possessed.* Cambridge, Mass.: Harvard Univ. Press, 1974.

Caporael, Linnda R., "Ergotism: The Satan Loosed in Salem?" *Science*, 192 (2 April 1976).

Caulfield, Ernest, "Pediatric Aspects of the Salem Witchcraft Tragedy," *American Journal of Diseases of Children*, 65 (May 1943).

Daly, Mary, *Gyn/Ecology* Boston: Beacon Press, 1978.

Demos, John, "Underlying Themes in the Witchcraft of 17th Century New England," *The American Historical Review*, 75, (June 1970).

Ehrenreich, Barbara, and Dierdre English, *Witches, Midwives and Nurses: A History of Women Healers.* New York: Feminist Press, 1973.

Erikson, Kai, *Wayward Puritans.* Wiley, 1966.

Gemmill, Wm. N., *The Salem Witch Trials.* A.C. McClurg, 1924.

Hansen, Chadwick, "Salem Witches and DeForest's *Witching Times*," *Essex Institute Historical Collections*, 104 (April 1968).

Hirschi, Travis, *Causes of Delinquency.* Berkeley, Calif.: University of California Press, 1969.

Hobbes, Thomas, *Leviathan.* New York: Macmillan, 1947. (o.d. 1651)

Karlsen, Carol F., *The Devil in the Shape of a Woman: Witchcraft in Colonial New England.* New York: W.W. Norton, 1987.

Kramer, Heinrich, and James Sprenger, *Malleus Maleficarum* (Montague Summers, trans.). Magnolia, Mass.: Peter Smith Pub., Inc., 1948 (o.d. 1486)

The Book of Job. *Holy Bible* (King James Version). World Publishing. (o.d. 1611).

Lewis, C.S., "The Abolition of Man." In L.W. Dorset (ed.), *The Essential C.S. Lewis.* New York: Collier, 1988 (o.d. 1943).

Lovejoy, Arthur O., *The Great Chain of Being.* Cambridge, Mass.: Harvard University Press, 1953 (o.d. 1936).

Macfarlane, Alan, *Witchcraft in Tudor and Stuart England.* London: Routledge and Kegan Paul, 1970.

Merton, Thomas, "Wilderness and Paradise," in his *The Monastic Journey.* New York: Image Books, 1978.

Mies, Maria, *Patriarchy and Accumulation on a World Scale.* London: Zed Books, 1986.

Miller, Perry, *Errand Into the Wilderness.* Cambridge, Mass.: Harvard University Press, 1956.

Murray, Margaret A., *The Witch Cult in Western Europe.* New York: Oxford University Press, 1921.

Nash, Roderick, *Wilderness and the American Mind.* New Haven: Yale University Press, 1982.

Pope, Alexander, *Essay on Man,* 1733.

Ruether, Rosemary Radford, "Woman, Body and Nature," in her *Sexism and God Talk: Toward a Feminist Theology.* Boston: Beacon Press, 1983.

Starhawk, *The Spiral Dance: A Rebirth of the Ancient Religion of the Great Goddess.* San Francisco: Harper & Row, 1989.

Thomas, Keith, *Religion and the Decline of Magic.* London: Weidenfield and Nicoesen, 1971.

Trevor-Roper, H.R., "The European Witchcraze and Social Change." In Max Marwick (ed.), in *Witchcraft and Sorcery.* New York: Penguin, 1970.

Turner, Frederick Jackson, *The Frontier in American History.* New York: Krieger, 1920.

White, Lynn, Jr., "The Historical Roots of Our Ecological Crisis," *Science* 155 (March 10, 1967) 1203–1207.

Woodward, W.E., *Records of Salem Witchcraft.* New York: DaCapo Press, 1969 (o.d. 1864).

DISCUSSION QUESTIONS
SECTION 2—HISTORICAL DEVELOPMENT OF WOMEN'S ISSUES

1. In public affairs, are women really treated as if they were inferior to men? What does the historical record pertaining to the law, education, suffrage, employment, and other aspects of public life show the relative status of women to be?

2. What does the statement mean that in a democracy, without the force of law behind them, women are civilly dead?

3. Many traditional male scholars see the Puritan witch hunt as a historical anomaly. How does looking at this event from a feminist perspective demonstrate that the behavior of the Puritans is in many ways quite similar to behaviors that we witness every day in contemporary society?

4. Can an argument be made that what was really at the heart of the witches' crime that occurred in Salem Village was a rebellion against the hierarchal order of society?

5. Can an argument be made that fundamental notions of traditional Christian thought are really sexist?

6. From a feminist perspective, how is taming the wilderness and taming wild women similar? How does a fear of wild nature translate into actions by the criminal justice system? What are some contemporary examples of man's attempt to maintain control over woman's nature?

Section 3 _____

Women, Drugs, and AIDS

The rights of women as persons and the obligations of women as mothers emerge in this section as irreconcilable differences that serve to generate issues and debates that are central to women and the treatment accorded them by the criminal justice system. If close attention is paid to the arguments presented in this section, you will find the underlying issues to be emotion-provoking, the problems to be quite complex, and the solutions to be less than clear. As pointed out by the authors in this section, the criminal justice system continues to rely principally on a simple-minded, punitive approach to solve very complex social problems. As a result, there are many serious and unanticipated consequences associated with treating drug-abusing mothers as criminals. Several of the articles in this section discuss problems generated by the debate over the rights and obligations of women in contemporary society.

As study is made of specific issues, try not to lose sight of the ramifications that particular problems and solutions have for women as a whole. The authors in this section agree that the criminalization of pregnancy is one front in a much larger political struggle over women's bodies. This larger struggle takes many forms, from abortion and surrogate mothers, to fetal surgery and maternal conduct. At stake are the rights of women to bodily integrity, reproductive choice, and personal freedom. The criminalization of pregnancy should also remind us that the study of women cannot escape the complexities of class, race, and ethnicity. It is the combined images of being black, being on welfare, and using drugs that drives the punitive reaction toward pregnant women of all classes and races.

So, too, we have a problem with American women, as a group, showing an increase in the rate of human immunideficiency virus (HIV) infection, as the Acquired Immune Deficiency Syndrome (AIDS) enters its second decade. It is estimated that by the end of the twentieth century, more than one million women will be affected by the AIDS virus. Women, in turn, are transmitting the virus to their children through prenatal events. Again, the criminal justice system, through the law, police, courts, and corrections, will increasingly find itself responding to the second wave of the AIDS epidemic as it deals with women offenders and women as victims. As the chapters in this section demonstrate, women who are seropositive for AIDS may very well be the next group to have the condition of pregnancy criminalized.

4

Women, AIDS, and the Criminal Justice System

Joan Luxenburg and Thomas E. Guild

The leading cause of HIV infection among women in the United States is intravenous drug use, followed by sexual contact with an infective IV drug user. This fact has tremendous policy implications for drug treatment programs as alternatives to incarceration, especially in cities where waiting lists for such treatment are prohibitive.

The association between non-IV drug use and AIDS cannot be ignored. Street prostitutes who are crack-addicted are more likely to exchange unprotected sex for crack. However, this group represents a very small percentage of prostitutes.

In the misguided belief that female prostitutes transmit the virus to their male clients, several states have enacted AIDS-specific statutes that target prostitutes. With no scientific evidence indicating that prostitutes are a vector for transmission of the virus, they suffer needless incarceration.

The criminal justice system has targeted sexual assault defendants for mandatory HIV antibody testing and disclosure to victims. With further expansion of these laws, women as the victims of rape will be granted medical information regarding the rapists. This seemingly necessary intrusion into the rights of defendants will no doubt be challenged on constitutional grounds.

Women as offenders and women as victims can be expected to play a significant role in the shaping of criminal justice policy to deter the spread of AIDS. This chapter explores these issues in detail, along with attendant issues.

Introduction and Background

The epidemic of Acquired Immune Deficiency Syndrome (AIDS) has had an impact on every facet of the criminal justice system (Blumberg 1990b). We address two legal issues surrounding AIDS that are very specific to women. One topic (prostitution) involves women as criminal offenders. The other topic (sexual assault) involves women as the victims of crime. While men are also arrested for prostitution, the offense is clearly a female-dominated activity. In fact, prostitution is the only crime for which the arrest rate for females is higher than the arrest rate for males (Yablonsky 1990, p. 84). Similarly, we recognize that men are the victims of rape. However, only an estimated 10 percent of rapes occur to men ("Face-to-Face," 1990). This percentage may be larger, since, overall, three to ten rapes go unreported for every one rape that is reported (President's Commission on the Human Immunodeficiency Virus Epidemic, 1988).

Our focus on prostitution and AIDS deals with whether prostitutes are at greater risk than other sexually active women for contracting the AIDS virus (also known as human immunodeficiency virus, or HIV), and whether prostitutes are vectors for transmitting the virus to their customers. We examine legislation that targets prostitutes for mandatory HIV antibody testing or that targets HIV antibody-positive prostitutes for enhanced criminal penalties. For the issue of sexual assault, we look at the debate over requiring HIV antibody testing of accused and/or convicted rapists and disclosure of such test results to the alleged and/or proven victims.

Women and AIDS

Women's concerns in the AIDS epidemic had gone virtually ignored until 1990. During the 1980s (the first decade of the AIDS epidemic), the public minimized the role of women and their relationship to this public health crisis. Women were merely viewed as the principal caregivers for Persons with AIDS (PWAs), for example, as nurses in hospitals or as mothers welcoming their homosexual sons home to spend their remaining days with family. This picture changed when, in 1990, AIDS was recognized as the leading cause of death among black women in New York and New Jersey, and it was predicted to become the fifth-leading cause of death among U.S. women of childbearing age, by 1991 ("AIDS deaths soaring" 1990, "More Women Getting AIDS" 1990). During the summer of 1990, the World Health Organization (WHO) estimated that 3 million women and children would die of AIDS during the 1990s, a figure representing more than six times their numbers of AIDS deaths in the 1980s ("More Women, Children" 1990). The rising death rate for women with AIDS is now apparent. While only eighteen women in the U.S. (between the ages of eighteen and forty-four) died of AIDS during the year 1980, for the year 1988, the number was 1,430 ("AIDS Deaths Soaring" 1990). In the U.S., prior to 1983, only ninety women (thirteen years old and older) had been diagnosed with AIDS (Miller, Turner, and Moses 1990, pp. 50–51). However, by November 1990, the cumulative figure for all women in the U.S. (regardless of age) was 16,394 (Oklahoma State Department of Health 1991).

In recognition of the increase in the number of women with HIV infection, "World AIDS Day" (December 1, 1990) proclaimed its focus to be on "Women and AIDS." Earlier that year, the sixth International AIDS Conference (held in San Francisco in June) became a forum for the Women's Caucus of the AIDS Coalition To Unleash Power (ACT-UP) to voice their grievances about women's issues related to HIV infection. By November 1990, the American Civil Liberties Union (ACLU) added to its staff a lawyer assigned to work exclusively with issues involving HIV infection among women and children (Herland Sister Resources 1990). Many of the ACLU's concerns deal with civil liberties debates not easily reconcilable.

Prostitution as a Transmission Category

The AIDS literature on prostitution has concentrated almost exclusively on female heterosexual prostitutes, rather than on male (homosexual) prostitutes. Because the clientele of male prostitutes are principally males, the AIDS literature treats male prostitutes for discussion under the heading of homosexuals (Centers for Disease Control 1987b; Turner, Miller, and Moses 1989, p. 14). Stereotypically, male and female prostitutes have been cast as intravenous drug users (IVDUs) or the sexual partners of IVDUs when, in fact, only a small percentage may fall into the category of IVDUs. In actuality, street prostitution accounts for an estimated 20 percent of all prostitution; and an estimated 5 to 10 percent of prostitutes are addicted (Cohen, Alexander, and Wofsy 1990, p. 92; Leigh 1987, p. 180). It is likely that those who are addicted (to IV drugs or to "crack") disregard safer sex practices in order to support their habit. For HIV-infected women in general, 75 percent of them acquired the virus through IV drug use or through sexual relations with IVDUs ("AIDS Deaths Soaring"

1990). The majority of U.S. women with AIDS live in New York, New Jersey, Florida, and California (Shaw 1988).

Self-reported findings suggest that prostitutes may be more likely to use a condom with their customers, rather than with their regular sex partners (Rowe and Ryan 1987, pp. 2–20; Miller, Turner and Moses 1990; Cohen and others 1990). However, when Project AWARE (Association of Women's AIDS Research and Education) conducted its San Francisco General Hospital comparison of prostitutes and other sexually active women, it found a slightly lower seropositive rate for prostitutes (Leigh 1987). The association between HIV-antibody-positive status and IV drug use (rather than with prostitution) was clearly found in the Centers for Disease Control (CDC)–coordinated seroprevalence studies of prostitutes in ten U.S. cities, including New York, San Francisco, Jersey City, Miami, and Los Angeles (Centers for Disease Control 1987a).

While our discussion focuses on street prostitution, it is worthwhile to note seroprevalence findings from other types of prostitution. In a study of New York City call girls, one in eighty was HIV-antibody-positive—and that individual was an IVDU ("Geraldo" 1990). When the state of Nevada conducted testing of all prostitutes employed in legal brothels, not a single case of HIV-antibody-positive results occurred in over 4,500 tests of approximately 500 prostitutes (Hollibaugh, Karp, and Taylor 1987, p. 135). Licensed houses of prostitution in Nevada (in addition to screening prospective employees for IV drug use) are required by law (since March 1986) to conduct preemployment HIV-antibody screening and monthly testing after employment; and employment is denied to HIV-antibody-positive applicants (Centers for Disease Control 1987a; "Infection not reported among legal prostitutes" 1987).

The CDC has not reported any documented cases of HIV transmission from a female prostitute to a male customer through sexual contact (Cohen and others 1990). Probably the most common means of an infected prostitute transmitting the virus to another individual is through sharing infected IV drug paraphernalia (AIDS and Civil Liberties Project 1990). In the U.S., female-to-male transmission of the AIDS virus through sexual contact is less efficient than is male-to-female transmission (Eckholm 1990a). For the period 1981 to October 1985, the CDC concluded that only one-tenth of one percent of all U.S. cases of AIDS were the result of female-to-male sexual transmission (Schultz, Milberg, Kristal, and Stonebruner 1986, p. 1,703). As of January 1988, only 6 of the 11,000 cases of AIDS in New York City males traced back to female-to-male sexual contact, although it is impossible to ascertain from the published data whether prostitutes were involved (AIDS and Civil Liberties Project 1990). Randy Shilts

(1987, pp. 512–513) reported on a case of a San Francisco IV drug-using prostitute who continued working while carrying the AIDS virus for ten or eleven years until her death in 1987; yet, during that same period, only two male heterosexual contact cases of AIDS had occurred in San Francisco.

In a CDC study of spouses of transfusion-acquired PWAs, 16 percent of wives were infected, while only 5 percent of husbands were infected; and although 10 percent of those studied had more than 200 sexual contacts with an infected partner, the uninfected spouse remained seronegative (Stengel 1987). It must be remembered that the chances of becoming infected are greater in repeated sexual contact (for example, with a spouse) as opposed to a one-time encounter (for example, with a street prostitute). The ACLU estimates that 200,000 female prostitutes participate in some 300 million sexual transactions per year in the U.S., and yet the incidence of men contracting the AIDS virus from prostitutes in the U.S. is virtually nil (AIDS and Civil Liberties Project 1990, p. 102). Early reports among U.S. servicemen are probably most responsible for having implicated prostitutes in the spread of the virus (Redfield, Markam, Salahuddin, Wright, Sarngadharan, and Gallo 1985). Critics of these reports were quick to reply that military men would be reluctant to report IV drug use or homosexual behavior (Potterat, Philipps, and Muth 1987).

AIDS Law and Prostitutes

The ACLU's position on coercive measures against prostitutes is that such measures are futile and serve to drive the disease further underground (AIDS and Civil Liberties Project 1990). History reveals that government crackdowns on prostitutes to stop the spread of other STDs have been ineffective (Brandt 1985, 1988, p. 370). Nevertheless, prostitutes have been the target in some states for mandatory HIV-antibody testing and for enhanced criminal penalties for HIV-antibody-positive prostitutes who continue to practice their trade while knowing their seropositive status.

By 1990, approximately twenty-two states had criminalized the act of knowingly exposing another individual to the AIDS virus ("More states" 1990). From the authors' own observations in Oklahoma, the utility of an AIDS-specific law seems questionable. The Oklahoma law (*Okla. Stat. Ann.* tit.21, Sect. 1192.1), which took effect July 1, 1988, states:

> A. It shall be unlawful for any person to engage in any activity with the intent to infect or cause to be infected any other person with the human immunodeficiency virus.

B. Any person convicted of violating the provisions of this section shall be guilty of a felony, punishable by imprisonment in the custody of the Department of Corrections for not more than five (5) years.

In January of 1990, the first individual to be charged under this new law was a thirty-four-year old Tulsa prostitute, Lynnette Osborne (a.k.a. Lynette Love). Osborne had apparently been reported to police by other prostitutes who work in the same general location (Tulsa's red-light district). Four undercover Tulsa police officers had interactions with Osborne, resulting in four counts of soliciting between October 1989 and Janaury 1990. Upon Osborne's arrest (under the new law), a search warrant was issued allowing authorities to test her blood for the HIV antibodies ("Charge filed" 1990; Brus 1990). Unfortunately, the Osborne case does not lend itself to us for analysis of the first trial of its kind in Oklahoma, because the defendant pled guilty in February 1990 to all four felony counts in exchange for four three-year prison terms, to run concurrently ("Prostitute goes to jail" 1990).

Several states have enacted AIDS legislation that specifically targets prostitutes. In Florida, as of October 1986, convicted prostitutes are mandatorily tested for HIV antibodies (and other STDs). In that state, engaging in prostitution after having been informed of one's seropositivity results in a misdemeanor, separate from the charge of prostitution [Centers for Disease Control 1987a; Bowleg and Bridgham 1989; *Fla. Stat. Ann.*, 14A, Sect. 381.609, 3(i)(1)(a)]. Georgia law provides that an individual who is aware of his or her seropositivity and subsequently offers to engage in sexual intercourse or sodomy for money, without disclosing (prior to the offer) the presence of the HIV infection, is guilty of a felony punishable upon conviction by not more than ten years. Georgia law also permits HIV-antibody testing by court order for anyone convicted of or pleading "no contest" to any HIV transmitting crime, including prostitution (Bowleg and Bridgham 1989). Idaho law mandates HIV-antibody testing for defendants being held in any county or city jail who are charged with certain offenses, including prostitution (Bowleg and Bridgham 1989).

Illinois law requires HIV-antibody testing for those convicted of a sex-related offense, including prostitution, solicitation, patronizing a prostitute, and operating a house of prostitution (Thomas 1988). One may question the relevance of testing the operator of a house, if he or she is not exchanging his or her own bodily fluids with the customers. Similarly, the state of Washington's law requires anyone convicted of prostitution or "offenses relating to prostitution under chapter 9A.88 RCW" to submit to HIV-antibody testing. Included (in

9A.88 RCW) are the offenses of "promoting prostitution" and "permitting prostitution" [*Wash Rev. Code*, Sect. 70.24.340, 70.24.340(1)(b)]. Under such a law, even individuals who engage in no actual sexual act, but who advance prostitution, are required to take the HIV-antibody test. The Washington law has yet to be subjected to a "reasonableness test," where probable cause (for example, that the defendant had actually engaged in an HIV transmitting act with his or her own bodily fluid) would need to be established (Weissman and Childers 1988–89).

Michigan's law provides that those convicted of crimes capable of transmitting the AIDS virus (including prostitution) shall be examined for HIV antibodies upon court order, unless the court determines such testing to be inappropriate (Bowleg and Bridgham 1989). Nevada law requires anyone arrested for prostitution to be tested for HIV antibodies. If the arrest results in a conviction, the defendant pays $100 for the cost of the testing. After receiving notification of a positive test, if the individual is subsequently arrested and found guilty of another charge of prostitution, the new conviction is for a felony punishable by one to twenty years in prison and/or a $10,000 fine (*Nev. Rev. Stat. Ann.*, Sect. 201.356, 201.358). Rhode Island and West Virginia each have laws requiring any individual convicted of prostitution to be tested for HIV antibodies (Bowleg and Bridgham 1989).

California's law requires convicted prostitutes (and certain other sex offenders) to be tested for the HIV antibodies. If a prostitute receives positive test results and later receives a subsequent conviction for prostitution, the subsequent conviction is a felony. (*Calif. Penal Code*, Sect. 647 f).

In spite of California's law, some counties in that state have opted not to conduct such testing. For instance, the Alameda County Health Department has declined to test convicted prostitutes, partly because that county's budget does not permit it. Recently Alameda County's policy came into the public limelight surrounding the highly publicized case of Oakland prostitute, Linda Kean (Bishop 1990). Kean had posed for a picture in a *Newsweek* article in which she claimed to be an HIV-antibody-positive, heroin-using prostitute, who continues to service customers (Cowley, Hager, and Marshall 1990). A zealous Oakland vice-squad sergeant, Mike Martin, read the *Newsweek* article and promptly arrested Kean for attempted murder, after he witnessed her getting into a car with a suspected customer. Dr. Robert Benjamin, Director of the Communicable Disease Division of the Alameda County Health Department referred to Kean's arrest as "scapegoating" and a "witch hunt." According to Benjamin, it is the customer's personal responsibility to use a condom. Benjamin further pointed out that testing prostitutes for HIV antibodies would send a "false message," suggesting to the public that those prostitutes who are still on the street have a clean bill of health.

Critics of the AIDS-specific laws targeting prostitutes suggest that enhancing penalties for subsequent convictions of HIV-antibody-positive prostitutes is an unproductive, punitive strategy aimed at a politically powerless group who show no epidemiological evidence that they are contributing significantly to the sexual transmission of the AIDS virus. The laws clearly stem from a false perception that prostitutes pose a major risk to their customers.

Alternatives to Coercion

The government's paternalistic concern can be helpful in assisting grassroots efforts to educate disenfranchised segments of the population to reduce risk behaviors. Among IVDUs, the Community Health Outreach Worker (CHOW) has been most successful in educating this population. These individuals are usually recovering addicts indigenous to the community and ethnically matched to the population which they try to reach. CHOWs provide referrals for drug-treatment programs, condoms, instructions for cleaning drug paraphernalia, and so on. Several organizations, such as Cal PEP (California Prostitutes Education Project) have utilized prostitutes and ex-prostitutes in a similar manner ("Geraldo" 1990). Clearly, funding and expansion of such programs appears to be a worthy area in which the government can invest its resources wisely. Education with dignity appears to have worked in Pumwani, a crowded slum in Kenya, where some 400 prostitutes can be found working on any given day (Eckholm 1990b). More than 80 percent of Pumwani prostitutes have tested positive for the HIV antibodies. Knowing that the HIV reinfection or other STDs can worsen their health, these woman have cooperated with health officials and are using condoms, reportedly 80 percent of the time (Eckholm 1990b). Since African prostitutes are transmitters of the AIDS virus, thousands of new HIV infections are being avoided by these efforts. Only about 30 percent of the male truckers at a nearby weighing station (outside of Nairobi) report that they "sometimes" use the free condoms handed to them; and one in four of those drivers (who consent to testing) show HIV antibodies (Eckholm 1990b). Stubborn male customers are not confined to Pumwani. In the U.S., there is a need to educate the clients of prostitutes, as well as to monitor these men to learn the incidence and prevalence of HIV infection among them (Miller, Turner, and Moses 1990).

While noncoercive government intervention shows promise for persuading prostitutes to reduce high-risk behaviors, the strategy may work only because we are dealing with consensual (though commercialized) sexual relations. For nonconsensual sexual relations, coercive measures may be appropriate.

AIDS Law and Sexual Assault

Several states have enacted legislation which requires either accused or convicted sexual offenders to submit to HIV-antibody testing; and, in some cases, the victim or alleged victim is entitled to the defendant's test results. Without AIDS-specific laws to address this topic, courts found themselves inconsistently deciding whether or not to permit testing of defendants accused of sexual assaults. In 1987, a Texas Court of Appeals ruled that a district court did not have the statutory (nor constitutional) power to order an HIV-antibody test for a defendant charged with aggravated sexual assault, nor did the district court have the authority to release the results to alleged victims on a "need to know basis" (*Shelvin* v. *Lykos* 1987) Subsequent to this appellate decision, Texas passed legislation (during a second special session in 1987) granting statutory power to trial courts to order such tests and to disclose to alleged victims the results (*Tex. Crim. Proc. Code Ann.*, art. 21.31; Thomas 1988). According to Texas law, a person indicted for sexual assault and aggravated sexual assault can be directed by a court to be examined and/or tested for an STD, AIDS, or HIV antibodies. The court can direct such examination and/or testing on its own motion or at the request of the alleged victim. The results may not be used in any criminal proceeding regarding the alleged assault. The court may not release the results to any parties other than the accused and the alleged victim.

In the state of New York, before similar legislation was introduced and defeated, that state's courts appeared to favor the victim's need to know over the defendant's right to privacy. In 1988, a New York Supreme Court ruled that it is not violative of a defendant's right to privacy for the state to divulge a rape defendant's HIV-antibody test results to the victim, when such testing is done during routine processing of the individual into the prison population (*People of New York* v. *Toure* 1987). Further, the court, in its "balancing test," decided that the fears and health concerns of the victims outweighed the minimal intrusion to the defendant. Similarly, a county court decided in New York in 1988 that a defendant, who had pled guilty to attempted rape, could be ordered to submit to HIV-antibody testing, and that the victim had a right to know the results (*People of New York* v. *Thomas* 1988). In that case, the court concluded that the testing was not an unreasonable search and seizure under the Fourth Amendment, and that the intrusion to the defendant was minimal.

Two New York City cases gained national attention in 1990 on the issue of the victim's need to know the accused sexual offender's HIV-antibody status. In one case, a seventeen-year-old Columbia University coed was raped at knife point in her dormitory room by a former Columbia University security guard, twenty-eight-year old Reginald Darby (Salholz, Springen, DeLaPena,and Witherspoon 1990; Glaberson 1990). In this case, a Manhattan assistant district attorney plea-bargained a first-degree rape case for a reduced sentence, contingent upon the defendant's submitting to an HIV-antibody test and making the results available to the district attorney's office and to "other appropriate parties." The reduced sentence was for no more than five to fifteen years, rather than the maximum sentence of eight and one-third to twenty-five years. One legal expert on women's rights criticized such agreements as creating a "windfall" for defendants and their attorneys (Glaberson 1990). Rape defendants and their attorneys will have additional leverage for striking plea agreements and can even imply an AIDS risk where there is none. Clearly, AIDS-specific legislation would be preferable to this type of plea bargain. However, bills requiring HIV-antibody testing of rape defendants (and disclosure to victims) were defeated in New York's legislature in 1990 (Glaberson 1990); and a principal opponent to the proposed laws was the Lambda Legal Defense Fund, a gay rights organization ("Face-to-Face," 1990). Lambda's position was that no one should be "forced" to take an HIV-antibody test. However, more recently Lambda is reportedly willing to support such testing when the rape victim is pregnant ("Face-to-Face," 1990). The other New York City case to gain attention in 1990 involved a victim of a March 31, 1988 burglary and rape, whose assailant was apprehended at the scene by police after he fell asleep in the victim's bed. The defendant (thirty-two-year old Barry Chapman), an IVDU and career offender on parole for rape and burglary, was eventually convicted. The victim, who had witnessed a hypodermic needle fall out of Chapman's jacket when police searched it, wanted him tested. Chapman refused two requests, by the Manhattan District Attorney's office, to be tested. Even after Chapman died of AIDS in Sing Sing Prison in 1990, the victim remained unaware of the cause of death, until CBS News obtained the autopsy report and informed the victim. More than two years after her attack, the victim continues to test negative for HIV antibodies.

In 1988, when Connecticut failed to pass a bill that would have forced rape defendants to be tested, those opposing the measure pointed out the unclear message that would result from a negative test (Hevesi 1988). Because of the long "window period"—the time between becoming infected and actually showing antibodies to the virus—a negative test does not rule out the presence of the virus in the rapist. For this reason, the victim is probably the most logical one to be tested (and retested every six months). With regard to repeated testing of the rapist, legislation can be worded to include this. For instance, Kansas law provides that if the test results are negative for persons convicted (of offenses capable of transmitting the AIDS virus), the court shall order the individual to submit to another HIV-antibody test six months after the first test (Bowleg and Bridgham 1989). This second test may actually be of dubious usefulness to the victim, because a positive test for the offender at this juncture may be the result of sexual activity after incarceration.

As of late 1990, very few states provide for HIV-antibody testing of accused sexual assaultists (prior to conviction). Colorado law provides that those who, after a preliminary hearing, are bound over for trial for sexual offenses (involving penetration) shall be ordered by court to be tested for HIV antibodies. The court reports the test results to victims, upon the victim's request. If the accused voluntarily submits to an HIV antibody test, such cooperation is admissible as mitigation of sentence if the offense results in conviction (*Colo. Rev. Stat.* 8B, Sect. 18-3-415). Florida law provides that any defendant in a prosecution for any type of sexual battery, where a blood sample is taken from the defendant, will have an HIV-antibody test. The results of the test cannot be disclosed to anyone other than the victim and the defendant. (*Fla. Stat. Ann.* 14A, Sect. 381.609 3(i)(6); "Rape Suspect" 1990). Idaho law requires the public health authorities to administer an HIV-antibody test to all persons confined in any county or city jail who are charged with "sex offenses" (Bowleg and Bridgham 1989).

The length of time between testing the accused and/or convicted offender and notifying the victim (where allowed) does not appear to be adequately addressed by most state's laws. A case profiled on national television ("Face-to-Face" 1990) illustrated the problem of timing. The case involved a victim of a rape and attempted murder in a suburban Seattle Park who was three months pregnant at the time of the knife-point attack. The conviction took place two days before the victim gave birth to a baby girl (six months after the attack). However, it took another six months until the victim was notified of the negative test results. The victim wanted to know the defendant's HIV-antibody status prior to his conviction, in order to decide whether to terminate the pregnancy. However, Washington is not one of the states where an accused rapist must be tested prior to conviction.

The President's Commission on the Human Immunodeficiency Virus Epidemic, in its June 1988 report, made several recommendations concerning HIV-antibody testing (and disclosure) in cases of sexual assault. Among its recommendations, the Commission favored mandatory testing "at the earliest possible juncture in the criminal justice process" (Blumberg 1990b, p. 76) and that there be disclosure to those victims (or their guardians) who wish to know. It is likely that the 1990s will see more states making such provisions in their laws.

As of January 1991, the CDC had no documented case of a rape victim becoming infected with the AIDS virus as a consequence of a sexual assault (Blumberg 1990a; "Sally Jessy Raphael" 1991). According to Mark Blumberg, who has written extensively on AIDS and the criminal justice system, the risk of HIV infection to female survivors of rape is remote. Most rape victims have been subjected to vaginal, rather than anal, intrusion—and (citing a 1988 *JAMA* article) Blumberg asserts that the chances are 1 in 500 for a female to contract the AIDS virus from a single male-to-female episode of vaginal intercourse (Blumberg 1990a, p.81). Nevertheless, rape has taken on an added threat to life in the AIDS epidemic and, consequently, places its survivors in a tormented frame of mind.

Summary and Conclusions

Since no scientific evidence implicates U.S. female prostitutes significantly in the transmission of the AIDS virus through sexual contact with their male customers, it may be a political and legal futility to use punitive legislative measures to "control" such activity. Coercive and punitive measures are unlikely to alter the behavior of women engaged in consensual sexual relations with their customers, especially where such activity constitutes their livelihood. Where they exist, it is unlikely that punitive strategies will stop the spread of the AIDS virus, since there has yet to be a documented case of a female U.S. prostitute sexually transmitting the virus to a male customer.

Certainly, noncoercive measures such as education would contribute at least as much to public health as coercive measures against such prostitutes. Since data indicate that transmission via IV drug use is a greater risk than sexual transmission as far as female prostitutes are concerned, education in this area as well as distribution of clean needles might do more to assure public health than all the coercive and punitive measures presently on the books.

Of course, proponents of the present trend of punitive legislation might point out that even if the risk of sexual transmission is small, all possible measures must be taken to check the AIDS virus. They might also argue that just because no cases have yet been documented, this does not mean sexual transmission has not occurred. Since many female prostitutes live a somewhat nomadic urban lifestyle, statistics and documentation may be extremely difficult to gather.

As far as state legislation requiring either accused or convicted sexual offenders (mostly male) to submit to HIV-antibody testing, several problems are raised. First, if we are testing accused offenders on an involuntary basis, we are eviscerating the presumption of innocence for the criminally accused. To conduct such testing, the government ought to have a compelling governmental interest before infringing on a criminal defendant's fundamental constitutional right to be presumed innocent. The right of a victim to obtain such information seems to fall short of such a compelling state interest.

As far as defendants who are convicted of sexual assault, convicts have traditionally lost many civil libertarian protections after conviction, and it seems more within the American constitutional tradition to then use coercive HIV-antibody testing. The contribution to public health and the victim's peace of mind seem to be sufficient justification for such postconviction testing and limited disclosure.

Clearly, the AIDS health crisis is a serious and growing epidemic. Rational and effective policies should be followed with a purpose of safeguarding both individual constitutional rights and the public health of the U.S.

REFERENCES

AIDS and Civil Liberties Project, American Civil Liberties Union, "Mandatory HIV testing of prostitutes: Policy statement of the American Civil Liberties Union." In M. Blumberg (ed.), *AIDS: The Impact on the Criminal Justice System.* Columbus, Oh.: Merrill Publishing, 1990, pp. 101–107.

"AIDS Deaths Soaring Among Women," *Daily Oklahoman,* July 11, 1990, p. 5.

Bennett, K. A., "Mandatory AIDS Testing: The Slow Death of the Fourth Amendment Protection" (Legislative Note), *Pacific Law Journal,* 20, 1413–1445.

Bishop, K., "Prostitute in Jail after AIDS Report," *New York Times,* p. 8.

Blumberg, M., "AIDS: Analyzing a New Dimension in Rape Victimization." In M. Blumberg (ed.), *AIDS: The Impact on the Criminal Justice System.* Columbus, Oh.: Merrill Publishing, 1990a, pp. 78–87.

Blumberg, M., *AIDS: The Impact on the Criminal Justice System.* Columbus, Oh.: Merrill Publishing.

Bowleg, I. A. and B. J. Bridgham, *A Summary of AIDS Laws from the 1988 Legislative Sessions.* Washington, D.C.: The George Washington University, Intergovernmental Health Policy Project, AIDS Policy Center, 1989.

Brandt, A. M., *No Magic Bullet: A Social History of Venereal Disease in the United States Since 1880.* New York: Oxford University Press, 1985.

Brandt, A. M., "AIDS in Historical Perspective: Four Lessons from the History of Sexually Transmitted Diseases," *American Journal of Public Health*, 78, no. 4 (April), 367–371.

Brus, B., "Tulsa Official Hopes Arrest to Slow AIDS," *Daily Oklahoman*, January 22, 1990, p. 1.

Calif. Penal Code. Sect. 647 f. (West. Supp. 1989).

Centers for Disease Control, (1987a) "Antibody to Human Immunodeficiency Virus in Female Prostitutes," *Morbidity and Mortality Weekly Report, 36*, no. 11 (March 27), 159.

Centers for Disease Control (1987b), "Human Immunodeficiency Virus Infection in the United States: A Review of Current Knowledge," *Morbidity and Mortality Weekly Report, 36*, nos. 5–6 (December 18), 8.

"Charge Filed under Anti-AIDS Law," *Sunday Oklahoman*, January 21, 1990, p. A18.

Cohen, J. B., P. Alexander, and C. Wofsy, "Prostitutes and AIDS: Public Policy Issues." In M. Blumberg (ed.), *AIDS: The Impact on the Criminal Justice System*. Columbus, Oh.: Merrill Publishing, pp. 91–100.

Colo. Rev. Stat. 8B. Sect. 18-3-415 (1990).

Cowley, G., M. Hager, and R. Marshall, "AIDS: The Next Ten Years," *Newsweek*, June 25, 1990, pp. 20–27.

Eckholm, E., "AIDS In Africa: What Makes the 2 Sexes so Vulnerable to Epidemic," *New York Times*, September 16, 1990a, p. 11.

Eckholm, E., "Cooperation by Prostitutes in Kenya Prevents Thousands of AIDS Cases," *New York Times*, September 18, 1990b, p. A6.

"Face-to-Face," Columbia Broadcasting System, December 10, 1990.

Fla. Stat. Ann., 14A, Sect. 381.609, 3 (i) (1) (a), 3(i)(6) (West 1990).

"Geraldo," "Have Prostitutes Become the New Typhoid Marys?" Tribune Entertainment, May 11, 1990.

Glaberson, W., "Rape and the Fear of AIDS: How One Case Was Affected," *New York Times*, July 9, 1990, p. A13.

Herland Sisters Resources, "ACLU AIDS Project to Focus on Women and Children with AIDS," *Herland Voice*, 7, no. 10, 4.

Hevesi, D., "AIDS Test for Suspect Splits Experts," *New York Times*, October 16, 1988, p. 30.

Hollibaugh, A., M. Karp, and K. Taylor, "The Second Epidemic." In D. Crimp (ed.), *AIDS: Cultural Analysis/Cultural Criticism*. Cambridge, Mass.: MIT Press, pp. 127–142.

"Infection Not Reported Among Legal Prostitutes," *AIDS Policy and Law*, November 18, 1987, pp. 2–3.

Leigh, C., "Further Violations of Our Rights," In D. Crimp (ed.), *AIDS: Cultural Analysis/Cultural Criticism*. Cambridge, Mass.: MIT Press, pp. 177–181.

"Man Tried to Spread AIDS Disease," *Edmond Sunday*, November 18, 1990, p. A15.

Miller, H. G., C. F. Turner, and L. E. Moses, *AIDS: The Second Decade*. Washington, D.C.: National Academy Press, 1990.

"More States Establishing Laws Allowing AIDS Assault Cases," *Daily Oklahoman*, October 22, 1990, p. 20.

"More Women, Children Expected to Die from AIDS," *Edmond Sunday*, July 29, 1990, p. A9.

"More Women Getting AIDS, Study Says," *Daily Oklahoman*, November 30, 1990, p. 6.

Nev. Rev. Stat. Ann. Sect. 201.356, 201.358, (Michie 1987).

Okla. Stat. Ann. tit. 21, Sect. 1192.1 (West 1989).

Oklahoma State Department of Health, *Oklahoma AIDS Update, 91*, no. 1 (January 1991), 6.

People of New York v. *Thomas*, 529 N.Y.S. 2d 439 (Co. Ct. 1988).

People of New York v. *Toure*, 523 N.Y.S. 2d 622 (Sup. 1987).

Potterat, J. J., L. Phillips, and J. B. Muth, "Lying to Military Physicians about Risk Factors for HIV Infections" (To the Editor), *JAMA*, 257, no. 13 (April 3, 1987), 1727.

Presidential Commission on the Human Immunodeficiency virus, "Sexual Assault and HIV Transmission: Section V of Chapter 9: Legal and Ethical Issues," *Report of the Presidential Commission on the Human Immunodeficiency Virus*. Submitted to the President of the United States, June 24, 1988. Reprinted in M. Blumberg, (ed.), *AIDS: The Impact on the Criminal Justice System*. Columbus, Oh.: Merrill Publishing, 1990, pp. 73–77.

"Prostitute Goes to Jail in AIDS Case," *Daily Oklahoman*, February 14, 1990, p. 31.

"Rape Suspect Due AIDS Test," *Daily Oklahoman*, July 23, 1990, p. 7.

Redfield, R. R., P. D. Markham, S. Z. Salahuddin, D. C. Wright, M. G. Sarngadharan, and R. C. Gallo, "Heterosexually Acquired HTLV-III/LAV Disease (AIDS-Related Complex and AIDS): Epidemiologic Evidence for Female-to-Male Transmission," *JAMA*, 254, no. 15 (October 18, 1985), 2094–2096.

Rowe, M., and C. Ryan, *AIDS: A Public Health Challenge: State Issues Policies and Programs, Volume I: Assessing the Problem*. Washington, D.C.: The George Washington University Intergovernmental Health Policy Project, AIDS Policy Center, 1987.

Salholz, E., K. Springen, N. DeLaPena, and D. Witherspoon, "A Frightening

Aftermath: Concern about AIDS Adds to the Trauma of Rape," *Newsweek*, July 23, 1990, p. 53.

"Sally Jessy Raphael," January 21, 1991, Multimedia Entertainment.

Schultz, S., J. A. Milberg, A. R. Kristal, and R. L. Stoneburner, "Female-to-Male Transmission of HTLV-III" (To the Editor). *JAMA*, 255, no. 13 (April 4, 1986), 1703–1704.

Shaw, N. S., "Preventing AIDS among Women: The Role of Community Organizing," *Socialist Review*, 18, no. 4 (October–December, 1988), 76–92.

Shelvin v. Lykos, 741 S.W. 2d 178 (Tex. App.-Houston 1987).

Shilts, R., *And the Band Played On: Politics, People and the AIDS Epidemic*. New York: St. Martin's Press, 1987.

Stengel, R., "Testing Dilemma: Washington Prepares a Controversial New Policy to Fight AIDS," *Time*, June 8, 1987, pp. 20–22.

Tex. Crim. Proc. Code Ann. art. 21.31. (Vernon 1988).

Thomas, C., *A Synopsis of State AIDS Laws Enacted During the 1983–1987 Legislative Sessions*. Washington, D.C.: The George Washington University, Intergovernmental Health Policy Project, State AIDS Policy Center, 1988.

Turner, C. F., H. G. Miller, and L. E. Moses, *AIDS: Sexual Behavior and Intravenous Drug Use*. Washington, D.C.: National Academy Press, 1989.

Wash. Rev. Code. Sect. 70.24.340, 70.24.340(1)(b) (Supp. 1988).

Weissman, J. L. and M. Childers, "Constitutional Questions: Mandatory Testing for AIDS under Washington's AIDS Legislation," *Gonzaga Law Review*, 24, (1988–89), 433–473.

Yablonsky, L., *Criminology: Crime and Criminality* (4th ed.), New York: Harper & Row, 1990.

5

The Criminalization of Pregnancy: Drugs, Alcohol, and AIDS

Susan O. Reed

Reproductive freedom consists of more than the right to an elective abortion. The right to become pregnant, refuse intrusive gynecological procedures, have custody of children after birth, and refuse intrusive monitoring of a fetus may also be considered reproductive issues. Balanced against the woman's right to privacy in these situations is the fragility of the development of the child in utero. The impact of new technologies to monitor fetal development, the rhetoric of the "war on drugs," and resistance to Roe v. Wade *by zealots may be seen in criminal and civil charges brought against women who use drugs or alcohol while pregnant. In some cases, the charges are brought on behalf of an abused "child," the fetus; in others, the mother is charged with criminal delivery of a drug.*

The use of child-abuse and drug statutes involves some heroic stretches of reasoning: the connection between chemical use and harm to the fetus is uncertain; women often do not know they are pregnant; appropriate prenatal and drug treatment are not available for all women; and it is not clear that a fetus is a person with rights that override the rights of the mother.

The use of criminal and civil charges to coerce women to seek prenatal care and abstain from drug and alcohol use may be counterproductive, instead causing them to avoid seeking care. This chapter posits that women with AIDS may be the next to have pregnancies criminalized. Many states have criminalized the transmission of AIDS, and history gives ample basis to expect scapegoating of women in times of epidemic sexually transmitted diseases.

The 1980s was a decade of increasingly bitter conflict about women's reproductive rights. *Roe* v. *Wade* became the focal point of the controversy about the woman's control of her reproductive system, and was the most visible combat arena. The purpose of this chapter is to explore other contests about reproductive rights that are less visible or politicized due to characteristics of the mother or circumstances of the pregnancy.

These civil and criminal cases center on the protection of children from harm because of the mother's addiction to drugs and alcohol. In some instances, the plaintiff is the child. What is new is that the child may not be born. This pits the rights of the woman-person-mother against the rights of the fetus-person-nonperson. In states where a fetus is considered a person, child-abuse statutes are used to take jurisdiction over the pregnancy; in states where the fetus is not a person, criminal-drug statutes are used. These cases seem to be based on a lesser standard of proof for child abuse and a move away from traditional centrality of "the benefit of the child" requirements.

The following discussion examines a survey of recent court actions against women on behalf of their fetuses through civil and criminal litigation; the movement to criminalize transmission of AIDS (HIV infection); the goals stated by advocates of this stream of litigation; impediments to the concise definition and achievement of these goals; a survey of knowledge about fetal damage from drug and alcohol use and from HIV infection; prevention and termination of pregnancy as a method of preventing prenatally damaged children; questions about the obtaining and standards of evidence used in cases against women; and an evaluation of the use of litigation to achieve goals here described.

Limitations of Reproductive Rights of Pregnant Women to Prevent Damage to a Fetus

Drug and Alcohol Use during Pregnancy

By mid-1990, the ACLU had identified fifty-one of these cases in nineteen states (Paltrow *et. al* 1990). In Michigan and Ohio, under child-abuse statutes, women have lost custody of newborns addicted to heroin, although the laws contained no language extending the definition of "abuse." A New York court defined alcohol use during pregnancy and failure to obtain prenatal care as child abuse sufficient to warrant loss of custody of the newborn child (*St. John's Law Review* 1987).

Pamela Rae Stewart was arrested in San Diego for "failing to follow her doctor's advice to stay off her feet, to refrain from sexual intercourse, refrain from taking street drugs [which could have been antihistamines], and to seek immediate medical attention" for problems with her pregnancy. Ms. Stewart's physician brought the case to the attention of the police. The charges against Ms. Stewart, a documented victim of spousal battering whose pregnancy had been compromised by placenta previa, were dismissed (Paltrow, Fox, and Guss 1990, pp. 15–16).

Jennifer Johnson was convicted in Florida of delivering illegal drugs to her child prenatally, not the using of illegal drugs herself (Mariner, Glantz, and Annas 1990). The matter of Ms. Johnson was referred to authorities by the staff of a prenatal care clinic when she came in for treatment. Ms. Johnson was found guilty.

Diane Pfannenstiel, fearing that a beating by her husband might have damaged her fetus, sought care in a Wyoming emergency room. Instead, the medical staff called the police who tested her for alcohol use, arrested her for criminal child abuse, and jailed her. Her husband was not arrested (Kolbert, Paltrow, and Goetz 1990).

In Nassau County, New York, women are routinely prosecuted for child abuse and repeated drug abuse on the basis of one positive toxicology report (Moss 1990). Other women who have tested positive for drugs or alcohol or whose newborns have tested positive have been charged with involuntary manslaughter, criminal neglect, and drug trafficking. In Charleston, South Carolina, twenty-one women were arrested and jailed on criminal charges of neglect immediately after giving birth. All cases were referred to the police by the medical staffs of hospitals after they tested positive for drugs (Pollitt 1990, *Drug Policy Letter* 1990). The women were not told they were to be tested or for what purpose.

As of February 1990, nineteen states have enacted statutes defining the killing of a fetus as homicide; some of these laws exclude the mother from prosecution, and some do not (Kolbert and others 1990). Former Senator Pete Wilson sponsored a federal bill that would criminalize "excessive" alcohol use during pregnancy (Pollitt 1990). With statutes such as these proliferating, the proposed Hyde Amendment to the Constitution will not be necessary to criminalize miscarriages and stillbirths (up to 900,000 per year) (Kolbert and others 1990).

Other Limitations of Reproductive Rights

> Reproductive rights will be taken to mean a woman's right to
> decide whether or not to bear children, and by whom, including
> decisions relating to prevention of conception, whether or not to
> carry a pregnancy to term and whether or not to keep the children
> she has chosen to bear, . . . and the decision to carry a pregnancy
> to term will encompass the right not to be committed or incar-
> cerated because of pregnancy, and to keep custody of the child
> unless parental rights-termination standards applicable to all
> parents are met. (Stefan 1989).

Using this expanded definition of reproductive rights, one finds
that the 1980s were characterized by limitations of those rights in
many areas. A seventeen-year-old Florida woman who killed her newborn baby was prohibited from becoming pregnant for ten years as
a condition of probation (Barringer 1990). Some state courts are again
authorizing sterilization of the "incompetent" ("Court Authorizes"
1990).

Angela Carder, a pregnant woman with cancer, was forced by
an attending physician and court order to have a caesarian section
to save a twenty-six-week-old fetus. She and the fetus died (Stefan
1989). Pollitt comments that the Carder case, notable only because
the woman is white and economically secure, serves to publicize a
decade of forced caesareans (1990). Another recent study of court-
ordered gynecological procedures found that all of the women studied
were receiving public assistance and/or being treated in teaching
hospital clinics. "Further, 81 percent were 'women of color and 24
percent did not speak English as a first language'" (Reed 1990,
p. 14).

The increasing ability to monitor fetal development and health
can transmute elective medical procedures into obligations and
make an exclusive class of "responsible parents."

> With the availability of the technology and know-how permit-
> ting prevention of many genetically based congenital abnor-
> malities, there may be developing as a corollary a social attitude
> which demands such use. (Bopp, Bostrom, and McKinney 1989,
> p. 468).

We may be seeing that attitude expressed as state legislators propose bills to force sterilization on women who are actively
addicted to drugs or alcohol. Some states offer the choice of
monitored birth control, sterilization, or drug treatment (Paltrow
1990).

Criminalization of HIV Transmission

Another area in which health-care problems are being litigated as criminal matters is the transmission of HIV disease or infection. Over one-third of the states have passed or are attempting to pass bills criminalizing HIV transmission (*Journal of Urban and Contemporary Law* 1990). These and other states are also using existing criminal statutes to prosecute persons who are HIV-positive who bite, splash blood, or throw feces or other body products on other persons.

Although no case has appeared in the literature surveyed for this chapter, the author posits that women who are seropositive for AIDS (HIV+, or HIV-positive)[1] may be the next group to have the condition of pregnancy criminalized or otherwise controlled by the courts. A study of public panic reactions to other sexually transmitted diseases lends support to this thesis. Historically, politically vulnerable groups such as prostitutes or those perceived as otherwise sexually immoral have been the target of "sweeps" by police as a means to control disease (Sullivan and Field 1988). By the end of 1988, seven states had written laws creating enhanced penalties for HIV-positive prostitutes (or sex workers), although research indicates that sex workers have not been defined as transmitters of HIV disease to more than 2 percent of their clients (Bergman 1988).

It is expected that these actions will be used more frequently against incarcerated or paroled women or women on probation. There exists ample precedent for great intrusions in convicted felons' rights of privacy, movement, and association. Further, the courts have so far supported most correctional agencies' initiatives to test, quarantine, or otherwise treat differently convicted persons who are HIV+ (Caruso and Messing 1990).

Goals Stated by Advocates of Criminalization

Debates over public policies that contain elements of sexual morality are hot and recurrent. Usually, little clarity or consensus is achieved because goals are not defined; assumptions substitute for definition. The goals as stated by advocates of criminalizing pregnancy are described below as a foundation for this discussion.

---

[1]"HIV+" (HIV-positive) and "HIV−" (HIV-negative) are used here to denote those whose blood tests indicate the presence or absence of HIV antibodies, or proof or lack of proof of exposure to the HIV virus.

Protect Fetuses and Other Children of the Substance-Abusing or HIV+ Women from Abuse and Injury

While this goal is often intertwined with the intent to punish the women for harming a child or for illegal chemical abuse, the belief in criminal penalties as a deterrent to injurious behavior (to the fetus) during pregnancy is powerful. It is stated that criminal penalties "may serve as a deterrent, and foster . . . the right of the fetus to be born healthy . . . [I]t logically follows that the state has the authority to deter that harmful conduct through the imposition of criminal sanctions" ("Developing Maternal Liability" 1987, p. 609).

This strategy usually requires that the fetus be treated as a person whether state laws have given the fetus that status or not. Some prosecutors admit that this use of drug laws is questionable.

> I'm not going to tell you I'm sitting on rock-solid legal ground. . . . All those legal issues about the fetus are interesting, but someone's got to do something about protecting the babies. (Lewin 1990, p. 14.)

Webster v. *Reproductive Health Services*, decided by the Supreme Court in 1989, is often cited to justify the expansion of the state's power. The case is interpreted to mean that viability is no longer a standard in defining a person. Therefore, once a woman has gone past the point at which she can legally choose to abort the fetus, the state can move to control her behavior so as to protect a fetus, viable or not (Logli 1990).

Deter and/or Punish Drug Abuse: The Zero-Toleration Philosophy

It is difficult to separate the rhetoric of the war on drugs from the war on "crack babies." Indeed, the image of the crack baby is a powerful one. Law-enforcement initiatives, rather than treatment services, have been endorsed at the highest levels of government. William Bennett, the first national drug "czar," called for mass removal of children from the custody of addicted parents, predicting that the war on drugs would produce "a dramatic increase in orphanages," and George Bush has vowed to fight drugs "block by block, child by child" ("Notes and Comments" 1990, p. 21).

Ignorance about Transmission of AIDS and Resultant Damage to Fetuses and Neonates

Public opinion surveys find that a majority are critical of HIV-positive women who bear children. Calls for punitive treatment are based on the underlying assumption that these women know of their HIV-positive status. This may not be true. Women are diagnosed later than are men for HIV disease. The reasons are myriad, ranging from protocols for diagnosis that are based on AIDS symptoms in men to biases about "the kind of woman" who is likely to become infected (Reed 1990). This was true in the early stages of the AIDS crisis and remains true. Although AIDS is the leading cause of death for New York City women ages 25 to 34, the federal disease-control agency, as late as fall 1990, did not recognize HIV-related symptoms found in the vagina, cervix, or uterus (Cole 1990).

Extreme Positions by Activists in the Abortion Rights Controversy

"Reproductive rights take on a new meaning when applied to AIDS and AIDS tends to turn the abortion issue on its head" (Campbell 1990, p. 410). To this statement can be added the issue of drug- and alcohol-damaged fetuses. Some antiabortion activists perceive the fetus as a person, thus defining the moral course of action as the salvation of the fetus to the exclusion of the salvation of the mother. It is likely that some of these activists are law-enforcement officials, prosecutors, health-care professionals, and judges. Sherry (1989) comments that the choice to abort or not may be interpreted as virtue or vice depending on the predicted condition of the child, not just one's stance about abortion. She warns, "Compelled life saving [of a fetus] is easier to enact (and for that very reason constitutionally suspect) when disfavored groups are forced to do the life saving" (1989, p. 1,595).

     At one extreme, we note the Catholic Church's refusal to support the use of condoms for the purpose of preventing AIDS, and Senator Jesse Helms filibustering for mandatory testing without confidentiality of result (Chandler and Dart 1989, and Getlin 1988). At the other pole, some, focused only on women's reproductive rights, state that threats to newborns are only interesting when those threats are caused by women (Pollitt 1990). The implication here is that the concern for the fetus is only a justification for further restraint of women's rights.

     Both camps can justify their stances by concern for the public weal. Both camps advocate limiting the right to privacy of a group of citizens in a new way. For example, a usual protocol for control of sexually transmitted disease is sex partner tracing, which requires some breach in total confidentiality of medical information. Yet, some groups oppose this despite the threat of AIDS. It is true that sexual and substance-abusing behaviors of fathers are linked to congenital defects in children (Nolan 1989, and Abel 1989), yet these findings are neither publicized nor are they the basis for funding future research. Some advocates for women's rights could theoretically justify an equal intrusion into the preconceptual behavior of men or a criminalization of sexual intercourse for chemical-abusing men.

Hurt Children: Fetal Alcohol Syndrome, Drugs, and AIDS

As a basis for a discussion of legal issues and effectiveness of child-injury prevention strategies, a summary of information about fetal damage associated with alcohol and drug abuse and HIV disease is presented below.

Fetal Alcohol Syndrome (FAS)

Reliable estimates of the number of FAS babies born per year do not exist. A recent estimate is from 6,000 to 8,000 FAS children born per year (Nolan 1990).

The mechanism that produces the damage is still unknown. While it is clear that heavy drinking causes FAS, the effects of alcohol on the fetus resemble damage caused by poor nutrition, smoking, or other class-related factors. A recent study of heavy-drinking women found FAS more likely among women of the lowest two economic levels (Waterson and Murray-Lloyd 1990). Other studies find alcohol abuse and subsequent FAS babies more prevalent among specific cultures; for example, Native Americans (Kolata 1989). Most studies emphasize that preventive efforts must begin immediately, since most FAS damage seems associated with drinking in the first trimester of pregnancy.

We do know that the costs of FAS are substantial. A 1987 estimate put yearly costs at $321 million, without including an additional 11 percent of the cost of institutionalizing mentally retarded persons (Waterson and Murray-Lloyd 1990).

Adolescents and Fetal Damage

A confounding dynamic is the combination of pregnant teenagers, AIDS, and drug abuse. Pregnancies in girls are routinely treated as pregnancies-at-risk. Infants born to adolescents are more likely to weigh dangerously less than those born to mature women; low birth weight is associated with infant mortality. In 1986, approximately 180,000 babies were born to those under seventeen years of age (Nolan 1989). Twenty-five percent of all black babies are born to black teenagers, most of whom will not receive adequate prenatal care (Davis 1989). Adolescents who are pregnant and live in neighborhoods in which drug use and AIDS are rampant face the same hazards as more mature women with chemical-abuse problems and/or AIDS.

Prenatal Transmission of AIDS and Fetal Damage

By June 1989, there were 8,727 women in the United States with AIDS; this does not include those who had less than full-blown AIDS ("ARC" or "HIV disease"). Over half of those women were exposed to the disease through intravenous drug use (IVDU) practices. Of the 30 percent of women exposed through heterosexual contact, 61 percent were exposed via sexual contact with an IVDU (Reed 1990).

There were 1,681 cases of pediatric AIDS (children under thirteen) by June 1989. Almost 80 percent of those were infected by a mother with AIDS prenatally. The majority of those women (75 percent) were infected by IVDU practices or through heterosexual contact with IVDUs. More than three-fourths of those women and those children were African-American or Hispanic nationwide, 93 percent in New York. The data cited above use the more limited definition of AIDS. Were one to use the more inclusive "AIDS-related illness" criterion, it is estimated that the total number of children affected could be three to five times greater (Reed 1990).

Alcohol, Drug Abuse, and HIV Disease

Obvious solutions to the problem of prenatally damaged children include prevention or termination of at-risk pregnancies. These solutions require that the mother know she is pregnant, understand that the pregnancy is compromised, and be able to terminate the pregnancy before the third trimester.

Awareness of Pregnancy and Ability to Prevent Pregnancy

Very young women, women who use heroin or methadone, and women who are malnourished because of drug or alcohol abuse may not have regular menses or menstruate at all (Verklan 1989). Thus, they may not be aware of their pregnancy. Because of multiple in-

cidents of sexually transmitted diseases, they may believe they are
infertile (Reed 1990). Many women may not be aware of the pregnancy until two periods have passed. Early awareness of pregnancy
is important to the establishment of culpability since damage to the
fetus from alcohol, drugs, nicotine, caffeine, and many other legal
substances occurs in the first trimester (Verklan 1989).

Other women, particularly young women or those who engage
in prostitution, cannot or will not assert demands that their sex partners use contraception. Indeed, some women invite assault if they
insist on the use of condoms. For poor women, the lack of access to
contraceptive devices or even knowledge of adequate contraception
means little control over pregnancies (Reed 1990). Further, most studies of attitudes about contraception indicate that men and women
believe it is the responsibility of women, not men, and most educational campaigns are oriented towards women. This is despite the
equally prevalent data that indicates that most men will not use
condoms or stop sex to allow some other form of contraception to be
used (Swanson and others 1990).

Women and Risk Behaviors during Pregnancy

It has been documented often that more women use legal drugs than
men. A survey of commercials and print ads demonstrates that
women are heavily targeted as purchasers of commercial drug products. As a consequence, women do use products with nicotine, anti-
histamines, caffeine, alcohol, and other harmful components without
understanding the risk to the developing fetus (Waterson and Murray-
Lloyd 1990, Verklan 1989). Women at the lower economic levels are
less likely to be informed about fetal damage caused by these substances and by alcohol.

Women do not always know that they are at risk for HIV infection. Dejarlais (in Campbell 1990) has documented the preference of
male IVDUs for non-IVDU female sex partners and their willingness
to lie about HIV infection to those partners. Thus, the women who
live in neighborhoods with high levels of drug abuse and HIV disease
are likely to contract the disease unknowingly, either because they
use drugs or are sex partners with male addicts who are HIV-positive.
Many discover their HIV-positive status when they seek prenatal care
(Reed 1990).

The unawareness of HIV infection is also caused by the ignorance
of doctors treating women, especially poor minority women, who do
not fit their stereotype of women who have AIDS. The doctors and
other health-care professionals may be unaware that HIV disease
manifests itself differently in women than in men (Reed 1990).

The Decision to Terminate a "Risky" Pregnancy

The decision to terminate the pregnancy is not informed just by knowledge of danger to a fetus. It is also guided by religious beliefs, desire for a child, level of self-esteem of the mother, and the counsel of important family members (Selwyn and others 1989). Women who have used drugs and alcohol or who are HIV-positive often choose to continue pregnancies because the fathers or other family members urge them to do so. Adolescents often see the coming child as the only thing that they can produce and so refuse abortion (Deisher and others 1989). Women who are told that the probability of bearing a child with HIV disease is lower than 50 percent see those odds as favorable, given the pressures to have a child.

Should they elect to terminate a pregnancy, women who live outside of population centers on the coasts may have a difficult time finding someone to perform the abortion (Gorney 1990). Should they be HIV-positive, they may find an abortion hard to achieve even in locales where the service is readily available. In March 1990, a study conducted in New York City found that two-thirds of the clinics surveyed refused clients who said they were HIV-positive ("Abortion and the Fear . . ." 1989). Another clinic raised its fee from $500 to $3,000 (Rosenthal 1990).

Criminalizing Pregnancy: Whose Crime and Whose Rights?

Targeted Testing, Arrests, and Prosecution

Minority community members are already sensitive to the threat of racist scapegoating with regard to the transmission of AIDS. Bayer suggests that similar "ethnically conscious [drug, alcohol and HIV] screening" would invoke great resistance because "the result would be an unacceptable stigmatization of poor black and Hispanic women . . . Only universalization [of screening] could prevent stereotyping and the imposition of the burdens associated with the historic legacy of racism" (1989, p. 501). If universal testing is not done, then retention of total confidentiality of results is the only protection against scapegoating. Other groups focused on women's reproductive rights fear that "there is not a very great distance between recommendations that infected women not have children and policies that would prevent then from becoming pregnant" (Bayer p. 502).

Paltrow (1990) suggests that testing and prosecution of pregnant women is discriminatory on the basis of gender as well as race. Prosecutions to date have primarily involved women of color. One study found that African-American women "were ten times more likely to be reported for child abuse . . . even though white women were more likely to have used drugs prior to their first visit to the doctor," (Moss, Paltrow, and Crockett 1990, pp. 15–16).

Finally, as noted above, there is considerable reason to believe that male drug and alcohol abuse and male refusal to practice safe sex result in the conception of birth of damaged children. The prosecution of only women for "child abuse" may be violative of the Fourteenth Amendment proscription against unequal treatment.

Child Abuse and Other Criminal Charges: The Standard of Proof and Validity of the Test Results

Women who are tested for drug or alcohol use while seeking prenatal care or at delivery of the child are rarely told they are being tested or informed about the consequences of a positive blood or urine sample (Moss 1990). Usually, the test for drugs or alcohol is initiated by medical personnel without the mother's informed consent. Prosecutors in California and Illinois have stated that they intend to use one positive urine sample taken from a newborn as evidence against the mother of the child (Moss 1990). This lapse in acceptable forensic protocols may be due to the newness of the role of prosecutor's assistant for medical professionals. Even should they improve in this regard, informing women during or immediately after labor and birth of the consequences of the tests in order to obtain permission may still result in questionably obtained evidence.

The reliability of standard drug tests may also be questioned. Women are being convicted of child abuse or delivery of controlled substances on the basis of one positive result. Even convicted prisoners, for whom there is a diminished standard of proof, are allowed double testing as a protocol ("Urine Testing Update" 1989). This is necessary because the tests used have a known false-positive rate and are shielded from liability in criminal cases (Moss 1990).

Standard of "Health"

The development of criminal laws to protect the fetus requires that a minimum standard of "health" be defined that is reasonably achievable by all pregnant women—for themselves and for their fetuses. For, if the state is to define certain behaviors as criminal, then legal behavior must be clearly understood and achievable. And, the connection between the criminal behavior and harm to the victim must be detectable and clear. Some authorities have suggested that poor nutrition, nicotine, and other conditions associated with the lives of impoverished women cause more damage to developing fetuses than alcohol or drugs at the most prevalent levels of use (Schnoll and Karan 1989, "Maternal Tort Liability" 1988). Because of these threats, the connection between act and harm becomes problematic.

In the absence of a clear connection between a mother's behavior and harm to the fetus, we see women being prosecuted for behavior that *may* be harmful without proof that the behavior *has been* harmful. As Mariner and others note, few cases are being prosecuted because of an injured newborn (1990). Rather, the failed duty of these women is of avoiding risk, not avoiding harm.

If the state sets the standard of avoidance of *all risk*, will the state ensure that this will be possible by providing the necessary nutrition, healthful housing, prenatal care, avoidance of airborne contaminants, and so on? Will the federal government ensure that women are included routinely, where now they are routinely excluded, in the testing of over-the-counter medications (Leary 1991)? Will the state go so far as to regulate intake of food, alcohol, drugs, sexual intercourse—amount and kind, type and amount of exercise? For, if there is a mother's duty to a fetus, then the state must monitor and, if necessary, control the body that contains the fetus ("Maternal Tort Liability" 1988).

Norman Fost (professor of pediatrics and director of a program in medical ethics) distinguishes between moral obligations and legal duties. "Does a woman have a moral obligation to protect her fetus from harm? . . . And if she does, the second question is whether that moral obligation should be transformed into a legal obligation" (Henig 1990). In order for the latter to occur, four conditions must exist:

> There must be a high risk of serious permanent harm to the baby, a low risk of serious permanent harm to the mother, a clear benefit from the recommended course of action, and the fetus' viability at the time the question arose. (Henig 1990)

Thus, Fost concludes that society has no ethical basis for forcing abstention in the third trimester from drugs, alcohol, or other risk behaviors on mothers (Henig 1990).

Timely Notice of Pregnancy

> Under a gross negligence standard, plaintiffs bringing actions against their mothers would have to meet four elements to prevail. They would first have to prove the defendant knew, or that it would have been obvious to a reasonable person in the defendant's situation, that she was pregnant at the time of the negligent act. Second, plaintiffs would have to prove that at the time of the negligent act, the defendant knew, or it would have been obvious to a reasonable person, that her action posed a serious threat to

the life or health of the fetus. ("Setting the Standard" 1989, p. 512).

As has been discussed earlier, many women do not learn of their pregnancies in time to prevent fetal damage. Those familiar with the literature describing adolescent pregnancies know how ignorant children are about the process of conceiving and bearing children. Further, women and girls may be very uninformed about what constitutes risky behavior—damage from smoking, caffeine, illicit medications. And, as stated previously, many women do not know that they are HIV-positive until they learn that they are pregnant or until they have the first appointment for prenatal care. For poor women, that can be late in the pregnancy. For example, in Los Angeles County, women often wait nineteen weeks for the first prenatal care appointment, certainly well after the time when prevention of damage to the fetus is probable (Moss 1990). Indeed, Nolan (1989) states that the HIV status of up to 42 percent of HIV-positive women is not detected in prenatal interviews and examinations, while Klieman (1988) warns of the high rate of false-negative results for HIV infection.

The Right to Appropriate Care: Pregnancy, Drugs, and AIDS

The high level of babies born with birth defects to poor women because of inadequate care, diet, healthful shelter, and understanding of risks to the fetus has been well documented. Poor women, without the compounding problems of drug and alcohol addictions, often cannot obtain adequate prenatal care. The situation is worse for the substance-abusing mother-to-be.

Evaluations of drug-treatment programs over the past decade have not found them to be very successful with most women. The program structures and philosophies, although suitable for male addicts, result in high failure-to-complete rates for women. Further, most programs refuse to allow women to contact their children for several weeks or keep their children with them. For women, giving up drugs means giving up their children (Reed 1990). Most surveys of treatment programs show that pregnant women in most areas of the country can find no program for drugs that will take them while they are pregnant. Those few that do treat pregnant women have waiting periods so long that many women bear children before they are accepted into the drug program (Kolbert and others 1990, Moss 1990).

Should the woman be arrested and incarcerated in jail or prison, the chances for adequate prenatal and drug treatment are diminished. Jails furnish minimal screening on entrance for gross medical problems, often with jailers doing the screening. Care for male jail inmates is poor; and for female inmates, often nonexistent. One jail in California had a miscarriage rate of 73 percent after the twentieth week, more than fifty times the rate for the state (Stefan 1989). Moreover, pregnant women may be assigned work duties that, because of the activities or substances involved in the work, are dangerous (Reed 1990).

The Availability of Abortion

Women now have the right to elective abortion through the first and second trimesters of pregnancy. This may make criminalization of pregnancy moot, because by the third trimester, it is often too late to benefit the fetus by forcing the mother to abstain from risky behaviors.

It is becoming more common for courts to order women convicted of crimes to prevent pregnancy, sometimes for as long as ten years. What then is the violation of that order—the conception, the continued pregnancy, the birth of the child, the presence of injuries in the newborn? If the woman is incarcerated or if she remains in the community, may she keep custody of that child?

Paltrow has stated that abortion may come to be the defense against criminal drug- and child-abuse charges (1990). If the pregnancy "disappears," so does the evidence. However, this action would be taken less by poor women who live in areas with no access to abortion. As stated earlier, doctors who are willing to perform abortions are becoming drastically fewer, and the woman who is HIV-positive may be refused service by available abortion services.

The Demise of Intrafamilial Tort Immunity

The doctrine of intrafamilial tort immunity has, until the present, protected a mother from suit by her child. That doctrine is weakening because of technology that demonstrates the role of the mother in protecting the child in utero ("Maternal Tort Liability" 1988) and because of a generalized retributive stance against women who use illegal drugs (Reed 1990). The waning of this legal doctrine pits the rights of the fetus against the right to privacy and safety of the mother.

Other litigation on the transmission of AIDS has weakened the doctrine of interspousal immunity long used to "maintain and strengthen" the bonds between spouses. Spouses and "life partners" are beginning to sue one another for transmitting AIDS, herpes and other sexually transmitted diseases ("Criminal Liability . . ." 1989). If these traditions weaken equally for men and women, we should see an increase in litigation against fathers who pass on defects via alcohol- or drug-damaged sperm, the AIDS virus, or who interfere with a woman's ability to carry her child safely to term.

Such equity was not demonstrated by prosecutors in the cases of Diane Pfannenstiel and Pamela Rae Stewart; only the women were charged.

The weakening of intrafamilial immunity and a new focus on the rights of the fetus have implications for doctors also. Who is the patient? Who speaks for the patient? How is the doctor to maintain the relationship of trust and privacy necessary for a flow of information between patient and doctor if she or he is now acting as an arm of the law-enforcement system? Is the doctor to use intrusive procedures to guard the fetus' health if the mother is a danger to the fetus?

John J. Ring, in a report by the American Medical Assocation Board of Trustees, examined the duty of a woman to give aid to her fetus. To raise this from moral obligation to legal duty makes the mother's duty override her own privacy and safety rights. It also creates an "adversarial relationship between doctor and patient," which is more likely to dissuade women from seeking prenatal care than from continuing practices harmful to the fetus (Ring 1990, p. 8). Ring also predicted that abortion might be sought as a defense against criminal charges.

Right to Refuse Abortion or Other Court-Ordered Procedures

Angela Carder refused a caesarean which was a danger to her but was supposed to save the life of her twenty-six-week-old fetus. She and the fetus died. The court explained that a child who would probably be "handicapped" had rights that outweighed the rights of a mother who had little life remaining. Other statements from those who were treating her predicted variously that the caesarean would lengthen her life, result in a nonviable newborn, or that the results could not be predicted. It should be noted that Ms. Carder had survived cancer for several years, despite medical predictions to the contrary.

The findings in this case could be generalized to situations involving HIV-positive or substance-addicted pregnant women. Certainly at this time we hear calls for "directive" counseling toward a decision to terminate the pregnancy for women who are HIV-positive. Some go farther, stating the belief that women should not have the right to continue a pregnancy in which the child is probably damaged. After advocating an expansion of wrongful-life suits on behalf of handicapped newborns [against physicians or women who chose to continue a compromised pregnancy], Schedler states:

> The duty to prevent a defective birth must be independent of any decision on the woman's part for two reasons—children with defects whose mothers never made up their minds about com-

pleting the pregnancy would have no wrongful life remedy and the physicians in such cases would seem to owe no duty to the child (1986, p. 372).

His policy, if implemented, would mean that women could be forced to have abortions because they had no right to become pregnant.

Evaluation of Strategies to Achieve Goals

The Court As the Mechanism to Prevent Fetal Damage

The court is a poorly fashioned tool to prevent fetal damage, for it should function slowly and cautiously. In comparison, decisions about protection of the fetus arise in emergency conditions requiring quick convening of actors and rapid deliberations. A study of court-ordered gynecological procedures finds that 88 percent of the court orders were obtained in six hours or less. The pressure on the mother, the lack of access to counsel for her, and forcing of the court to decision without thorough examination of all factors means that the decision process is weighted against the woman's interest. As mentioned above, this is particularly true for minority women. Indeed, 81 percent of these court-ordered procedures involve minority women (Ring 1990). In addition, the rapidity of the process may allow free play of doctors' and judges' peculiar biases about the nature of families, parenting, or motherhood ("The Effect of AIDS . . ." 1989). The overriding of the mother's wishes or of medical need to avoid hazardous intrusive procedures is justified by a regard for the fetus. It is this "Galahad" mentality on behalf of the fetus that makes dissent difficult.

Criminalizing Pregnancy to Prevent Child "Abuse" to the Fetus

Most women who typically are at risk for damaged pregnancies due to alcohol and drug abuse will probably not be informed of *certain* damage to the fetus until after the period in which they have the right to abort. Punishing the mother at that time does not prevent damage to the child. The same results may be anticipated with regard to AIDS babies. One study of HIV-positive pregnant women found that two-thirds of the pregnancies were unplanned due to failure to use contraception (Selwyn and others 1989). These women were at risk also for drug-impaired fetuses and did not learn of the risks until they sought prenatal care.

The history of failed attempts to control epidemics by use of intimidation should give us pause. Indeed, many authorities believe that the use of criminal statutes or other methods of intimidation are ineffective for a population of persons who believe that they are dying. Some go farther and suggest that such tactics will push women away from early diagnosis and treatment of AIDS (Sullivan and Field 1988). Women must know they have AIDS before they can be intimidated into preventing pregnancies. As discussed above, the late diagnosis, lying by infected sex partners, and confusion about presenting symptoms in women all work to retard timely diagnosis of HIV-positive status.

Loss of Custody of Living Children and Prevention of Child Abuse

The foster-care system for children is overloaded, unmanageable, and underfunded. The usual criticism is that the foster-care system does not move quickly enough to protect children. What is of concern here is that children who do not need to be removed from parental custody may be thrown into the overloaded and dangerous foster system. On the basis of one positive toxicology report, Nevada child-care workers removed children from a home without a home visit to examine the conditions there. Other newborns wait in hospital nurseries because of litigation or legislation that makes drug-exposed newborns "abused" and places them in state custody (Moss, Paltrow, and Crockett 1990).

Recent studies suggest that the chronically homeless, chemical-abusing, and at-risk-for-AIDS persons who live in shelters and the streets are products of the foster-care system. One study found that one-third of former foster children existed in this unstable manner. Another project in San Francisco found that half of the foster children studied found their way into the streets as sex workers ("When Foster Care Ends . . ." 1991).

Estimates of further burdens on the foster-home system must include the "AIDS orphans." One estimate anticipates that from 50,000 to 100,000 children in New York City will lose one parent ("AIDS Legacy" 1990). If that parent is the mother, the child will probably need a home. The stigma of AIDS makes it difficult to place these children. As the public hears more about the horror of "crack babies" and "FAS babies," the author anticipates a similar reluctance to foster these children.

Finally, those children taken from mothers whose pregnancies were crimes are not necessarily served better than they were in the care of their mothers. They will be moved from home to home and separated from siblings because of the rules on the ages of children and numbers of children in households. One study of prenatally drug-exposed children found that thirteen children had been in thirty-five foster homes before the age of three (Moss 1990).

Containment of Costs for Treatment

Costs of treatment for AIDS in prison communities are rising steeply. The need to contain costs means that persons with AIDS do not receive the most currently approved treatments while incarcerated (Hammett and Moini 1990). The courts, in disposing of litigation by inmates on this issue, have consistently "respected the expertise" of correctional administrators. This has meant that treatments that are routine for free citizens and are effective in delaying full-blown AIDS are not available to prisoners. This is probably penny-wise and pound-foolish in the cases of prisoners with long sentences. Comparisons demonstrate that prison-hospital care costs are vastly greater than nonprison acute care.

Costs for the "boarder babies" left by untreated addicts who come into hospitals to deliver and then leave, or who are taken from women on the basis of a toxicology report, are spiraling. All of the costs for the babies, of course, are not subject to measurement in dollars. Costs for AIDS babies whose mothers are too ill to care for them or are dead are compounding. Clearly, the costs of treatment for these damaged children are not being contained. Instead, we see an increasing number of boarder babies with AIDS and babies with damage due to drug and alcohol abuse. The cost of readily accessible prenatal care and education is less than any of the responses to the problem described above.

Other Strategies

Drugs, Alcohol, and AIDS as a Public Health Problem

> AIDS is a disease in which fears of contamination and death have been united with fears of sex, drug use and race ... [The] voluntary modification of sexual and drug-using behavior is the only effective, acceptable method of stopping the AIDS [and chemical abuse] epidemic. . . . (Barnes 1989, pp. 701, 699).

Barnes's comments are focused on the AIDS crisis, but the suggestion falls in the mainstream of opinion about solutions to the intertwined problems of AIDS, drugs, alcohol abuse, and pregnancy. Jessup (1990) notes that communities where the criminalization of pregnancy is occurring are communities with few to no resources for women with drug and alcohol problems. Sederer warns of the dangers of custodial management as a cure for complex social problems, the decay of effective treatment and growth of the targeted problem (Reed 1990). Certainly one result of criminalizing pregnancy is increased use of institutions for mothers and children, but in separate institutions.

With regard to the relationship between physician and pregnant women, the Committee on Ethics of the American College of Obstetricians and Gynecologists issued a report stating:

> Because of the urgency of situations in pregnancy, the courts are often petitioned for a speedy decision, which may have serious limitations and unexpected outcomes . . . [R]esort to the courts is almost never justified. . . . Obstetricians should refrain from performing procedures that are unwanted by a pregnant woman. Furthermore, inappropriate reliance on judicial authority may lead to undesirable societal consequences. . . . (ACOG 1987, p. 2)

Most of the health-care authorities surveyed for this work recommend classic public health education campaigns, tailored to subgroups within the greater group at risk for AIDS-, drugs- or alcohol-threatened pregnancies (Waterson and Murray-Lloyd 1990, and Bergman 1988). This would necessitate taking the information to where the women are, not waiting until they show up at clinics for prenatal care or for delivery. It also requires that programs for chemical abuse be moved into prenatal care programs or prenatal care programs be moved into chemical-abuse programs. Encouraging results may be found where this meshing of treatment needs and services has occurred.

A FAS education and prevention effort funded by the Indian Health Service, was targeted for Native American and Alaska Native communities. Designed at the local level and utilizing local community leaders, the education program by local trainers had success in educating school children, prenatal groups and others about Fetal Alcohol Syndrome (May and Hymbaugh 1989). Other programs for women at risk for AIDS and chemical abuse build on the role of helper, into which most women are socialized.

Each of these programs has overcome some of the barriers to treatment found in existing programs. The programs have overcome racism by a variety of means. They are tailored for women, not for men, and for women who have children. The chemically dependent clients are not stigmatized or fearful of criminal consequences. Rather, a central goal of these programs is to incorporate all of the living problems faced by women as they struggle with their maternal responsibilities. This, of course, means that drug programs also become prenatal care and well-baby programs, or that programs for pregnant women take responsibility for providing assistance in the fight against addiction and AIDS. Simple, inexpensive components of these programs assure that women can follow through on medical regimens: coordination of health-care appointments in time and location, child-care provisions, appropriate transportation arrangements, location of some aspects of treatment (education, for example) in sites in the local community, and selection of information providers from the local community. Such programs are sensitive to local norms.

Impediments to Reform; Research Agenda for the Future

As none of these responses to the need are heretofore undocumented or costly, it is difficult to defend a continuing reliance on the current ineffective and costly strategies described previously. Enough has been written about the health-care funding problem that it need not be discussed here. It is sufficient to say that the pregnant woman with children and AIDS, addictions, or both is fractionated as a patient by the pattern of service given by big hospital centers. Further, ancillary needs (child care, transportation) are not included in current funding sources. The costs incurred by not providing these services (injured newborns, or otherwise compromised pregnancies exacerbated by lapses in abstinence or poor prenatal care) surely outweigh the costs to provide the services.

Another impediment to reform is an uninformed public that believes that the police and prosecutorial functions can successfully intimidate poor pregnant women. The intimidation is to result in noncompromised pregnancies. Giving officials in these professions the benefit of doubt, we may attempt to educate them about the causes of damages to fetuses and effective drug and alcohol treatment for women. Should we be less sanguine about motivations to criminalize pregnancy, we may focus funding and effort on illuminating the fragile legal foundations of this strategy.

The latter requires that we better define the population of women so treated. This author is concerned about the *undocumented* cases of restriction on reproductive rights.[2] She suspects that many women on probation and parole are being inappropriately restricted and sanctioned with regard to reproductive issues. Another group of women deserving of study is women with AIDS in correctional institutions. The deference of federal courts to correctional administrators in litigation brought by male prisoners with AIDS is not heartening. Given what is known about health-care treatment for women prisoners, treatment of free women with AIDS, and the reproductive rights (as defined for this work) of women prisoners, we should be focusing on women in jails and prisons.

---

[2]Thanks to Kary Moss and Lynn Paltrow of the ACLU whose work was the impetus to assemble this information.

REFERENCES

Abel, Ernest L., "Paternal Behavior Mutagenesis," *Neurotoxicology*, 10, no. 3 (1989), 335–345.

"Abortion and Fear of AIDS," *Family Planning Perspectives*, 21, no. 6 (1989), 246.

"AIDS Legacy: A Growing Generation of Orphans," *New York Times*, July 17, 1990, p. A1.

Andiman, W. A., Simpson, J., and others, "Rate of Transmission of Human Immunodeficiency Virus Type 1 Infection from Mother to Child and Short-Term Outcome of Neonatal Infection, *American Journal of Diseases of Children*, 144, no. 7 (1990), 758–766.

Barnes, Mark, "Toward Ghastly Death: The Censorship of AIDS Education," *Columbia Law Review*, vol. 89 (1989), 698–724.

Barringer, Felicity, "Sentence for Killing Newborn: Jail Term, Then Birth Control," *The New York Times*, November 11, 1990, pp. 1, 21.

Bayer, Ronald, "Perinatal Transmission of HIV Infection: The Ethics of Prevention," *Clinical Obstetrics and Gynecology*, 32, no. 3 (September 1989), 497–505.

Bergman, Beth, "AIDS, Prostitution, and the Use of Historical Stereotypes to Legislate Sexuality," *The John Marshall Law Review*, 21, no. 755 (1988), 777–830.

Bopp, J., B. A. Bostrom, and D. A. McKinney, "The 'Rights' and 'Wrongs' of Wrongful Life: A Jurisprudential Analysis of Birth Related Torts," *Duquesne Law Review*, 27 (Spring 1989), 461–515.

Campbell, Carole A., "Women and AIDS," *Journal of Social Science and Medicine*, 30, no. 4 (1990), 407–415.

Caruso, G., and H. Messing, "AIDS Caselaw Slowly Developing in Favor of Institution, But Cases Still Surprisingly Few," *Correctional Law Reporter*, 11, no. 2 (1990), 17, 22–24.

Chandler, R., and J. Dart, "Bishop's Panel Rejects Condoms in AIDS Battle," *Los Angeles Times*, October 13, 1989, pp. 3, 27–28.

Cohn, Victor, "Rationing Our Medical Care: Whatever We Call It, We're Already Doing It," *The Washington Post National Weekly Edition*, August 13–19, 1990, p. 11.

Cole, Rebecca, "Women and AIDS," *Women and AIDS Project*, New York State Division for Women, Fall, 1990, pp. 1–31.

"Court Authorizes Forcing Sterility," *New York Times*, February 18, 1990, p. 1.

"Criminal Liability for Transmission of AIDS: Some Evidentiary Problems," *Criminal Law Journal*, 10, no. 41 (1989), 69–97.

Davis, Richard A., "Teenage Pregnancy: A Theoretical Analysis of a Social Problem," *Adolescence*, 24, no. 93 (1989), 19–28.

Deisher, R., J. Farrow, K. Hope, and C. Litchfield, "The Pregnant Adolescent Prostitute," *AJDC*, 143 (October 1989), 1162–1165.

"Developing Maternal Liability Standards for Prenatal Injury," *St. John's Law Review*, 61, no. 592 (1987), 592–605.

"Doctors and Others Criticized over Fetal Alcohol Problem," *New York Times*, December 11, 1990, p. 15.

Embree, J. E., M. Braddick, and others, "Lack of Correlation of Maternal Human Immunodeficiency Virus Infection with Neonatal Malformations," *Pediatric Infectious Disease Journal*, 8, no. 10 (1989), 700–704.

Gieringer, Dale, "How Many Crack Babies?" *The Drug Policy Letter*, March/April 1990, pp. 4–6.

Getlin, Josh, "AIDS Testing, Research Bill Blocked by Helms," *Los Angeles Times*, October 12, 1988, p. 14.

Gorney, Cynthia, "Getting an Abortion in the Heartland," *The Washington Post National Weekly Edition*, October 15–21, 1990, pp. 10–11.

Graham, K., D. Dimitrakoudis, E. Pellegrini, and G. Koren, "Pregnancy Outcome Following First Trimester Exposure to Cocaine in Social Users in Toronto, Canada," *Veterinary and Human Toxicology*, 31, no. 2 (1989), 143–148.

Hammett, Theodore M., and Sairi Moini, "Update on AIDS in Prisons and Jails," *AIDS Bulletin*, National Institute of Justice, September 1990, pp. 1–11.

Henig, Robin Marantz, "Making Mothers-to-Be Abstain: As Drug Risks to the Fetus Become Clear, Can Mothers' Rights Be Threatened?" *The Washington Post*, 1990 (n.d.).

Jessup, Marty, "The Treatment of Perinatal Addiction: Identification, Intervention, and Advocacy," *Western Journal of Medicine*, 152, no. 5 (1990), 553–558.

Klieman, Mark A. R., "AIDS, Vice and Public Policy," *Law and Contemporary Problems*, 51, no. 1 (1988), 315–368.

Kolata, Gina, "Alcohol Abuse by Pregnant Indians [*sic*] Is Crippling a Generation of Children," *New York Times*, July 19, 1989.

Kolbert, K., L. Paltrow, and E. Goetz, "Discriminatory Punishment of Pregnant Women," *ACLU Memorandum*, February 15, 1990, pp. 1–7.

Leary, Warren E., "Inquiry Sought on Drug Tests That Exclude Women," *New York Times*, February 28, 1991, p. 20.

Lewin, Tamar, "Drug Use in Pregnancy: New Issue for the Courts," *New York Times*, February 5, 1990, p. 14.

Logli, Paul A., "Drugs in the Womb: The Newest Battlefield in the War on Drugs," *Criminal Justice Ethics*, Winter/Spring 1990, pp. 23–29.

Mahan, Sue, and D. A. Prestwood, "Policy and Treatment for Cocaine Mothers: A Community Study of Volusia County, Florida." Unpublished Report for the Academy of Criminal Justice Sciences Annual Conference, Denver, Colo., March 13, 1990.

Mariner, W. K., L. H. Glantz, and G. J. Annas, "Pregnancy, Drugs and the Perils of Prosecution," *Criminal Justice Ethics*, Winter/Spring 1990, pp. 30–40.

"Maternal Tort Liability for Prenatal Injuries," *Suffolk University Law Review*, 22, no. 719 (1988), 747–777.

May, Philip, and Karen Hymbaugh, "A Macro-Level Fetal Alcohol Syndrome Prevention Program for Native Americans and Alaska Natives," *Journal of Studies on Alcohol*, 50, no. 6 (1989), 508–518.

Moss, Kary L., "Legal Issues: Drug Testing of Postpartum Women and Newborns as the Basis for Civil and Criminal Proceedings," *Clearinghouse Review*, March 1990, pp. 1406–1414.

Moss, K. L., L. M. Paltrow, and J. Crockett, "Testimony on Behalf of the American Civil Liberties Union before the Select Committee on Children, Youth and Families," May 17, 1990, pp. 1–24.

Nolan, Kathleen, "Protecting Fetuses from Prenatal Hazards: Whose Crimes: What Punishment? *Criminal Justice Ethics*, Winter/Spring 1990, pp. 13–23.

Nolan, Kathleen, "Ethical Issues in Caring for Pregnant Women and Newborns at Risk for Human Immunodeficiency Virus Infection," *Seminars in Perinatology*, 13, no. 1 (1989), 55–65.

"Notes and Comments," *The New Yorker*, July 23, 1990, p. 21.

Paltrow, Lynn M., "When Becoming Pregnant Is a Crime," *Criminal Justice Ethics*, Winter/Spring 1990, pp. 41–47.

Paltrow, L., H. Fox, and A. Guss, "State by State Case Summary of Criminal Prosecutions against Pregnant Women and Appendix of Public Health and Public Interest Groups Opposed to These Prosecutions," *ACLU Memorandum*, 1990 (n.d.), pp. 1–19.

Paltrow, L., K. Moss, and J. Crockett, "Testimony on Behalf of the American Civil Liberties Union on the President's National Drug Abuse Strategy before the Subcommittee on Health and the Environment of the United States House of Representatives Committee on Energy and Commerce," April 30, 1990, pp. 1–51.

Pollitt, Katha, "Fetal Rights: A New Assault on Feminism," *The Nation*, March 26, 1990, pp. 409–418.

"Putting Crack Back into Perspective," *The Drug Policy Letter*, March/April 1990, pp. 1–12.

Reed, Susan O., "Reform by Decree," *Critical Issues in Psychiatry: Mental Health Services to Correctional Facilities*, vol. IV. New York: Plenum, 1988.

Reed, Susan O., *Women, Drugs, and AIDS: Refocusing Prevention and Treatment*. Forthcoming.

Ring, John J., "Legal Interventions during Pregnancy: Court-Ordered Medical Treatments and Legal Penalties for Potentially Harmful Behavior by Pregnant Women," *Report: 00* (A-90). Chicago: Board of Trustees, American Medical Association, 1990.

Rosenthal, E., "Abortions Often Denied to Women with AIDS Virus," *New York Times*, October 23, 1990, p. A16.

Schedler, George, "Women's Reproductive Rights: Is There a Conflict with a Child's Right to Be Born Free from Defects?" *The Journal of Legal Medicine*, 7, no. 3 (1986), 357–384.

Schnoll, S. H., and L. D. Karan, "Substance Abuse," *JAMA*, 261, no. 19 (1989), 2890–2892.

"Selective Prosecution: A Viable Defense Against a Charge of Transmitting AIDS?" *Journal of Urban and Contemporary Law*, 37, no. 337 (Spring 1990), 337–350.

Selwyn, A., R. Carter, E. Schoenbaum, and others, "Knowledge of HIV Antibody Status and Decisions to Continue or Terminate Pregnancy among Drug Users," *JAMA*, 261, no. 24 (1989), 3567–3571.

"Setting the Standard: A Mother's Duty during the Prenatal Period," *University of Illinois Law Review*, (1989), 493–519.

Sherry, Suzanne, "Women's Virtue." *Tulane Law Review*, 63 (1989), 1591–1598.

Stefan, Susan, "Whose Egg Is It Anyway?: Reproductive Rights of Incarcerated, Institutionalized and Incompetent Women," *Nova Law Review*, 13 (1989), 405–456.

Sullivan, K. M., and M. A. Field, "AIDS and the Coercive Power of the State," *Harvard Civil Rights–Civil Liberties Law Review*, 23 (1988), 140–197.

Swanson, J. M., I. Swenson, D. Oakley, and S. Marcy, "Community Health Nurses and Family Planning for Men," *Journal of Community Health Nursing*, 7, no. 2 (1990), 87–96.

"The Effect of AIDS on Child Custody Determinations," *Gonzaga Law Review*, 23, no. 167 (1990), 167–191.

"Urine Testing Update," *Correctional Law Reporter*, 1, no. 4 (1989), 57–59.

Verklan, M. Therese, "Safe in the Womb? Drug and Chemical Effects on the Fetus and Neonate," *Neonatal Network*, 8, no. 1 (1989), 59–65.

Waterson, E. J., and I. M. Murray-Lloyd, "Preventing Alcohol Related Birth Damage: A Review," *Social Science and Medicine*, 30, no. 3 (1990), 349–364.

"When Foster Care Ends, Home Is Often the Street," *New York Times*, January 6, 1991, pp. A1, A10.

"Winds of Change in the United Kingdom," and "Italy Mobilizes Public Opinion to Defeat Craxi Bill," *Anti-Prohibitionist News*, 1 (1990), 1–7.

6

Babies Born with Drug Addiction: Background and Legal Responses

Inger J. Sagatun

The concept of "fetal abuse" raises complex legal and ethical questions. Society has responded to these dilemmas in three different ways: (1) holding that fetal abuse is a form of child abuse with criminal prosecution of the mother, (2) juvenile court dependency intervention for the purpose of protecting the child, and (3) social services and medical treatment approaches with no court intervention. Often two or more of these approaches may be combined.

Focusing on the problem of maternal substance abuse during pregnancy, this chapter discusses the rationales and legal bases for each of these approaches. Relevant court cases and legislation are described. The chapter concludes that criminal prosecution of fetal abuse violates important constitutional rights for the mother and does not promote the well-being of the child. Fetal abuse should not automatically come under mandatory child-abuse reporting laws, and juvenile court intervention should be used only in the most serious cases to protect the child. Comprehensive treatment is the best approach to this growing and costly problem.

In recent years, women have been charged with "fetal abuse" or with the crime of endangering their children while still in the womb. This chapter focuses on substance abuse during pregnancy which, in turn, may affect the fetus. These children may later be born with multiple handicaps and suffer lifelong pain and frustration, and they may require continuous services from an already overburdened society.

The concept of fetal abuse raises complex legal and ethical questions. Meeting obligations to the unborn child may require placing limitations on the mother's conduct that would not be there if she were not pregnant (Robertson 1989). The mother's right to privacy and her autonomy must be balanced against her baby's welfare. Should the right of the fetus be recognized at the risk of sacrificing the rights of the mother? Is the mother's right of privacy worth the lifelong suffering of the child and the staggering costs to society?

Numerous public policy issues are raised by the births of drug-exposed or drug-addicted infants. Should the state intervene on behalf of the baby? Should the child welfare system take action to protect the baby? Should the criminal justice system take action to punish the mother for her conduct? Or, should the mother be left to the medical and public health systems, which should deal with the problem?

Society has responded to these dilemmas in three different ways, the first of which is the most serious: (1) allegations of "fetal abuse" with criminal prosecution of the mother, (2) juvenile court dependency intervention, which could result in taking custody of the child away from the mother, and (3) drug treatment according to a medical model. In some cases, combinations of these approaches may be used.

Maternal Substance Abuse during Pregnancy

National hospital studies have estimated that in 10 to 25 percent of all live births, babies have been exposed to drugs before birth (Chasnoff, Burns, Burns, and Schnoll 1986; Dixon 1989). A study conducted at Hutzel Hospital in Detroit's inner city found that 42 percent of that hospital's newborns test positive on a toxic screen for illicit drugs (Hundley 1989). The entry of a large number of drug-exposed infants into an already overloaded welfare and court system presents a great challenge. Children born with drug exposure are likely to be at much greater risk for child abuse and future delinquency unless effective treatment strategies can be established. Prenatal substance abuse can cause a wide range of serious medical complications for the infant, including withdrawal, physical and neurological deficits, low birth weight, growth retardation, cardiovascular abnormalities, spontaneous abortion and premature delivery, as well as long-term developmental abnormalities (Howard, Kropenske, and Tyler 1986; Petitti and Coleman 1990; Weston, Ivens, Zuckerman, Jones, and Lopez 1989).

Although drug exposure during pregnancy does not harm every

child, those that are affected may become "problem children" for their parents and schools who may be unable to meet their children's special needs (Coulborn, Faller, and Ziefert 1981). For example, many drug-exposed babies resist cuddling and cry easily. Their symptoms of irritability, lethargy, and poor feeding and sleeping habits are extremely stressful for their caretakers. They are severely disturbed by changes in routine and are easily aroused, overreacting to any stimulation. They do not like to be touched. It is frequently difficult to form a strong attachment to such babies (Lacayo 1989).

Traditional Fetal Rights

Whether a fetus has any rights is a controversial issue. What actions can be taken against a pregnant mother during her pregnancy to protect the health of the unborn child? What actions can be taken after birth if the baby has been harmed? Current laws seek to protect children from harm after their birth, and the applicability of current child-abuse and neglect laws to prenatal conduct is uncertain. Fetuses have few, if any, legal rights since, as fetuses, they are not considered to be children in most jurisdictions. The fetus, therefore, has a precarious legal position. A much-debated issue is whether prenatal conduct that affects the fetus should come under the same legislation intended for children after birth, or if new laws should be created that are specifically directed at the protection of the fetus.

The nonrecognition of the fetus as a legal entity is embodied in the "born alive" rule, which states that the fetus has to be born alive as a precondition to legal personhood. Underlying this rule is the assumption that the mother and fetus constitute a unit whose legal interests are co-extensive (McNulty 1988). Historically, the law declined to extend any legal rights to the fetus except in narrowly defined situations and except when the rights were contingent upon live births (*Roe* v. *Wade* 1973). Since the law viewed the fetus as part of the mother, it was only after birth that the child acquired any legal rights independent of those of the mother (Rickhoff and Cukjati 1989).

To be actionable child abuse under traditional criminal law, the conduct that causes the injury or creates the dangerous situation must occur after the birth of a live child (*Reyes* v. *Superior Court* 1977). In this case, the court found that child-endangerment statutes did not apply to prenatal conduct, since this was not expressly stated in the relevant statute (California Penal Code 1989).

Increasingly, however, the "born alive" rule in child-abuse and neglect laws has come under attack. In *Commonwealth* v. *Cass* (1984), the court held that a viable fetus was a person within the protection of the state's vehicular homicide statute. Several states, including California, Illinois, Iowa, Michigan, Mississippi, New Hampshire, Oklahoma, Utah, Washington, and Wisconsin now have "feticide" statutes.[1]

In civil law, fetal rights have already been well established. A majority of states consider fetuses that have died in utero to be "persons" under wrongful death statutes, and, therefore, parents may sue people who harmed the fetus in utero, causing the death (McNulty 1988). Courts have also long recognized "wrongful life" actions.

In *Grodin* v. *Grodin* (1981), a child brought suit against his mother for prenatal injuries because of the mother's negligence in failing to secure prenatal care. The court held that the injured child's mother should bear the same liability as a third person for negligent conduct that interfered with the child's rights to begin life with a sound mind and body (Balisy 1987).

The Criminalization of Maternal Substance Abuse

Some case law demonstrates that in contexts other than maternal substance abuse, the courts have already found that the state's interests in protecting the fetus may overcome a woman's autonomy rights. In 1964, the New Jersey Supreme Court recognized the rights of a fetus to have the mother submit to blood transfusions against her religious beliefs (*Raleigh Fitkin-Paul Morgan Memorial Hospital* v. *Anderson* 1964). In another case, the Georgia Supreme Court affirmed a lower court's order authorizing the hospital to perform a caesarian section in the event that the woman could not safely deliver the child naturally (*Jefferson* v. *Spalding County Hospital Authority* 1981). In this case, the court found that the interests of the fetus outweighed those of the pregnant woman.

Many efforts have been made to expand the legal sanctions available for abuse to the fetus to include criminal sanctions. Maternal and fetal rights are now often perceived as being in conflict, and as such, the interests of one must be balanced against the other. More and more, the interests of the fetus are being seen as more important than those of the mother. The movement to see the fetus as a "pa-

---

[1]State codes containing feticide statutes include: Cal. Penal Code, sect. 187 (1986); Illinois Ann. Stat. ch. 38, Sect. 9-1.1 (1985); Iowa Code Ann., sect. 707.7 (1979); Mich. Comp. Laws Ann., sect. 750.322 (1968); Miss. Code Ann., sect. 97-3-37 (1973); N.H. Rev. Stat. Ann, sect. 585:13 (1974); Okla. Stat. Ann. tit. 21, sect. 713 (1983); Utah Code Ann. sect. 76-5-201 (1983); Wash. Rev. Code Ann. Sect. 9A. 32.060 (1977); Wis. Stat. Ann. Sect. 940.04 (1987).

tient," separate from that of the pregnant woman, has resulted in a tendency to view the mother simply as "the maternal environment," instead of two patients with access to one through the other (McNulty 1988).

Women in states such as Florida, Massachusetts, and South Carolina have faced criminal prosecutions stemming from their use of cocaine, heroin, or alcohol while pregnant. A mother was convicted in Florida under a drug-pushing statute for "pushing" drugs to the fetus via the umbilical cord and sentenced to fourteen years probation (*Florida* v. *Johnson* 1989). The mother's two children were both born with cocaine derivative in their systems because the mother was a crack addict when she was pregnant. Since Florida does not recognize a fetus as a person, prosecutors had to prove that cocaine was pumped into the infants during the sixty to ninety seconds after they were delivered from the birth canal, but before the umbilical cords were cut. The terms of the mother's probation included reporting any future pregnancies to law-enforcement authorities and obtaining approval for her program of prenatal care ("Florida Ruling" 1989).

In California, at least one county has begun using positive toxicology tests on mother and child as prima facie evidence of a violation of the Health and Safety Act (Section 11550) which prohibits being under the influence of a drug (Rosen 1989). This is based on the assumption that mothers will not seek treatment unless the alternative is criminal punishment.

Some who favor prosecution of maternal substance abuse argue that the use of alcohol is a mere privilege, and the use of illicit drugs is a crime, not a "fundamental right." Balisy (1987) argues that the state has a compelling interest in protecting "potential life." Such compelling state interests include both preventing the societal costs of mother's conduct and preventing injury to the fetus. Therefore, states should be permitted by statutory interpretation to proscribe a pregnant woman's tobacco, alcohol, and drug abuse to protect a viable fetus. Johnson (1990) argues that there is a societal interest in protecting the health of unborn citizens who will one day be citizens, and that not prosecuting women for drug abuse during pregnancy leads to the "monstrous moral conclusion" that a pregnant woman has the right to engage in conduct that severely and permanently damages a developing unborn child.

Opponents of criminalizing "fetal abuse" argue that prosecuting women for their conduct during pregnancy is not only unconstitutional, but a waste of resources (Paltrow 1990). From this perspective, no criminal statute could be tailored narrowly enough to protect a woman's right to privacy or her due process rights. At all stages of pregnancy, the fetus is completely dependent on the woman. According to Paltrow (1989), recognizing "fetal abuse" as a crime moves us toward criminalizing pregnancy itself because no woman can provide the perfect womb. A woman should not give up her legal rights just because she chooses to become pregnant.

The creation of "fetal rights" mandating state intrusions in regulating a woman's conduct during pregnancy would necessarily intrude in the most private areas of a woman's life (Johnsen 1986). Criminalization of maternal conduct during pregnancy would also violate a woman's right to equal protection under the law. A statutory requirement that women resolve all health-care decisions in favor of the fetus would hold women to a much higher standard of self-care than men (McNulty 1988). Even a statute that only criminalized a pregnant woman's conduct after she had been informed of possible harm and had been offered treatment without subsequently changing the damaging behavior would still raise serious constitutional questions about rights to privacy and equal protection.

The view that the mother cannot be prosecuted criminally for abuse to the fetus was given support in a 1988 Illinois Supreme Court decision (*Stallman* v. *Youngquist* 1988). In this case, the Illinois Supreme Court refused to adopt "the legal fiction" that the fetus is a "separate legal person with rights hostile to the woman." The court found that holding a mother liable for negligent infliction of prenatal injuries infringes on her right to privacy and bodily autonomy.

Traditionally, criminal laws require that punishment be imposed when there is both a criminal act and a culpable mental intent. Assuming that the state has a right to maintain a reasonable standard of fetal health, it seems logical that the state could only punish those women that willfully, intentionally, or knowingly create a substantial risk of harm to their fetus. However, women who harm their fetuses generally do not do so because they want to. Sometimes women do not even know that they are pregnant when they use the harmful drugs. Therefore compliance with a principle of "fetal health" would require that women be criminally punished for unintended or unknowing harm to their fetuses. Often women who are addicted to drugs or use drugs may be unaware of the harm done to their babies. They may be too poor to afford proper prenatal care, they may be afraid to seek such care for fear of being reported and having their babies taken away, or such prenatal care may not be available. A reasonable community standard of care is hard to determine under such adverse conditions.

Prosecution might discourage a woman from seeking prenatal care and dissuade her from providing accurate information to health-care providers. Both the California Medical Association and the Ethical Committee of the American College of Obstetricians and Gynecologists have therefore opposed the notion of "fetal abuse" (Paltrow 1989). But according to Logli (1990) the concern that pregnant women who abuse drugs would not seek health care because of fear of prosecution is not enough to overcome the state's duty to protect the newborn. If such were the case, then mandatory reporting laws for child abuse would have to be reconsidered for fear that parents would not seek medical care for their children. He concludes that prosecution may help deter future criminal behavior and protect the best interests of the child.

There are many practical arguments against criminalization. For example, the mother might go underground at birth. How can one control the mother during pregnancy? If she should be locked up, when should the incarceration start? Should it start at three months or six months? Incarceration of drug-using mothers after delivery would prevent early bonding and virtually guarantee that the child be raised by a nonparent (Nolan 1990).

Thus, not only can criminalizing the effects of drugs on the fetus be seen as an intrusion on women's fundamental rights, it may also further no interest in the woman's health or well-being and be nearly impossible to enforce.

Juvenile Court Dependency Intervention

Until recently, juvenile law and the jurisdiction of Juvenile Court did not extend to unborn children. In *In re Stevens S.* (1981), the Court of Appeals in California overturned a juvenile court decision, finding that an unborn fetus was not a person within the meaning of the child-abuse or neglect statutes.

Today, however, many cases of drug-exposed and drug-addicted infants reach the dependency side of the Juvenile Court. The first point of entry of drug-exposed infants and their families into the juvenile court system is often right after birth. Many hospitals now routinely perform neonatal toxicology screens when maternal substance abuse is suspected. Typically, such screens are performed when the newborn shows signs of drug withdrawal, when the mother admits to drug use during pregnancy, or when the mother has had no prenatal care. Based on a positive toxicology test, the hospital may report the results to the child protective services agency, which, in turn, may ask the court to prevent the child's release to the parents while an investigation takes place. If further investigation reveals a risk to the child, the court may assume temporary custody of the child, and eventually the child may be placed in foster homes, with the mother under court supervision.

Since 1974, most states have instituted mandatory reporting laws which require health-care professionals, teachers, day-care providers, child protective services agencies, and other professionals dealing with children to report any reasonable suspicion of child maltreatment to the authorities. Failure to do so is typically a criminal offense at the misdemeanor level. These statutes, when written, did not extend to the effects of prenatal behavior or to "fetal abuse" (Moss 1989). The current problem of fetal abuse has therefore led to a movement to include prenatal substance abuse under the reporting statutes.

Legislation specifically requiring physicians to test and report pregnant women for illicit substance abuse has already been passed in several states. For example, Minnesota, Florida, Massachusetts, Oklahoma, Utah, and Illinois have included fetal abuse under their mandatory child-abuse reporting laws.[2] Such statutes require that reports be made to child protective services agencies when infants are born drug-dependent or when toxicology tests on pregnant women or newborns are positive. The Minnesota statute, for example, requires physicians to test mothers and the newborns if they think the mother has used a controlled substance for nonmedical purposes prior to birth (English 1990).

A recently enacted California law (SB 2669), also known as the Perinatal Substance Abuse Services Act of 1990, does *not* endorse automatic reporting of positive toxicology screens, and it emphasizes the desirability of treatment and medical services.[3] This law modified the existing child-abuse reporting laws in California to specify that a positive toxicology screen at the time of delivery of an infant is not in and of itself a sufficient basis for reporting child abuse or neglect. Instead, any indication of maternal substance abuse shall lead to an assessment of the needs of the mother and her infant. Any indication of risk to the child as determined by the assessment shall then be reported to county welfare departments.

Courts have also addressed the issues of whether positive toxicology tests performed on newborns should come under the mandatory reporting laws. An earlier case in California (*In re Troy D.* 1989) addressed the issues of mandatory reporting and juvenile court jurisdiction for drug-exposed infants. In *Troy*, the California Supreme Court let stand an earlier appellate decision that the use of drugs

---

[2]Fla. Stat. Ann., section 415.503 (Supp. 1988); Mass. Laws Ann. Ch. 119, sect. 51A (West Supp. 1988); Omnibus Crime Bill, Chapter No. 290, H.F. No. 59, Minnesota statutes 1988 at 626.5561 and 5562; Okla. Stat. Ann. tit 21, sect. 846 (A) (West Supp. 1988); Utah Code Ann. sect. 78-36-3.5 (1989 Cum. Supp); Ill. H.B. 2590, P.A. 86-659 sect. 3 (1989).

[3]California Senate Bill no. 2669, amended in Assembly, August 23, 1990; Perinatal Substance Abuse Services Act of 1990, effective July 1, 1991.

during pregnancy is alone sufficient basis to trigger a child-abuse report and to support juvenile court dependency jurisdiction (English 1990). The 1990 law negated this ruling.

A related issue is whether maternal substance abuse during pregnancy is indicative of future child abuse and neglect. Legislation defining newborns with toxic substances in their systems as neglected, triggering deprivation of custody and potential criminal prosecution, has been passed in Illinois, Minnesota, Florida, Massachusetts, Indiana, and Oklahoma.[4] In Michigan (*In re Baby X* 1980), an appellate court reasoned that since prior treatment of one child can support neglect allegations regarding another child, prenatal treatment can be considered probative of a child's neglect as well. The *Troy* case also found that prior neglect during pregnancy constituted future risk to the living child. This argument was later reinforced in another appeals court case from California (*In re Stephen W.* 1990).

Robin-Vergeer (1990), however, argues that while the state should concern itself with future harm, there is no reason to assume that pregnant drug users will be incapable of raising their own children. While the criminal justice system is inherently backward-looking and could indeed punish a woman for "fetal abuse" if such a crime existed, the juvenile system is forward-looking and must look for real indicators of future risk to the child. Juvenile courts and legislation intended to protect children cannot automatically characterize as abuse to the child the harms inflicted upon the fetus.

Conclusion

The growing incidence and awareness of drug-exposed infants warrant careful examination and efforts by policymakers, the legal system, and service providers. So far, a wide variety of respones has emerged. Efforts range from the criminalization of "fetal abuse" movement, to a mandatory reporting with dependency proceedings under child-protective laws, to a medical-service-oriented (nonpunitive) approach (English and Henry 1990). The growing practice of testing pregnant women for drug use, and the use of criminal prosecution and neglect proceedings based on these results, has created a serious health and civil-liberties crisis (Moss 1989).

The desirability of postbirth sanctions should depend on the

---

[4]Fl. Stat. Ann., sect. 415.503 (Supp. 1988); Illinois Ann. Stat. Ch. 37, sect. 802-3 (1); Ind. Code Ann. sect 31-6-4-3.1 (Burns 1987); Mass. Gen. Laws Ann. Ch. 119, Sect 51A (West Supp. 1988); Omnibus Crime Bill, Chapter 290, H.F. No. 59, Minn. Stat. 1988 at 626.5561 and 626.5562; Okl. Stat. Ann. Tit. 10, sect. 1101 (4) (Supp. 1989).

gains to the children relative to the harms that might arise from such a policy. While the health of the fetus is important, criminalizing "fetal abuse" does not serve the intended purpose. It would probably jeopardize, rather than secure, the fetal health. Women at risk would not seek medical advice for fear of being punished and of losing their children. More important, the mother's important constitutional guarantees of right to liberty and privacy would be violated.

The constitutionally protected rights to liberty, privacy, and equality prohibit any legal recognition of the fetus that would diminish women's decision-making autonomy on the basis of their ability to bear children. The fetus is a physical part of the pregnant woman, and it is completely dependent upon her for its development. A woman has to make countless decisions about her conduct during pregnancy, many of which will affect the fetus. While a pregnant woman certainly has a moral obligation to her future child, the state should not attempt to transform a pregnant woman into an ideal "baby-making machine."

Protection of children after birth is important. The states should have the right to interfere under Juvenile Court Jurisdiction once family maintenance programs and other treatment forms of intervention have been explored. Infants who have severe symptoms of drug addiction and whose mothers appear unable to care for them for other reasons should come under the mandatory child-reporting statutes and neglect and abuse laws. This should only be a last resort. Since after birth a mother's drug use cannot directly harm the child, any intervention on behalf of the drug-exposed infant must be predicated on other indications of future harm, not the past prenatal drug use. Such indicators might include the mother's care of siblings, her willingness and ability to participate in drug treatment, parenting classes, and the availability of a support system. The goal should be to provide pregnant women with effective drug treatment and comprehensive prenatal care with continued services after birth, so that they may maintain custody of their own children. Intervention should be limited to protect children who are at great risk, so that loss of constitutional rights and societal costs may be prevented.

REFERENCES

Balisy, S., "Maternal Substance Abuse: The Need to Provide Legal Protection for the Fetus," *Southern California Law Review,* 60 (1987), 1209–1238.

California Penal Code, Section 273 a(1). St. Paul, Minn.: West Publishing, 1989.

California Welfare and Institutions Code. St. Paul, Minn.: West Publishing, 1990.

Chasnoff, I. J. (ed.), *Drugs, Alcohol, Pregnancy and Parenting*. Boston, Mass.: Kluwer Academic Publisher, 1989.

Chasnoff, I. J., K. A. Burns, W. J. Burns, and S. H. Schnoll, "Prenatal Drug Exposure: Effects on Neonatal and Infant Growth and Development," *Neurobehavioral Toxicology and Teratology*, 8, no. 4 (1986), 357–362.

Commonwealth v. Cass, 392 Mass. 799, 467 N.E.2d 1324 (1984).

Coulborn, Faller, K., and M. Ziefert, "Causes of Child Abuse and Neglect," *Social Work with Abused and Neglected Children*, 32 (1981), 43–44.

Dixon, S., "Effects of Transplantal Exposure to Cocaine and Methamphetamine on the Neonate," *Western Journal of Medicine*, 150 (1989), 436–442.

English, A., "Prenatal Drug Exposure: Grounds for Mandatory Child Abuse Reports?" *Youth Law News*, 11, no. 1 (1990), 3–8.

English, A., and M. Henry, "Legal Issues Affecting Drug-Exposed Infants," *Youth Law News*, 11, no. 1 (1990), 1–2.

Grimm, B., "Drug-Exposed Infants Pose New Problems for Juvenile Courts," *Youth Law News*, 11, no. 1 (1990), 9–14.

Grodin v. Grodin, 102 Mich. App. 369, 301 N.W. 2d 869 (1981).

"Florida Ruling Won't Deter Addicts," *Atlanta Constitution*, July 20, 1989, p. A-14.

Florida v. Johnson, No. E-89-900-CFA (Fla. Cir. Ct. 1989).

Howard, J., "Developmental Patterns for Infants Prenatally Exposed to Drugs." Paper presented at the Assembly Ways and Means Committee Perinatal Substance Abuse Educational Forum, Sacramento, Calif., February 23, 1989.

Howard, J., V. Kropenske, and R. Tyler, "The Long-Term Effects on Neurodevelopment in Infants Exposed Prenatally to PCP," *National Institute of Drug Abuse Monograph Series*, 64 (1986), 237–251.

Hundley, I., "Infants: A Growing Casualty of the Drug Epidemic," *Chicago Tribune*, October 16, 1989, p. 1.

In re Baby X, 97 Mich. App. 111, 293 N.W. 2d 736 (1980).

In re Stephen W., 221 Cal. App. 3d 629 (1990).

In re Stevens S., 126 CA 3d 23, 178 Cal. Rptr. 525 (1981).

In re Troy D., 215 Cal. App. 3d 889, 263 Cal. Rptr. 868 (1989).

Jefferson v. Spalding County Hospital Authority, 247 Ga. 86, 274 S.E. 2d 457 (1981).

Johnsen, D., "The Creation of Fetal Rights: Conflicts with Women's Constitutional Rights to Liberty, Privacy, and Equal Protection," *Yale Law Review*, 95 (1986), 599–602.

Johnson, P. E., "The ACLU Philosophy and the Right to Abuse the Unborn," *Criminal Justice Ethics*, 9, no. 1 (1990), 48–51.

Lacayo, R., "Nobody's Children," *Time*, October 9, 1989, pp. 91–92.

Logli, P., "Drugs in the Womb: The Newest Battlefield in the War on Drugs," *Criminal Justice Ethics*, 9, no. 1 (1990), 23–28.

McNulty, M., "Pregnancy Police: The Health Policy and Legal Implications of Punishing Pregnant Women for Harm to their Fetuses," *Review of Law and Social Change,* 16, no. 2 (1987–1988), 277–319.

Moss, K. L., *Legal Issues: Drug Testing of Post-Partum Women and Newborns as the Basis for Civil and Criminal Proceedings.* San Francisco, Calif.: Women's Rights Project, American Civil Liberties Union, 1989.

Nolan, K., "Protecting Fetuses from Prenatal Hazards: Whose Crimes? What Punishments?" *Criminal Justice Ethics,* 9, no. 1 (1990), 13–23.

Ostrea, E. M., C. J. Chavez, and M. E. Strauss, "A Study of Factors that Influence the Severity of Neonatal Narcotic Withdrawal," *Journal of Pediatrics,* 88 (1976), 642–645.

Paltrow, L., "Fetal Abuse," *American Bar Association Journal,* August 1989, p. 39.

Paltrow, L., "When Becoming Pregnant Is A Crime," *Criminal Justice Ethics,* 9, no. 1 (1990), 41–47.

Petitti, D., and M. Coleman, "Cocaine and the Risk of Low Birth Weight," *American Journal of Public Health,* 80, no. 1 (1990), 25–28.

Raleigh Fitkin–Paul Morgan Memorial Hospital v. Anderson, 42 N.J. 421, 201 A.2d (1964).

Reyes v. Superior Court, 75 Cal. App. 3d 214, 141 Cal. Rptr. 912 (1977).

Rickhoff, T., and C. Cukjati, "Protecting the Fetus from Maternal Drug and Alcohol Abuse: A Proposal for Texas," *St. Mary's Law Journal,* 21, no. 2 (1989), 259–300.

Robertson, J., "Fetal Abuse," *American Bar Association Journal,* August 1989, p. 38.

Robin-Vergeer, R., "The Problem of the Drug-Exposed Newborn: A Return to Principled Intervention," *Stanford Law Review,* 42, no. 3 (1990), 745–809.

Roe v. Wade, 410 U.S. 113 (1973).

Rosen, J., "The Saga of Butte County," *California Advocates for Pregnant Women Newsletter,* January/February 1989, p. 1.

Senate Select Committee on Children and Youth, *Task Force on Substance Exposed Infants (Final report).* Sacramento, Calif.: California Legislature, 1990.

Stallman v. *Youngquist,* Ill. 531 N.E. 2d 355 (1988).

Suffet, F., and R. A. Brotman, "A Comprehensive Care Program for Pregnant Addicts: Obstetrical, Neonatal and Child Development Outcomes," *Journal of Addiction,* 19, no. 2 (1984).

Weston, D. R., B. Ivens, B. Zuckerman, C. Jones, and R. Lopez, "Drug Exposed Babies: Research and Clinical Issues," *National Center for Clinical Infant Programs Bulletin,* 9, no. 5 (1989), 7.

7

Mothers and Children, Drugs and Crack: Reactions to Maternal Drug Dependency

Drew Humphries

*Prosecutors have charged drug-using pregnant women with drug traf-
ficking and child abuse. But health-care providers, bound to report suspected cases of drug use among pregnant women, have brought far more
women into family court where they risk forfeiting their children to foster
care. This chapter reviews the lack of drug-treatment programs for
women and concludes by recommending community-based drug treatment that keeps families together and provides a full range of social
services.*

Fear that prosecutors are making pregnancy a crime rests on a hand-
ful of highly publicized cases. Brenda Vaughan, an African-American
woman, was charged with and convicted of second-degree theft for
check forgery in Washington, D.C. Although probation is the normal
sentence for first-time offenders like Vaughan, the judge decided to
imprison the pregnant woman after she tested positive for cocaine.
"I'm going to keep her locked up until the baby's born," said Judge
Peter Wolf at the time of sentencing (Churchville 1988, p. A1). No
drug charges were brought against Vaughan nor did the prosecution
seek a trial on possession or use of illegal drugs.

This article was originally published in *Women and Criminal Justice* (Fall 1991),
copyright © 1991 by The Haworth Press, Inc., Binghamton, NY.

When she was charged with and convicted of two counts of delivering drugs to a minor, the prosecution alleged that Jennifer Johnson, an African-American woman, had passed cocaine to her newborn child through the umbilical cord after the baby was delivered, but before the cord was cut (Curriden 1990). Prosecutor Jeff Deen defended the move. "We needed to make sure this woman does not give birth to another cocaine baby. The message is that this community cannot afford to have two or three cocaine babies from the same person" (Curriden 1990, p. 51). The Florida court gave Johnson fifteen to twenty-four years probation, mandatory drug rehabilitation, and drug and alcohol prohibitions, and required her to report subsequent pregnancies to her probation officer and to enter a court-approved prenatal care program (Curriden 1990, Sherman 1989).

In Rockford, Illinois, Melanie Green, African-American, became the first woman to be charged with manslaughter for the death of her two-day-old infant due, allegedly, to her cocaine use during pregnancy. Apparently, doctors at the hospital where Green gave birth reported that the child had tested positive for cocaine (Curriden 1990, Sherman 1989). When an Illinois grand jury refused to indict Green, the charges were dropped.

In other words, pregnancy combined with drug use, especially cocaine use, has been made grounds for punitive sentencing and novel application of criminal and child-protection statutes. These developments give meaning to the phrase "criminalizing pregnancy." This chapter reviews practices that make pregnancy a crime. Because the prosecutions are a response, the chapter begins with the perceived problem, drug-dependent mothers, and then returns to reactions, both legal and medical, before discussing treatment and policy issues.

Maternal Drug Use and Cocaine-Exposed Children

The perceived problem consists of (1) the presumably large number of infants born to drug-using mothers, (2) the damaging effects of drug use on fetal and infant development, and (3) the fear that the long-term needs of these infants will overwhelm social, health, and educational systems.

Maternal Drug Use

The widely publicized claim that 375,000 babies are born annually to mothers who use drugs[1] is the basis of fears about crack and crack-

---

[1]Health providers determine drug use in three ways. The mother may tell the health provider she has used or is currently using drugs. The health provider may, in

addicted babies. The 375,000 figure, reported by Chasnoff,[2] a leading researcher in the field of perinatal drug exposure, represents about 11 percent of births in the United States. It has been extrapolated from case studies of urban hospitals where one might expect that drug use, especially the use of illicit drugs, might be relatively high (Chasnoff 1988, 1987). A Los Angeles study cited by Chasnoff reported that 9 percent of the births surveyed involved neonatal withdrawal due to maternal drug use (Chasnoff 1988). Another case study conducted at Harlem Hospital showed that 10 percent of the newborns (3,300) tested positive for cocaine in their urine (Chasnoff 1987). By 1988, trends suggested that maternal drug use was on the increase. In New York City, it increased from 8 percent in 1980 to 30 percent in 1988, affecting from 20 to 25 percent of all women giving birth (Drucker 1989).

Cocaine use is of special concern. Not only have estimates of cocaine use spawned a moral panic; the awareness that women, including pregnant women, use cocaine and crack contributes to the medical and legal reactions. The 1990 National Drug Control Strategy Report singled out pregnant cocaine users, estimating that 100,000 cocaine babies[3] are born each year (Kusserow 1990). This figure is consistent with the results of an eight-city survey conducted by the U.S. Department of Health and Human Services (Kusserow 1990). The eight-city survey found that 9,000 babies had been born addicted to crack in 1989.

Effects of Exposure

There is ample evidence that maternal cocaine use adds avoidable risks to pregnancy (Chasnoff and others 1986). Cocaine increases maternal blood pressure and the risk of stroke. When used by a pregnant woman, the drug crosses the placenta, exposing the fetus, which cannot excrete the foreign substance quickly enough. Cocaine stimulates fetal movement, increasing the risk of miscarriage during the first

---

addition, screen the mother's urine or that of the newborn for drugs. Among the estimated 375,000 babies exposed to drugs (both licit and illicit drugs), some suffer withdrawal symptoms at birth.

[2]Dr. Ira Chasnoff, head of the Perinatal Center for Chemical Dependency at Northwestern University Medical School, is founder of the National Association for Perinatal Addiction Research and Education, a group which advocates mandatory testing of pregnant women for drug use.

[3]Of the 375,000 drug-exposed newborns, 100,000 are thought to have been exposed to cocaine. The U.S. Department of Health and Human Services uses the term *addicted* to refer to these infants, presumably on the basis of tremors produced when the umbilical cord is cut and the drug supply stops.

trimester and risking premature labor during the last trimester. Cocaine has been associated with an abstinence syndrome (Chasnoff 1987). If the mother abruptly stops taking the drug, the fetus experiences withdrawal-like symptoms. Shortly after birth, the cocaine-exposed infant experiences withdrawal symptoms which can persist for two to three weeks (Chasnoff 1988). Symptoms include wakefulness, irritability, trembling, body temperature variations, rapid breathing, hyperactivity, exaggeration of reflexes, and increased muscle stiffness. Neonates suffer diarrhea, sweating, respiratory distress, runny nose, apneic attacks (failure to breathe), and failure to gain weight. The babies have a high-pitched, persistent cry, are painfully sensitive to sound, cannot suck properly, and are very difficult to comfort (State of Oregon 1985).

In addition to withdrawal symptoms, infants delivered to mothers who used cocaine during pregnancy are smaller in size, tend to be shorter, and have lower birth weights. Their smaller-than-normal head size, indicative of growth retardation, is thought to result from cocaine-induced constriction of the blood supply to the uterus. Babies born addicted to cocaine can develop convulsions and strokes. They are also at significantly higher risk for Sudden Infant Death Syndrome (Chasnoff 1988).

While no one would dispute the toll maternal cocaine use may take, two points require attention. First, the studies reviewed for this chapter point out that the women in question are polydrug users, using, among other drugs, heroin, methadone, marijuana, tobacco, alcohol, and over-the-counter medications. Polydrug use makes it difficult to trace all but a few newborn symptoms to cocaine, these being irritability and the risk of premature delivery (Chasnoff 1986, 1987). Other effects, such as low birth weights or growth reductions, may have social roots in the lack of prenatal and health care, or can be traced to other legal or illicit drugs.

Second, Koren and others recently reported what they call "the bias against the null hypothesis" in the literature on cocaine effects. In other words, studies that fail to show that cocaine has adverse effects on pregnancy tend to be ignored (Koren and others 1989). Of fifty-eight abstracts on fetal outcomes following exposure to cocaine that were submitted for presentation at the Society of Pediatric Research conference, nine reported no effects and twenty-eight reported adverse effects. Only one of the abstracts reporting no effects was accepted for presentation, despite the fact that these studies verified cocaine use and used control cases more often than the other studies. Reviewers, however, accepted over half of the abstracts reporting adverse effects. Findings led researchers to conclude that there may be a "distorted estimation of the teratogenic risk of cocaine" (Koren and others 1989, p. 1440).

Long-Term Needs

Predictions about the long-term needs of cocaine exposed infants are dire. According to a 1989 survey by the U.S. Department of Health and Human Services, the cost of caring for 9,000 crack-addicted children from infancy through age five would be $500 million (Kusserow 1990). To mitigate this cost, the U.S. Department of Health and Human Services recommends that state and local governments provide prenatal care for pregnant women at risk for addiction. It further recommends revising laws on child custody to make it easier to place "boarder babies" in foster care and adoptive homes. The report also estimates that the additional cost of preparing the 9,000 crack babies for school could exceed $1.5 billion. With confirmation of the national estimate of 100,000 crack babies a year, the annual cost could come to $10 billion.

It may be difficult to reconcile spending such sums on children thought to have suffered permanent, irreversible damage, including emotional detachment, inability to relate to others, and neurological impairment. The results of long-term studies are not yet in. But whatever their outcome, one thing is clear: investments that improve a child's environment pay off in minimizing drug-related damage. Environment, not drugs, has the larger influence on development. A two-year study of three groups of newborns (opiate-addicted, nonopiate-addicted, and a control group) showed a downward trend in mean developmental scores, a phenomenon not uncommon in infants from low socioeconomic circumstances (Chasnoff 1986). A study of methadone-exposed infants from birth to four years of age produced similar findings (Kaltenbach and Finnegan 1984). The strongest correlates of developmental status were again social factors. Biological risk, researchers concluded, is either attenuated or potentiated by the child's social environment. The point is, biological risk, including drug-related ones, can be minimized.

Criminalization, Drug Trafficking, and Child Abuse

State and federal prosecutors have argued that pregnant women who use drugs are engaging in illegal activity, and that they ought to be arrested, prosecuted, and convicted. The purpose, they claim, is to stop maternal drug use by incarcerating the women or by forcing them into drug treatment. Patricia Toth[4] of the National Center for

---

[4]The prosecution of drug-using pregnant women has produced unlikely alliances. While Patricia Toth might be expected to take the prosecutors side, she prefers treatment provided the pregnant drug-user takes advantage of it. Otherwise, Toth argues

the Prosecution of Child Abuse says, "Prosecutors seem to agree that the ultimate solution is not criminal prosecutions, but prevention and treatment" (Curriden 1990, p. 53). Lynn Paltrow of the American Civil Liberties Union's Reproductive Freedom Project argues, however, that these prosecutions, in effect, "criminalize" pregnancy. She asserts that "none of these women have [sic] been arrested for the crime of illegal drug use or possession. Instead, they are being arrested for a new and independent crime, becoming pregnant while addicted to drugs" (Paltrow 1990, p. 41–42).

Clearly, the debate over how to handle the problem of maternal drug abuse has aroused passionate feelings on both sides of the issue. Those who favor prosecution state that women must be held accountable for prenatal conduct that may injure the fetus. Those who oppose it feel that the creation of a "prenatal police force" would only succeed in driving the problem underground, preventing many women from obtaining the help that they desperately need (Paltrow 1990). In examining this issue, it is important to outline the theories behind the prosecutions and explore the consequences of prosecuting pregnant addicts.

Of the more than forty cases reported around the country between 1987 and 1990, over half are based on the mother's alleged violation of drug-trafficking laws (Paltrow, Fox, and Goetz 1990). In the case of Jennifer Johnson, the state of Florida succeeded in convicting her of passing cocaine to her newborn through the umbilical cord (Curriden 1990). A drug-trafficking conviction can carry with it a prison sentence of up to ten to fifteen years. Only three women have been successfully prosecuted on these grounds, and all three cases are currently on appeal at the state level.

Other methods of prosecution center on the issues of child abuse or infant neglect. This is the instance in nearly every case cited in the ACLU's summary of criminal proceedings involving pregnant women (Paltrow, Fox, and Goetz 1990). Prosecutors allege that maternal drug use during pregnancy imposes serious health risks on the developing fetus or can result in postnatal trauma including narcotic withdrawal and physical and mental defects (Chasnoff 1987). This type of prosecution is more likely to result in a conviction, although these decisions are also later appealed, since most states do not have child-abuse statutes that pertain to prenatal conduct.

Civil and women's rights advocates have denounced these proceedings and offer many reasons why they may be considered unethical, unproductive, and, in some ways, unconstitutional. First and

---

that pregnant women do not have a license to use drugs nor immunity against prosecution as child abusers.

foremost, there are the problems of legislative intent and due process of law. Specifically, it is argued that prosecutions based on drug trafficking go beyond the expressed intention of the law. In other words, these laws are designed to apply to the sale or exchange of controlled substances between "born persons." Arbitrarily using them to convict pregnant women violates due process, since there has been no notice that these laws are applicable to this situation (Paltrow 1990). Using existing child-abuse statutes also falls under this criticism. Since the fetus is not legally defined as a child, these types of prosecutions violate the due-process rights of the mother. While evidence concerning the negative effects of drug use during pregnancy exists, prosecutors are not always able to prove that the mother's drug use is the cause of specific postnatal defects, if indeed such defects occur at all.[5]

The child-abuse issue leads us into the area of "fetal rights." In her article, "Fetal Rights: A New Assault on Feminism," Katha Pollit discusses the problems created by placing the interests of the unborn above those of the mother. Not only does this kind of action violate the constitutionally guaranteed right to privacy, she argues; it also places an undue burden, a "duty of care" on the pregnant woman (Pollit 1990). Prosecutors, like University of Texas law professor John Robertson, insist that "if [the pregnant woman] decides to go to term, she takes on additional responsibilities so the child will be born healthy" (Curriden 1990, p. 52). But Pollit (1990) insists that the emphasis on the woman's responsibility is merely a convenient way of dismissing the multitude of factors that affect pregnancy but which are beyond the ability of the woman to control.[6] If prosecutors succeed in establishing fetal rights, she argues, women will come to be seen as "incubators," unable to control pregnancies or maintain bodily integrity.

Prosecuting drug-addicted pregnant women leads inevitably down a "slippery slope." Lynn Paltrow suggests that "prosecutions . . . cannot rationally be limited to illegal conduct because many legal behaviors cause damage to developing babies. Women who are diabetic or obese, women with cancer or epilepsy who need drugs that could harm the fetus, and women who are too poor to eat adequately or to get prenatal care could all be categorized as fetal abusers" (Paltrow 1990, p. 7). She also points out that the more than

---

[5]See Chasnoff. Studies have not conclusively established the extent of the harm posed by prenatal drug use. Ill effects are not always exhibited by the infant and the effects of poor nutrition and lack of obstetrical care are not emphasized by prosecutors.

[6]Pollit (1990) discusses the lack of adequate medical care for poor minority women, substandard living conditions, spousal abuse, and poor diet as factors that have significant impact on pregnancy but which legislatures have refused to address.

900,000 women who suffer still births and miscarriages each year could be subject to these same types of criminal proceedings (Kolbert and others 1990).

The overwhelming majority of prosecutions involve poor women of color. The criminal justice system may accentuate the class-racial bias, but it originates in the requirement that medical providers report drug use among pregnant women. Cases normally come to the prosecutor's office from the police, but few maternal drug-use cases come to prosecutors this way. This is what makes Brenda Vaughan's case unusual. She entered the system through conventional channels: she was arrested for and charged with forgery; her pregnancy and drug use were discovered in the course of criminal processing. In contrast, most of the women against whom prosecutors have pressed charges enter the system through hospitals and clinics.

Medicalization: Reporting Child Abuse

The wave of prosecutions described in the introduction began not with drug arrests, but as doctors or other health workers reported the positive results of drug tests for women who, like Melanie Green, had just delivered babies. Such practices reflected the medical providers' belief that without law-enforcement assistance, they could do little to halt the increasing numbers of drug-exposed infants (Goetz, Fox, and Bates 1990). They supported the "reporting laws," which, by the mid-1980s had already imposed a legal and ethical duty on medical providers to report infants born addicted to drugs (Angel 1988). The purpose of such laws, according to Catherine Tracy of Los Angeles County Children's Services, was to prevent child abuse, child neglect, or health-endangering situations (Angel 1988). But, in creating a "duty," reporting guidelines, even in states without applicable child-abuse statutes, turned health-care providers into medical police officers (McNulty 1988).

The procedures developed to implement child-abuse statutes require medical providers to report evidence of abuse or neglect to social service agencies that have the authority to remove the infant from the mother's custody. Evidence of neglect consists of the mother's admission of drug use, positive drug screens for the mother, and positive drug screens for the newborn (Chasnoff 1990).

When the mother admits to drug use, the medical provider has a duty to report. The admission, which is in other circumstances a condition for getting help, jeopardizes the mother's custody of the newborn and, depending on local prosecutors, places her at risk for criminal prosecution. The focus of reporting is unrelated to maternal health or illness. If it were, the Supreme Court's definition of drug addiction as an illness would bar prosecution (Chavkin 1989). Instead, the duty to report arises from the newborn's exposure to drugs. So, in addition to the mother's admitted use of drugs, courts accept the positive results of drug tests on mothers or newborns as evidence of abuse.

Drug testing, however, has limited value in identifying the drug-exposed newborns protected by the abuse laws. It is important to understand what drug tests can and cannot tell us (see Chasnoff 1990). What drug tests can tell is that a drug was ingested by the mother within the last twenty-four to seventy-two hours (Moss and Crockett 1990). They do not indicate the quantity of drug, nor do they reveal the prevalence of its use (Chasnoff 1990). They cannot discriminate between the habitual and the occasional user. They cannot determine whether miscarriage, neonatal death, or early childhood illness or injury are due to maternal or paternal drug use (American Public Health Association, n.d.). Finally, drug tests do not always tell exactly what drug was used. In one case, a woman tested positive for an illegal substance which was actually an antihistamine (Moss and Crockett 1990). Laboratory technicians are not infallible, and false positives can occur.

Nonetheless, drug testing takes place. In public hospitals drug testing is periodic or routine (Chavkin 1989; Moss and Crockett 1990), but many private hospitals test only when drug use is suspected (Angel 1988). Guidelines like those established in South Carolina (Goetz, Fox, and Bates 1990) reveal the circumstances that justify testing: no prenatal care, late prenatal care, incomplete prenatal care, abruptio placentae, intrauterine fetal death, preterm labor, intra-uterine growth retardation, previously known drug or alcohol abuse, or unexplained congenital abnormalities. Some criteria pertain to medical emergencies where maternal and infant health depend on the physician knowing what drugs, if any, a woman may have taken. But other criteria, like the deviations from the monthly and weekly visits to the obstetrician, are rooted in the way the poor use the health-care system. Poor women tend to delay prenatal care, which risks the pregnancy and turns them into candidates for drug testing.

To evaluate bias in drug testing and reporting, a Florida study identified the drug-using pregnant women in the community and then compared them to the group of women selected by public and private hospitals for drug testing (Chasnoff 1990). The study first collected urine samples from black and white women receiving obstetrical care in private and public hospitals. It found no significant difference in the prevalence of positive results beween private and public patients or between black and white women. It did, however, identify a sig-nificant difference between drug choice, socioeconomic status, and race. Middle-income, white women tested positive for marijuana, while low-income black women tested positive for cocaine. The second phase of the study reviewed the characteristics of pregnant women that medical providers tested under the Florida child-abuse statute. The women actually tested by medical providers came from poorer socioeconomic backgrounds than the middle- and low-income women whose urine samples had tested positive for drugs. But the strongest bias revealed by the study was racial. The rate of reporting was ten times higher among black women than among white women. The racial discrepancy held true for black women receiving care in both public and private hospitals. The research team suggested that discrimination reflects (1) the reluctance of private physicians to risk alienating affluent patients and (2) stereotypes about minority drug use held by doctors practicing in large urban hospitals.

Despite technical deficiencies and discrimination, drug tests are the vehicle by which medical providers refer drug-exposed infants to social service agencies. Under Florida's child-abuse statute, medical providers must report exposed infants to the Department of Health and Rehabilitative Services (as reported by Chasnoff 1990). Community health nurses are then required by the Florida statute to determine the suitability of the home and whether the agency should continue supervision or recommend to family court that the child be placed in foster care. The foster-care solution is well documented in New York (Chavkin 1989). In New York, a positive drug-screen, evidence of maternal drug use and child neglect, must be reported to Special Services for Children. The agency investigates, files charges in Family Court, and places neglected children in foster care. The number of children, shortage of foster homes, and delays in investigating have created the so-called boarder-baby crisis, the approximately 300 babies under the age of two that are to be found on any given day boarding in New York City hospitals.

Treatment: From Limited Options to One-Stop Shops

Both the child-abuse and drug-trafficking approaches rest on the assumption that current drug programs can accommodate the pregnant women referred for drug treatment by family or criminal courts. There is, however, widespread recognition that this assumption is false. Congressman George Miller, Chairman of the Select Committee on Children, Youth, and Families, reports that "two-thirds of the hospitals have no place to refer substance-abusing pregnant women" (Kolbert and others 1990, p. 5). The need for drug-treatment programs that include prenatal care is urgent.

Existing treatment programs discriminate against pregnant women. In recent survey of seventy-eight drug-treatment programs in New York City, Wendy Chavkin found that 54 percent refused to treat pregnant women; of those that treated pregnant women, 67 percent refused to treat pregnant women on Medicaid, and 87 percent had no services available for Medicaid patients who were both pregnant and addicted to crack (Chavkin 1989). The bias against admitting pregnant women reflects the perception that obstetrical care adds unacceptable risks to drug rehabilitation (McNulty 1988, Moss 1990).[7]

In Michigan, where the situation is similar to that as described above, only nine of the thirteen residential treatment programs available to women will "consider" pregnant women (McNulty 1988). Long waiting lists, delayed examinations, and admission policies restricting treatment to women who are less than three months pregnant deter pregnant women attempting to get help. A Detroit study found that the average lag time for an initial prenatal appointment at Detroit hospitals was 4.2 weeks (Potti 1990). The initial appointment does not ordinarily include an obstetrical examination, which is scheduled about two weeks later, making the total waiting time, from first contact to initial examination, anywhere from three to thirteen weeks (Potti 1990).

Limited treatment facilities and restricted admissions cast doubt on official responses to the problem. Katha Pollit mentions that Jennifer Johnson had sought admission to a drug-abuse clinic, but was turned away, presumably because she was pregnant (Pollit 1990). Punishing women who are not likely to get the treatment they seek, Paltrow argues, "raises serious questions about prosecutorial ethics" (Paltrow 1990, p. 11). Similarly, the lack of programs that admit pregnant women creates untenable choices. If a woman has a drug problem and a family to care for, she must choose between helping herself or caring for her family (McNulty 1988). Typically, there is no choice. When women coming before the criminal or family court are ordered into drug rehabilitation, their children are placed in foster care.

Despite inadequate facilities, our survey of available literature has identified programs combining prenatal care and drug treatment. Born Free, associated with the San Diego Medical Center, is the country's first residential treatment program for pregnant addicts. It now has several homes for women and their children. The women are required to undergo detoxification either in the program or under another auspice before entering residential treatment (Abraham 1988). Harlem Hospital Center, one of the first in the country to care

---

[7]According to a 1985 study on prenatal care in Orlando, Florida, "It's safer for a baby to be born to a drug abusing, anemic or diabetic mother who visits the doctor throughout her pregnancy than to be born to a normal mother who does not" (Paltrow 1990, p. 8).

exclusively for pregnant addicts, has had some success (French 1989). In Detroit, the Hutzel Hospital takes virtually all high-risk pregnancies in the city, including pregnant addicts, and provides prenatal, delivery, and postpartum care. It encourages women to enter day or residential treatment in the Hutzel Recovery Center. Patients enter treatment on a voluntary basis, but patients facing court dates chose treatment in order to retain custody of their older children (Teltsch 1990). Also, the Neil J. Houston House in the Roxbury section of Boston cares for pregnant addicts who have been convicted of crimes and who would have normally served at least five months in state prison. The program requires detoxification, covers delivery of the baby, and then requires participation in a one-year follow-up program ("Trying to Free Children" 1989). Finally, the Family Center at Thomas Jefferson Medical College of Thomas Jefferson University, like Hutzel Hospital, has a self-referred, high-risk obstetrical clinic (Reagan and others 1987). Other programs that rely on court referrals for patients include MABON, Hale House, and CARE.

The programs which hold out the most hope are voluntary, involve family-centered treatment, and offer a variety of social services in addition to prenatal care and drug therapy. Pregnant drug-users voluntarily seeking help with the pregnancy and for the drug problem have the greatest chance of recovery. Short of self-admissions, court referrals that offer women a choice between entering treatment or serving custodial sentences represent more difficult trade-offs. The element of coercion introduced by court orders reduces the likelihood of recovery, but the terms of the choice are important. Entering a treatment program that keeps the mother, her newborn, and older children together is better than remanding the mother to prison and forcing her to surrender the children to foster care. But little is gained if the treatment option looks like boot camp or participation entails loss of her children. Such punitive choices serve to drive women away from prenatal care and drug treatment almost as much as prison. On the other hand, the chance for maternal or family recovery disappears entirely when women have no control over what happens to them or their children.

Social therapies that keep families together fare better than those that treat family members in isolation. High on the list are the residential treatment and follow-up programs that admit the mother, the newborn, and older siblings. Such programs attend to the needs of the whole family, although the focus on the mother unfortunately overlooks the role that adult male's drug use may play. Nonetheless, the principle operating in these programs keeps children out of the already overburdened and frequently dangerous foster-care system.

And, finally, programs that recognize that drug abuse is a medical problem with deeper social roots stand to contribute more than others. Most programs offer classes in prenatal and infant care, parenting, nutrition, and general health care as well as drug, alcohol, and AIDS education. Others add coping skills, day care, and job training. And still others combine all these services in "one-stop shopping centers." By most accounts, community-based, one-stop shops are the vehicle for delivering the range of services required by a particular community (Abraham 1988, French 1989, Teltsch 1990, "Trying to Free Children" 1989, Reagan and others 1987).

Conclusion

Two ill-conceived national policies have greatly exacerbated, if not produced, maternal drug use. Aimed at eliminating cocaine production in South America, the national drug policy limits the drug-treatment facilities that ought to accommodate all who seek rehabilitation, including pregnant women. Rehabilitation ranks third after domestic enforcement and international drug-control efforts, according to national priorities set in the early 1990s. So, too, the health-care system's collapse, precipitated by withdrawal of federal funds, makes health care the province of the insured. Hospitals and clinics that continue to serve the poor risk bankruptcy. Being poor and pregnant may still get you prenatal care, that being a public-health priority; but being poor, pregnant, and drug-dependent puts you in jail, your children in foster care. Humane alternatives have neither been created nor defended in the decade-long attack on social services.

It is easy to oppose the prosecution of drug-using pregnant women. Medical and public-health organizations condemn the prosecutions as discriminatory. Women's groups have cited violation of fundamental reproductive rights. Such prosecutions, some medical and health-care professionals argue, are detrimental to the health and safety of women and their children. They undermine the trust in the confidentiality of the physician-patient relationship. They drive women at high risk of complications during pregnancy away from the health-care system, creating a situation that is potentially harmful to women and their children.

While the prosecutions have received more attention, it is fair to say that the reporting laws have done more harm. Defining drug use as child abuse and requiring medical providers to report drug use admittedly allows more room for debate. There is something compelling in the fact that these laws are designed to protect newborns. But consider the following: defining the use of controlled drugs as child abuse does not, as some think, solve the problem. It only shifts the burden from the criminal courts to the family court, breaks up families, and produces boarder babies, half of whom go into congregate or foster care. The boarder-baby crisis makes a mockery of claims that the statutes protect children.

The drug-use-as-child-abuse formula ought to be opposed for several other reasons. Although this chapter focused on controlled drugs, some states have included alcohol use in the definition of child abuse, raising the possibility that a range of otherwise legal behaviors during pregnancy may fall within the meaning of child abuse. Additionally, reporting procedures under the child-abuse statutes are discriminatory, undermine patients' confidence in physicians, and drive the women in need of help away from care facilities. Finally, drug testing is an unwarranted invasion of women's right to privacy. The decision to test rests on subjective standards, its application is discriminatory, and evaluation of results are plagued with technical problems.

The most telling criticism that can be made against the drug-trafficking and child-abuse approaches, however, is the lack of treatment programs for pregnant drug-users. Without treatment, prosecutions are simply punitive stopgaps, and reporting laws force minority, poor women to surrender their children. Health care, drug treatment, and social services must be, as we have already argued, among the first priorities. Health and drug rehabilitation must target women in the community, rely on voluntary admissions, strive to keep families together, and offer the support of social services in local community centers.

REFERENCES

Abraham, Lauris, "They Cure Their Habits to Save Their Babies: Unique Program Helps Women Stay Off Drugs," *American Medical News*, January 8, 1988, p. 2, 50–51.

American Public Health Association, Legal Brief to *People of the State of Michigan* v. *Kimberly Hardy*, n.d.

Angel, Carol, "Addicted Babies: Legal System's Response Unclear," *Los Angeles Daily Journal*, February 29, 1988, p. 1, 24.

Chasnoff, Ira J., "The Prevalence of Illicit-Drug or Alcohol Use during Pregnancy and Discrepancies in Mandatory Reporting in Pinellas County, Florida," *New England Journal of Medicine*, April 1990, pp. 1202–1208.

Chasnoff, Ira J., "Newborn Infants with Drug Withdrawal Symptom," *Pediatrics in Review*, 9 (March 1988), 273–277.

Chasnoff, Ira J., "Perinatal Effects of Cocaine," *Contemporary OB/GYN*, May 1987, pp. 163–176.

Chasnoff, Ira J., Kayreen Burns, William J. Burns, and Sidney H. Schnoll, "Prenatal Drug Exposure: Effects on Neonatal and Infant Growth and

Development," *Neurobehavioral Toxicology and Teratology* 8 (1986), 357–362.

Chavkin, Wendy, Testimony presented to House Select Committee on Children, Youth, and Families, U.S. House of Representatives, April 27, 1989.

Churchville, Victoria, "D.C. Judge Jails Women as Protection for Fetus," *Washington Post*, July 23, 1988, pp. A1, A8.

Curriden, Mark, "Holding Mom Accountable," *American Bar Association Journal*, March 1990, pp. 50–53.

Drucker, Ernest, "Notes from the Drug Wars," *The International Journal on Drug Policy* 1, no. 4 (1989), 10–12.

French, Howard W., "For Pregnant Addicts: A Clinic of Hope," *New York Times*, September 29, 1989, p. B1.

Goetz, Ellen, Hilary Fox, and Steve Bates, "Poor and Pregnant? Don't Go to South Carolina . . . ," ACLU Memorandum: Initial Report on RFP's [Reproductive Freedom Project] Carolina Investigation, February 1, 1990.

Kaltenbach, Karol, and Loretta P. Finnegan, "Developmental Outcome of Children Born to Methadone Maintained Women: A Review of Longitudinal Studies," *Neurobehavioral Toxicology and Teratology*, 6 (1984), 271–275.

Kolbert, Kathryn, Lynn Paltrow, Ellen Goetz, and Kary Moss, "Discriminatory Punishment of Pregnant Women," ACLU Memorandum, February 15, 1990.

Koren, Gideon, Karen Graham, Heather Shear, and Tom Einarson, "Bias Against the Null Hypothesis: The Reproductive Hazards of Cocaine," *The Lancet*, December 1989, pp. 1440–1442.

Kusserow, Richard P., *Crack Babies*. Washington, D.C.: U.S. Department of Health and Human Services, Office of the Inspector General, OEI-03-89-01540, June, 1990.

McNulty, Mollie, "Pregnancy Police: The Health Policy and Legal Implications Punishing Pregnant Women for Harm to their Fetuses," *New York University Review of Law and Social Change*, 16 (1988), 277–319.

Moss, Kary, and Judy Crockett, Testimony on Children of Substance Abusers before Subcommittee on Children, Family, Drugs and Alcoholism, U.S. Senate, February 22, 1990.

Paltrow, Lynn, "When Becoming Pregnant is a Crime," *Criminal Justice Ethics*, 9 (Winter/Spring 1990), 41–47.

Paltrow, Lynn, Hilary Fox, and Ellen Goetz, "State by State Case Summary of Criminal Prosecutions Against Pregnant Women," ACLU Memorandum, April 20, 1990.

Pollit, Katha, "Fetal Rights: A New Assault on Feminism," *The Nation*, March 16, 1990, pp. 409–418.

Potti, Lisa, Testimony before the House Select Committee on Children, Youth, and Families, U.S. House of Representatives, April 23, 1990.

Reagan, D. D., S. M. Ehrlich, and Loretta P. Finnegan, "Infants of Drug Addiction: At Risk for Abuse Neglect and Placement in Foster Care," *Neurotoxicology and Teratology*, 9 (1987), 315–377.

Sherman, Rorie, "Keeping Babies Free from Drugs," *The National Law Journal*, October 1989, pp. 1, 28.

State of Oregon, "Women, Drugs, and Babies," Unpublished survey conducted by the Division of Youth and Family Services, 1985.

Teltsch, Kathleen, "A Drug Recovery Center that Welcomes the Pregnant Addict," *New York Times*, March 20, 1990, p. A4.

"Trying to Free Children From Shackles of Crime," *New York Times*, August 30, 1989, p. A9.

8

Pregnant Substance Abusers: The New Female Offender

Alida V. Merlo

Pregnant women who use drugs have received a great deal of attention in recent years. They have been officially sanctioned for such behavior under a variety of statutes. One of the more controversial approaches utilizes the criminal law. Although drug use during pregnancy poses a major public-health concern, the government's efforts appear to be directed more at prosecution rather than treatment and prevention. Providing good-quality prenatal care for all pregnant women is one step that the government can take to help ameliorate the problem.

All of us have been made aware of the scourge of drugs in America. We are reminded daily of the government's interest in the "War on Drugs," and the various attempts that have been undertaken to reduce drug use. Recently, we have begun to recognize the serious implications of drug use on fetal development, and our attention has been focused on the behavior of pregnant women. This chapter will elucidate the legal approaches to the problem and examine the increasing utilization of the criminal law and its negative consequences on pregnant women.

Society has competing interests in the area of fetal abuse. On the one hand, no one can doubt the importance of preventing children from being born with mental and physical damage. Such an interest is strengthened when the damage is caused by the mother's inges-

This chapter is a revision of a paper that was presented at the American Society of Criminology Annual Meeting in Baltimore, Maryland, on November 10, 1990.

tion of toxic substances like drugs, alcohol, and tobacco during pregnancy. Conversely, society recognizes and upholds the rights of privacy and bodily integrity that citizens have to be free from governmental invasion. There also is a social interest to protect the traditional mother-fetus relationship from unnecessary intrusion and interference.

It is estimated that two drugs, cocaine and crack, affect approximately 10,000 to 100,000 babies born each year (Nolan 1990, p. 14). In fact, one hospital in Oakland, California reports that about one-fifth of its babies are born addicted to drugs and 90 percent of these are cocaine-addicted ("Crack Babies" 1989). The effects of cocaine addiction are serious, but it is not the only illegal drug to impact the fetus. Babies of women who use marijuana during pregnancy experience problems from prematurity and low birth weight to congenital abnormalities and perinatal problems (Lester and Dreher 1989, p. 765).

There are a number of legal substances like alcohol that are also related to retardation and serious birth defects (Anderson and Grant 1984). Nolan (1990) reports that 6,000 to 8,000 infants are born with Fetal Alcohol Syndrome each year. Additionally, maternal contact with other dangerous legal substances like carbon monoxide and lead are just now beginning to be evaluated (Nolan 1990). The long-term costs to these children and society because of their involuntary exposure are indeed troublesome.

State Intervention and Enforcement

Confronted with these preliminary findings, the government is in the unenviable position of having to decide which course of action to pursue. Some legal scholars argue that the government has a compelling interest to intervene in the lives of pregnant women and coerce them, if necessary by utilization of criminal sanctions, to refrain from certain behaviors. These scholars point to the case law in the area of court-ordered caesarean sections and forced blood transfusions (Balisy 1987). Because the state has an interest in potential life, the courts have intervened in these situations to resolve maternal-fetal conflicts. They contend that there is a similar basis for such interference when the mother is abusing alcohol, narcotics, or tobacco (Balisy 1987).

Proponents of state intervention and criminalization of maternal conduct during pregnancy suggest that once the woman has made a decision not to abort, she has ". . . a legal and moral responsibility to bring the child into the world as healthy as is reasonably possible" (Robertson 1983, p. 438). Women are, of course, finding it increasingly difficult to obtain abortions. States are restricting the availability of abortions and some abortion clinics are discouraging certain patients from treatment. Recently, a study conducted by the New York City Commission on Human Rights has confirmed that when women who identified themselves as HIV-positive called abortion clinics in New York to schedule abortions in 1988, more than half of the centers refused them. During the spring of 1990, fifty more sites were called, and 42 percent either refused to provide services or required excessive fees (Rosenthal 1990, p. 14). Since the relationship between testing positive for HIV and intravenous drug use is widely known, it would appear that drug-dependent pregnant women who want to abort are being denied equal access to abortion services. One might wonder to whom these women can turn for help.

State intervention advocates also cite the court's recognition of prenatal tort liability and wrongful death actions when states allow the wronged infant or its survivors to recover damages. They conclude that fetal rights have been long recognized and might even result in the substance-abused infant's right to initiate civil action against both parents (Balisy 1987).

Opponents of state intervention adopt a different stance. They contend that the state does not have an interest in fetal life sufficient to override a woman's rights of privacy and bodily integrity (Nelson, Buggy, and Weil 1986, p. 757). They suggest that the case law on abortion clearly indicates that statutes that encroach upon a constitutionally protected right would be authorized only if they are narrowly drafted to meet a compelling state interest (Note 1988, p. 996).

State enactment of fetal-abuse laws affects two different areas of the right to privacy. They include the right to make decisions that affect the areas of marriage, family, and procreation and the right to control one's own body (Note 1988, p. 998). Pregnant women make a number of decisions every day with respect to their bodies that can affect the fetus. They make decisions about eating, taking medication, exercising, and consulting a doctor, for example. Any of these behaviors may harm the fetus and could be legally significant in the criminalization of fetal abuse. Opponents of state intervention contend that even though the state believes that a woman has made a bad choice by choosing to drink alcohol during her pregnancy, that does not allow it to criminalize her procreative decision making (Note 1988, p. 998–1001).

Opponents of criminalization also question the constitutionality of laws that infringe upon the individual's right to control her own body. The right to bodily integrity rests on an application of the Fourth Amendment prohibition against unreasonable search and seizure. That has been interpreted to mean the right to control one's own physical self (Note 1988, p. 1002). Fetal-abuse law limits that right of the woman because of the state's interest in protecting the fetus.

Intervention opponents point out that the state must also consider the special relationship that exists between mother and fetus. State intervention to regulate the mother's conduct or to punish the mother for actions affecting the fetus during her pregnancy may result in mother and child becoming legal adversaries (Field 1989, p. 124–125). There is the additional risk that women would forego medical treatment for fear of criminal prosecution (Field 1989).

Given the competing positions, the state must decide how to proceed. As is typical in such dilemmas, public opinion plays a role. A survey conducted by the *Atlanta Constitution* polled 1,500 people in fifteen southern states on the question of criminalization of fetal abuse. Predictably, in this conservative climate of law and order, 71 percent favored criminal penalties for women whose ingestion of illegal drugs injured their babies. Additionally, 45 percent were in favor of prosecuting women for alcohol and cigarette use during pregnancy that harms their infants (Curriden 1990).

Such a position also seems to have the support of some government officials. The former federal official in charge of drug enforcement, William Bennett, recommended removing children from every woman who uses drugs (Mariner, Glantz, and Annas 1990, p. 37). Similarly, former Senator Pete Wilson proposed a bill that would have mandated three years incarceration in a custodial rehabilitation center for women convicted of using drugs during pregnancy (Johnsen 1989). There appears to be little resistance to prosecuting women with fetal-abuse laws. Since 1987, nineteen states and the District of Columbia have begun more than fifty criminal proceedings against women for drug use during pregnancy (Hoffman 1990, p. 35).

The state's recent interest in fetal versus maternal rights conflicts with women's rights to privacy and autonomy articulated in abortion case law. Perhaps these actions are indicative of a social climate in which women who are pregnant or might get pregnant are subject to greater regulation and control.

Recent Legislation and Litigation

States have three courses of legislative action. They can attempt to apply existing criminal narcotics statutes to prohibit fetal abuse (narcotics laws). These prosecutions usually employ narcotics laws pertaining to the distribution of drugs to minors, which are interpreted to include a woman providing drugs to her fetus or newborn. Alternatively, they can draft new fetal-abuse laws (criminalization laws). The new criminal-code provisions attempt to address directly the

woman's behaviors (primarily drug use) during a specific time period—her pregnancy—that may in some way harm the fetus. Lastly,
they can amend or interpret existing child-abuse laws to include
maternal transmission of drugs *in utero*. These actions usually require
the cooperation of hospital staff to screen the infant and/or mother
and then to contact the authorities at the time of delivery (informant
laws).

Attempted prosecutions that employ the narcotics laws to acts
committed during pregnancy have had mixed results. Some states
have successfully prosecuted such cases, while others have not
been able to indict or convict. Recently, a Superior Court judge
in Massachusetts dismissed a drug-distribution indictment against
Josephine Pellegrini for cocaine found in her child's blood at birth.
Ms. Pelligrini had been charged in 1989 with distributing cocaine
to a minor (her newborn) and possession. The judge ruled that the
defendant's right to privacy was violated by the criminal charge
and advocated treatment instead of prosecution in her opinion
("Judge Clears Woman" 1990). In Illinois, a grand jury refused to
indict Melanie Green with involuntary manslaughter and delivery
of a controlled substance. Her daughter died two days after birth,
and both Ms. Green and the baby had evidence of cocaine in their
blood (Logli 1990, p. 24). A Michigan prosecutor charged two mothers,
Lynn Bremer and Kim Hardy, with the felony of drug delivery instead of possession (a misdemeanor) because they used drugs while
pregnant.

Some states are enacting new legislation designed to address
fetal abuse. These legislatures have moved quickly to criminalize the
mother's use of illicit drugs during pregnancy. These new criminalization laws are designed to prosecute women for felonies committed
during their pregnancies by use of illegal drugs such as cocaine. Illinois developed such legislation in 1989, the Infant Neglect and Controlled Substances Act, making it a felony to "inflict or create a
substantial risk of physical injury to a newborn infant" by the pregnant woman's use of drugs during pregnancy (Curriden 1990). To
date, the legislation has focused on illegal drugs and has not included
legal substances like alcohol and tobacco use during pregnancy.

According to Hoffman (1990, p. 35), at least eight states have
approached the problem differently; they have expanded their definition of child abuse and neglect to include drug exposure *in utero*.
Informant laws now require hospital officials to contact some state
social-service agency when a baby is born with cocaine or other illicit
drugs in its system.

Florida has enacted these informant laws. Under legislation
which became effective in 1987, the state's child-abuse laws have

been amended to include children born drug-dependent. Hospital staff members are mandated to immediately notify Florida's Department of Health and Rehabilitative Services when a child is born with drugs in its system (Spitzer 1987, p. 865). Minnesota also requires hospital staff members to inform the local welfare agency of any pregnant women ". . . who have or are believed to have used a controlled substance during pregnancy" (Paltrow 1990, p. 44). New York follows a similar procedure. This approach, utilizing the presence of drugs in a newborn as the basis of a request for a neglect hearing, has been upheld by the Appellate Court in New York (Baquet 1990).

Procedures for intervention differ from state to state, and they may even vary within the same state. According to Robin-Vergeer (1990, p. 753–761), hospitals in California have discretion regarding whether toxicological screens will be administered, whether the mother is to be notified that she or her infant will be screened, and what the result of a positive screen will be. In some counties, a positive screen of an infant provides the child-welfare authorities with the basis for automatic removal of a child, while in other counties, a more detailed investigation is necessitated before temporary custody of a child can be granted. In other counties, no screening is done.

Arguments against Criminalization

One of the most significant criticisms of the prosecution of women for conduct during their pregnancies is that it occurs after the fact and is not preventative. The dearth of drug-treatment programs for pregnant women is well documented (Johnsen 1989; Mariner, Glantz, and Annas 1990). It seems particularly untimely for the state to express its concern for the fetus's well-being after the child has been delivered. The intervention of the state to prevent the fetus from being exposed to drugs appears to be a more logical and coherent approach. Criminalization is all the more unreasonable when one considers the inability to determine cause and effect. In the child-abuse cases, cause and effect and intent are usually obvious. In many instances of fetal abuse, cause and effect may only be speculative. For example, smoking cigarettes may be correlated with low birth weight and learning disabilities. However, it cannot be said conclusively that the mother's use of tobacco resulted in her child's learning disabilities (Blumberg 1987, p. 41).

In addition to substance abuse, women who use drugs usually are experiencing problems related to lack of housing and income and family difficulties. All of these factors can play a part in poor birth outcomes. Unfortunately, it is easier to blame the mother's ingestion of a particular drug than to consider all the factors that might have contributed (Mariner, Glantz, and Annas 1990; Nolan 1990).

Sentencing pregnant women who test positive for drugs at the time of arrest to incarceration is not a solution either. Women who are pregnant and drug users are likely to enter prison or jail with high-risk pregnancies. They need to be closely monitored and have emergency services available (Stein and Mistiaen 1988). The lack of adequate services for pregnant offenders has resulted in civil lawsuits in California, Massachusetts, and Connecticut. The Santa Rita jail in California and the California Institution for Women have implemented drug-treatment programs and better obstetrical/gynecological services as a result of lawsuits (Stein and Mistiaen 1988).

If the rationale for enacting new criminalization legislation is that it will deter women from taking drugs or using other substances during their pregnancies, it is misguided. Possession of illicit substances is already a crime. If existing legislation is ineffective in deterring drug use during pregnancy, there is no reason to suspect additional prohibitions will be any more effective. When the mother's fear of being prosecuted is that overwhelming, she will simply avoid prenatal care issues completely. Providing optimal prenatal care to cocaine-using pregnant women requires health-care professionals to get detailed histories from their patients and to examine them (Chasnoff 1989). Unfortunately, women who feel that their doctors are really law enforcers may be inclined to avoid seeing doctors (Thompson 1989; Note 1988; McNulty 1987–1988).

Currently, women who are convicted of drug charges face possible confinement in jail or prison. Since there is already a significant chance that the woman will lose custody of her child through incarceration, it seems unnecessary to sponsor new legislation or interpret existing legislation to discourage pregnant women from using drugs. It is conceivable that such legislation might be a manifestation of the government's interest in attempting to regulate and control the lives of pregnant women, to single them out for special treatment. Recently, in Wyoming, a woman contacted authorities to get protection from an abusive partner. She was jailed for prenatal child abuse because the police detected the smell of alcohol on her breath (Stellman and Bertin 1990, p. A19).

Opponents of criminalization also question the discriminatory manner in which the laws are being enforced. According to ACLU statistics on prosecutions for using drugs while pregnant, 80 percent of the women were black, Hispanic, or members of other minorities (Kolata 1990b). They also tended to be poor. It is especially tragic that criminal sanctions are being utilized on that segment of the population that is least able to defend itself or resist governmental intrusion. Apparently, poor women are more likely to go to public hospitals for care, and these hospitals are most likely to do drug testing and to report the pregnant abusers (Kolata 1990b). One wonders if their vigilance in testing and reporting might discourage women from seeking treatment.

Arguments for Alternative Approaches

Providing all pregnant women with quality prenatal care and establishing educational programs designed to deter their use of alcohol, tobacco, and illicit drugs or other harmful substances appear to be more rational and realistic approaches to this problem. The United States government has not been very successful in assisting pregnant women. According to 1987 data, the United States ranks twentieth in infant mortality when compared to other industrialized countries (Friend 1990, p. A1). For every 1,000 live births in 1987, the overall infant mortality rate was 10.1. For blacks, the rate was 17.9, and for whites, it was 8.6 (Pear 1990, p. B9). These rates are inexcusable for one of the wealthiest countries in the world.

Every year, over 200,000 low-birth-weight infants are born (Nolan 1990, p. 15). In 1985, one-third of all women who gave birth did not receive adequate prenatal care (Johnsen 1989, p. 210). Based upon these data, there appears to be plenty of room for improvement. In fact, almost any effort to enhance prenatal care would be assured of having a modicum of success.

When a pregnant woman is using drugs, it is usually an indication of far more complex problems. Drug use in pregnancy is not an isolated phenomenon. One study of eighty-one Hispanic and non-Hispanic pregnant adolescents in California suggested that factors like changes in living situations, high stress, lack of social support and parental substance use, rather than ethnicity, were related to substance use (Moss and Hensleigh 1988). Substance use is frequently accompanied by inadequate nutrition, poor prenatal care, lack of housing and poorly timed pregnancies (Nolan 1990; Mariner, Glantz, and Annas 1990).

Pregnant addicts have also been shown to be depressed and anxious. In their study of fifty-four pregnant addicts, Burns and others (1985) found that over 50 percent of the women were moderately to severely depressed. The state should commit its resources to support groups, parenting classes, treatment programs, and outreach programs to encourage women to get help (Kahn 1987). Rather than focus our anger and dissatisfaction on the pregnant women, Paltrow

(1990) suggests that we should express our concern over the lack of funding committed to treatment programs and the exclusion of pregnant women from these programs.

It seems unfortunate that the state is uninvolved throughout the woman's pregnancy, an important period of a woman's and her fetus's life, and then suddenly intervenes at childbirth to prosecute her. There is some research that indicates that pregnancy is an especially effective time to diagnose and treat such problems as maternal alcoholism. The combination of a decrease in drinking and the mother's concern for the developing fetus creates an ideal time for treatment and future prevention (Anderson and Grant 1984). Governmental interest and action in education and treatment programs, rather than prosecutions, would appear to be a more positive and effective response.

Based upon the available evidence, it seems to be a waste of governmental resources for the state to persist in enacting and enforcing criminalization laws. Having recognized the deleterious effect of toxic substances on fetuses, there is a more humane and reasonable approach. Society needs to be convinced of the importance of prenatal care in order to commit the necessary resources to provide it for everyone. Paltrow (1990, p. 39) reports that 25 percent of all women in America have no health insurance coverage for prenatal care or delivery. All women from all social and economic classes deserve the best prenatal care society can provide. It is only through such care that problems like poor nutrition, low birth weight, stress, lack of exercise, and insufficient support can be addressed.

In addition, society needs to stop giving lip service to drug education and prevention and start creating and supporting programs. For example, mental deficiency related to Fetal Alcohol Syndrome is preventable (Anderson and Grant 1984). Providing reliable information to prospective parents, advising them of the need to take proper precautions, counseling, and assistance will go a long way in reducing drug use and promoting healthy babies (Kahn 1987, Field 1989, Note 1988).

Also, society needs to strengthen and maintain family ties. Any action by the state that potentially pits mother against fetus in an adversarial way is to be avoided. Recognizing opposing fetal rights affects maternal-fetal bonding by suggesting that there is a potentially antagonistic relationship between mother and fetus. The fetus is thus viewed as an object that restricts the mother's legal rights (Note 1988, Field 1989).

Every action a pregnant woman takes should not be subject to scrutiny, and she should not be held accountable for every bad outcome. Some infants will be born with physical, mental, and psychological abnormalities. Punishing a parent for what she may or may not have done prenatally can serve no benefit for the child (Blumberg 1987, p. 41). Women should not be made to feel that they are responsible for every birth defect because of something they did or were exposed to during their pregnancy (Blumberg 1987).

Finally, society must realize that there is no "quick fix" to this problem. There are no shortcuts to improve the staggering mortality rate of American babies. Prosecuting women may give the illusion of dealing with the problem, but it does not. The real solution will not result in a lot of media attention for prosecutors, judges, and victims. The real solution is a long-term commitment designed to prevent and treat substance abuse during pregnancy and to provide the best in prenatal care to all women.

Conclusion

By a combination of advances in medical technology and research, we are now able to understand more fully the maternal-fetal relationship and the need to provide a healthy environment for the developing fetus. Society has to decide how to deal with this new knowledge. It seems we can proceed in a variety of ways.

One approach involves the state further criminalizing maternal conduct like drug possession by enacting new fetal-abuse laws or prosecuting women under existing felony statutes, such as those intended for drug distribution, instead of those for simple possession of drugs. The main focus of these actions is the mother's conduct prior to the actual birth. The fact that an infant tests positive at birth for cocaine or some other illicit drug results in the mother being criminally prosecuted.

Another approach utilizes recently revised or previously drafted child-abuse and neglect laws and may take a newborn infant's manifestation of drugs in its system as an indication of abuse and/or neglect. Some states may even employ a combination of the two: authority to declare a newborn drug-dependent or neglected and remove it from the mother's custody and, simultaneously, to initiate formal criminal charges against the mother under new or existing legislation.

A less punitive approach involves the state taking an active interest in the education and treatment of women who may be using or inclined to use toxic substances during pregnancy. Such an approach would necessarily include the provision of quality prenatal care for all women, special assistance and counseling services to women and their families experiencing stress, child care where needed, and residential and nonresidential drug-treatment programs. These activities would seem to be the most effective and the least disruptive to family life.

If our goal is to prevent Fetal Alcohol Syndrome, drug-addicted newborns, and the transmission of other potentially toxic substances to fetuses, the government needs to commit the resources and the energy to assist women before and throughout their pregnancies. Unfortunately, these problems will not abate overnight. They require more than rhetoric and "get-tough" philosophies designed to deter, prosecute, and punish pregnant women. In return, they hold the promise of a lower infant-mortality rate, fewer low birth weight babies, and healthier mothers and babies who will have less need for long-term government expenditures and services.

REFERENCES

"Aids, Abortion and Fairness," *New York Times,* October 27, 1990, p. 14.

Anderson, Sandra C., and James Fraser Grant, "Pregnant Women and Alcohol: Implications for Social Work," *Social Casework,* 65 (1984), 3–10.

Balisy, Sam S., "Maternal Substance Abuse: The Need to Provide Legal Protection for the Fetus," *Southern California Law Review,* 60 (1987), 1209–1238.

Baquet, Dean, "New York City Neglect Hearings Upheld in Newborn Cocaine Cases," *New York Times,* May 30, 1990, p. A13.

Blumberg, Lisa, "Why Fetal Rights Must Be Opposed," *Social Policy,* 18 (1987), 40–41.

Burns, Kayreen, Jacob Melamed, William Burns, Ira Chasnoff, and Roger Hatcher, "Chemical Dependence and Clinical Depression in Pregnancy," *Journal of Clinical Psychology,* 41 (1985), 851–854.

Chasnoff, Ira, "Cocaine, Pregnancy, and the Neonate," *Women & Health,* 15 (1989), 23–35.

Chavkin, Wendy, "Drug Addiction and Pregnancy: Policy Crossroads," *American Journal of Public Health,* 80 (1990), 483–487.

"Crack Babies," *The Economist,* 311 (1989), 28.

Curriden, Mark, "Holding Mom Accountable," *American Bar Association Journal,* 76 (1990), 50–53.

Field, Martha. "Controlling Women to Protect the Fetus," *The Society,* 17 (1989), 114–129.

Friend, Tom, "Infant Mortality Could Soar," *USA Today,* March 11, 1990, p. A-1.

Hoffman, Jan, "Pregnant, Addicted—and Guilty?" *New York Times Magazine,* August 19, 1990, pp. 33–36, 44.

Jeruchimowicz, Rita Jeremy, and Victor J. Bernstein, "Dyads at Risk: Methadone-Maintained Women and Their Four-Month-Old Infants," *Child Development*, 55 (1984), 1141–1154.

Johnsen, Dawn, "From Driving to Drugs: Government Regulation of Pregnant Women's Lives after *Webster*," *University of Pennsylvania Law Review*, 138 (1989), 179–215.

Johnson, Phillip E., "The ACLU Philosophy and the Right to Abuse the Unborn," *Criminal Justice Ethics*, 9 (1990), 48–51.

"Judge Clears Woman of Fetal Drug Charge," *New York Times*, October 18, 1990, p. B11.

Kahn, Judith, "Of Women's First Disobedience: Foresaking a Duty of Care to Her Fetus—Is This a Mother's Crime?" *Brooklyn Law Review*, 53 (1987), 807–843.

Kolata, Gina, "N.I.H. Neglects Women Study Says," *New York Times*, June 19, 1990, p. B10.

Kolata, Gina, "Racial Bias Seen on Pregnant Addicts," *New York Times*, July 20, 1990, p. A13.

Lester, Barry M., and Melanie Dreher, "Effects of Marijuana Use during Pregnancy on Newborn Cry," *Child Development*, 60 (1989), 765–771.

Logli, Paul A., "Drugs in the Womb: The Newest Battlefield in the War on Drugs," *Criminal Justice Ethics*, 9 (1990), 23–29.

Mariner, Wendy K., Leonard H. Glantz, and George J. Annas, "Pregnancy, Drugs, and the Perils of Prosecution," *Criminal Justice Ethics*, 9 (1990), 30–41.

McNulty, Molly, "Pregnancy Police: The Health Policy and Legal Implications of Punishing Pregnant Women for Harm to Their Fetuses," *Review of Law & Social Change*, 16 (1987–1988), 277–319.

Moss, Nancy, and Paul A. Hensleigh, "Substance Use by Hispanic and White Non-Hispanic Pregnant Adolescents: A Preliminary Survey," *Journal of Youth and Adolescence*, 17 (1988), 531–544.

Muraskin, Roslyn, "Mothers, Children and Drugs." Paper presented at the American Society of Criminology Annual Meeting, November 10, 1990, Baltimore.

Nelson, Lawrence J., Brian P. Buggy, and Carol J. Weil, "Forced Medical Treatment of Pregnant Women: 'Compelling Each to Live As Seems Good to the Rest," *The Hastings Law Journal*, 37 (1986), 703–763.

Nolan, Kathleen, "Protecting Fetuses from Prenatal Hazards: Whose Crimes? What Punishments?" *Criminal Justice Ethics*, 9 (1990), 13–23.

Note: "Maternal Rights and Fetal Wrongs: The Case against the Criminalization of 'Fetal Abuse'," *Harvard Law Review*, 101 (1988), 994–1012.

Paltrow, Lynn, "Fetal Abuse: Should We Recognize It As a Crime? No," *American Bar Association Journal* 75 (1989), 39.

Paltrow, Lynn M., "When Becoming Pregnant Is a Crime," *Criminal Justice Ethics*, 9 (1990), 41–47.

Pear, Robert, "Study Says U.S. Needs to Battle Infant Mortality," *New York Times*, August 6, 1990, pp. A1, B9.

Robertson, John, "Fetal Abuse: Should We Recognize It As a Crime? Yes," *American Bar Association Journal,* 75 (1989), 38.

Robertson, John, "Procreative Liberty and the Control of Conception, Pregnancy, and Childbirth," *Virginia Law Review,* 69 (1983), 405–464.

Robin-Vergeer, Bonnie I., "The Problem of the Drug-Exposed Newborn: A Return to Principled Intervention," *Stanford Law Review,* 42 (1990), 745–809.

Roden, Nancy K., "The Judge in the Delivery Room: The Emergence of Court-Ordered Cesareans," *California Law Review,* 74 (1986), 951–2030.

Rosenthal, Elisabeth, "AIDS Infection Often Blocks Abortion Access, Study Says," *New York Times,* October 23, 1990, pp. A1, B2.

Sagatun, Inger J., "Babies Born with Drug-Addiction: Background and Legal Response." Paper presented at the American Society of Criminology Annual Meeting, November 10, 1990, Baltimore.

Smith, Steven R., "Disabled Newborns and the Federal Child Abuse Amendments: Tenuous Protection," *The Hastings Law Journal,* 37 (1986), 765–825.

Spitzer, Brian C., "A Response to 'Cocaine Babies'—Amendment of Florida's Child Abuse and Neglect Laws to Encompass Infants Born Drug Dependent," *Florida State University Law Review,* 15 (1987), 865–884.

Stein, Loren, and Veronique Mistiaen, "Pregnant in Prison," *The Progressive,* 52 (1988), 18–21.

Stellman, Jeanne Mager, and Joan E. Bertin, "Science's Anti-Female Bias," *New York Times,* June 4, 1990, p. A19.

Thompson, Elizabeth L., "The Criminalization of Maternal Conduct During Pregnancy: A Decision-Making Model for Lawmakers, *Indiana Law Journal,* 64 (1989), 357–374.

DISCUSSION QUESTIONS
SECTION 3: WOMEN, DRUGS, AND AIDS

1. What is the leading cause of HIV infection among women in the United States? Is there an association between non-IV drug use and AIDS?

2. Should there be mandatory testing for AIDS of all defendants accused of rape? Are prostitutes at higher risk than other sexually active women for contracting the AIDS virus? Would mandatory testing drive the disease underground?

3. Should the government criminalize pregnancy? By prosecuting women who use drugs prior to or during pregnancy, are we masking the real drug crisis in America? Are the courts the proper mechanism to prevent fetal damage?

4. Does a woman have a right to privacy to refuse intrusive gynecological procedures when suspected of drug use? Can she refuse intrusive monitoring of the fetus? Is the use of criminal and civil charges to coerce women to abstain from drug and alcohol use counterproductive? Will the threat of criminal sanctions cause women to avoid seeking prenatal care?

5. Should the "right" of the fetus be recognized at the risk of sacrificing the rights of the mother? Is the mother's right of privacy worth the lifelong suffering of the child and the staggering costs to society? What actions, if any, should be taken against a pregnant mother during her pregnancy to protect the health of the unborn child? What actions, if any, can be taken after birth if the baby has been harmed?

Section 4

Women and Policing

Police work, probably better than any other social role, serves as an aspect of social life in which men have traditionally predominated. The work of the police, especially patrol activities, has long been a bastion of male dominance. Power, assertiveness, force, and authority are central elements of the job. In addition, patrol activities take place in the public arena. Police officers are expected to demand respect, establish control, and enforce rules under adverse and even hostile conditions. A central topic of this section is how well women perform those duties that were once considered to be the exclusive domain of men.

Until the extension in 1972 of Title VII of the Civil Rights Act of 1964, women in American policing were restricted to nonpatrol assignments—primarily those involving clerical work, crime prevention, and work with juveniles. The articles in this section discuss not only the litigation that occurred as a result of this legislation, but its contribution to the literature on women in policing as well.

The number of problems that women have faced in policing is astounding. Women have found themselves to be the subject of ridicule and mockery. Gaining the confidence of their fellow officers is only one of the many hurdles that women police officers must overcome. Can women perform as well as men in the full range of police activities? This section should help in answering this most important of questions.

9

A Perspective on Women in Policing

Sean Grennan

This chapter reviews the history of women in policing. It analyzes relevant legal decisions, problems in the workplace, and theoretical perspectives concerning women entering what is considered the male workplace or male domain. The findings of this research indicate that women are performing quite well and, in some areas, better than their male counterparts.

The sexual revolution has brought with it an overdue increase in the number of women actively employed as sworn officers by law-enforcement agencies. Today, women represent approximately 10 percent of the law-enforcement work force, but this proportion is quite a bit lower than the proportion of women in society. Recent research findings indicate that the ratio of women in policing has increased, but the total outlook for women in policing is far from encouraging (Martin 1989).

Female participation in patrol work has been minimal until recently, even though the first American female officer was appointed in 1910. Historically, female officers were assigned to low-visibility positions in most police departments; for the most part, they were

The author would like to thank the Academy of Criminal Justice Science's *Police Forum* for granting permission to reprint parts of a research note that appeared in vol. 1, no. 2 (1991), pp. 9–10.

used as matrons, traffic-enforcement officers, clerical personnel, or juvenile officers until the Equal Employment Opportunity Act (Title VII) was passed in 1972 amending the Civil Rights Act of 1964. The 1972 amendment made it mandatory for all state and local governments to follow the same guidelines as the federal government in relation to discriminatory practices in employment. Henceforth, state and local governments could no longer use race, creed, color, or sex as a condition of employment. Since the enactment of Title VII, eleven female officers have been killed in the line of duty. The first was killed by a robbery suspect in Washington, D.C. in 1974, and five of the other ten were killed without any warning that they were in any type of imminent danger. Four of these officers were assassinated and one was shot and killed by a sniper (Milton 1972, Horne 1980, Keefe 1981, and Bell 1982).

The view of most police executives in the United States is that women, for the most part, do not belong on patrol because of their lack of physical strength and their inability to maintain an imposing presence in the face of challenges to police authority.

History of Women in Policing

Women have been employed as police matrons since 1880 in order to satisfy the legal requirements related to the confinement of female offenders. The 1890s brought about the appointment of Marie Owen, the widow of a Chicago police officer, as an assistant to Chicago investigators handling cases involving women or children. This appointment, made directly by Chicago's mayor, was probably a way of taking care of police widows rather than a change in police philosophy toward women in policing. Early in the twentieth century, women's responsibilities increased to include social work, juvenile work, and clerical work. In 1905, the city of Portland, Oregon gave Lola Baldwin police powers to cope with the problems created by the large influx of workers arriving during the Lewis and Clark Expedition. In 1910, Alice Stebbins Wells, a social worker, petitioned and addressed the Los Angeles City Council and the Police Commissioner on the problems the city was facing concerning women and children and the need for female personnel to handle these problems. Wells was convincing and was appointed to the Los Angeles Police Department to work with women and children, but was not permitted to perform field work outside police facilities. This breakthrough created opportunities for women to be hired by police departments throughout the United States. One other major breakthrough took place in 1914 when the city of Milford, Ohio appointed Mrs. Dolly Spencer as the first female police chief in the United States. The total number of women appointed, however, remained small, and women's impact on the male-dominated profession was, at best, minimal. Whatever gains women made in the early years of this century were dissipated with the reduction in police personnel caused by the Great Depression of the 1930s (Buwalda 1945, Perlstein 1971, Milton 1972, Crites 1973, Connolly 1975, Horne 1980, and Linn and Price 1985).

At the end of World War II, poor police working conditions and low wages created significant police labor shortages in many southern police departments. Lacking sufficient men, departments hired women to perform the tasks of traffic control and parking enforcement. The solution was so successful that it led to the employment of women by departments in many other jurisdictions throughout the United States. Although the job the women were hired to perform was basically traffic duty, it provided movement in the right direction for those women wanting to enter law enforcement (Milton 1972, Horne 1980).

Gradually, the social-worker role of women disappeared and, during the 1960s, vanished entirely as women started to become actively engaged in more typical police field work. In 1968, women were officially assigned to perform patrol duties in Indianapolis, Indiana. Much more instrumental than the Indianapolis experiment in putting substantial numbers of women on police forces was the Equal Rights Amendment of 1972, expanding the Civil Rights Act of 1964 (Title VII) to include public employees. The *Griggs* v. *Duke Power Co.* (1971) case established the principle that a plaintiff in a job-discrimination case need not prove discriminatory intent. Instead, the Supreme Court held, once it is evident that job qualifications appear out of proportion in relation to a group or class of people, the employer must prove that the said requirement is a "bona fide occupational qualification" (BFOQ) that is directly related to the occupation and that no other standards could reasonably replace this criterion. Sex could not be proven as a BFOQ, simply because many police departments had never hired women, and thus had no way of comparing the performances of men and women. For just about every standard— height, weight, age, and so on—*Griggs* made a winner of most actions by plaintiffs against police. In *Reed* v. *Reed* (1971), the Supreme Court banned discrimination on the basis of a person's sex. Taken together, legislation and court rulings have had more of an impact in opening employment to women than isolated experiments by police departments (Milton 1972, Martin 1980, Horne 1980, Remmington 1981, and Keefe 1981).

Prior to 1970, very few large police departments placed women in significant positions in policing. In the 1970s women started to be integrated into the patrol ranks in most major police departments in the United States. In St. Louis County, Missouri, women were appointed to the police department and trained for one-person patrol units in 1975. One restrictive hiring practice, a height requirement, was abolished by many of the large urban police departments in the 1970s. This was a significant step for women officers who were frequently eliminated from hiring considerations because they did not pass the height requirement. The elimination of the height requirement in New York City led to the hiring of more female officers, and, ultimately, the placing of more women on patrol in 1973. Once the precedent was set by the New York City Police Department, many other large departments arranged similar guidelines to place women on patrol (Sichel and others 1978, Horne 1980, Colgrove 1983).

Gaining appointments to police departments has not been the only problem women have faced in their efforts to pursue careers in law enforcement. Having passed written, physical, and medical examinations, they were still placed in menial positions within most departments and denied the right to compete for promotion. In 1961, Felicia Shpritzer, a member of the New York City Police Department, took her case to court. She had previously been denied the right to take the sergeant's examination. By 1963, she had won several court decisions, but the police department still refused to let her take the promotional exam. Finally, in 1964, the police department followed the court decision in *Shpritzer* v. *Lang* that gave women an equal opportunity to take promotional tests. Shpritzer was permitted to take the exam and was subsequently promoted to sergeant (Milton 1972, Keefe 1981).

In 1967, Shpritzer and Gertrude Schimmel both passed the lieutenant's test and were the first women in New York City promoted to that rank. In 1971, Schimmel was the first woman to attain the rank of captain. In 1972, the police department assigned fifteen female officers to patrol duties under a pilot project established by Police Commissioner Patrick F. Murphy. On January 1, 1973, the Commissioner changed the designation of "policewoman" to "police officer." Further progress was evident when the Policewomen's Bureau was abolished in 1973. This was significant because women were to be assigned throughout the department and were placed in the same category as their male counterparts on patrol.

The major problem faced by female officers in New York City during this period was the lack of acceptance they received from male officers. An additional setback occurred in 1975 when a city fiscal crisis resulted in the layoff of 3,000 police officers. At that time, there were approximately 500 female officers. With the city's fiscal crisis in 1975, most of the newly appointed officers, male and female, were dismissed because of an inverse seniority rule under the New York State civil service law requiring the last person hired to be the first person laid off. The state law also contained a ruling on veteran's preference that gave a person thirty months seniority, provided that person had served in the United States Armed Forces and had one year of police service. This ruling obviously favored the male officers. The numerical gains that female officers had attained dissipated until the city was able to get back on its feet financially (Acerra 1978, Keefe 1981, and Linn and Price 1985). The female officers had fallen victim to the last-hired/first-fired rule.

The New York City Police Department has more than tripled its total number of female members since 1979. The 1988 figures for the NYPD show a total of 3,071 women, compared to a total of approximately 600 female members of the department in 1979 (NYPD 1988). The recruitment and hiring of women suggests that this police department does not accept the questionable view that only male officers can handle the vigorous and dangerous work of policing. More women are entering police work than ever before, but, as most other police departments, the NYPD is failing to address the question of promoting women in proportion to their representation within the police population. The following two tables indicate the disproportionate number of women in supervisory positions within the NYPD.

Theoretical Considerations

The entry of women into police work in more substantial numbers than ever before has caused considerable controversy in the law-enforcement community. Studies have been conducted on female ability to perform in the patrol environment. Most of these studies indicate that while women can properly function within that envi-

TABLE 1 Population of NYPD by Gender and Rank

RANK	MEN	WOMEN	TOTAL
Detective/Police Officer	19,939	2,910	22,849
	87.3	12.7	84.2
Sergeant	2,766	149	2,915
	94.9	5.1	10.7
Lieutenant	888	11	899
	98.8	1.2	3.3
Captain	304	0	304
	100.0	0.0	1.1
All Ranks above Captain	164	1	165
	99.4	.6	.7
Total	24,061	3,071	27,132
	88.7	11.3	100.0

Source: New York City Police Department, *Employment Statistics for 1988.*

TABLE 2   Population by Gender and Rank—Actual/Expected

RANK	MEN		WOMEN	
	ACTUAL	EXPECTED	ACTUAL	EXPECTED
Detective/Police	19,939	20,262.78	2,910	2,586.22
Officer	87.3	88.7	12.7	11.3
Sergeant	2,766	2,585.06	149	329.94
	94.9	88.7	5.1	11.3
Lieutenant	888	797.24	11	101.76
	98.8	88.7	1.2	11.3
Captain	304	269.59	0	34.41
	100.0	88.7	0.0	11.3
All ranks above	164	146.33	1	18.67
Captain	99.4	88.7	.6	11.3
Total	24,061	24,061	3,071	3,071

Source: New York City Police Department, *Employment Statistics for 1988.*

ronment, they may have problems when handling violent confrontations with citizens.

In discussing the evolution of the American image of the female role, Epstein theorizes that its roots are in European literature and the arts. Despite the fact that women of lower classes have always worked inside or outside the home, the ideal feminine attributes were the ones "glorified by the urban middle or upper class role ideas, in which the expectation of what women should be and do was linked with the man's desire for beauty and pleasure and his demand for order and relaxation after work" (Epstein 1970, p. 21).

Epstein notes that many of the so-called feminine traits, such as passivity, nonaggression, and practicality are found in all humans but have come to be "sexualized and are assumed, asserted, or expected to correlate with sexual differences" (Epstein 1970, p. 22).

For the woman entering the work world, conflict is inevitable, as the traits most necessary to a successful career (such as competitiveness, aggressiveness, active persistence, emotional detachment) are considered to be masculine (Epstein 1970).

A result of the process of socialization and consequent polarization of the sexes is the limitations placed upon women entering the work field. She is limited not only by societal pressures but by real external barriers (discriminatory policies, sex typing, or particular jobs) in certain occupations, as well as by her own "internal barrier"—a limiting view of herself (Lipman-Blumen and Tickamyer 1975).

Thus, for the woman entering a male-dominated occupation, conflict is not only inevitable, it is highly stressful. Epstein characterizes this stress as:

> ... sociological ambivalence ... the social state in which a person, in any of his statuses (as wife, husband, or lawyer, for example), faces contradictory normative expectations of attitudes, beliefs, and behavior which specify how any of these statuses should be defined. (Epstein 1970, p. 19)

Traditional family roles divided family functions into instrumental and expressive roles for male and female, respectively. At its worst, this division "reinforces sex role stereotyping. At its best, this instrumental-expressive dichotomy fails to perceive the dysfunctional aspects of the traditional order into which men and women are socialized" (Lipman-Blumen and Tickamyer 1975, p. 306). Thus, the traditional role-casting of the male and female has failed to provide modern women with the prescriptive behavior and role models necessary for her successful entry into a male-dominated society.

Studies have concurred that, for the most part, men and men's needs take precedence in a marriage. The husband's time, interests, and career are dominant over those of the wife. While the wife's professional status does not seem to have much effect on the family, her income does, if it is greater than her husband's (Lipman-Blumen and Tickamyer 1975). Certainly, it raises the family's standard of living, but, in addition:

> The attitudes of social scientists have lent considerable legitimation to the popular suspicion that women who seek an independent identity outside the home are women with problems and that women who do not feel a strong drive to establish a family first and foremost should wonder what is wrong with them. Women who choose careers react to the cultural expectations of femininity by trying to prove themselves in all spheres. They attack all the role expectations attached to their female status, feeling that to lack any is to deny they are feminine. (Epstein 1970, p. 31)

A woman entering a typically male profession may be subject to status inconsistency. She would also encounter a problem of dominance. Men tend to have the dominant sex status and, for many purposes, sex tends to be the most salient determinant of status: in many contexts, the female executives are accorded less status than male secretaries. Further, the public may look to a male police officer for confirmation of a female sergeant's orders, or a female sergeant's orders may be questioned by a male subordinate. Thus, sex is often a factor in establishing status. Sex status and racial status are among those statuses that are "central in controlling the choices of most individuals" (Epstein 1970, p. 35).

Organizational Theory and the Female Role

Social theory gives us reason to anticipate gender-related differences in police-citizen encounters. The police, after all, are in the business of getting people to defer to their authority (Muir 1977), and we should expect that, by virtue of the traditionally higher social status and authority accorded them, men might do this more easily than women. Martin (1980) analyzed the role of officers' sex on their general behavior as police officers and found that sex influences the exchange of deference when police officers interact with citizens. When male police officers, by virtue of their higher male status, interact with female citizens, citizen deference is likely. Conversely, the expectation of deference to the male can work to the disadvantage of female officers when encountering male citizens.

Prior research reports two broad types of behavior styles on the part of female police officers. The first is an aggressive posture, usually interpreted as an effort to compensate for their relatively weak physical stature. Aggressiveness is used in an effort to "outmacho" male peers, and, within the police world, it is commonly assumed that female officers who adopt this proactive style of policing will be quicker to use deadly force than their male counterparts (Martin 1980). To date, no evidence supports this belief. The second behavioral pattern, in which female officers perform their work, according to Martin, is a stereotypical and exaggerated feminine manner, an excessively passive style; more passive, in fact, than the average woman's behavior seen in work environments that do not require the exercise of authority. Thus, Martin (1980) and Remmington (1981) suggest that there are female officers who exhibit a passive style of policing and may fail to take any action when a citizen does not comply with directions or otherwise resists. When such passive female officers work with male partners, they tend to rely on the male officer to gain citizen compliance and to maintain control (Martin 1980, Remmington 1981).

Kanter points out that management is a male category; those women who hold managerial positions tend to be concentrated in the lower-paying positions, in certain fields, and in less-powerful organizations. Office work, on the other hand, is a predominantly female function: "women are to clerical labor as men are to management" (Millman and Kanter 1976, p. 39). A "masculine ethic" early on became associated with the ideology of the managerial idea. It incorporated supposedly masculine qualities such as a "hard-line" approach to solving problems; analytical planning abilities; an ability to set aside the personal, emotional point-of-view in dealing with a task; and the intellectual approach to problem solving and decision making. This ethic defined a place for women in management in the people-handling staff functions, where the intuitive-emotional approach was appropriate; thus, the feminine stereotyping became operative (Kanter 1977).

A woman entering a male-dominated profession encounters several problems related to tokenism. She may be categorized into one of the four stereotyped roles, which Kanter has given the self-explanatory labels of *mother, sex object* or *seducers, pet,* or *iron maiden.* She may also be treated as average or stereotypical, as when a female executive is assumed to be a secretary. The result is that the woman may be less likely to behave competently, and she may have a longer or more difficult time establishing her competence, due to the pressures of the role-defined situation (Kanter 1977).

"Cultures demand that one must do masculine work to be considered a man, and not do it to be a feminine woman" (Epstein 1970, p. 154). Women entering a masculine profession are thus seen as deviant and subject to social group sanctions. The salient status may be an irrelevant one; for example, a female lawyer may be perceived as a woman first and a lawyer second; while a male lawyer is seen first as a lawyer. The male lawyer thus has the advantage, as his professional mode is not diffused by the intrusion of sex-role status (Epstein 1970). For the woman, each new professional encounter usually begins with the focus on sex status: she is first received as a female, with the appropriate surprise and accompanying uncertainty of a favorable reception. Attention and energy are leeched away from the professional role, as "the working environment is always transmitting messages that she is unique, and she anticipates them" (Epstein 1970, p. 23).

Women respond to sex-role typing and the correspondent status discrepancies by unobtrusive behavior, attracting as little attention as possible, and by overachievement. One professional woman expressed the conflict thus: ". . . if you're a woman, you have to make less [sic] mistakes . . . a woman must put greater effort into her work . . . because if you make a fool of yourself, you're a damn fool woman instead of just a damn fool" (Epstein 1970, pp. 191–192).

Women in the Police Organization

Women entering police organizations find the same kinds of obstacles to advancement found in other occupations. Martin notes that, in this transitional period, many women still lack the seniority to be eligible for upper-level positions:

. . . a low promotion rate for women is likely to continue, however, since in most departments, promotion is based on both written examinations and ratings by one's supervisors; the criteria on which officers are evaluated are often unclear; and sponsorship by a [male] supervisor is, in fact, a necessity—few female officers are likely to gain such support. (Martin 1980, p. 48)

Price and Gavin point out that the police management hierarchy is rigid and very narrow at the top, with a limited number of middle-management and administrative positions. This pyramid structure, and the emphasis on crime fighting and a good arrest record as the best means to promotion serve to "perpetuate the attitudes about policing being man's work" (Price and Gavin 1982, p. 406).

In answer to the question of why women are not fully accepted in the police organization, Price and Gavin theorize that there are two major sources of resistance:

(1) the social change process and the critical role that attitudes play in it; and (2) the impact of police attitudes shaped by the organizational structure, and in turn, reinforcing its social structure. (pp. 404–405)

An important aspect of police officers' attitudes and feelings about their work is the deep-rooted conviction that it is men's work, requiring physical strength and bravery. Historically, the police task was defined as "maintaining order by intimidation." Those officers who are performing according to the old criteria are responsible for propagating this traditional attitude, rather than acknowledging the fact that 80 to 85 percent of police work today is made up of service-related tasks, in which women have proven themselves to be equally capable (Price and Gavin 1982).

Studies have shown that, traditionally, policemen come primarily from working-class and lower-middle-class backgrounds (Neiderhoffer 1969 and Westley 1970). Even those who do not:

tend to adopt a working-class perspective toward the meaning of masculinity as a result of the recruitment process, the nature of their work and the frequent interaction with working and lower-class citizens—the primary users of police services and the targets of patrol efforts. . . . The police share with such males an emphasis on toughness, and seek to be smarter and tougher than the "street dudes" whose values and postures they often mirror. (Martin 1980, p. 90)

Remmington's Atlanta study evidenced perhaps the most stereotypical attitudes and corresponding behaviors in male officers. "Women do not belong on the streets" was a frequent remark made in the presence of female officers and in conversations among male officers. Male officers expressed and demonstrated a lack of confidence in female peers. A male officer was present at every violent call during the year of observation and took charge in nearly every case. Female officers, on the other hand, seemed to fall into a stereotypical mode as well. When asked whether they would prefer a male or female partner, every female chose a male partner. "Most of the women expressed greater trust in the policing capabilities of males" (Remmington 1981, p. 167). Male officers complained extensively of the need for extra protection for female peers.

Men tended to take the initiative and tended to take a protective role with a female partner. On the other hand, a strong female partner tended to threaten the male:

> The men are caught in a bind: they want a partner who will be "tough," fight, and back them up and whom in turn, they are willing to back up. But women are not supposed to fight, be tough or protect a man. The more a female partner acts like a police officer, the less she behaves like a woman. On the other hand, the more she is as a partner—although such behavior preserves the man's sense of masculinity. (Martin 1980, pp. 93–94)

There is also the issue of occupational status. "Traditionally, male occupations that seek out women recruits frequently suffer a decline in prestige, while traditionally female occupations become more prestigious following the entry of males" (Martin 1980, p. 100). A female patrol partner is also in a double bind: as a strong partner, she is a threat to the male partner's ego; as a weak partner, she is a threat to his safety and well-being. Male officers have also expressed the fear that because female officers lack virility and authority, they will weaken the police image with the public, and potentially endanger the male officer during a stand-off with a criminal (Martin 1980).

For the female police officer, the additional stresses of role ambiguity, the conflicting demands of home and job, and other factors, such as male hostility and nonacceptance on the job, take their toll.

Women on Patrol: Physical Strength Considerations

A number of studies have examined the issues arising from women's entrance into the police profession. Milton (1972) examined problems women faced when dealing with male officers who, for the most part, felt that women were incapable of performing police work. Men cited the physical-strength factor as a reason for the perceived unsuitability of women for police work, but the men also noted that women may possess superior psychological skills. The results of the studies indicated that women may approach and handle situations differently from men, but men and women obtained the same outcomes. Bloch and Anderson (1974) concluded that women were more than capable of performing patrol duties.

Conclusion

The percent of women in policing has increased considerably in the past ten years, and, at the same time, police administrators in city after city have assigned women to patrol duties.

Positive changes have been noted in the status of female police officers. The total number of females in policing has increased dramatically since the early 1980s. Yet, the opportunities for females in some police agencies are lacking, and there is a considerable need for improvement. This is especially prevalent in the areas of promotion and turnover rate. As far as promotional policy is concerned, most police departments have made few, if any, efforts to promote according to the proportional rate of women in their departments. As the tables in this chapter indicate, the advancement in rank for female officers is proportionately lower than that of male officers, and, therefore, female officers are finding it difficult to attain leadership positions in policing. Police executives must find a way to fill the void created by the lack of female supervisors in policing. Police agencies must develop auspicious promotional policies related to female officers. This can be done by eliminating or minimizing the value of the seniority and superior-officer evaluation variables, which play a major role in the advancement programs of most police departments. The exclusion or reduction of the seniority variable would benefit most female officers because a major portion of all female officers have less than five years' experience in policing.

Martin (1989) states that ". . . women have higher turnover rates than men, and thus more women are needed to enter policing even to maintain current sex ratios" (p. 7). This high turnover rate can be reduced if police departments take the time to create a professional and affirmative work environment for both male and female officers. A professional and positive work atmosphere would help remove a major part of the animosity and offensiveness that is directed toward female officers in most police settings.

REFERENCES

Acerra, Lucy, "From Matron to Commanding Officer: Woman's Changing Role in Law Enforcement." In Robert A. Scanlon (ed.), *Law Enforcement Bible*, South Hackensack, N.J.: Stoeger, 1978, pp. 131–140.

Bell, Daniel J., "Policewomen: Myths and Reality," *Journal of Police Science and Administration,* 10 (1982), 112–120.

Bloch, Peter B., and Deborah Anderson, *Policewomen on Patrol: Final Report.* Washington, D.C.: Police Foundation, 1974.

Buwalda, Irma W., "The Policewomen: Yesterday, Today and Tomorrow," *Journal of Social Hygiene,* 31 (1945), 290–293.

Colgrove, Susan B., "Personality and Demographic Characteristics as Predictors of Burnout in Female Police Officers." Doctoral dissertation, University of California at Berkeley, 1983.

Connolly, Harriet, "Police Women as Patrol Officers: A Study in Role Adaptation." Doctoral dissertation, City University of New York, 1975, unpublished.

Crites, Laura, "Women in Law Enforcement," *Management Information System,* 5 (1973), 1–16.

Epstein, Cynthia, *A Woman's Place.* Berkeley, Calif.: University of California Press, 1970.

Gavin, Susan, and Barbara Raffel Price, "A Century of Women in Policing." In Donald O. Schultz (ed.), *Modern Police Administration.* Houston, Texas: Gulf Publishing Co., 1979, pp. 109–122.

Griggs v. Duke Power Co., 91 S. Ct. 849 (1971).

Horne, Peter, *Women in Law Enforcement.* Springfield, Ill.: Charles C. Thomas, 1980.

Kanter, Rosabeth M., *Men and Women of the Corporation.* New York: Basic Books, 1977.

Keefe, Mary L., *Overview of Equal Opportunity in Policing for Women.* Washington, D.C.: National Institute of Justice, 1981.

Linn, Edith, and Barbara Raffel Price, "The Evolving Role of Women in American Policing." In A. S. Blumberg and A. Neiderhoffer (eds.), *The Ambivalent Force.* New York: Holt, Rinehart and Winston, 1985, pp. 69–78.

Lipman-Blumen, Jean, and Ann R. Tickamyer, "Sex Roles in Transition: A Ten Year Perspective," *Annual Review of Sociology,* 1 (1975), 297–337.

Martin, Susan E., *Women on the Move: A Report on the Status of Women in Policing.* Washington, D.C.: Police Foundation, 1989.

Martin, Susan E., *Breaking and Entering: Policewomen on Patrol.* Berkeley, Calif.: Sage Publications, 1980.

Millman, Marcia, and Rosabeth Moss Kanter (eds.), *Another Voice.* New York: Octagon Books, 1976.

Milton, Catherine, *Women in Policing.* Washington, D.C.: Police Foundation, 1972.

Muir, William Der, Jr., *Police: Street Corner Politicians.* Chicago: University of Chicago Press, 1977.

Neiderhoffer, Arthur, Behind the Shield: *The Police in Urban Society.* Garden City, N.Y.: Anchor/Doubleday, 1969.

New York City Police Department, *Employment Statistics for 1988.* New York: NYPD, 1988.

Perlstein, Gary R., "An Exploratory Analysis of Certain Characteristics of Policewomen." Doctoral dissertation, Florida State University, 1971.

Reed v. Reed, 92 S. Ct. 251 (1971).

Remmington, Patricia, *Policing: The Occupation and The Introduction of Female Officers.* Washington, D.C.: University Press of America, 1981.

Shpritzer v. Lang, 234 N.Y.S.2d 285 (1963).

Shpritzer v. Lang, 234 N.Y.S.2d 422 (1963).

Sichel, Joyce, Lucy Friedman, Janet Quint, and Michael Smith. *Women on Patrol: A Pilot Study of Police Performance in New York City.* Washington, D.C.: Police Foundation, 1977.

Westley, William, *Violence and the Police: Sociological Study of Law, Custom and Morality.* Cambridge, Mass.: M.I.T. Press, 1970.

10

Discrimination and Harassment: Litigation by Women in Policing

Donna C. Hale and Daniel J. Menniti

This chapter presents the history of litigation brought by women who are sworn police officers. The court cases discussed here concern employment discrimination and sexual harassment of policewomen.

Until 1972, when Title VII of the Civil Rights act of 1964 was extended to cover state and local governments and their agencies, positions for women in policing were limited to duties related to the care of children and women. Women did not perform patrol duties. And, seventeen years later, women working as sworn officers comprised a mere 7.9 percent of our nation's patrol force. (United States Department of Justice 1989). Although the Equal Opportunity Act (EEOA) in 1972 opened the doors of the police station, the integration of women into police patrol obviously has been limited.

The explanation for this limited use of women in police patrol appears to be sex discrimination. Sex discrimination may be defined as "the unequal and harmful treatment of individuals or groups because of their gender" (Benokraitis and Fagan 1986). Benokraitis and Fagan indicate that "women more frequently are discriminated against because of their gender [rather] than other variables, including age, race, religion, intelligence, achievement, or socio-eco-

The authors wish to thank Kellee Kissinger for her library research assistance.

nomic status." These authors distinguish between three forms of sex discrimination: overt, subtle, and covert.

They say that overt sex discrimination is "readily apparent, visible, and observable and can be easily documented." Examples include sexist language and jokes, physical violence and violation, unequal salaries in comparable jobs, lack of promotion opportunities, sex-segregated labor markets, and—what has become a highly contentious issue—sexual harassment.

In late 1980, the Equal Employment Opportunity Commission (EEOC) issued guidelines[2] establishing that sexual harassment in the workplace is a violation of Title VII of the Civil Rights Act of 1964. Sexual harassment is defined in Section 1604.11 as "unwelcomed sexual advances, requests for sexual favors, and other verbal or physical conduct of a sexual nature." Employers, under EEOC guidelines, are liable for the sexually harassing conduct of their supervisors, other employees, and even nonemployees (Plitt and Summers 1983).

Benokraitis and Fagan describe subtle sex discrimination as visible but often not noticed since so much sexist behavior has been internalized as normal, acceptable custom. They say that covert sex discrimination is treatment that is clandestine and maliciously motivated. It is hard to document.

In the literature, the most frequently cited complaints of overt sexual harassment of women include "comments, innuendos, jokes of a sexual nature, unwelcome invitations to engage in physical touching that is sexually suggestive, and—the most serious of all—pressure to engage in sexual activity that is held out as the basis for continued employment, a promotion, or other tangible job benefit" (Plitt and Summers 1983).

In the mid-1970s, Martin (1978) studied patrol officers in a single patrol district in Washington, D.C. She described the various forms of overt sexual discrimination, including verbal (language, jokes, put-downs) and nonverbal messages (touching) and sexual harassment. Sexual harassment occurred "when a man in a position of control hampered or affected the job or career of a woman who refused his offer, used his authority or power to coerce a woman into sexual relations, or punished her rejection."

Policewomen on Patrol: Can They Do the Job?

The literature regarding the performance of women as patrol officers is replete with comments that policing is a man's job (Milton 1975,

---

[2]29 C.F.R. Part 1604, et. seq.

Charles 1982, Remmington 1983, and Jones 1986). Despite research indicating that the bulk of police work is service-related and order-maintenance, with very little of it involving physical or violent confrontations, the principal physical requirements used in police officer selection prior to the passage of the Civil Rights Act of 1964 were based on standards of height and weight (Booth and Hornick 1984). These standards, no longer used in selection, adversely affected employment of women (Booth and Hornick 1984). Regarding the physical ability of women to do police work, Charles and Parsons (1978) and Charles (1982) point out that women can be trained to do police work. Evaluation studies on performance (Bloch and Anderson 1974) support the contention that overall, women are as effective as men.

Stereotypes persist, however, as Bell (1982) and Van Wormer and Whaley (1982), and Pogrebin (1986) discovered. These stereotypes include perceptions that women are not authoritative, aggressive, or physically strong enough to handle police work, especially the violent offender; cannot handle shift work; and that if male and female police officers are partners, they may become involved in sexual and emotional situations.

Disproving some of these stereotypes, Grennan (1987), analyzed over 3,500 incidents of firearms discharge/assaults from official police department reports. He found no difference in the injury rates between male and female officers, no difference in the number of injuries to male or female partners in patrol teams during violent confrontations with citizens, and that the male partner in male-female teams was more likely to discharge a firearm than the female partner. He concluded that female officers reacted in the same way as male officers to violent situations and that female officers are more emotionally stable than male officers because they do not have to project the "macho" image that is part of the male personality (see also Horne 1979).

The literature on work performance clearly supports the proposition that women are as capable as men of performing patrol duties. However, the acceptance and advancement of women on patrol have been impaired by discrimination: subtle, overt, and covert. Remedies to these injustices have been extended by litigation in the courts.

To give an indication of the extent of litigation in this area, the following cases have been selected from a myriad of examples of discrimination against women in policing. Their selection was based on the belief that they reflect the most common types of documentation faced by women who desired to be efficient members of police departments. Moreover, the cases were selected to illustrate the requirements for successful litigation based on antidiscrimination statutes and the rationale of court decisions in this sensitive area.

The Status of Sexual Discrimination/Harassment Litigation

> There is no place for rivalry between male and female officers.
> While their specific duties may vary, they are all servants of the
> people, doing the same job, and working toward the same end.
> They should join forces and work as a unit. The policewoman is
> a regular member of the department, and as such should be gov-
> erned by the same rules and regulations, assume the same re-
> sponsibilities, and share the same rights and privileges as male
> officers who are doing the same kind of work. A policewoman will
> be accepted as a "good officer" by her coworkers when she earns
> their approval and respect. (Tenny 1953, p. 239)

Debra Webb was hired as a police officer in Chester, Illinois on
February 1, 1982. When the mayor left to get her a badge, a member
of the Board of Fire and Police Commissioners expressed very clearly
his opinion of women police officers: "I don't want you here, you have
no business being here, you are a woman, and a woman has no business being a police officer." *Webb* v. *City of Chester, Illinois* (1987).

Despite this inauspicious beginning, Ms. Webb, who was at the
top of the list of applicants, enrolled in the six-week training program
at the Police Academy in Belleville, Illinois. She completed her program with high grades on March 19 and began working as a police
officer in Chester on the following day. On April 7, however, two and
one-half weeks after her graduation, the Chester Chief of Police recommended to the Board of Fire and Police Commissioners that she
be fired because she was "observed of being incapable and physio-
logically remissed [sic] to perform police functions in the City of
Chester" (*Webb*, p. 827). The Board voted to fire Ms. Webb on the
Chief's recommendation and eventually hired a man to fill her position as a police officer. When Ms. Webb requested the reasons for
her dismissal, she was told that the Board was not required to give
reasons because she was a probationary officer. Ms. Webb countered
by filing a lawsuit alleging sex discrimination.

The legal basis for the suit was founded in Title VII of the Civil
Rights Act of 1964, which is considered the most important civil-
rights legislation of the twentieth century. When Title VII was first
passed, it was viewed by the Congress which passed it solely as a
prohibition against disparate treatment based on race, color, religion,
sex, or national origin. The United States Equal Employment Act of
1972 extended the application of Title VII to state and local
governments and their agencies. Section 703(a) of Title VII states that
it is an unlawful employment practice to discriminate on the basis
of sex.

The legal standards in a sex discrimination case require that a
plaintiff like Debra Webb prove that (1) the defendants acted with

discriminatory intent; (2) the defendants acted under color of state law; (3) the defendants deprived plaintiff of her rights; and (4) the defendants' conduct caused plaintiff's deprivation. Once a plaintiff shows that these elements are present, a prima facie case of discrimination is made and the burden then shifts to the defendants to articulate a legitimate nondiscriminatory reason for taking the alleged discriminatory action (*Webb*, p. 828).

The defendants alleged that Debra Webb was fired for incompetence, not because she was a woman. The jury decided that she was the victim of discrimination, and she was awarded $20,250 for embarrassment and humiliation and $9,750 as compensation for lost wages. The appeals to the district court and the circuit court by defendants were denied and the judgment stood.

Discrimination against women in hiring, however, has not always been as blatant as in the *Webb* case, because agencies have set up specific employment conditions that are not directly discriminatory, such as weight and height requirements. Title VII of the Civil Rights Act, Section 703(e), permits the exclusion when the position has a "bona fide occupational qualification reasonably necessary to the normal operation of an enterprise."

The Supreme Court, in *Dothard* v. *Robinson* (1977), dealt with the bona fide occupational qualification (BFOQ). The Alabama Board of Corrections, with BFOQ as a legal basis, excluded prison guards from "contact positions" in state prisons if they were not the same gender as the inmates. The Board was apprehensive about women's safety. Women were, as a result, excluded from all but approximately 25 percent of positions available in the prisons. The Supreme Court approved of the practice of the Alabama Board of Corrections, despite its holding that "the BFOQ exception was in fact meant to be an extremely narrow exception to the general prohibition of discrimination on the basis of sex" (*Dothard*, p. 334).

The BFOQ exception, however, was occasionally abused in the hiring of police officers to discriminate against female applicants. Unlike the *Webb* situation, in which the only reason for the dismissal was the officer's sex, more subtle approaches are found in the cases based on the BFOQ exception. The most common are requirements of minimum height and/or weight or the passing of physical agility tests.

Such was the situation in *Thomas* v. *City of Evanston* (1985). Applicants for the police force had been required to pass a physical agility test for a position on the force. The test was claimed to result from a "job analysis" of the work done by police officers in various Illinois cities. Only a small percentage of women had been able to pass the test. A class suit was instituted by several women claiming that the use of the physical agility test violated Title VII. The court sided with the complainants, noting that the city could not prove that the physical agility test was a valid test. The court's conclusion is well worth repeating:

> In so concluding, we would like to emphasize that by this opinion the Court does not presume to exercise the prerogatives of police superintendent or to second-guess the police superintendent's exercise of his professional discretion. It is well within the police executive's authority to devise a physical agility test which would be justifiable as a device to screen police applicants. Certainly the job demands some minimum level of coordination and strength. Too often tests which on the surface appear objective and scientific turn out to be based on ingrained stereotypes and speculative assumptions about what is "necessary" to the job. (*Thomas*, p. 432)

Other governmental units have utilized physical agility tests in a similar discriminatory manner and the courts have struck them down. In *Burney* v. *Pawtucket* (1983), a female police cadet, Gail Burney, a resident of Pawtucket, Rhode Island, had graduated from the law-enforcement program of Bryant College and applied for a position on her home city's police force. A condition of employment was the successful completion of the program of the Academy which was established by the Rhode Island General Assembly. On December 16, 1982, Gail Burney reported to the Academy. She was the only woman in her class. A number of calisthenics and expected times for distance runs were part of the physical-training program. When Ms. Burney was unable to keep up with the physical-training program, she was told that she could either withdraw or be dismissed. She then signed a resignation form. The day after she resigned, however, she pointed out that her resignation had not been voluntary and she applied for readmittance but was refused. Her civil suit was her response.

The trial court found that the pass rate on the physical-agility requirements for women was generally 50 percent, while for men it was 90 percent. The conclusion of the court was:

> Based on the overwhelming weight of the testimony of the experts (much of which stands uncontroverted), the lay testimony in the case, and the statistical evidence, this Court concludes that plaintiff has convincingly established a prima facie case, and has proved that the physical agility requirements of the Academy as a whole have a disproportionate, adverse impact on women. (*Burney*, p. 1099)

It should be noted, however, that the court in Burney's case also held that it is not discriminatory for both men and women to complete a course in self-defense in which the emphasis is on technique rather than physical strength. Similarly, a federal court in St. Louis held that it was not illegal not to hire police officers who are unable to run, jump, hop, stoop, turn, pivot, or perform similar movements (*Simon* v. *St. Louis County*, 1981). Such requirements were not a denial of equal protection because these requirements were "rationally related" to having physically fit police officers.

The foregoing illustrate that the facts of individual cases are essential determinants for the courts to render decisions in discrimination complaints. But the courts are quick to outlaw artificial barriers to women in policing. Where the courts find a pattern of discrimination, they are swift to strike them down. The courts have a great amount of discretion in determining the relief given to those who are the victims of discrimination. 42 U.S.C. 2000 e 5 (g) gives the courts broad discretion in the rehiring of employees, back pay, punitive damages, and other appropriate equitable relief. It is important to note other practices that have been examined by the courts.

Generally, minimum height-or-weight requirements have been adjudged to constitute illegal sex discrimination. In *Vanguard Justice Society* v. *Hughes* (1979) the Court held that a height of five feet, seven inches with weight proportioned to height as required by a city police department constituted a violation of Title VII and the Fourteenth Amendment of the Constitution. The state highway patrol of North Carolina was enjoined from requiring troopers to be at least five feet, six inches in height. This minimum height eliminated 77.3 percent of women between eighteen and thirty-four years of age from consideration for employment on a force which had only one female trooper on the patrol force (*U.S.* v. *North Carolina*, 512 F. Supp. 968, E.D.N.C. 1981). This case was affirmed without opinion by the Fourth Circuit and was denied certiorari by the Supreme Court.

It is well to note that the Courts adhere to the so-called "80 percent rule" in determining whether physical agility tests or height-and-weight requirements discriminate against female applicants. (See *Thomas*, p. 428.) This simply means that where the success rate of a plaintiff class is less than 80 percent, a finding of a disparate impact is appropriate for the courts. Thus, in *Eison* v. *Knoxville* (1983), this disparate impact was not a factor when a police academy's physical qualification test consisted of sit-ups, push-ups, leg lifts, squat thrusts, pull-ups, and a two-mile run. The pass rate of women did not contravene the "80 percent rule," and the tests were considered related to effective police work.

In *Thorne* v. *El Segundo* (1983), Deborah Lynn Thorne appealed the decision of the district court, which held that she was not a victim of discrimination. At the time of the trial, the El Segundo police department had eighty-three officers, of whom only two were women. In the previous nine years, only three women had been hired. In 1978,

Ms. Thorne received the second-highest score on combined oral and written tests. (The highest score was received by another female.) After the rankings were published, Ms. Thorne passed the physical agility test as well as psychological screening. Later, she submitted to a polygraph testing, which resulted in her revealing she had suffered a miscarriage of a child fathered by a married officer of the El Segundo police department.

Ms. Thorne was turned down by the department for the following reasons:

> First, she had a poor record of tardiness and sick time. Second, she had "barely passed" the physical agility test and was "a very feminine type person who is apparently very weak in the upper body." Third, Thorne had only a very recent interest in police work. (*Thorne*, p. 463)

On appeal, the circuit court reversed the decision, pointing out that she had met the appropriate legal standards (See also *Webb* 1987). The decision of the court is well worth repeating:

> She is a member of a group protected by Title VII. She applied for a position as a police officer with the City. She ranked second among applicants on the oral and written tests for the job. She was rated qualified to be a police officer following psychological testing and she passed the physical agility test required of applicants. In addition, she submitted to the polygraph testing demanded by the police department and there is no indication that her answers on this test were unacceptable or false. Under these circumstances, the district court's finding that plaintiff was not qualified for the position of police officer was clearly erroneous. (*Thorne*, p. 464)

The difficulties of women in policing obviously do not end once they have been hired. In *Curl* v. *Reavis* (1984), women officers were precluded from achieving detective status. The court struck down this practice and noted that the sheriff had acted illegally when he intimidated the complaining officer, fired her, and gave her an unsatisfactory job reference after she filed a complaint with the Equal Employment Opportunity Commission. In *Gibbs* v. *Pierce County Law Enforcement Support Agency* (1986), the court held that Title VII was clearly violated when consolidation of several police agencies resulted in different job classifications with different salaries for similar functions, where the lower-paid employees were all female and the higher-paid were all male.

In Ward County, North Dakota, the Sheriff had fourteen deputies, one of whom was female. The records in the case show that the female, Deputy Sheriff Howard, was third in seniority and no lower than fifth in the chain of command. She was, however, *fifteenth* in salary. Her duties were virtually the same as all other deputies, and the chief deputy characterized her work as equal to all the other deputies. The court in *Howard* v. *Ward County* (1976) ordered the county compensate her for back pay and enjoined them from discriminating against a female deputy with respect to compensation.

The difficulties for women in policing go beyond salary problems. A violation of Title VII is basically established when an employee is subjected to unwelcome sexual harassment that affects conditions of employment. In *Henson* v. *Dundee* (1982), a female dispatcher requested permission from the chief of police to attend the police academy. The chief insisted on sexual favors as a condition for granting permission. She declined. Male dispatchers were allowed to attend the academy. The court had no difficulty in concluding that the facts clearly established a violation of Title VII.

Sexual harassment, however, requires more than a superior officer's single effort to have a female officer go out with him (*Sapp* v. *Warner Robins* 1987). The latter case required repeated or continuous requests with some effect on the plaintiff's psychological well-being to establish proof of sexual harassment.

In *Arnold* v. *Seminole* (1985), a female officer was subjected to derogatory comments as well as vicious jokes about her. Moreover, pornographic cartoons were posted in officers' quarters and were directed to Ms. Arnold, who was the first female police officer hired by the department. The court found that the chiefs had knowledge of the harassment and took no significant action to correct the problem. In fact, as in the *Webb* decision, one of the defendants informed Ms. Arnold that he did not believe in women officers and refused to speak to her. He also told her that he would harass her until she quit or was fired. Many nude pictures were placed in public view with plaintiff's name placed on them. In addition, the court found that Ms. Arnold had to defend herself against many false charges of misconduct. Her son, in fact, was arrested and detained in jail without justification, and she and her husband were warned that, if they filed discrimination charges, both their jobs would be in jeopardy. The court ruled that the police officer clearly carried her burden of proving sexual harassment in violation of the Civil Rights Act of 1964.

In addition to the many cases spawned by discrimination before and after the hiring of women police officers, there are also cases concerning the training and classification of women hired by police departments. In 1975, a federal court ordered the Pittsburgh Police Department to conform its hiring procedures to the requirements of Title VII. In *Pennsylvania* v. *Flaherty* (1982), the court held that the classification of female officers in the special position of "police women" was a violation of the law. Women officers received the same initial training as the men, except that they did not receive firearms training. Consequently, because they lacked firearms training, the women were routinely assigned to the missing-persons section. Despite the lack of training with firearms, the women were occasionally assigned to participate in dangerous assignments without carrying weapons. The lack of firearms training also precluded some promotional opportunities.

In a similar vein, three black female recruits were terminated for inability to meet firearms proficiency standards (*Griffin* v. *Omaha* 1986). The court ordered reinstatement under Title VII because there was ample evidence that only black females ever failed the marksmanship test and that the firearms training they received was not equal to that given to other recruits. Moreover, the record shows that, after termination, they easily passed the marksmanship test following competent private instructions.

These court cases reflect that women who enter the police department as sworn officers have encountered both blatant sexism (rumor, sexual innuendo, and harassment), as well as subtle sexism (height-and-weight requirements and denial of promotion). The courts have remedied these particular situations by decisions finding that the police departments involved had, in fact, discriminated against these female police officers. Therefore, these decisions are precedents in the legal field.

The court decisions have resulted in changes in both hiring and promotional standards of police departments.

Conclusion: Implications of Legal Cases

Plitt and Summers (1983, p. 19) point out that most cases based on EEOC guidelines state that prevention is the best tool for eliminating sexual harassment. Several preventive measures are suggested by Plitt and Summers as approaches administrators may utilize to minimize potential liability. They include:

1. Publishing a policy on the prevention of sexual harassment and disseminating policy on prevention of sexual harassment from highest officer to all levels of employees throughout the agency;

2. Instituting training seminars to sensitize the employees to this type of potential misconduct;

3. Implementing grievance procedures and publicizing their existence (personnel offices would receive and settle complaints in-house, on an informal basis, thereby avoiding costly litigation); and

4. Publicizing the sanctions that would be imposed on violators.

Although it is clear from official statistics that women as sworn officers are nowhere near Milton's projection of 50 percent by the year 2078, it is obvious that the courts are dealing with overt and subtle discrimination cases brought to their attention by policewomen. The courts' decisions have remedied these injustices and have set precedents for future litigation. Police administrators must be aware of these decisions and establish departmental policies to prevent discrimination of any form (overt, subtle, and covert) against women police officers.

Tenny's (1953) remarks, presented earlier, regarding the similarities of male and female officers' duties in the 1950s, are interesting to note today. She emphasized that although their duties were different, they were equals in the department. From the early 1900s until the early 1970s, policewomen were primarily responsible for prevention-protection work with women and children. Only policemen handled patrol work. Today, because of the Equal Employment Act, the duties are the same, and as the legal cases discussed herein reflect, discrimination against policewomen is not permissible. What is most pertinent today—from Tenny's earlier comment—is that women will be accepted in work when they achieve the respect and approval of their male peers. Lack of peer and supervisory approval are still the greatest obstacles that women encounter in the police department (Milton 1975, Horne 1979, Johns and Barclay 1979, and Bell 1982). Male officers still perceive police work as man's work, and they stereotype female police officers as unable to do the job because they lack the physical strength to do so. However, the research on women in policing (see Hale 1992) supports the claim that women can do, or can be trained to do, the job. Perhaps more important, however, are the court decisions. These decisions have guaranteed women equal access to police positions.

CASES CITED

Arnold v. Seminole, 614 F. Supp. 853 (E.D.OK. 1985).

Burney v. Pawtucket, 559 F. Supp. 1089 (D.C.R.I. 1983).

Curl v. Reavis, 740 F. 2d 1323 (4th C. 1984).

Dothard v. Robinson, 433 U.S. 321 (1977).

Eison v. Knoxville, 570 F. Supp. 11 (E.D. Tenn. 1983).

Gibbs v. Pierce County Law Enforcement Support Agency, 785 F. 2d 1396 (9th C. 1986).

Griffin v. Omaha, 785 F. 2d 620 (8th C. 1986).

Henson v. Dundee, 682 F. 2d 897 (11th C. 1982).

Howard v. Ward County, 418 F. Supp. 494 (D.C.N.D. 1976).

Pennsylvania v. Flaherty, 532 F. Supp. 106 (W.D. Pa. 1982).

Sapp v. Warner Robins, 655 F. Supp. 1043 (M.D. Ga. 1987).

Simon v. St. Louis County, 656 F. 2d 316 (8th C. 1981).

Thomas v. City of Evanston, 610 F. Supp. 422 (N.D. Ill. 1985).

Thorne v. El Segundo, 726 F. 2d 459 (9th C. 1983).

U.S. v. North Carolina, 512 F. Supp. 968 (E.D.N.C. 1981).

Vanguard Justice Society v. Hughes, 471 F. Supp. 670 (1979).

Webb v. City of Chester, Illinois, 813 F. 2d 324, 829 (7th C. 1987).

REFERENCES

Bell, Daniel J., "Policewomen: Myths and Reality," *Journal of Police Science and Administration*, 10 (1982), 112–120.

Benokraitis, Nijole V., and Joe R. Feagin, *Modern Sexism: Blatant, Subtle, and Covert Discrimination.* Englewood Cliffs, N.J.: Prentice-Hall, 1986.

Bloch, P. B., and D. Anderson, *Policewomen on Patrol: Final Report.* Washington, D.C.: Police Foundation, 1974.

Booth, Walter S., and Chris W. Hornick, "Physical Agility Testing for Police Officers in the '80s," *Police Chief*, January 1984, pp. 39–41.

Charles, M. T., "Women in Policing: The Physical Aspect." *Journal of Police Science and Administration*, 102 (1982), 194–205.

Charles, M. T., and Kevin Parsons, "Female Performance in the Law Enforcement Function: A Review of Past Research, Current Issues and Future Potential," *Law and Order*, 26, no. 1 (1978), 18–74.

Grennan, Sean A., "Findings on the Role of Officer Gender in Violent Encounters with Citizens," *Journal of Police Science and Administration*, 15, no. 1 (1987), 78–85.

Hale, Donna C., "Women in Policing." In Gary W. Cordner and Donna C. Hale (eds.), *What Works in Policing.* Cincinnati: Anderson, 1992, pp. 125–142.

Horne, Peter, "Policewomen: 2000 A.D.," *The Police Journal*, 52, no. 1 (1979), 344–357.

Johns, Christina J., and Andrew M. Barclay, "Female Partners for Male Police: The Effect on Shooting Responses," *Criminal Justice and Behavior*, 6, no. 4 (December 1979), 327–338.

Jones, Sandra, "Women Police: Caught in the Act," *Policing* 2, no. 2 (1986), 129–140.

Martin, Susan E., "Sexual Politics in the Workplace: The Interactional World of Policewomen," *Symbolic Interaction*, 1 (1978) 44–60. Reprinted in Mary Jo Deegan and Michael R. Hill (eds.), *Women and Symbolic Interaction.* Boston: Allen and Unwin, 1987, pp. 303–321.

Milton, Catherine H., "Women in Policing." In James T. Curran and Richard

H. Ward (eds.), *Police and Law Enforcement 1973–1974*, vol. II. New York: AMS Press, 1975, pp. 230–245.

Milton, Catherine H., "The Future of Women in Policing." In Alvin W. Cohn (ed.), *The Future of Policing*, vol. 9 of *Sage Criminal Justice System Annuals*. Beverly Hills, Calif.: Sage Publications, 1978, pp. 185–204.

Plitt, Emory A., Jr., and William C. Summers, "The Chief's Counsel: Sexual Harassment," *Police Chief*, 1 (December 1983), 18–19.

Pogrebin, Mark, "The Changing Role of Women: Female Police Officers' Occupational Problems," *The Police Journal*, 59, no. 2 (April-June 1986), 127–133.

Remmington, Patricia Weiser, "Women in the Police: Integration or Separation?" *Qualitative Sociology*, 6, no. 2 (1983), 118–135.

Tenny, Evabel, "Women's Work in Law Enforcement," *Journal of Criminal Law, Criminology and Police Science*, 44 (1953–54), 239–246.

United States Department of Justice. *Uniform Crime Reports for the United States*, Washington, D.C., 1989.

Van Wormer, Katherine, and Marie Annala Whaley, "Men in Police Work: A Feminist Assessment," *American Journal of Police*, 2, no. 1 (1982), 91–99.

DISCUSSION QUESTIONS
SECTION 4: WOMEN AND POLICING

1. Historically, how have women advanced in the performance of police duties? Create a timeline marking significant new roles and events in the advancement of women in policing. Analyze each of these points in time and how these events have served to expand the roles of women in policing.

2. What do the terms "role casting" and "status inconsistency" mean? Can an argument be made that women are at a disadvantage with men due to the way women have been socialized? In your opinion, can training overcome the traditional roles women have been socialized to perform? Why, or why not?

3. What is it that police officers actually do on a day-to-day basis? Which of these activities can a man perform better than a woman? Which duties of a police officer can't a woman perform? Given the overall job duties of a police officer, how well do women compare to their male counterparts?

4. In what aspects of policing do men have distinct advantages? In what aspects of policing do women have distinct advantages? Prepare an argument for or against the employment of women in policing.

5. Identify the legislation that has advanced women in policing and the specific effect that this legislation has had on the role of women as police officers. Today, just what role do women play in American policing?

Section 5

Women and Prisons

Since the 1980s, the number of women imprisoned in the United States has doubled. Approximately 75,000 women are now locked up in American jails and prisons. Increases in the number of women incarcerated have surpassed the male rates of increase for the past decade, and an unprecedented number of expensive prison spaces are being built for women.

In the past, women prisoners were often ignored because they were few in number. Now, with increasing numbers of female prisoners and overcrowded facilities, the number of women's prisons is continuing to grow. Since the extraordinary increases in women's imprisonment have been a product of criminal justice policy shifts rather than significant changes in women's criminal behavior, dramatic reductions of incarcerated women ought to be within reach. But, significant prison population reductions through the use of alternatives to incarceration are not yet to be realized.

Women present a special challenge as prisoners because their needs and interests are different from men. Socially, women come from situations where they are already "imprisoned" through lower wages, inadequate housing, and unequal opportunities for education and jobs. Prison provides an atmosphere that doubly and often triply imprisons women, particularly when they are separated from their children. As we shall see, the social consequences of imprisoning large numbers of women is magnified when the effects on families and dependent children is taken into consideration.

On the other side of prison walls are those women whose husbands or boyfriends are behind bars. These women also "do time." They suffer hardships, have financial and emotional struggles, and need to cope with their feelings. These women, too, undergo identity crises. The stigmatization that these women and their families feel are not dealt with by the system. A study of women who have men behind bars demonstrates that they, too, become incarcerated by prison policies.

The treatment of women in prison is in many ways an extension of the way women are generally treated in society. The images, roles, and stereotypes of women carry over into our jails and prisons where women are either ignored and treated as unimportant, or given that special attention that casts them as dependent beings who must be "rehabilitated" to their traditional, familial roles as wives and mothers. The ways in which women are treated as prisoners and the roles they are assigned as correctional officers reflect, in a rather direct way, the inequality and subservience of women in general. Prison, and its policies, represents a fertile area of research of women and their roles in society.

11

Women's Prisons: Issues and Controversies

Imogene L. Moyer

This chapter utilizes a feminist perspective to explore the impact of the patriarchal social structure on the history of women's prisons. It examines the programs in women's prisons in light of the needs of the current population of women incarcerated in institutions in the United States and other countries. Finally, the chapter explores the policy implications of the data presented in the chapter for both prison programs and community-based programs for women offenders.

Women's prisons have been a highly neglected part of the various systems of justice throughout the world. Most prisons for women have been located in rural, isolated areas so that travel to the prisons is quite difficult, if not impossible, for most family and friends of women prisoners. In addition, most women's prisons reflect the sex-role stereotyping of a chauvinistic and patriarchal society both in their physical structure and administration and programming.

One reason frequently given by researchers and prison administrators for the neglect and isolation of women's prisons has been the small number of women prisoners. Researchers (for example, Simon 1975 and Sobel 1982) in the United States have indicated that women comprise only 3 to 4 percent of all persons incarcerated in criminal justice settings. Women also comprise a very small proportion of prison populations in many other countries: India (Sikka 1986, p. 201), 1.7 percent; Venezuela (deCastro 1981, p. 220), 1.7 percent; Finland (Anttila 1981, p. 64), 8 percent; Norway (Jensen 1981, p. 85),

3 percent; Argentina (Kent 1981, p. 191), 3.2 percent; and Australia (Hancock 1986, p. 101), 3.7 percent. These small numbers of women prisoners usually mean that each legal jurisdiction has only one institution for women, which further creates problems for incarcerated women. For example, in Hawaii, long-term women prisoners have been moved alternately to the men's facility at Oahu Community Correctional Center and to the Women's Community Correctional Center during the last decade. The decisions to move the women have been made primarily on the basis of available bed space.

This chapter examines the history of women's prisons and the current population of women prisoners in the United States and other countries in which research studies are available to determine if the prison structures and programs are designed to meet the needs of most women prisoners. Finally, the chapter explores policy implications for creating meaningful societal responses to women offenders.

The History of Women's Prisons

The history of women's prison reflects our chivalrous and patriarchal society in which images of women suggested a dual nature—either as madonnas or as whores. This duality placed women in subservient positions to men, who assumed the role of protectors of the madonnas and punishers of the whores (Feinman 1980, p. 2). The chivalrous image of a spiritually pure wife/mother brought demands for laws to punish the nonconforming woman as unnatural. Women who violated the moral and sexual codes of society were referred to as "fallen women." But, eventually, the term was used to refer to any woman who violated the law, including women charged with drunkenness, vagrancy, and streetwalking, as well as murder, manslaughter, burglary, and larceny (Freedman 1981, p. 11). The fallen woman was considered more depraved than her male counterpart and beyond hope because she had denied her own pure nature (Freedman 1981, p. 17).

Early penitentiaries in America were not designed for women. As a result, women were often crowded into small, secluded sections of a men's prison. For example, the women prisoners at Auburn, New York in the 1820s were lodged together, unattended in a one-room attic, the windows sealed to prevent communication with men. The twenty to thirty women prisoners were neglected in this overcrowded area (Freedman 1981, p. 15). Rafter (1985, p. 6) further indicates that "once a day a steward delivered food and removed the waste, but otherwise prisoners were left to their own devices." These conditions sharply distinguished women's care from that of men in the nearby cellblocks. Visiting the Auburn prison in the early 1830s, Harriet Martineau reported a scene of almost complete chaos:

> The arrangements for women were extremely bad. . . . The women were all in one large room, sewing. The attempt to enforce silence was soon given up as hopeless; and the gabble of tongues among the few who were there was enough to paralyze any matron. . . . There was an engine in sight which made me doubt the evidence of my own eyes; stocks of a terrible construction; a chair, with a fastening for the head and for all the limbs. Any lunatic asylum ought to be ashamed of such an instrument. (quoted by Rafter 1985, p. 6)

Rafter (1985) suggests that reports such as Martineau's—together with the scandal that ensued when one Auburn inmate became pregnant, was flogged while five months into her pregnancy and later died—finally forced New York to construct regular quarters for its female felons. Freedman (1981, p. 15), however, indicates that changes for women prisoners occurred when a group of women reformers became interested in the plight of these women in the early 1840s. These predominantly middle- and upper-middle-class women questioned the condemnation of the fallen woman and made efforts to change the neglect and abuse of women in prison.

In contrast to most male prison officials and reformers, who condemned the fallen woman as a social outcast, these women reformers insisted on removing the stigma that separated them from their "fallen sisters." As one of their reports explained:

> . . . we would approach the fallen woman, and when all the world turns away with loathing from her misery, we would take her by the hand, lift her from her degradation, whisper hope to her amid her despair, teach her lessons of self-control, instill into her ideas of purity and industry, and send her forth to work her own way upward to her final destiny. (Freedman 1981, p. 32).

These women reformers argued for the separation of women prisoners from male prisoners, male officers, and male gaurds. As argued by one reformer, "It is natural that a Christian motherly heart should· have more influence with these girls than a man would have . . ." (Freedman 1981, p. 200). These female administrators created reformatories for women that provided a homelike environment with a mother-child relationship between matron and inmate. Sex-role stereotypes of women were perpetuated by these women reformers as staff assumed the roles of loving but demanding mothers who taught these erring inmates to be good homemakers and to assume their proper roles in society as pure wives and mothers.

While some progress has been made in improving the physical conditions for women's prisons in America, in other countries (for example, India and Australia) women are still housed in the same facilities as men. Shekar (1981, p. 347) and Sikka (1986, p. 202) note that in India today, women are mostly housed in separate yards or segregated wings of male prisons. In these prisons, "the very structure and fabric . . . the working tools, mechanisms, philosophies, policies, methodologies and procedures that form the backbone and flesh of our penological system have all, without exception been born, raised and have sometimes died, male . . ." (Sikka 1986, p. 202). Because women are less dangerous or disruptive, and easier to deal with, they are easily neglected.

Hancock (1986, p. 101–102) notes that in Australia, small inmate numbers and high turnover have resulted in the neglect of female prisons. In Victoria, the abysmal conditions of imprisoned women have been the subject of complaint for over twenty years. At the Pentridge prison, for example, women are kept in appalling conditions, locked up in small unhygienic cells from 4 P.M. until 8 A.M. each day. In emergencies, it may take up to ninety minutes to unlock the cells. Hancock further indicates that, until recently, there has been little governmental recognition of the substandard conditions in the state prison system or of the inequalities experienced by imprisoned women.

In America, however, nineteenth-century women reformers, saved women from the harshness of cellblocks and steel bars. Women's prisons often have the appearance of a castle, a hospital, college campus, or a motel (Giallombardo 1966, Heffernan 1972, Moyer 1978 and 1980; and Ward and Kassebaum 1965). The following statement is a description of a typical architectural design of a modern women's prison:

> . . . most inmates live singly in rooms with curtained windows, bedspreads, rugs, and wooden doors. These buildings with soft chairs, couches, and a fireplace, picture and open-out windows for each inmate's room, give the appearance of a convalescent hospital. The design and appearance of Frontera has also been likened to a motel. . . . (Ward and Kassebaum 1965, p. 7)

The casual, naive visitor and uninformed state administrators are often deceived by this environment into believing that women are receiving better treatment than men in prison. Moyer (1984, p. 45) reports one young college student visiting a midwestern women's prison where the buildings have the appearance of a castle made the following naive statement: "Wow! If I ever have to go to prison, I hope they send me to a women's prison." And again Moyer (1984, p. 45) notes that the Director of Corrections in a southeastern state justified the neglect of the women's prison by saying, "I've been out to see that prison. The grounds are beautiful . . . just like a college campus." Although the architectural structure of women's prisons provide a casual appearance, research has demonstrated that this is deceptive. Studies by Giallombardo (1966), Heffernan (1972), Moyer (1980 and 1984), and Ward and Kassebaum (1965) provide evidence that women prisoners find the entrance procedures to be frightening and denigrating. Furthermore, women have paid a price for the chivalrous environment of their prisons in rigid regimentation and control of virtually all of their movements and activities. In addition, stereotypical programs intended to prepare them to be good wives and mothers have failed to provide women offenders with meaningful vocational programs. In the words of Chapman (1972, p. 47), "Where women offenders are concerned there is no systematic planning; there is no systematic program development; and there is no systematic resource allocation." More recent researchers (for example, Leonard 1983, Shaw and others, 1981, and Sobel 1982) have pointed to serious deficiencies in health-care services in women's prisons. Thus, as Moulds (1978) has suggested, women offenders have paid a price for the chivalrous treatment of the criminal justice system. This is especially true in most women's prisons.

A Profile of Women Prisoners

Social-Economic Characteristics

Researchers have consistently reported that women prisoners are largely composed of young women from poor economic and educational backgrounds with an overrepresentation of racial/ethnic minorities (Chesney-Lind and Rodriguez 1983; Connolly 1983, Crawford 1988, Giallombardo 1966; Glick and Neto 1977; Goetting and Howsen 1983; Leonard 1983; Moyer 1980; Pollock-Byrne 1990; and Ward and Kassebaum 1966). These studies include data from national surveys, state and federal prisons, as well as local jails.

Several national surveys of American women prisoners have been completed (for example, Glick and Neto 1977; and Goetting and Howsen 1983). Of the 6,500 women studied by Glick and Neto in 1976 in prisons and jails in fourteen states, two-thirds were under thirty years old; over half were black; 56 percent had been on welfare; 60 percent had not graduated from high school; and 73 percent had children (Leonard 1983, p. 46). In another study, Goetting and Howsen (1983, p. 28) analyzed interview data for a sample of 2,255 women who comprised a subsample of the 1979 Survey of Inmates of State Correctional Facilities conducted by the U.S. Bureau of the Census. Goetting and Howsen's data support Glick and Nato's findings regarding age, race, and educational level. In addition, Goetting and Howsen (1983, p. 29) report that most of the women were either never married, separated, or divorced, with only 21.5 percent reporting that they were married. A more recent survey of a sample of 2,094 inmates conducted under the auspices of the American Correctional Association and reported by Crawford in 1988, found few changes in the characteristics of women prisoners (Pollack-Byrne 1990, pp. 57–58). The women continued to be young women in their early thirties and late twenties who were disproportionately black and Hispanic, few of whom were currently married. In addition to finding that most of the women had not completed high shcool, Crawford reported that more than one-third of the women who quit high school quit because they were pregnant and that 80 percent of the women had at least one child. The studies of state prisons by Chesney-Lind and Rodriguez (1983), Moyer (1980), and Ward and Kassebaum (1965); the federal prisons by Giallombardo (1966), and local jails by Connolly (1983) report profiles of women offenders that closely resemble the characteristics of female offenders that emerged in the survey studies discussed above. Studies in Hawaii (Chesney-Lind and Rodriguez 1983, and State of Hawaii Department of Corrections, 1989), however, indicate that because of the unique cultural diversity, the prison population in that state consists of Asians, Pacific Islands, Caucasians, and Hawaiians. Thus, Hawaiians, Samoans, and those of mixed ancestry (as the disadvantaged class in Hawaii) are overrepresented in the Hawaii women's prison. Chesney-Lind and Rodriguez (1983, p. 53) further report that although 88 percent of their small sample (sixteen to eighteen) were unemployed at the time of arrest, they had tried a good many of the traditional female occupations, most of which were dead-end jobs. For example, the authors report that the job history of a thirty-one-year-old part-Hawaiian woman included: cannery worker (one and one-half months), car wash (one and one-half months), interior cleaners (three months), hotel maid (one and one-half months), perfume factory (two weeks), bar maid (five months), and go-go dancer (her first job, which she obtained at fourteen years of age).

Criminal Backgrounds

The profile of women presented by the research studies in the previous section suggests that these women have experienced economic deprivation. The economic, phsyical, and psychological oppression of women by the patriarchy is evidenced in the types of offenses for which women are incarcerated. Most of the studies in the United States (Chesney-Lind and Rodriguez 1983; Connolly 1983; Giallombardo 1966; Hancock 1982; Moyer 1980; and Ward and Kassebaum 1965) and other countries (Anttila 1981, p. 69; Bhanot and Misra 1981, p. 233; Gibbens 1981, p. 103; Hancock 1986, p. 104; Jensen 1981, p.

89; Kent 1981, p. 191; Plenska 1981, p. 142, and Sato 1981, p. 263) reported that most women were incarcerated for minor economic crimes (for example, larceny-theft, forgery, fraud, shoplifting, and robbery).

Goetting and Howsen (1983, p. 32), in their analysis of United States survey data, stated that "nearly half of the women inmates (48.68 percent) were serving sentences . . . for violent offenses. Research in Hungary by Rasko (1981, p. 147) also found a predominance of "crimes against life" by women who were experiencing prolonged crisis situations. As pointed out by Browne (1987), Kuhl (1985), Mann (1988), and Pollock-Byrne (1990), many of these women in prison for violent crimes are serving sentences for killing their abusive husbands. Kuhl (1985, pp. 200–201) and Pollock-Byrne (1990, p. 60) argue that the woman who has been physically battered and psychologically abused by her husband or boyfriend for a period of time often is not only economically dependent on the batterer but also may see no other way out of her pain and personal danger than to kill him. Chesney-Lind and Rodriguez (1983, p. 12, 52) found that women in their small sample in the Hawaii prison reported severe childhood beatings and sexual abuse. These authors (Chesney-Lind and Rodriguez 1983, p. 54) report that many of these women ran away from home as children, became involved in drugs and prostitution, and thus had extensive criminal records and previous incarcerations for minor offenses. Other researchers, such as Goetting and Howsen (1983, p. 32), report that drug abuse is related to the offenses for which women are incarcerated.

Programs for Women Prisoners

The greatest evidence of the neglect and misunderstanding of women offenders is found when one examines programs in women's prisons. Most of the programs are inadequately funded and, thus, fail to meet the needs of women prisoners. The sex-role stereotyping established in women's prisons by the early women reformers in their efforts to save the "fallen women" by teaching them to be good wives and mothers (Freedman 1981) has resulted in pitifully inadequate and inappropriate programs in women's prisons today. Thus, the prison population, which is mostly comprised of economically disadvantaged women with low educational and vocational skills who are the sole support for their children, are provided with few of the programs they need to build new lives in society upon release from prison. The inadequacies of the medical, parenting, and vocational/educational programs have been well documented by feminist researchers (for example, Goetting and Howsen 1983; Hancock 1986, Leonard 1983,

Ross and Fabiano 1986; Shaw and others 1981, Shekar 1981, Sikkar 1986, and Sobel 1982).

Medical/Health Care Programs

Health care in all prisons tends to be disorganized and crisis-oriented, with a heavy reliance on part-time doctors and mental-health personnel. Sobel (1982, p. 111) suggests that personnel providing health services in women's prisons are less available and not as well trained as those providing services in men's prisons. Hancock (1986, p. 102) stressed her concern for the inadequate attention given to the diet and to nutritional needs of women in Australian prisons as well as the failure to provide meaningful drug programs for addicts.

Although Glick and Neto's 1977 study of American prisons revealed that the most frequent medical complaints for women prisoners were gynecological problems, few prisons for women have a full-time gynecologist on staff (Sobel 1982, p. 111). Sikka (1986, p. 204) also reports that women's prisons in India give very limited prenatal and postnatal care for pregnant prisoners. The quantity of gynecological complaints may be a result of the failure to provide trained gynecologists, the age of most of the women in prison (late twenties and early thirties), poor previous diagnosis and treatment, and the psychological disability and stress of being incarcerated. Sobel (1982, p. 111) suggests that psychosomatic disorders are frequently associated with deprivations. This is an important factor, particularly in light of Glick and Neto's (1977) finding that the second most frequent medical complaints were nerves (anxiety and depression), which researchers (Moyer [Simmons] 1975; Resnick and Shaw 1980; and Shaw and others 1981) have noted frequently are handled by the use of tranquilizers.

Leonard (1983, p. 50) further points out that inadequate medical care presents particularly acute problems for pregnant women. These women require specialized care for an extended period of time. Since most prisons do not have full-time gynecologists on duty, there is no routine health-care program for pregnant women or for the infants. This is a serious problem as many women enter prison pregnant and a few become pregnant while incarcerated.

A successful class-action suit reported by Leonard (1983, p. 49) was brought by women at the Bedford Hills Correctional Facility in New York. *Todaro* v. *Ward* (1977) established that medical care at Bedford Hills was inadequate and violated Eighth Amendment protections against cruel and unusual punishment. Although the medical staff and the facilities themselves were adequate, prisoners were often denied access to medical help through arbitrary procedures. The court noted, for example, that one woman with a tumor in her uterus was denied treatment for eleven months.

According to Ross and Fabiano (1986, p. 52), in addition to standard medical examinations, particular concern needs to be given to detection and treatment of sexually transmitted infections, cancer examinations (breast and pelvic), general gynecological care, prenatal, childbirth and postpartum care, abortion, menstrual problems, and problems associated with poor nutrition and the abuse of drugs.

Sikka (1986, p. 204) has noted that the Prison Model Jail Manual in India "enjoins that every woman offender shall be examined by a Lady Medical Officer once a month, besides on initial admission and readmission after bail, leave, or emergency release." Ross and Fabiano (1986, p. 52) also recommend that prison doctors in women's prisons in America should be female and have special training in gynecology. They urge that medical staff should be particularly concerned about the perils of dispensing tranquilizers and psychotropic medications, especially when this is done for the well-being of the institution and not for the patient's physical or psychological well-being. They also condemn the use of tranquilizers as a substitute for programs. Finally, Ross and Fabiano (1986, p. 53) call for a systematic health-education program in women's prisons to provide general health information and specific training on sex and reproduction, nutrition, infant care, effects of drugs and chemicals, contraception, first aid, and obtaining medical services.

Mother-Child Programs

One of the most important problems facing women in prison is the loss of their families, particularly their children (Baunach 1985, Giallombardo 1966, and Ward and Kassebaum 1965). This issue takes on added significance when one recognizes that between 50 percent and 70 percent of incarcerated women are mothers (Baunach 1985; McGowan and Blumenthal 1976; and Moyer [Simmons] 1975) and that most of them are the sole support of their children (Baunach 1985, Chapman 1980, and Moyer [Simmons] 1975).

Hancock (1986, p. 105) suggests that the greater hardship suffered by women in Australia when they are imprisoned and experience forced separation from their children reflects the trend in outside society for women to be primarily responsible for caring for and supporting their children. When the mother is imprisoned, families are disrupted and children are often put into state care. In her research study of mothers in prison in Kentucky and Washington (1985, pp. 19 and 37) Baunach documents through interviews the mother's feelings of shame, guilt, and embarrassment that their behavior led to their imprisonment and separation from their children.

Mothers in America and in most other countries primarily maintain the ties with children while they are in prison through letters, phone calls, and intermittent brief visits. In some European countries and in India (Shekar 1981, and Sikka 1986) mothers have been allowed to keep their children with them in prison. The Maharashtra Prison Manual in India provides that a woman admitted to a prison with a child depending on her for nursing or otherwise for whom no friend or relative can be found to take charge, or to whom a child is born while in prison, shall be allowed to retain the child with her until the child completes the age of four years. Both Shekar (1981, p. 352) and Sikka (1986, p. 205) report that children in prisons in India are subject to the same kind of regimentation as their mothers. They report that instead of being fondled and played with, children of two or three are made to sit in orderly rows with arms folded (for the benefit of visitors).

Since 1970, there have been efforts in the United States to unite prison mothers and their children. Washington, Wisconsin, Nebraska, Kentucky, and New Jersey have programs permitting children to visit their mothers for weekends (Baunach 1985 and Leonard 1983). Several other states provide nurseries, including Bedford Hills, New York, Muncy, Pennsylvania, and Raleigh, North Carolina (Leonard 1983, p. 51). The need for parenting skills training has been cited by several authors (for example, Baunach 1985, and Ross and Fabiano 1986). Ross and Fabiano (1986, p. 59) note that prison programs in parenting skills need to include training in nutrition, health care, child growth and development, parent-child relations, birth control, methods of discipline, welfare, budgeting, and maternal rights. These authors further point to the inmate mother's need for crisis-intervention skills and knowledge about legal and financial aid (Ross and Fabiano 1986, p. 60). While most researchers note that inmate mothers need training in parenting skills, Chapman (1980) and Ross and Fabiano (1986) emphasize that survival skills to enable them to function as the head of a household and as the principal or only wage earner are equally important.

Educational/Vocational Training Programs

It is obvious that most women who come to prison are the principal wage earners for their children and that these same women come to prison without the educational and vocational skills and experience necessary to support their children. It is also clear from historical accounts (Feinman 1983 and Freedman 1981) that the women reformers of the nineteenth century created a philosophy of rehabilitation that did nothing to prepare most women to lead productive lives upon release from prison. As pointed out by Feinman (1983, p. 20):

> The failure to reform the majority of imprisoned women's lives, in part, is society's failure to recognize the historic fact that not all women have been given the socioeconomic opportunities that would enable them to conform to the idealized role of true womanhood. . . . Ignoring the fact that women who are sentenced to prison or jail usually come from a low socioeconomic background, from a slum/ghetto environment, and from minority or immigrant groups, and ignoring the fact that they will return to conditions with the additional burden of carrying the stigma of being an ex-offender, rehabilitation programs have attempted to teach these women to be honest, law abiding members of society as wives/mothers or homemakers who have husbands to support them.

A survey of vocational training programs in adult prisons in the United States nearly twenty years ago by Arditi and Goldberg supports Feinman's concerns that programs in women's prisons are not meeting the socioeconomic needs of the women offenders. Arditi and Goldberg reported finding an average of ten vocational training programs available to inmates in men's prisons compared to an average of only 2.7 programs available to women in prison (Ross and Fabiano 1986, p. 27). Furthermore, numerous researchers (for example, Giallombardo 1966; Goetting and Howsen 1983; Moyer 1984; and Ross and Fabiano 1986) noted that the few programs that are available to most women in prison are in sex-stereotyped fields such as cosmetology, food service, laundry, nurse's aide work, housekeeping, sewing, garment manufacturing, clerical work, and keypunch operation. Ross and Fabiano (1986, p. 29) also state: "Ironically, more than fifty percent of adult female offenders have had prior training in the same fields that are typically taught in correctional institutions—cosmetology, clerical, and nursing." Opportunities for meaningful vocational training in women's prisons also are reduced by the fact that classes in cosmetology, clerical work, and computers are usually limited to ten to twelve students who have high-school-equivalency credentials.

Pollock-Byrne (1990, pp. 39–91) reports some evidence that both the number and variety of vocational programs in women's prisons have increased. Beginning in the 1970s, nontraditional programs (for example, photocopy machine repair, meatcutting, auto repair, appliance repair, construction work, carpentry, and welding) began to be available in some institutions for women (Chapman 1980, p. 116, and Pollock-Byrne 1990, p. 92). Many of these programs are project-funded for short periods of time, with little or no administrative continuity, and they are seldom integrated into the criminal justice system in any meaningful way. Pollock-Byrne (1990, p. 93) reports a more recent study of vocational programs available to women incarcerated in the California Institution for Women at Frontera, California. In this study, Taylor found that women had access to thirteen vocational programs, but five of those programs had slots for only five women.

Nontraditional programs also present low-enrollment problems. Although research indicates preparing women in prison for traditional roles as housewives and mothers does not fit the socioeconomic needs of most women in prison, other research (for example, Fortune and Balbach 1985; and Pollock-Byrne 1990) further suggests that women offenders may be more committed to the traditional feminine-role-type vocational programs. When women on probation in the midwest failed to participate in a positive way in the nontraditional programs in a state-funded, community-based Model Employment Training project, Fortune and Balbach (1985, p. 125) concluded:

It is suggested that perhaps a different approach be taken in offering nontraditional training to women with this background than has been attempted previously. Past efforts, including this project, seem to approach the woman offender with the "here it is, come and get it" perspective. What appears to be needed is an intermediate component that deals with increasing the woman's awareness of the benefits of such occupations and her acceptance of female participation in such occupations. Although she may view her role as secondary to the male in the family, the facts are that she is often the primary supporter of the family and needs to have opportunities equal to the male functioning in the primary position.

Pollock-Byrne (1990, p. 92) also states that: "Institutions that have instituted nontraditional programs have found they need to do public relations work and 'consciousness-raising' to get women interested." One successful nontraditional program used for women in prisons in Washington, D.C. and New York, Wider Opportunities for Women (WOW), combines nontraditional jobs with self-assertion training to help women learn to be independent. This program promotes nontraditional careers in such areas as carpentry, welding, electrical work, and so on because they are far more lucrative than traditional women's work. WOW places women in construction jobs and helps with day-care and housing (Pollock-Byrne 1990, p. 93). While the programs just discussed suggest that there has been some improvement in vocational programs for women prisoners, programs for women are still too few, and most of these programs lead to traditional sex-stereotyped, low-paying, dead-end jobs that do not prepare women to be self-supporting upon release from prison.

Conclusions and Policy Implications

Women's prisons today reflect the patriarchal history described earlier. In a patriarchal social structure, men are in control of society and become the protectors of women who follow the traditional sex roles and the punishers of those who violate tradition. Prisons, it may be asserted, are designed to force the wayward "fallen woman" into the powerless, subservient role of wife and mother. The architectural design of women's prisons attests to society's recognition that these women are not a danger to society. Research on women prisoners provides strong evidence that most of these women commit the less serious property offenses or violent crimes in domestic situations in which many of them have been battered and/or sexually abused by their mates.

Precisely because women are less dangerous and have historically been arrested and incarcerated for fewer and less serious offenses, women in prison have been neglected and have suffered inequities that become obvious when one examines programs in women's prisons. Pollock-Byrne (1990, p. 183) argues that parity with men's prisons is not an adequate solution. As indicated in the research studies cited previously in this chapter, women have *different* medical and health-care needs than men. Along with adequate diagnosis and treatment of gynecological health problems, special provisions must be made for maintaining the contact of mothers with their children. Although most children still suffer the pains of separation from their incarcerated mothers, more progress has been made in this area than in health-care programs for women prisoners. In addition to programs to maintain the ties between mothers and children, research studies demonstrate that there is a critical need to provide women with the training and work skills to care for their children economically. Although research has demonstrated not only that women's vocational-training programs are still primarily aimed at developing domestic skills, women also have fewer vocational training opportunities than men in prison.

But it should be noted that programs in all American prisons were undermined by the "lock-them-up-and-throw-away-the-key" mentality that dominated the 1980s in America. Prison populations in federal and state institutions reached a record high of 710,054 in 1989 (*Prisoners in 1989* 1990, p. 5). Immarigeon and Chesney-Lind (1990, p. 1) suggest, "Overall, we have one of the highest rates of incarceration in the world."

The percent of women incarcerated in the United States increased from 4 percent to 5.7 percent (*Prisoners in 1989* 1990, p. 4). This increase in percentage of the prison population that is female has resulted in some controversy over the correct interpretation of these data. Simon (1990, p. 8) utilized Bureau of Justice Statistics data to analyze prison populations from 1963 to 1987 and concludes that "while a higher percentage of women have been arrested for serious offenses between 1963 and the present, the rate at which they have been sentenced to state prisons has remained relatively stable." In contrast, Immarigeon and Chesney-Lind (1990, pp. 5–6) argue that:

> Women have been hard hit by our nation's punitive policies. In recent years, female populations in jails and prisons have increased disproportionately to the increase in women's involvement in serious crime. The U.S. Bureau of Justice Statistics (BJS) reports that the average daily population of women confined in local jails rose by 82 percent between 1984 and 1988. The number of men in jail increased by 44 percent during this period. . . . In 1979, there were 12,005 women in our nation's prisons. By 1988, that number had grown to 32,691, an increase of 172 percent. In 1979, there were 289,465 males in prison. This number grew to 594,711, an increase of 105 percent.

Immarigeon and Chesney-Lind (1990) argue that these numbers reflect changes in law enforcement and a greater willingness of the criminal justice system to incarcerate women. Part of the reason for the lack of clarity regarding the meaning of the growth in women incarcerated is that, in absolute numbers, the proportion of women in prison is relatively small.

There is consensus, however, among most researchers that most women in prison are not dangerous and that criminal justice systems should be seeking alternative policies and programs for handling these less-serious women offenders. In discussing the local jail population, Connolly (1983, p. 113) states, "there is enough evidence that as many women are jailed for being socially undesirable or a 'problem' as are being jailed for their criminality." The result of the in-depth interviews of a small sample of women incarcerated in Hawaii (Chesney-Lind and Rodriguez 1983, p. 82) suggest that women in prison today are minor offenders, who, while they have extensive histories with the criminal justice system, are imprisoned largely for nonviolent property offense. Support for this statement is provided by the American Correctional Association's recommendation that the Hawaii Women's Correctional Facility should release 50 percent of its prison population to community-based programs on the grounds that these women were convicted of property and nonviolent offenses and were not a danger to society (*Honolulu Star Bulletin* 1991, p. A-5).

Researchers in Australia (Hancock 1986) and India (Sikka 1986) are also suggesting that less-serious offenders should be placed in community-based programs. Hancock points to the families that are disrupted and children who are often put into state care when women are incarcerated and then argues, ". . . on the purely legal grounds of their less serious offenses, family disruption and suffering could be avoided in many women's cases by a non-custodial sentence instead of imprisonment" (Hancock 1986, p. 105). Sikka (1986, p. 205) also states:

> It is legitimately argued that since the number of female prisoners is still small, it should be conducive to experimental methods of treatment. Intensified rehabilitative efforts, aimed at this small group, may well lead to improved methodologies and strategies.

> Supervised diversionary programmes of probation and parole treatment should be expanded by the criminal justice system and bail should be more liberally granted to women. Imprisonment should be imposed only in cases where it is absolutely necessary for the protection of the community, obviating in its wake the use of short term sentences.

Whether the researchers are calling for new programs in prison for women or for greater use of community-based programs, criminal justice policy makers are being asked to seriously examine society's reaction to the female offender. Criminal justice and correctional administrators must begin to analyze research findings and utilize that data to establish policies regarding systematic planning, systematic program development, and systematic resource allocation for the female offender.

REFERENCES

Adler, Freda (ed.), *The Incidence of Female Criminality in the Contemporary World*. New York: New York University Press, 1981.

Anttila, I., "Female Criminality in Finland—What Do the Statistics Show?" In Freda Adler (ed.), *The Incidence of Female Criminality in the Contemporary World*. New York: New York University Press, 1981, pp. 64–84.

Baunach, Phyllis Jo, *Mothers in Prison*. New Brunswick, N.J.: Transaction Books, 1985.

Bhanot, M. L., and Surat Misra, "Criminality Amongst Women in India: A Study of Female Offenders and Female Convicts." In Freda Adler (ed.), *The Incidence of Female Criminality in the Contemporary World*. New York: New York University Press, 1981, pp. 228–258.

Browne, Angela, *When Battered Women Kill*. New York: Free Press, 1987.

Chapman, Jane, *Economic Realities and Female Crime*. Lexington, Mass.: Lexington Press, 1980.

Chesney-Lind, Meda, and Noelie Rodriguez, "Women Under Lock and Key: A View from the Inside," *Prison Journal*, 63, no. 2 (1983), 47–65.

Connolly, Janet, "Women in County Jails: An Invisible Gender in an Ill-Defined Institution," *The Prison Journal*, 63, no. 2 (1983), 99–115.

de Castro, L. Aniyar, "Venezuelan Female Criminality: The Ideology of Diversity and Marginality." In Freda Adler (ed.), *The Incidence of Female Criminality in the Contemporary World*. New York: New York University Press, 1981, pp. 215–227.

Feinman, Clarice, "An Historical Overview of the Treatment of Incarcerated Women: Myths and Realities of Rehabilitation," *The Prison Journal*, 63, no. 2 (1983), 12–26.

Feinman, Clarice, *Women in the Criminal Justice System*. New York: Praeger, 1986.

Fortune, Eddyth P., and Margaret Balbach, "Project MET: A Community Based Educational Program for Women Offenders." In Imogene L. Moyer (ed.), *The Changing Roles of Women in the Criminal Justice System: Offenders, Victims, and Professionals*. Prospect Heights, Ill.: Waveland Press, 1985, pp. 111–128.

Freedman, Estelle B., *Their Sisters' Keepers: Women's Prison Reform in America, 1830–1930*. Ann Arbor: University of Michigan Press, 1981.

Giallombardo, Rose, *Society of Women: A Study of a Women's Prison*. New York: Wiley, 1966.

Gibbens, T. C. N., "Female Crime in England and Wales." In Freda Adler (ed.), *The Incidence of Female Criminality in the Contemporary World*. New York: New York University Press, 1981, pp. 102–121.

Glick, Ruth, and Virginia Neto, *National Study of Women's Correctional Programs*. Washington, D.C.: U.S. Government Printing Office, 1977.

Goetting, Ann, and Roy Michael Howsen, "Women in Prison: A Profile," *The Prison Journal*, 63, no. 2 (1983), 27–44.

Hancock, Linda, "Economic Pragmatism and the Ideology of Sexism: Prison Policy and Women," *Women's Studies International Forum*, 9, no. 1 (1986), 101–107.

Heffernan, Esther, *Making It in Prison: The Square, the Cool, and the Life*. New York: Wiley, 1972.

Honolulu Star Bulletin, April 23, 1991, p. A-5.

Immarigeon, Russ, and Meda Chesney-Lind, *Women's Prisons: Overcrowded and Overused*. Washington, D.C.: National Council on Crime and Delinquency, 1991.

Jansen, A., "Norwegian Women in Court." In Freda Adler (ed.), *The Incidence of Female Criminality in the Contemporary World*. New York: New York University Press, 1981, pp. 84–101.

Kent, J. N., "Argentine Statistics on Female Criminality." In Freda Adler (ed.), *The Incidence of Female Criminality in the Contemporary World*. New York: New York University Press, 1981, pp. 188–214.

Kuhl, Anna F., "Battered Women Who Murder: Victims or Offenders." In Imogene L. Moyer (ed.), *The Changing Roles of Women in the Criminal*

Justice System: Offenders , Victims, and Professionals. Prospect Heights, Ill.: Waveland Press, 1985, pp. 197–216.

Leonard, Eileen B., "Judicial Decisions and Prison Reform: The Impact of Litigation on Women Prisoners," *Social Problems*, 31, no. 1 (1983) 45–58.

Mann, Coramae Richey, "Getting Even? Women Who Kill in Domestic Encounters," *Justice Quarterly*, 5 (1988), 33–51.

Moulds, Elizabeth, "Chivalry and Paternalism: Disparities of Treatment in the Criminal Justice System," *Western Political Quarterly*, 31 (1978), 416–430.

Moyer, Imogene L., "Deceptions and Realities of Life in Women's Prisons," *The Prison Journal*, 64, no. 1 (1984), 45–56.

Moyer, Imogene L., "Differential Social Structures and Homosexuality Among Women in Prison," *Virginia Social Science Journal*, 13 (1978), 13–19.

Moyer, Imogene L., "Leadership in a Women's Prison," *Journal of Criminal Justice*, 8 (1980), 233–241.

Moyer [Simmons], Imogene L., "Interaction and Leadership Among Female Prisoners." Unpublished doctoral dissertation, University of Missouri, Columbia, 1975.

Plenska, D., "The Criminality of Women in Poland." In Freda Adler (ed.), *The Incidence of Female Criminality in the Contemporary World*. New York: New York University Press, 1981, pp. 134–145.

Pollock-Byrne, Joycelyn M., *Women, Prison, & Crime*. Pacific Grove, Calif.: Brooks/Cole, 1990.

Prisoners in 1989. Washington, D.C.: U.S. Department of Justice, Bureau of Justice Statistics Bulletin, May 1990.

Rafter, Nicole Hahn, *Partial Justice: Women in State Prisons 1800–1935*. Boston: Northeastern University Press, 1985.

Rasko, G., "Crimes Against Life Committed by Women in Hungary." In Freda Adler (ed.), *The Incidence of Female Criminality in the Contemporary World*. New York: New York University Press, 1981, pp. 145–157.

Resnick, Judith, and Nancy Shaw, "Prisoners of Their Sex—Health Problems of Incarcerated Women," *Prisoners' Rights Sourcebook*, vol. 2, New York: Clark Boardman, 1980.

Ross, Robert R., and Elizabeth A. Fabiano, *Female Offenders: Correctional Afterthoughts*. Jefferson, N.C.: McFarland & Company, 1986.

Sato, K. S., "Emancipation of Women and Crime in Japan." In Freda Adler (ed.), *The Incidence of Female Criminality in the Contemporary World*. New York: New York University Press, 1981, pp. 258–272.

Shaw, Nancy S., Irene Browne, and Peter Mayer, "Sexism and Medical Care in a Jail Setting," *Women and Health*, 6 (1981), 5–24.

Shekar, Sanober, "Special Problems of Women in Correctional Institutions," *The Indian Journal of Social Work*, 42, no. 4 (1981), 347–356.

Sikka, K. D., "Women in Indian Prisons: Major Issues," *The Indian Journal of Social Work*, 47, no. 2 (1986), 201–206.

Simon, Rita J., *Women and Crime*, Lexington, Mass.: D. C. Heath, 1975.

Simon, Rita J., "Women and Crime Revisited," *Criminal Justice Bulletin*, 5, no. 5 (1990), 1–11.

Sobel, Suzzanne B., "Difficulties Experienced by Women in Prison." *Psychology of Women Quarterly*, 7, no. 2 (1982), 107–118.

State of Hawaii Department of Corrections, "A Statistical Report on Hawaii's Sentenced Felons: Fiscal Years 1975–76 to 1987–88." Honolulu: Administrative Services Office, Correctional Information and Statistics Office, Research and Records Section, 1989.

Todaro v. Ward, 431 F. Supp. 1129, S.D. N.Y., 1977.

Ward, David A., and Gene G. Kassebaum, *Women's Prison: Sex and Social Structure*, Chicago: Aldine, 1965.

12

Disparate Treatment in Correctional Facilities

Roslyn Muraskin

It is estimated that one-half million women are locked up in local jails across our nations annually. On a daily basis, approximately 16,000 women are detained in jail to await trial or to serve sentences of less than one and one-half years. In prisons, female inmates constitute a small percentage of the total inmate population. These female inmates must live in correctional institutions established for men. Litigation has been the means used in an effort to eliminate what has been claimed to be discriminatory treatment against delivery of services for women. Even when legal action is successful, there is no guarantee that compliance as well as implementation will occur.

The providing of services and programs is all part of good detention practice; it ensures that those inmates returning to society can be reintegrated into society. The equality or parity of treatment between men and women still does not exist in correctional facilities. This chapter outlines how women prisoners have sued and have taken their cases to court. It is demonstrated here that services legally mandated by the states are not being delivered.

In the United States, no constitutional obligation exists for all individuals to be treated alike. The government, frequently, and in fact, does "treat disparate groups differently. What is required is that where unequal treatment exists, the inequalities must be rational, and related to a legitimate interest of the state" (Pollack and Smith 1978, p. 206). Laws create categories in which some individuals may be treated unequally. These categories include women incarcerated in correctional facilities. The question that arises is "whether the inequalities created by the law are justifiable—in legal jargon, whether the person upon whom the law's burden falls has been denied equal protection of the law" (Pollack and Smith 1978, pp. 206–207).

Since the decision in *Holt* v. *Sarver* (1970), in which the court declared an entire prison to be in violation of the Eighth Amendment and imposed detailed remedial plans, the judiciary has taken an active role in the administration of correctional facilities. Some of the most recent cases challenge the inequity of treatment between male and female prisoners.

Ostensibly, the needs of male and female prisoners would appear to be the same. They are not. While some inmate interests are similar, others are separate and distinct. In many institutions, criteria developed for men are automatically applied to women, with no consideration for gender differences. Research shows that female inmates experience more medical and health problems than male inmates. Classification officials note that female offenders need help in parenting skills, child welfare, pregnancy and prenatal care, home stability, and understanding the circumstances of their crime. But, typically, assignments to programs and treatment resources in the correctional facilities are based more on what is available than what should be available (Clements 1986, p. 38).

A review of the literature of the cases and issues dealing with disparity of treatment reveals that each takes note of the fact that women represent a small minority in both prisons and jails. Yet, the effects of incarceration are in many but not all respects similar for men and women. Each suffers the trauma of being separated from family and friend. When either a man or a woman becomes imprisoned, he or she experiences a loss of identity as well as a devaluation of his or her status. Regardless of the inmate's sex, prison life coerces conformity to an environment alien to the individual and in which one's every movement is dictated each and every minute (Muraskin, 1989).

Most challenges to prison conditions have neglected the special needs of female prisoners. Historically, correctional facilities for women have not received funding comparable to that of correctional facilities for men. Education and vocational-training programs for the women have been seriously underfunded. "Benign neglect [has] . . . created a situation of unequal treatment in many states" (Hunter 1984, p. 133). Correctional administrators have insisted that "the small number of female offenders [has] made it too expensive to fund such programs." The courts, however, have ruled "that cost is not an acceptable defense for denying equal treatment" (Hunter pp. 133–134). Women have been subjected to policies designed for the male offender. "Women have deferred to males in the economic, social, political spheres of life. In the legal realm, more specifically in the imprisonment of the female, women have been forced into the status of being less than equal" (Sargent 1984, p. 83).

Review of Cases

When inmates similarly situated find themselves being treated differently, there may exist a violation of equal protection. A review of the cases discussed below shows that "discretion in such matters as classification, work assignments, and transfers may not be exercised discriminatorily or in an arbitrary or capricious manner" (Gobert and Cohen 1981, p. 293).

Constitutionally, no obligation exists for the government to provide any benefits beyond basic requirements. However, this will not excuse invidious discrimination among potential recipients (Gobert and Cohen pp. 294–295). Case law indicates that benefits afforded some cannot be denied others solely based on race or sex.

In any equal-protection challenge, the central question raised is the "degree of state interest which can justify disparate treatment among offenders" (*Reed* v. *Reed*, 1971). As established, the "classification must be reasonable, not arbitrary and must bear a fair and substantial relation to the object of the legislation or practice" (*Reed* v. *Reed*, 1971). Courts, for example, have found sex classifications to be irrational because they appear to be solely enacted for the convenience of correctional administrators (See *Craig* v. *Boren*, 1976[1]; *Weinberger* v. *Wisenfeld*, 1975[2]; and *Eslinger* v. *Thomas*, 1973)[3]. Exist-

---

[1]In *Craig* v. *Boren* (1976) it was held that to "withstand (a) constitutional challenge under the equal protection clause of the Fourteenth Amendment, classification by gender must serve important governmental objectives and must be substantially related to achievement of those objectives."

[2]*Weinberger* v. *Wisenfeld* (1975) was a case in which a widower was denied benefits for himself on the ground that survivors' benefits were allowable only to women under 42 USCS sec. 402(g)—"a provision, headed 'Mother's insurance benefits,' authorizing the payment of benefits based upon the earnings of a deceased husband and father covered by the Social Security Act, to a widow who has a minor child in her care." The Court held that "(1) the sex-based distinction of 42 USCS sec. 402(g), resulting in the efforts of women workers required to make social security contributions producing less protection for their families than was produced by the efforts of men, violated the right to equal protection under the due process clause of the Fifth Amendment, and (2) the distinction could not be justified on the basis of the 'noncontractual' character of social security benefits, or on the ground that the sex-based classification was one really designed to compensate women beneficiaries as a group for the economic difficulties confronting women who sought to support themselves and their families."

[3]*Eslinger* v. *Thomas* (1973) was an action brought by a female law student who alleged she was denied employment as a page because of her sex. Citing Reed, the Court indicated that "(T)he Equal Protection Clause (denies) to States the power to

ing differences in conditions, rules, and treatment among inmates have proven fertile ground for equal protection challenges. Administrative convenience is not an acceptable justification for disparity of treatment (*Cooper* v. *Morin*, 1979, 1980). Lack of funds is not an acceptable justification for disparate treatment (*State ex rel Olson* v. *Maxwell*, 1977).

Legal uprisings against intolerable conditions in correctional facilities and the prisoner's rights litigation were initiated by male attorneys and male prisoners. In the early stages of this litigation, female inmates did not turn to the courts nor did officials at female institutions fear lawsuits, condemnation by the public, or inmate riots. With so few women incarcerated, there was little the women felt they could do. This situation has changed. Female prisoners have sued and have demanded parity with male prisoners (Aron 1981, p. 191). The Fourteenth Amendment of the Constitution, in particular the equal protection and due process clauses, is the legal basis for presenting issues of disparity in correctional facilities. The Fourth Amendment is the source for issues of violation of privacy, while the Eighth Amendment is used for cases involving cruel and unusual punishment.

Differential sentencing of similarly situated men and women convicted of identical offenses has been found to violate the equal protection clause. A review of cases dealing generally with sentencing in correctional institutions include *United States ex rel Robinson* v. *York* (1968), which held that it was a violation of the equal protection clause for women who were sentenced to indeterminate terms under a Connecticut statute to serve longer maximum sentences than men serving indeterminate terms for the same offenses. In *Liberti* v. *York* (1968), the Court held that female plaintiff's indeterminate sentence of up to three years violated the equal protection clause because the maximum term for men convicted of the same crime was one year. In *Commonwealth* v. *Stauffer* (1969), a Pennsylvania court held that the practice of sentencing women to state prison on charges for which men were held in county jail to be a violation of a woman's right to

---

legislate that different treatment be accorded to persons placed by a statute into different classes on the basis of criteria wholly unrelated to the objective of that statute."

The Court quoted from an article by Johnson and Knapp that "on the one hand, the female is viewed as a pure delicate and vulnerable creature who must be protected from exposure to criminal influences; and on the other, as a brazen temptress, from whose seductive blandishments the innocent must be protected. Every woman is either Eve or Little Eva—and either way, she loses" (Johnson and Knapp 1971, pp. 704–705).

The decision of the lower court was reversed, there being no " 'fair and substantial' relation between the object of the resolution, which was to combat the appearance of impropriety, and the ground of difference, which was sex. . . ."

equal protection. In a reverse of disparate treatment in *U.S.* v. *Maples* (1974), a male codefendant's sentence of fifteen years was held to violate his equal protection rights when his female codefendant received only a ten-year term. The trial judge had expressly stated that sex was a factor in imposing the lighter sentence.

In *Williams* v. *Levi* (1976), dealing with disparate treatment in the issue of parole, male prisoners in the District of Columbia were placed under the authority of the D.C. Board of Parole while women prisoners were placed under the authority of the U.S. Board of Parole's stricter parole standards for women. In *Dawson* v. *Carberry* (1971), it was held that there must be substantial equivalence in male and female prisoners' opportunities to participate in work-furlough programs.

In *Barefield* v. *Leach* (1974), women at the Women's Division of the Penitentiary of New Mexico claimed that the conditions there violated their rights to an uncensored press, to have their persons free from unreasonable searches, to be free from cruel and unusual punishment, to be allowed due process and equal protection of the law regarding disciplinary procedures and rehabilitative opportunities respectively. The court held that:

> What the equal protection clause requires in a prison setting is parity of treatment as contrasted with identity of treatment, between male and female inmates with respect to the conditions of their confinement and access to rehabilitative opportunities.

Barefield is especially important as it was the first case to enunciate the standard against which disparity of treatment of men and women in prison was to be measured.

Still further, in *McMurray* v. *Phelps* (1982), there was a challenge to conditions for both men and women at the Ouachita County Jail, where the court ordered an end to the disparate treatment of female detainees.

And, in *Mary Beth G.* v. *City of Chicago* (1983), a strip-search policy under which female arrestees underwent a full strip-search while men were not stripped without reason to believe that a weapon or contraband was present was ruled to be a violation of the equal protection clauses as well as the Fourth Amendment.

In *Bounds* v. *Smith* (1977), the court held that access to the courts by prisoners was a fundamental constitutional right. The court noted there existed an affirmative obligation on the part of state officials to insure that access by providing adequate law libraries or some alternative involving a legal-assistance program. It was further noted in the court's decision that female inmates had less access to library facilities than male inmates. This situation was ordered remedied. In *Cody* v. *Hillard* (1984), the court held that inmates at the state women's correctional facility which had neither a law library nor law trained assistants were denied their constitutional right of meaningful access to the courts.

In a case dealing with the tranfer of female inmates out of state because of a lack of facilities (*State ex rel Olson* v. *Maxwell* 1977), female inmates filed a petition for a supervisory writ challenging the North Dakota practice of routinely transferring them to other states to be incarcerated, alleging a denial of equal protection and due process. It was held that North Dakota must not imprison women prisoners outside of the state unless and until a due process waiver hearing is held or waived, and the state admits that it cannot provide women prisoners facilities equal to those of male prisoners. While in *Park* v. *Thompson* (1972), the court ruled that there must be substantial equivalence for male and female prisoners in the distance of the place of incarceration from the place of sentencing.

"From a policy perspective, discriminatory distribution of prison privileges . . . will appear counter-rehabilitative, fueling inmate-administration animosity and generating inmate-peer jealousies" (Gobert and Cohen 1981, p. 295). Male prisoners may be assigned to maximum, medium, or minimum security units, while female prisoners, regardless of the severity of their crimes, will be sent to the same institution. Problems arise with providing proper treatment as well as the need for rehabilitative programs. The cases indicate a need for parity of treatment. This is evidenced in *Molar* v. *Gates* (1979), a class action challenging the county's practice of providing minimum-security jail facilities for men but not for women. It was held that the practice violated the equal protection clauses of the state and federal Constitution. Women prisoners have the same right of access to minimum-security facilities as men do. The courts have been very critical of differences in men's and women's correctional facilities (*Mitchell* v. *Utreiner*, 1976).

In *Canterino* v. *Wilson* (1982, 1983), it was indicated that "restrictions imposed solely because of gender with the objective of controlling the lives of women inmates in a way deemed unnecessary for male prisoners" would not be tolerated. In areas such as work programs, vocational education, and training and community programs, disparate treatment was found to exist between male and female prisoners. Inferior programs as they existed and discrimination in the area of privileges had to be remedied. The court concluded that "males and females must be treated equally unless there is a substantial reason which requires a distinction be made" (1982). Such a distinction could not be found. Case law has established that discriminatory selection for work release when based on race, religion, sex, or even mental impairment is not an acceptable practice. Any arbitrary or capricious selection for participation in work programs has been prohibited by the courts.

Due to the small numbers of women in men's correctional facilities, services and treatment programs appear to be reduced. These reduced services include medical services. Generally, there is a wider range of medical services for male than for female inmates. Thus, in both *Todaro* v. *Ward* (1977) and *Estelle* v. *Gamble* (1976), the issues were medical. In the former case, the medical system in Bedford Hills Correctional Facility was found to be unconstitutionally defective, while in the latter, there was found to be deliberate indifference to the medical needs of the females. This was found to be a violation of the Eighth Amendment.

In *Bukhari* v. *Huto* (1980), it was held that no justification existed for disparate treatment based on the fact that women's prisons serviced a smaller population and the cost would be greater to provide programs equivalent to the men's institutions. Cost could not be claimed as an excuse for paucity of services.

The landmark case on women's prison issues was *Glover* v. *Johnson* (1979). This was a comprehensive case challenging a disparate system of educational, vocational, work, and minimum-security programs in the Michigan prison systems based on due process and equal protection violations as well as First and Eighth Amendment violations. The Court ruled that female prisoners must be provided program opportunities on a parity with male prisoners. The case resulted in an order requiring the state to provide postsecondary education, counseling, vocational programs, and a legal-education program (in a companion case, *Cornish* v. *Johnson* 1979) as well as other relief. ". . . 'institutional size is frankly not a justification but an excuse for the kind of treatment afforded women prisoners' " (*Glover*, 1979).

And in a facility in Nassau County, New York, in the case of *Thompson et al* v. *Varelas*, Sheriff, Nassau County et al (1985), the plaintiffs asked for:

> declaratory and injunctive relief regarding the discriminatory, oppressive, degrading and dangerous conditions of . . . their confinement within the Nassau County Correctional Center. . . . alleged in their action was the existence of inadequate health care, lack of private attorney visiting facilities, inadequate and unequal access to employment, recreation and training; unequal access to library facilities and newspapers, and excessive confinement; unsanitary food preparation and service; and, inadequate and unequal access to religious services . . .

all of which they claimed violated their rights as guaranteed by the First, Fifth, Sixth, Eighth, Ninth, and Fourteenth Amendments to the

Constitution of the United States and various provisions of the state law. The *Thompson* case began in 1979, but it was not until September 1985 that a consent judgment was entered in the *Thompson* case. *Thompson* makes a further argument for the need of a checklist of standards against which to assess what constitutes disparate treatment in the correctional facilities.

Prior to these cases the female prisoner was the "forgotton offender." Testimony by a teacher in the *Glover* case indicated that, while men were allowed to take shop courses, women were taught at a junior-high level because the attitude of those in charge was "keep it simple, these are only women."

While litigation provides an opportunity for inmates to have a role in altering conditions of their confinement, a judicial opinion requiring comprehensive change does not necessarily bring about change. Viewed from a nonlegal perspective, litigation is but a catalyst for change, rather than an automatic mechanism for ending wrongs found. All of the cases reviewed in this section hold that invidious discrimination cannot exist. A review of the nonlegal literature in the field indicates that social scientists support the reasoning of the courts.

Review of the Literature

There are indications that significant differences have existed at all levels of men's and women's services in relation to living conditions, medical and health, vocational and educational programs, religious practices, psychological counseling, work-release programs, legal and recreational services, post-release programs, drug and alcohol counseling, and the actual management of the correctional facilities.

Before discussing the literature, it is necessary to note the distinctions between jails, prisons, and reformatories. A jail is generally defined as a facility "which detains persons for more than forty-eight hours, [and is] used both as a detention center for persons facing criminal charges and as a correctional facility for persons convicted of misdemeanor and felony crimes (American Correctional Association 1985, p. xvii). Such facilities usually hold individuals convicted of a crime for up to one year. It is generally intended for adults, although it sometimes contains juveniles. Jails hold both individuals detained pending adjudication of their cases and individuals who are sentenced to one year or less. A prison is defined as a facility housing those individuals who are sentenced to one year or more. Prisons tend to have more programs than jails due to the lengthier prison sentences. The reformatory is a type of prison and has been called ". . . an historical fad that merely reflects the spirit of the times" (Williams, Formby, and Watkins 1982, p. 387). These "prisons" were built during a time when penologists wanted to stress their commitment to their idea of rehabilitation" (Williams 1982). The reformatory era represents a treatment philosophy of corrections. The view was that offensive behavior represented manifestations "of various 'pathologies' and psychological 'maladies'" all of which could be corrected by therapeutic intervention (Inciardi 1984, p. 582). The importance of these three distinctions is that the courts have accepted different standards for different types of institutions.

The first penal institution for women opened in Indiana in 1873. By the beginning of the twentieth century, women's correctional facilites had opened in Framingham, Massachusetts, in Bedford Hills, New York, and in Clinton, New Jersey. The Federal Institution for Women opened in Alderson, West Virginia in 1927, and the House of Detention for Women (the first separate jail for women) opened in New York City in 1932. These institutions all shared one thing in common, "traditional values, theories and practices concerning a woman's role and place in society. . . . The staffs, architectural design and programs reflected and perpetuated the culturally valued norms for women's behavior" (Feinman 1986, p. 38).

Historically, disparate treatment of male and female inmates started when state penitentiaries first opened. "Female prisoners . . . were confined together in a single attic room above the institution's kitchen. [They] were supervised by the head of the kitchen below. Food was sent up to them once a day, and once a day the slop was removed. No provision was made for privacy or exercise and although the women were assigned some sewing work, for the most part they were left to their own devices in the 'tainted and sickly atmosphere'" (Rafter 1983, p. 135). Female convicts were morally degraded to a greater extent than were male convicts. The reformatories built for female prisoners "established and legitimated a tradition of deliberately providing for female prisoners treatment very different from that of males" (Rafter 1983, p. 148).

Lown and Snow describe the disparate treatment of females in prison. "Traditional theories of women's crime and imprisonment tend to focus on biological, psychological and social factors to explain criminal activity. From Lombroso to the present, criminological thought has been wrought with the sexism inherent in assuming that there exists only two distinct classes of women—those on pedestals and those in the gutter" (1980, p. 195). A double standard has persisted traditionally in both the law and treatment of inmates.

Overlooking, letting go, excusing, unwillingness to report and to hold, being easy on women are part of the differential handling of the adult female in the law enforcement process from original complaints to admission to prison. The differential law enforcement handling seems to be built into our basic attitudes toward women. The operation of such attention can be called euphemistically the chivalry factor. (Reckless and Kay 1967).

This chivalry factor meant that women should be treated more leniently than men. The nature of treatment and programs for female inmates appears to indicate the assumption of such a theory. Theories abound concerning the causes of criminality by female offenders. Certainly the chivalry factor does not appear to be held in favor today. Once the female enters the correctional facility, she does not necessarily benefit from the benevolence of the criminal justice system. The theories of female crime continue to emphasize the natural differences between men and women, but fail to explain why women commit the crimes they do. Sarri concludes that "discrimination and sexism are serious and pervasive problems in statutes, law enforcement, courts, and correctional agencies. All society is being harmed by a serious overkill in the processing of females and by the inhuman conditions which continue to prevail in correctional agencies" (Sarri 1979, p. 194). It is clear that female prisoners are treated differently and sometimes worse than are male prisoners. Often, as an alternative to differential treatment, the model followed is that of the men's prison that frequently ignores the obvious physical differences of female inmates. An almost total lack of enforcement of standards exists for the confinement of women. What occurs then at the local correctional facility represents but a sample of those problems characterizing state prisons for women. The literature and cases both indicate that "the plight of the female behind bars is often a difficult one" (Allen and Simonsen 1978, pp. 325–327).

In addition to the poor quality and minimal services available to the female inmate, she still suffers the same miserable conditions of prison as do male inmates. Women suffer even more because in jails, regardless of classification, they are normally housed together in the same area, while men, who are classified according to minimum, medium, and maximum security, find themselves housed in separate areas. Women live in crowded facilities, often in squalid cells, lack privacy, are faced with insensitive visiting rules, callous treatment, and the threat of or actual sexual abuse. Two other stresses upon the female inmate stem from her being separated from her children and from having special health and medical needs (Wood 1982, p. 11).

In 1971, suggestions were made by the National Advisory Commission for the Correctional Facilities to reexamine policies, procedures, and programs with the objective of making them relevant to the problems and needs of female inmates. At that time, it was strongly urged that:

> Facilities for women offenders should be considered an integral part of the overall correctional system. . . .
>
> Each state should determine differences in the needs between male and female offenders and implement differential programming.
>
> Appropriate vocational training programs should be implemented.
>
> Classification systems should be investigated to determine their applicability to the female offender.
>
> Adequate diversionary methods for female offenders should be implemented.
>
> State correctional agencies with such small numbers of women inmates as to make adequate facilities and programming uneconomical should make every effort to find alternatives to imprisonment for them.
>
> Programs within the facility should be open to both sexes (where both sexes were being held). (Flynn 1971, p. 113)

Much of the neglect in assessing disparate treatment is attributed to writers believing that the experiences in prison for both men and women are the same and are not areas calling for special investigation. As Rafter points out in her article, "Prisons for Women, 1790–1980," it was not until the 1970s that literature dealing with women in prison began to take notice of their special problems (Rafter 1983, p. 130). Singer's bitter protest regarding the treatment afforded women inmates and her indictment of the criminal justice system's refusal to even recognize the existence of women is quite evident (1979). Arditi and associates compiled a staggering catalog of sex discrimination in prisons throughout the country (1973). Gibson in his work took a "first step toward historical research on women's prisons. . . ." (1973). Feinman indicates that, for the most part, programs in correctional facilities for women continue to be based on the belief that "the only acceptable role for women is that of wife/mother" (Feinman 1983, p. 12). The female offender has been described as being poor, black or Hispanic, undereducated, and lacking in both job skills and self-confidence. Indications are that more women are involved in criminal acts today, especially in the selling and possession of drugs (Bureau of Justice Statistics 1988). And yet when women are released back into the community, studies show that men still represent a disproportionate majority in community programs. The way these community programs are structured provide evidence of lack of sensitivity and the differential treatment afforded women (Lewis 1982, p. 49).

Rafter (1983, p. 132) points out that the women's prison system is not a replica of the men's, but rather "differs radically along a number of key dimensions, including its historical development, administrative structures, some of its disciplinary techniques and the experience of its inmates." In her work, "Women in Prison: Sexism Behind Bars," Suzanne Sobel assesses the mental-health needs of inmates and concludes that "women incarcerated in state or federal prisons are the victims of a sexist correctional system that delivers fewer services and offers fewer opportunities than those available to male prisoners" (Sobel 1980, p. 336).

Jessica Mitford (1973) has written that "the entire criminal justice system for all offenders in the United States could not be characterized as a just or humane system, but in the case of the female offender its ineffectiveness and inhumanity are even more apparent."

Fabian points out as well that "the reform movement for women prisoners was aimed at refining their standards of sexual mobility to a level acceptable to society, while that for men was aimed at reaching the young felon before he became a permanent danger to the community" (Fabian 1980, p. 173). It is specifically this attitude that persists throughout the literature dealing with disparate treatment. Historically, women have been regarded as moral offenders, while men assert their masculinity. ". . . institutional incarceration needs to become more reflective of the ongoing changing social climate" (Sargent 1984, p. 42). Most states have but one prison facility for women which, of necessity, must be of maximum security; local jails house both men and women. Population size has become a justification for ignoring females. However, size is but "an excuse for the kind of treatment afforded women prisoners" (*Glover* v. *Johnson*, at p. 1078, 1979). The disparate treatment of male and female prisoners "is the result of habitual and stereotypic thinking rather than the following of a different set of goals for incarceration" (Lown and Snow 1980, p. 210).

If administrators in corrections continue to assign women's corrections low priority in budget allocation, staff development, and program development, continued conflict can be expected between the needs of the warden of the correctional facility and the treatment afforded or not afforded women. It may well be that because of overcrowding in both types of facilities, men's and women's equality will become less of an issue, thereby producing equally undesirable conditions for both. Whatever the reasons, as demonstrated in the research findings reported in the literature, disparate programs and facilities permeate the correctional institutions today.

CASES CITED

Barefield v. Leach, Civ. Action No. 10282 (1974).

Bounds v. Smith, 430 U.S. 817 (1977).

Bukhari v. Huto, 487 F. Supp. 1162 (E.D. Va. 1980).

Canterino v. Wilson, 546 F. Supp. 174 (W.D. Ky 1982) and 562 F. Supp. 106 (W.D. Ky. 1983).

Cody v. Hillard, 799 F. 2d 447 (1986).

Commonwealth v. Stauffer, 214 Pa. Supp. 113 (1969).

Cooper v. Morin, 49 NY2d 69 (1979), cert denied, 446 U.S. 984 (1980).

Cornish v. Johnson, No. 77-72557 (E.D. Mich. 1979).

Craig v. Boren, 429 U.S. 190 (1976).

Dawson v. Carberry, No. C-71-1916 (N.D. Cal. 1973).

Eslinger v. Thomas, 476 F. 2d (4th Cir. 1973).

Estelle v. Gamble, 429 U.S. 97 (1976).

Glover v. Johnson, 478 F. Supp. 1075, 1078 (1979).

Holt v. Sarver, 309 U.S. F. Supp. 362 (E.D. Ark. 1970).

Liberti v. York, 28 Conn. Supp. 9, 246 A2d 106 (S. Ct. 1968).

McMurray v. Phelps, 535 F. Supp. 742 (W.D.L.A. 1982).

Mary Beth G. v. City of Chicago, 723 F. 2d 1263 (7th Cir. 1983).

Mitchell v. Untreiner, 421 F. Supp. 887 (N.D. Fla. 1976).

Molar v. Gates, 159 Ca. Rptr. 239 (4th Dist. 1979).

Park v. Thompson, 356 F. Supp. 783 (D. Hawaii 1973).

Reed v. Reed, 404 U.S. 71 (1971).

State ex rel Olson v. Maxwell, 259 N.W. 2d 621 (Sup. Ct. N.D. 1977).

Thompson et al. v. Varelas, Sheriff, Nassau County et al., 81 Civ 0184 (JM) (September 11, 1985).

Todaro v. Ward, 431 F. Supp. 1129 (S.D. N.Y. 1977).

United States v. Maples, 501 F.ed. 985 (4th Cir. 1974).

United States ex rel Robinson v. York, 281 F. Supp. 8 (D. Conn. 1968).

Weinberger v. Wisenfeld, 420 U.S. 636, 43 L.Ed. 2d 514. (1975).

Williams v. Levi, Civ. Action No. Sp. 792-796 (Superior Court of D.C. 1976).

REFERENCES

Allen, Harry E., and Clifford E. Simonsen, *Corrections in America: An Introduction.* Encino, Calif.: Glencoe Criminal Justice Series.

American Correctional Association, "Standards for Adult Local Detention Facilities," 2nd ed., in cooperation with the Commission on Accreditation for Corrections, April 1985.

Arditi, Ralph R., Frederick Goldberg, Jr., John Peters, and William R. Phelps, "The Sexual Segregation of American Prisons." *The Yale Law Journal.* 6, no. 82, pp. 1229–1273.

Aron, N., "Legal Issues Pertaining to Female Offenders," (from Representing Prisoners). New York: Practicing Law Institute, 1981.

Fabian, S. L., "Women Prisoners Challenge of the Future," (from Legal Rights of Prisoners). Beverly Hills, Calif.: Sage Publications, 1980.

Feinman, Clarice, *Women in the Criminal Justice System.* New York: Praeger, 1986.

Flynn, Edith E., "The Special Problems of Female Offenders." Paper presented at National Conference on Corrections, Williamsburg, Va.: Virginia Division of Justice and Crime Prevention, 1971.

Gibson, Helen, "Women's Prisons: Laboratories for Penal Reform," *Wisconsin Law Review* (1973).

Glick, Ruth M., and Virginia V. Neto, "National Study of Women's Correctional Programs." In Price & Sokoloff (eds.), *The Criminal Justice System and Women.* New York: Clark Boardman, Ltd., 1977.

Gobert, James J., and Neil P. Cohen. *Rights of Prisoners.* New York: McGraw-Hill, 1981.

Hunter, Susan, "Issues and Challenges Facing Women's Prisons in the 1980's," *Prison Journal,* 64, no. 1 (Spring/Summer 1984).

Inciardi, James A., *Criminal Justice.* Orlando, Fl.: Academic Press, 1984.

Johnson and Knapp, "Sex Discrimination By Law: A Study in Judicial Perspective," 46 *N.Y.U.L. Rev.* 675, 704–5, 1971.

Lewis, Diane K., "Female Ex-Offenders and Community Programs," *Crime and Delinquency,* 28 (1982).

Lown, R. D., and C. Snow, "Women, the Forgotten Prisoners—*Glover* v. *Johnson,*" (from Legal Rights of Prisoners). Beverly Hills, Calif.: Sage Publications, 1980.

Mitford, Jessica, *Kind and Usual Punishment.* New York: Knopf, 1971.

Muraskin, Roslyn, *Disparity of Correctional Treatment: Development of a Measurement Instrument.* Unpublished doctoral dissertation, City University of New York, 1989.

Pollack, Harriet, and Alexander B. Smith, *Civil Liberties and Civil Rights in the United States,* St. Paul, Minn.: West Publishing, 1978.

Rafter, Nicole, "Prisons for Women, 1790–1980." In Michael Tonry and Norval Morris (eds.), *Crime and Justice—An Annual Review of Research,* vol. 5. Chicago: University of Chicago Press, 1983.

Reckless, Walter. 1967. The crime problem. New York: Appleton Century Croft.

Sargent, John P., "The Evolution of a Stereotype: Paternalism and the Female Inmate," *Prison Journal,* no. 1 (Spring/Summer 1984).

Sarri, Rosemary C., "Crime the Female Offender." In Edith S. Gomberg and

Violet Frank (eds.), *Gender and Disordered Behavior—Sex Differences in Psychopathology*. New York: Brunner/Mazel, 1979.

Singer, Linda. "Women and the Correctional Process." In Freda Adler and Rita Simon (eds.), *The Criminality of Deviant Women*. Boston: Houghton Mifflin, 1979.

Sobel, S. B., "Women in Prison: Sexism Behind Bars," *Professional Psychology*, no. 2 (1980).

Williams, Vergil L., William A. Formby, and John C. Watkins, *Introduction to Criminal Justice*. Albany, N.Y.: Delmar Publishers, 1982.

Wood, D., *Women in Jail*. Milwaukee, Wis.: Benedict Center for Criminals, 1982.

13

Female Guards in Men's Prisons

Rita J. Simon and Judith D. Simon

In addition to a review of the literature, two recent studies are reported. One assesses the legitimacy of the role of female guards in men's prisons, and the other describes the experience of one female guard in a men's medium-security prison. The first-person account serves as a basis for generalizing about some aspects of the status of female guards in men's prisons.

This chapter has three sections. The first summarizes the major work in the field, Lynn Zimmer's study *Women Guarding Men*.[1] The second reports the results of a study that assessed the relative legitimacy of female guards compared to male guards in one medium-security men's prison. The third section is based largely on a first-person account of how female guards perform their roles and how they are perceived as performing their roles by inmates and male guards. It couches personal experiences within the context of observations that have been made about female guards and about the relationships between inmates and guards in total institutions.

---

[1]Lynn E. Zimmer, *Women Guarding Men* (Chicago: University of Chicago Press, 1986), p. 164.

Summary of Women Guarding Men

Women began working as guards in men's prisons in the early 1970s. Before 1972, Virginia and Idaho were the only two states that hired women as guards in men's prisons. According to Zimmer:

> The job of prison guard is an extremely nontraditional occupation for women. Because the literature on occupational choice suggests first, that people choose careers that match their personality and areas of expertise and, second, that women who choose nontraditional occupations tend to have nontraditional sex-role attitudes, one might expect female prison guards to espouse rather "liberated" attitudes concerning male and female roles in society. This is not the case. Female guards are a diverse group, especially with regard to sex-role attitudes. Only a small minority defined themselves as "liberated" or claimed to favor major changes in sex-role patterns. Many have extremely conservative views about sex roles; a few even suggested that guard jobs in men's prisons should not be given to women. If there is one generalization to be made about these women, it is that they become guards primarily because of extrinsic rewards—money, security, and fringe benefits. In this respect, the women are probably quite similar to their male counterparts.[2]

Male guards and male administrators of men's prisons were either openly and strongly opposed to the presence of women or were concerned about the consequences of their presence in the institutions. The parties involved that were most receptive and welcoming toward women in their midst were the male inmates; but even with this group, there was strong opposition.

In describing the impact of women on the male guards, Zimmer observed:

> The large majority of male guards are unhappy with the introduction of women into their ranks, fearing that their own safety and the security of the institution are threatened by women's presence. But it is obviously not just the actual performance of female guards that causes so much disapproval, because many men oppose even the few women they admit can outperform a large portion of their male colleagues. What male guards seem additionally to resent is elimination of their all-male world, disturbance of the camaraderie they have enjoyed with coworkers, and destruction of the notion that masculinity is a necessary requirement for the job. The presence of women, then, calls into question not only their assumptions about the nature of men and women, but also their assumptions about the nature of their work.

---

[2]Zimmer, *Women Guarding Men*, p. 50.

The introduction of female guards into the male prison has also been unsettling to male guards because it requires them to alter their behavior on the job. Regardless of women's wishes with regard to male behavior in their presence, most men (consciously or unconsciously) behave quite differently when women are present.[3]

As for the prison administrators, Zimmer noted:

The mandate to hire women as guards has similarly created new administrative burdens for prison managers at every level.

Even in states that choose to comply with Title VII, the law's exact requirements had to be determined. Title VII clearly prohibits discrimination against women in matters of employment opportunity, but because it does not explicitly require identical treatment of males and females once they are on the job, decisions about women's deployment had to be made. Especially in states where women were hired shortly after the legal change, high-level administrators had little assistance or guidance in deciding how to legally (and efficiently) use female staff.

Virtually none of the early policy decisions for deploying women diminished administrative attention to the "female guard problem" because they were almost immediately attacked from all affected groups. First, policies that limited women to noncontact positions were attacked by male guards on the grounds that such policies discriminated against men by excluding them from those jobs considered the least dangerous (and therefore most desirable) in the prison. There was a considerable amount of complaining by male guards, and in states with strong seniority systems, a barrage of formal challenges to these policies through the union's grievance procedures.

Policies that limited the assignment possibilities for women were also attacked, in some cases, by female guards who desired a wider range of assignment options. Some women wanted access to more jobs so they would have a better chance of obtaining a desired shift or a transfer to another facility, perhaps one closer to home. Other women, hoping to advance within the organization, wanted to obtain assignments that would broaden their experience. Still others just wanted to be equal members of the guard force, with no special privileges or differential treatment. For a variety of reasons, then, some women also attacked administrative policies that limited their deployment options; they complained, filed union grievances, and in some cases, filed or threatened to file lawsuits claiming illegal sex discrimination.[4]

---

[3]Zimmer, *Women Guarding Men*, p. 155.
[4]Zimmer, *Women Guarding Men*, pp. 160–161.

In describing the mixed reactions of inmates to female guards, Zimmer commented:

> Some men claim that their presence represents a nice change—that it is pleasant to look down the hall and see a woman coming; it gives them a reprieve from the all-male world. Some inmates claim to prefer female guards because they treat them better than the male guards—they are more helpful, more compassionate, and more understanding. They are easier to talk to and more willing to listen to problems. They can share family problems with female guards. They talk with them about their wives, girl friends, and children.

> But even inmates who favor the use of women as guards recognize some disadvantages to their presence. Some fear is expressed that female guards will not be able to protect them if they are attacked by another prisoner.

> Those who dislike being guarded by a woman believe it violates their sense of the rightful place of men and women in society. Several inmates said, "it's just not right," or claimed that women belong either in the home or in female occupations. These inmates do not so much resent the presence of women as oppose, on the basis of their ideology, the hiring of women for all "male" occupations. A number of inmates complained that the use of women as guards invades their privacy.[5]

An important question raised by Zimmer toward the end of her monograph is whether women guards "have the authority to enforce the rules and regulations against recalcitrant inmates." In 1987, we sought to answer that question by doing an empirical test of the legitimacy of women's authority to enforce prison rules.

Legitimacy of Female Guards' Authority

The setting for the study was a medium-security state institution in the midwest that housed some 650 male prisoners and had a staff of 160 corrections officers.[6] The inmates had been convicted for crimes that include murder, rape, armed robbery, assault, and a wide range of property and drug-related offenses.

The data collected for testing the legitimacy of the female officer's authority were the reports or tickets that were filed by the of-

---

[5]Zimmer, *Women Guarding Men*, pp. 61–63, 65.

[6]Judith Simon was employed as a corrections officer at the prison and collected the data described in this article during her period of employment from July 1986 to August 1987. This section appeared in Rita J. Simon and Judith D. Simon, "Female COs: Legitimate Authority," *Corrections Today*, August 1988, pp. 132–134.

ficers against inmates whom they claimed had violated a prison rule and the consequences of such reports.[7] Each report described an incident or disturbance that led to the writing of the report, the inmate(s) involved, and who reported the violation. The reports were reviewed by prison officials (reviewing officers) who held the rank of sergeant or higher. They then determined whether a hearing should be conducted. Their reasons for deciding to destroy the ticket or to go ahead with the hearing were based on substantive considerations (for example, the information on the ticket does not substantiate the charges made by the corrections officer, or the ticket refers to physical evidence such as contraband and the evidence is not provided), as well as procedural considerations (for example, the prisoner's identification number on the ticket does not match the name of the prisoner, or the ticket had not been reviewed within twenty-four hours after it had been issued). During the hearing, the inmate had the opportunity to present his case and to provide written testimonials that he had obtained from witnesses. The hearing officer, an attorney employed by the state, acted as a judge and decided both the validity of the charges and, if the charges were upheld, the appropriate punishment.

The study design involved comparing the total number of tickets filed by all of the male and female correction officers, the charges on the tickets, the pleas the inmates made at the time of the incident, and whether the tickets were eventually upheld or denied by the hearing officers. Tickets written by civilians and supervisory personnel with the rank of sergeant and higher were excluded. Each of those groups contributed less than 7 percent of the total number of tickets.

The information collected was expected to indicate (1) whether women correction officers filed as many tickets as male officers, and (2) whether the female officers' tickets were as likely to be upheld at the hearing as those filed by the male officers. If there was little or no difference in the number of tickets filed and in the rate at which they were upheld, then, we would argue, the female corrections officer's authority was as legitimate as that of her male counterpart.

In total, we examined 1,170 tickets written by 45 female officers and 115 male officers. Women officers accounted for 28 percent of the corrections officer staff, and they wrote 24 percent (275) of the

---

[7]Prison personnel other than corrections officers may write tickets. We found that counselors and other civilian employees, along with sergeants, lieutenants, and captains did exercise that prerogative, but that over 71 percent of the tickets were written by the corrections officers.

tickets. The difference in mean number of tickets by gender, 6.1 for women and 7.8 for men, was not significant.[8]

Men and women wrote tickets for the same types of violations, as the table below describes in detail. "Being in the wrong place" and "refusing to obey a direct order" accounted for 55 percent of the men's tickets and 54.5 percent of the women's tickets. The only behaviors for which women seemed to write more tickets than men were "insolence" and "sexual conduct" (for example, reaching out to touch, or verbal misconduct). But, even for those behaviors, the differences between men and women did not reach statistical significance. More tickets were written in the dormitories (59 percent) than anywhere else by both male and female officers: 72 and 56 percent. The school and the dining room were the next most frequent places in which violations were ticketed.

Eighty-six percent of the prisoners entered pleas of not guity to the violations for which they were ticketed, with no difference by the gender of the officers writing the tickets.

The crucial questions for establishing the legitimacy of the women's authority are what percentage of the prisoners were *found guilty* by the hearing officers after they stated their case; and whether female officers' tickets were less likely to be upheld than male officers. The

TABLE 1   Violations for Which Tickets Were Written, by Sex of Corrections Officers

Violations	MALE	FEMALE
	(PERCENT)	
Physical Attack with Weapon	3.0	4.1
Physical Attack without Weapon	10.6	6.4
Insolence	7.1	12.2
Refused to Obey Orders	23.2	25.5
Alcohol and Drugs	4.2	3.7
Disturbance	1.3	2.0
Wrong Place	31.9	29.0
Threatening Behavior	4.9	6.4
Sexual Misconduct	0.8	4.7
Other	13.0	6.0
Total	100.0	100.0

[8]One of the women guards wrote more tickets (20) than anyone else. Before coming to work at the prison described in this study, she had worked at a maximum security men's prison in the same state where she had been badly beaten by inmates who used bricks.

results shown in Table 2 clearly indicate that there was *no* difference in the likelihood of female guards' tickets, as opposed to male guards' tickets, being upheld or rejected.

The sanctions following the guilty verdicts also showed no clear differences on the basis of the gender of the guard. Loss of privileges was the most frequently applied sanction received by 70 percent of the prisoners who received tickets from male officers and 81 percent for tickets written by female officers.

Finally, we also compared the decisions made by the three male hearing officers as opposed to the three female hearing officers for tickets that were written by male and female corrections officers. Again, only the tickets of prisoners who pleaded not guilty were included. The figures in Table 3 are the "Percent Found Guilty"; that is, the percentage of tickets that were upheld.

Clearly, gender makes no difference! The three male hearing officers were just as likely to uphold the female corrections officers' tickets as they were the male officers' tickets, and the three female hearing officers also made no distinction in upholding the tickets written by male and female guards. On the basis of the data collected in this study, the answer to the concern raised by Lynn Zimmer is that the authority of the women corrections officers is as legitimate as that of their male colleagues.

Female Guard in a Men's Prison: A First-Hand Account

This last section of the chapter consists of a first-person account of a young, middle-class, white female guard's experiences in a men's

TABLE 2   Percent of Prisoners Found Guilt, by Sex of Correction Officer Writing Ticket

Corrections Officers	Of Those Prisoners Who Pleaded Not Guilty, Percent Found Guilty
Female	73.6
Male	74.5

TABLE 3   Percent of Prisoners Found Guilty, by Sex of Corrections Officer Writing Ticket and Hearing Officer

Hearing Officers	Corrections Officers (Percent Found Guilty)	
	Male	Female
Male	75.1	74.3
Female	75.2	70.6

prison.[9] The interview focuses on two controversial issues concerning female roles in the criminal justice system: (1) the quality of the interaction between the male and female corrections officers, and (2) the relationships between the inmates and the female officers.

A Brief Biographical Statement

At twenty years old, I was the second-youngest officer and the youngest female corrections officer assigned to the men's prison that housed 650 inmates. Four weeks into the four-month training program, I was still finishing my bachelor's degree in sociology. Prior to this experience, I had never seen the inside of a prison. My closest experience was doing volunteer work in Madison, Wisconsin with delinquent adolescents.

I am five feet, three inches in height and weigh 110 pounds. Although I was twenty years and six months when I started working in the prison, I heard later that when the assistant deputy warden saw me enter the facility with other newly hired officers, he commented, "Here comes trouble." He said later that I looked more like sixteen than twenty, and the fact that I was "pretty," white, and female all added up in his mind to a complicated and troublesome situation. I left my job as a corrections officer thirteen months later to go to law school. During my stay at the prison, I received a letter of commendation from my shift commander for my role in a practice emergency mobilization; I graduated in the top 10 percent of the officer's training class of 240; and I believe I gained the respect of the assistant deputy warden, the deputy warden, and the other administrators at the prison.

A Brief Description of the Prison Staff and the Size and Composition of the Inmate Population

When I started working, there were 150 corrections officers, about 40 of whom were women. I was the second-youngest officer and one of two white female guards. The administrative staff consisted of the warden, two assistant deputy wardens, the inspector, three captains, six lieutenants, and ten sergeants. All of them were men except for two female lieutenants and one sergeant. The first woman corrections officer was hired about a decade earlier, in the late 1970s. Prior to that, women had worked in the prison as teachers, secretaries, nurses, and in a social-service capacity.

---

[9]A shortened and edited version of this section appeared in Judith Simon and Rita J. Simon, "Some Observations on the Status and Performance of Female Correction Officers in Men's Prisons," in Muraskin and Kushner (eds.), *Issues In Justice* (Indiana: Wyndham Hall Press, 1990), pp. 140–148.

The inmate population in the fall of 1986 was 650; one year later the number had been reduced to 500, the maximum permitted under state regulations. Under the state classification system, the facility was a medium-security prison that specialized in parole violators. That meant that most of the inmates had served time earlier and were somewhat older than the typical state prisoner. The offenses for which they had violated their parole were primarily drug-related property crimes. There was also a fairly large group of violent offenders who had been found guilty of murder, manslaughter, armed robbery, and aggravated assault. At least 80 percent of the inmates were black, there was a small group of Hispanics, and all the others were white males.

Duties and Responsibilities of Male and Female Officers and Guards

There was no difference between the duties and responsibilities of the male and female commanding officers. They included scheduling the custody staff, reviewing and updating employee personnel files, insuring that the daily operations of the prison ran smoothly, and filing reports on all critical incidents. Additionally, the commanders reviewed disciplinary "tickets" (reports) that officers wrote on the prisoners, occasionally heard prisoners' complaints, and monitored the on-the-job training of new officers. One member of the command staff was required to monitor each meal in the dining hall, and at least once during their eight-hour shift, they made rounds and inspected all the housing units. There was one commander in the control center at all times.

According to Department of Corrections' policy, commanding officers were supposed to assign staff to positions without consideration of the officer's sex. The extent to which this policy was followed depended on which commander was doing the scheduling. At the beginning of my thirteen months' tenure, I noticed that women were always assigned to the information desk, the control center, and the front gate, and that men were always assigned to the arsenal, the alert-response vehicles, and the yard. But after a few months, I noticed a change. Men, as well as women, were regularly assigned to the information desk and the control center, and women were just as likely to be assigned to the arsenal and to the alert-response vehicles as the male officers were. This change was the result, I think, of an influx of new officers and several changes in the command staff.

Attitudes of Male Guards toward Female Colleagues

I found that there was a dramatic difference between the attitudes of the men who had recently completed coursework at the training academy and those who had been with the state for many years or who had worked for the city. The men who were new to the system generally accepted women as equals and respected the women officers and commanders. There was a sense of camaraderie and teamwork among the young officers (in experience, not necessarily in years) who had completed work at the academy. But since the academy had only been in existence for a few years, there were only a limited number of officers who shared this experience. I experienced very little animosity from these men and I heard few stories of these men complaining about women being incompetent or burdensome. That is not to say that they did not complain about a particular woman, but the complaints did not stem from the officer being a woman. The male guards who had either worked for the city or had been with the state for many years were more likely to resent women generally, and many of these officers indicated that they would have preferred that women not work inside the prison at all.

For example, many of the women were housing unit officers. They were in charge of running a unit of forty to fifty-five men for eight hours. The yard crew, frequently all male officers, were in charge of relieving these unit officers for their restroom breaks as well as their regular meal breaks. Often times the yard crew would complain that the women officers would demand many more restroom reliefs than the male officers. These men would accuse the women of demanding these breaks even when they did not need to use the restroom. It is possible that the women did abuse the system. However, it is important to note that the male officers often did not ask for restroom reliefs because they were able to use the restrooms in the housing units since the prisoners and the guards were all men. The only women's restrooms were located in the kitchen and in the administration building.

The shift commander occasionally remarked that female officers had a better overall record of reporting for work on time than men officers. One explanation offered was that the women officers were less likely "to stay out drinking until late at night." The occasions when female officers failed to report to work were usually because their children were sick or because there were other family problems.

Occasionally, there were disturbances in the yard or in the housing units to which several officers were required to respond immediately. All officers who were in a position to do so were expected to respond, men and women alike. As a general rule, officers were anxious to come to the aid of their fellow officers and responded quickly. However, there were some officers who were notorious for disappearing during emergencies. There were several men and women who enjoyed this reputation. There were also male and female officers whom their fellow officers preferred not to have on the scene. Generally, the male officers who were not welcomed were feared because they tended to get the prisoners riled up and to escalate the situation. The unwelcome female officers were not desired because they were ineffective. The prisoners made fun of these women and thus it was more difficult to quell the disturbance.

Relations between Prisoners and Female Guards

In general, the prisoners tended to relate to each officer as an individual. They tried to play on the officer's weaknesses in the hopes of receiving favorable treatment, of getting the officer to do favors for them, or of allowing them to get away with prohibited acts. The prisoners would play on women officers' appearance or sex appeal by complimenting them, by making suggestive remarks, and by asking a lot of personal questions. For example, the inmates made many comments about my age and the fact that I was white. They asked a lot of questions about my feelings towards black men and about my marital status. I was given several letters full of compliments on my appearance, my charm, and my friendliness.

For the first several weeks of a new officer's tenure, the prisoners would "pull out all the stops" to try and "set up" a new officer, be it a man or a woman. They tried hard to treat the officer as a "special" person.

The prisoners' primary concern is their personal safety and the safety of their belongings. Any other preferences or desires are secondary to these concerns for survival and safety. Thus, any consideration a prisoner might give to liking a male or female officer is secondary to his concern that the officer be able and willing to protect him and his property.

Protecting the prisoners does not necessarily involve great physical strength or size; rather, it involves the guard's ability to maintain order and enforce the prison's rules. Initially, prisoners are skeptical of any officer's ability to maintain order. Once an officer proves him or herself, most prisoners are ready to accept that officer. Some prisoners do not like women in general, and they especially resent women in positions of authority. Some think all women officers are reformed prostitutes. Still others dislike women officers because they claim that some women purposely set out to tease them and thus are a source of great frustration; for example, women who wear their clothes too tight, use too much makeup, or have on too much jewelry. Finally, there are those who dislike certain women officers because they think they are too "manly," perhaps indicating they think they are lesbians. These inmates were unwilling to concede that a female officer was able to maintain order and they caused trouble whenever a woman was in charge. But, they were a small minority of the inmates.

Once a female officer established her competency, many of the prisoners were pleased to have her in place of a man. Many of the inmates believed that women treated them with more respect and more care than the male guards. They believed that the women guards did not need to constantly affirm their power over the prisoners, as opposed to the male officers who saw power and control as symbols of their manhood. Many of the prisoners were also more anxious to talk to women officers about their personal situations, once they were past their initial "wooing" stage discussed previously. In general, then, male prisoners like female officers.

Fear and Stress

Working at the prison was always stressful. There is a constant fear that the prisoners would riot and take control of the prison. I became accustomed to this type of fear and stress, such that I did not notice it on a daily basis. However, if there was a break in my schedule, such as vacation, I would suddenly become aware of how different I felt without the fear and stress.

In addition to this general constant stress, there were often specific incidents that occurred throughout the day that were stressful. Anytime I had a confrontation with a prisoner, it was frightening and stressful. Would they "get me" when I turned my back? Would they continue wandering around the cellblock and not enter the cell? Would they give me the knife they were holding?

There were two particular incidents that occurred that frightened me more than any others. The first incident occurred in the dining hall, in which there were several hundred inmates and ten or fifteen officers monitoring the meal. One prisoner, as he entered the food line, began picking up trays and dropping them on the floor so that they made a loud noise. He continued doing this for several minutes, one tray after another. Many of the other prisoners became angry because the loud noise was disturbing. Other prisoners were clapping and laughing, apparently in support of the prisoner's behavior. It became clear, very quickly, that either the prisoners who were upset were going to put an end to the noise or the other prisoners would begin dropping trays as well. The officers in the dining hall needed to remove the tray-throwing prisoner from the dining hall immediately, but they had to do it without the other prisoners becoming involved. If a battle broke out, the outnumbered officers would not have much of a chance.

I was in the control center listening to the action on the radio.

The lieutenant, the only commander on duty, and I were trying to figure out a plan of action. We were concerned that the prisoner might begin throwing trays at the inmates, and that if an officer approached him he might direct his violence at the officers. Additionally, we were concerned about how the other prisoners would react to any action we might take against the disruptive prisoner, in light of some recent events at another prison in the state system. Several days earlier, an inmate had been beaten to death and five corrections officers, a sergeant and a lieutenant were all held responsible for the beating death.

My role in the "plan" was to operate the video camera in order to make sure there was a record of the incident in case of lawsuits. I was also to be one of two officers responsible for preventing the prisoners in the dining hall from interfering with the officers trying to apprehend the disruptive prisoner.

Just as the prisoner stopped dropping the trays and turned to walk out of the dining hall, five officers and the yard sergeant approached him. The prisoner did not react to the presence of the officers. The sergeant and officers walked with the prisoner down the walkway toward the cellblock. There was a large group of prisoners on the walk ahead of the prisoner and there was another large group leaving after the prisoner. The lieutenant, another officer and I (equipped with the video camera) stepped out onto the yard. As the prisoner and officers walked past me and the other young officer, we stepped onto the walk in front of the approaching prisoners. As soon as the prisoners saw me holding the video camera, they were aware that something unusual was taking place. They began shouting questions and accusations as to what the officers were going to do to the prisoner. As the prisoners came closer to where the other officer and I were standing, I wondered how we were going to keep 100 angry prisoners from marching over us into the cellblock.

Inside the cellblock the officers and sergeant escorting the prisoner grabbed him for the first time. They quickly handcuffed him and marched him off to the control center. He did not resist. I had managed to film the action by running from where I had been standing on the walk into the cellblock. Once the prisoner and officers were on their way to the control center, I ran back to help the lone officer restrain the prisoners from coming inside. The prisoners had advanced almost to the cellblock. We could not yet let them in for fear they would push through the gate and try to overtake the officers and the cuffed prisoner. During the entire time, two scenarios kept running through my mind. One was that they would grab me and the other officer, pick us up, carry us to another part of the yard, and kill us. The other was that they would just knock us to the ground and trample over us.

Those scenarios were not without foundation. Two young, relatively inexperienced officers in the yard preventing 100 cold prisoners from getting back to the warm cellblock on a Sunday morning is not a stable situation. In addition, there was the equivalent of a stick of dynamite thrown on the scene because one prisoner began recounting to the others information he had about the incident at the other prison where the officers had beaten an inmate to death. Suddenly, all the prisoners became convinced that the same thing was taking place in our cellblock, which was just five feet away. As loudly and clearly as we could, we tried to convince the prisoners that nothingn of the kind was going to happen, that the lieutenant and sergeant had merely handcuffed the prisoner and taken him to the control center to try and find out what inspired the tray throwing.

The incident passed without anyone getting hurt. We were fortunate that the prisoner stopped throwing trays and walked out of the dining hall on his own because we really had no plan for getting him to stop. We all knew that if the officers grabbed the prisoner in the dining hall in full view of the other inmates, there could have been a riot. Some of the prisoners would have come to his aid, while others might have tried to help get the disruptive prisoner out of the dining hall.

In retrospect, I can still remember how frightened I felt standing in the yard in front of 100 angry inmates. But, as the incident was occurring, I also knew I had no choice but to stand there and try to talk the prisoners out of any violent action they might take and hope that the sergeant would get the prisoner up to the control center before the prisoners in the yard decided to get me! As it turned out, both my instincts and my record of behavior with the prisoners worked in our favor. Because I had a reputation of being straightforward with the prisoners, many of them, instead of pushing toward me, stood still and asked me a lot of questions that I must have answered to their satisfaction. "Ms. Simon, what's going on?" "Ms. Simon, why are you making us stand out here in the cold?" "Ms. Simon, why do you have the video camera?" "Ms. Simon, you all are going to beat him up, aren't you?" Perhaps the fact that I was a woman, and a woman for whom they had some respect, helped defuse the situation.

The second particularly frightening experience occurred late one night in the segregation unit. I found working the midnight shift more frightening than either of the other two shifts because usually I worked alone and, except for dim safety lights, the cellblock was dark. There are many fewer officers assigned to midnights because there are no activities that take place during the night and there is no prisoner movement.

On this particular night, I was making my rounds through the segregation unit to which I had been assigned. As I walked past each cell, I pulled on the bars to make sure the cell door was securely locked. Just as I reached the last cell, one of the prisoners called my name. I was startled because I thought they were all sleeping. I turned around quickly and saw a prisoner standing in the middle of the cell walkway, the cell door wide open. I was about five feet from the gate leading out of the cell block and about twenty feet from the prisoner. I knew I did not have time to run out of the cell block, open the lock box, close the cell gate behind me, and lock it. The prisoner could jump on me if he wanted to before I ever made it out the gate.

I looked at the prisoner and asked him to please step back into the cell. I stood where I was and tried not to shake with fear. The prisoner did not move. Because it was quite dark, I could not see his face. Several of the other prisoners were awakened by the exchange between me and the prisoner.

The prisoner did not move. I decided I had better get closer to him if I were going to speak so that I would not wake any more of the prisoners. The fewer people involved the better. Even though the other inmates were locked up, they might encourage the prisoner to do something—perhaps grab me! When I got within several feet of the prisoner, but not, I hoped, within arm's reach, I again asked him to step back into his cell and shut the door. He began to chuckle, but he did not move. We both stood there looking at each other. The prisoners who had awakened remained quiet, aside from saying hello when I passed their cells. Finally, and slowly, the prisoner walked into his cell and pulled the door shut. I wanted to run out of the cellblock gate as fast as I could and lock it behind me. But I knew that I had to check to be sure the prisoner's cell was, in fact, locked so that he could not step out of it again if he so desired. Very hesitantly, I walked up to his cell door and pulled on the door. It did not open.

I said goodnight and walked down the long hallway and out of the gate. It seemed as if it took me twice as long as usual to get to the gate and lock it. When I finally made my way back to the officer's station, I was shaking so hard I could not write.

Assessment

In retrospect, my overall assessment of whether female corrections officers carry their weight in a men's prison and whether they are accepted by their male colleagues is positive. I never saw a male officer threatened or endangered by having to work alongside a female officer. Female officers were as likely to assume their responsibilities, stand up to the prisoners, and enforce the rules as the male officers were; and for the most part, the male and female officers recognized the absence of differences. As for the prisoners, most of them like having women around: it humanizes the institution.

Working within the system gives you a clear understanding of correctional facilities and their workings. More importantly, it proves that men and women alike can do the job. All it takes is a willingness to accept the responsibility and not think in terms of man or woman, but rather of a person who is capable of doing the job.

14

Women's Prisons: Overcrowded and Overused

Russ Immarigeon and Meda Chesney-Lind

Since 1980, the number of women imprisoned in the United States has nearly tripled. Approximately 75,000 women are now locked up in American jails and prisons. Increases in the number of incarcerated women have surpassed comparable rates of increase for men for the past decade, and an unprecedented number of expensive prison spaces are currently being built for women.

This chapter argues that these trends should not go unquestioned and that construction of new women's prisons should be halted until several crucial questions can be answered. Specifically, is imprisoning increasing numbers of female offenders the best or most cost-effective method of addressing the substantial social problems that underlie female criminality? What alternatives to incarceration exist that can improve the ability of female offenders to lead law-abiding lives? And, how can states shift from a growing reliance on incarceration to more frequent use of community resources as criminal sanctions?

This chapter presents evidence to suggest that the current level of women's imprisonment is disproportionate to the absolute need for such confinement and the emerging consensus that scarce jail or prison space should be reserved for those offenders who are clear public-safety risks. In the past, women prisoners were ignored because they were few in number. Now the primary corrections response to overcrowding in women's prisons has been to build more prison cells rather than to review

---

This article is reprinted with permission of the National Council on Crime and Delinquency.

the specific needs of female offenders to determine whether traditional incarceration is necessary.

There is a need to expand the growing number of community-based programs rather than building cells to incarcerate women. A review of these programs demonstrates that women in conflict with the law can be turned away from crime by addressing issues such as economic marginality and substance abuse, as well as women's assorted health, parenting, and self-esteem needs.

America's Imprisonment Binge

The United States imprisons more people than at any time in its history. Currently, more than 710,054 men and women are imprisoned in federal and state prisons, and local jails house at least 395,553 prisoners. According to a recent study by the Sentencing Project ("U.S. Leads World" 1991), we have the highest rate of incarceration in the world. Furthermore, the National Council on Crime and Delinquency estimates that the nation's prison population will grow by about 68 percent in the next five years (Austin and McVey 1989).

Women Get More Than Equal Time

Women have been hit hard by our nation's punitive policies. In recent years, female populations in jails and prisons have increased disproportionately to the increase in women's involvement in serious crime. The U.S. Bureau of Justice Statistics (BJS) reports that the average daily population of women confined in local jails rose by 95.3 percent between 1984 and 1989. The number of men in jail increased by 51 percent during this period (*Census of Local Jails* 1990).

Similarly, BJS reports that women's imprisonment has expanded disproportionately to prison population increases experienced by men during the last decade. In 1989, for example, the number of women incarcerated in federal and state prisons grew by

Several persons offered, and were frequently asked for, guidance and direction in the completion of this chapter. Jan Elvin, editor of *The National Prison Project Journal*, encouraged one of the authors to examine women's imprisonment in the United States. Parts of this chapter were originally published in the *Journal*. Later, the National Council on Crime and Delinquency, especially Marci Brown, its director of communications, gave steadfast support. Others who shared their time and experience with the authors include: Patt Adair, James Austin, Sandra Kay Barnhill, Louise Bauschard, Barbara Bloom, Kathleen Daly, Laura Fishman, Mary E. Gilfus, Donna Ginther, The Rev. Deborah Hafner, Tracey Huling, Dan Le Clair, Joycelyn M. Pollack-Byrne, Joan Potter, Nicole Hahn Rafter, Chase Riveland, and Mary Scully. We are also grateful to those academics, policy makers, practitioners, and researchers who sent us materials for use in this chapter.

24.4 percent over the previous year. The number of men in prison increased by 12.5 percent (*Prisoners in 1989* 1990).[1]

Women made up 4 percent of the nation's imprisoned population shortly after the turn of the century. By 1970, the figure had dropped to 3 percent. By 1989, however, more than 5.7 percent of those incarcerated were women—an 81 percent increase in women's proportional share of the total prison population in less than two decades. In fact, the rate of women's imprisonment grew from 6 per 100,000 in 1925 to 29 per 100,000 in 1989 (Calahan 1986).

In 1980, there were 12,331 women in our nation's prisons. By 1989, that number had grown to 40,566, an increase of 229 percent. In 1980, there were 303,643 males in prison. This number grew to 669,498 in 1989, an increase of 120 percent (Calahan 1986 and *Prisoners in 1989* 1990).

By contrast, total arrests of women (which might be seen as a measure of women's criminal activity) increased by 65.5 percent between 1980 and 1989. The FBI reports that Part One arrests (including murder, rape, aggravated assault, robbery, burglary, larceny/theft, motor-vehicle theft, and arson) of women increased by about 51.5 percent during the same time period, while Part One arrests for men increased by about 32 percent (*Uniform Crime Reports* 1990). While these trends in women's crime may sound serious, it should be noted that most of the increase in women's arrests is accounted for by more arrests of women for nonviolent property offenses such as shoplifting, check forgery, welfare fraud, as well as for deportment offenses, such as driving under the influence of alcohol, and drug offenses.

A look at national data on the characteristics of women in state prisons also confirms that women are not being imprisoned because of a jump in the seriousness of their offenses. Indeed, the proportion of women imprisoned for violent offenses actually dropped. In 1979, nearly half (48.9 percent) of the women in prison were incarcerated for a violent offense; by 1986, this figure had fallen to 40.7 percent. By contrast, the number of women incarcerated for property offenses increased from 36.8 percent of women's commitments in 1979 to 41.2 percent in 1986, with most of the increase accounted for by a jump in the number of women committed for larceny/theft. Increases were also noted in the percentage of women imprisoned for public-order offenses. Women were also slightly more likely to be incarcerated for drug offenses, but the Bureau of Justice Statistics reports the increase was explained by a jump in the number of women incarcerated for

---

[1]In 1990, however, this pattern slowed and shifted, with only a 7.9 percent increase in the number of women in prison and an 8.3 percent increase in the number of men (see *Prisoners in 1990*).

possession of rather than trafficking in drugs (*Profile of State Prison Inmates, 1986* 1988).

Figures 1 and 2 show the disproportionate increase in both male and female jail and prison populations compared to the number of arrests during the same period. In one five-year period (1984 through 1988), arrests of women increased about 19.7 percent, while arrests of men increased by 9.7 percent. Arrests for Part One, or crime index offenses, showed slightly larger increases (24.3 percent for women and 18.5 percent for men) (*Uniform Crime Reports* 1989). Jail popu-

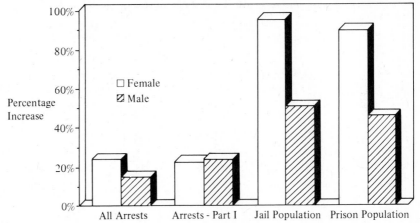

Figure 1 Percent Increase, Male & Female, 1985–1989

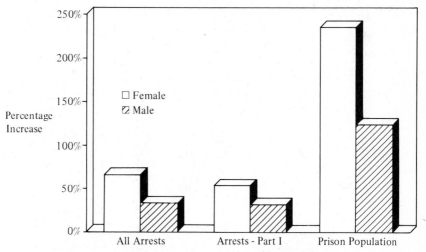

Sources: Federal Bureau of Investigation, 1990, *Crime in the United States*, pp. 177, 179; Bureau of Justice Statistics, 1990, *Jail Inmates 1989*, p. 2; Bureau of Justice Statistics, 1990, *Prisoners in 1989*, p. 4.

Figure 2 Percent Increase, Male & Female, 1980–1989

lations for both men and women grew significantly during the same time—the women's jail population increased 82 percent, while the men's grew by only 36 percent (*Census of Local Jails* 1990). The prison population grew by 69 percent for women, and only 37 percent for men (*Prisoners in 1988* 1989).

Why More and More Women Are Imprisoned

Women are arrested and imprisoned in greater numbers because of changes in legislative responses to the "war on drugs," law-enforcement practices, and judicial decision making, rather than a shift in the nature of the crimes they commit. Recent information on the characteristics of women in prison systems in different parts of the country suggests that the war on drugs, in particular, with its emphasis on increasing the penalties for drug use and selling, may be having a significant effect on women's imprisonment.[2] Simply put, the criminal justice system now seems more willing to incarcerate women.

In 1970, 45 percent of women charged with murder were imprisoned. By 1975, this figure surged to 73 percent. Likewise, the percentage of women imprisoned for robbery rose from 25 percent in 1970 to 61 percent in 1975. In a five-year period, the number of women imprisoned for writing bad checks increased from 15 to 33 percent (Chapman 1980). A recent California study observes that the proportion of females incarcerated for the commission of felonies increased from 54 percent to 79 percent between 1978 and 1987 (*Women in Crime* 1988).

The growth in the number of women's prisons in the U.S. is another measure of our willingness to incarcerate more women. In the early 1970s, only twenty-six states, Puerto Rico, and the District of Columbia had separate prisons for women—a pattern representing decades of reluctance to incarcerate women. Recent research, however, indicates that this pattern has changed abruptly in the last two decades (see Figure 3).

---

[2]A study done by the Rhode Island Justice Alliance ("Female Offender Survey, Rhode Island Adult Correctional Institution, Women's Division") incarcerated in Rhode Island which has had 1,000 percent increase in women's imprisonment in the last five years, for example, shows 33 percent of the women incarcerated for a drug crime. Research conducted by the Massachusetts Department of Correction (Daniel LeClair, "The Incarcerated Female Offender: Victim or Villain?" Research Division, Massachusetts Division of Correction, October 1990) on women incarcerated in Massachusetts shows that fully 47 percent of the female state sentenced offenders, but only 19 percent of the male offenders are incarcerated for some sort of drug offense in 1990. Tracy Huling ("Breaking the Silence," Correctional Association of New York, March 4, 1991) reports that in New York's prisons, only 23.3 percent of women inmates were incarcerated for drug offenses between 1980 and 1986. By February 1991, that proportion had risen to 62 percent.

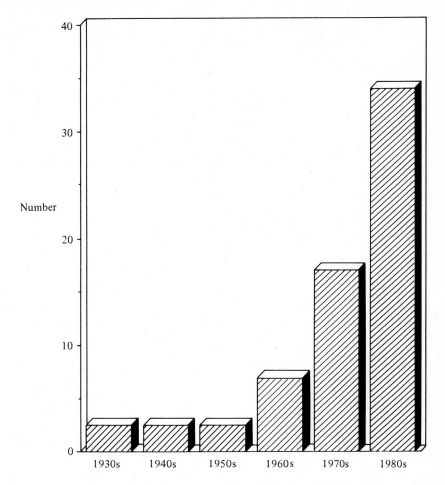

Source: Rafter, Nicole, & Kahn, *Partial Justice.* Transaction Books, 1990, pp. 181–182.

Figure 3 Creation of State Prison Facilities for Women, 1930-1980

Prison historian Nicole Hahn Rafter observes that between 1930 and 1950, roughly two or three prisons were built for women each decade. In the 1960s, the pace of prison construction picked up slightly with seven units opening, largely in southern and western states. During the 1970s, seventeen prisons opened, including units in states such as Rhode Island and Vermont, which once relied on transferring women prisoners out of state. In the 1980s, thirty-four women's units or prisons were established (Rafter 1990).

This growth in the number of women's prisons during the 1980s is the result of inadequate planning. Few states have made a comprehensive assessment of which women really require incarceration and which women could be cared for safely using community resources. Instead, women have been housed in abandoned hotels, motels, mental hospitals, nurses' dormitories, and youth training schools.

In the past decade, California, Michigan, Minnesota, and Wyoming were among the states that have built new prisons for women. Hawaii and Oklahoma have converted former men's or youth facilities into women's prisons. In New Mexico, women were housed in a converted motel. In West Virginia, officials used a remodeled hospital to house women when the state's prison for women was closed because of fire and safety-code violations (DeConstanzo and Scholes 1988). New York State doubled its capacity to imprison women in the space of three years at a cost of $300 million.

Those states that failed to develop sufficient community resources experienced severe overcrowding. In Massachusetts, cells meant for one person held as many as eight. In Hawaii, over 100 women were crowded into a building designed to hold 36 juvenile females (Chesney-Lind 1987).

The Women We Imprison

The American Correctional Association (ACA) recently conducted a national survey of imprisoned women in the U.S. and found that they were overwhelmingly young, women of color, and mothers of children (American Correctional Association 1990). About half of these women ran away from home as youths, about one-fourth of them had attempted suicide, and a sizeable number had serious drug problems. One-half of the women used cocaine; about a quarter of them used it daily. One-fifth said they used heroin daily.

The ACA survey found that over half were victims of phsyical abuse and 36 percent had been sexually abused. Another study of women in prison in Massachusetts indicates that, if anything, these figures are conservative. Mary Gilfus found that when childhood physical abuse, childhood sexual abuse, adult rape, and battering were combined, fully 88 percent of her sample had experienced at least one major form of violent victimization (Gilfus 1988). About one-third of the women in the ACA study never completed high school, and a similar number quit because they were pregnant. Twenty-two percent had been unemployed in the three years before they went to prison. Just 29 percent had only one employer in that period. Largely, they had worked in traditional women's service, clerical, and sales jobs. Two-thirds had never earned more than $6.50 per hour for their labor.

Generally, these women were first imprisoned for larceny/theft or drug offenses. At the time of the survey, they were serving time for drug offenses, murder, larceny/theft, and robbery. Research indicates that a considerable number of women convicted of murder or manslaughter had killed husbands or boyfriends who repeatedly and violently abused them. A survey found that 40 percent of 132 women incarcerated in Chicago between 1975 and 1976 had killed boyfriends or husbands who had been battering them (Lindsey 1978).[3] Studies of women charged with robbery also show that they were usually less active, noninitiators of these crimes (Fenster 1977 and Ward 1968).

Current Policies Rarely Address Needs of Women Offenders

States must begin now to support existing community-based resources for women and to create new ones where none now exist. Fortunately, there are a few models of how this process should occur. The Georgia Department of Corrections established a planning division for female offenders in the late 1970s. Then, a continuum of programs stressing economic independence was designed to take a balanced approach toward multidimensional problems faced by women offenders. Several years later, the Minnesota Department of Corrections also set up a planning division responsible for developing programs based on the special needs of women offenders.

Unfortunately, such systemic planning is rare. More typical is the lack of attention given women offenders by most policy and planning groups. In the 1980s, for instance, task forces in more than twenty states forged recommendations to reduce prison overcrowding. Only four of these states made recommendations specifically for incarcerated females. Three states focused on expanding prison space for women or the use of cocorrectional institutions. Only one state suggested the use of more halfway houses for women. Finally, even where planning has been done, incarcerative policies may still dominate. Georgia's continuum of programs has not been fully implemented, and, in Minnesota, a second facility for women prisoners has been opened at Moose Lake State Hospital to eliminate the overcrowding at the state's Correctional Facility at Shakopee.

Innovative Policies Towards Women Offenders

Several states have begun to examine how criminal justice policies affect women offenders in their jurisdictions. Studies in Connecticut, Delaware, Illinois, Maryland, Massachusetts, and New Jersey have

---

[3]More recently, outgoing Governor Richard Celeste of Ohio granted clemency to 25 women who had been convicted of killing or assaulting abusive husbands or boyfriends after reviewing "records of more than 100 women" (*New York Times*, December 22, 1990).

reviewed the characteristics and treatment of female prisoners as they begin to identify and address the specific circumstances and needs of imprisoned women (Avallone and Talisano 1989; Miller 1990; and Herr and others 1988).

The Connecticut Correctional Institution at Niantic, the state's only women's prison, has been overcrowded throughout the 1980s and has been the subject of a lawsuit by the Connecticut Civil Liberties Union for much of this period. Nonetheless, the Governor's Task Force on Jail and Prison Overcrowding, established in 1981 to define and implement programs and policies to reduce correctional overcrowding, has failed, in nine annual reports, to specifically address alternatives for female offenders.

Two noncorrectional groups have filled this void. In 1985, a task force formed as part of a legal settlement with the state's Department of Corrections identified the need to explore alternatives to confinement for women imprisoned for victimless and nonviolent crimes. In 1989, a report prepared by the state's Permanent Commission on the Status of Women found that less than 10 percent of imprisoned women were incarcerated for violent offenses (Avallone and Talisano 1989). Most imprisoned women were confined for probation violations, failure to appear, prostitution, and operating a vehicle under suspended license or registration. The Commission also found that communities had severely limited services designed for women offenders' special needs and circumstances, and that neither the state's Bail Commission nor its Office of Adult Probation had specialized units for female offenders.

The Commission recommended a comprehensive range of pretrial sentencing, residential, and out-patient services to reduce the number of incarcerated women in the state. These options include: a specialized bail unit; expanded nonincarcerative options for women; the reclassification of offenses such as prostitution and the possession of small amounts of marijuana; supervised home release for women who have a history of being physically or sexually abused and who were imprisoned for violent behavior; and increased drug and alcohol counseling and treatment services.

Numerous policy and program initiatives to reduce correctional crowding were undertaken in Connecticut in the 1980s, yet little changed for women offenders in the state. State policy makers supported the renovation and expansion of antiquated prison facilities through new construction or the use of modular units. The Governor's Task Force on Jail and Prison Overcrowding constantly referred to the need for additional halfway houses (1981–1989). Yet, while the state's halfway house capacity expanded during this time, only six of the additional beds were made available for women.

In Illinois, the Dwight Correctional Center, the state's only women's prison, has been overcrowded throughout the 1980s, despite the 1988 transfer of seventy-two women to a men's facility, where women now comprise 9 percent of the total population. Women transferred to the men's facility report that they have lost time for good behavior that would have been considered a minor rule violation when they were incarcerated at Dwight. They have also had difficulty continuing vocational programs begun at Dwight, and have been frustrated by excess unscheduled and unstructured free time. One consequence of the inadequately planned mixing of male and female correctional populations, however, was that twelve pregnancies occurred within ten months of the transfer.

The Citizens' Assembly, a bipartisan legislative agency, supported a study of the feasibility of sentencing program alternatives for women offenders (Citizens' Council on Women 1987 and 1988). They found that over 80 percent of incarcerated women in the state are mothers and that 82.7 percent of them are single-parent heads-of-household. Most of the women at Dwight are from Chicago, eighty miles away, and transportation services between the two places is inadequate. Forty-three percent of the women housed at Dwight are classified as minimum-security.

In this context, the Citizens' Assembly's Citizens' Council on Women concluded the following: the forced separation of women prisoners from their children causes long-lasting and severe psychological harm; county jails and work-release programs now being used to alleviate prison crowding merely complicate the parent-child reunification process; and community-based alternative sentencing programs are cost-effective and result in less recidivism than imprisonment.

Why Fewer Women Should Be Imprisoned

Many men are needlessly incarcerated, but women's imprisonment stands in stark contrast to most widely accepted reasons for incarcerating anyone. State and national groups that have studied women's imprisonment agree that female offenders overwhelmingly commit crimes that, while unacceptable, pose little threat to the physical safety of the community at large.[4]

---

[4]Several years ago, the Governor's Advocacy Council on Children and Youth in North Carolina observed that many corrections professionals agree that imprisonment is particularly counterproductive for nonviolent offenders. More recently, the American Correctional Association, in a policy statement approved by its membership, stated that few female offenders are a public-safety risk. [American Correctional Association, *Public Policy for Corrections: A Handbook for Decision-Makers* (College Park, Md.: ACA, 1986); and Milgram, Ruky B., *Women, Families and Prison* (Raleigh, N.C.: Governor's Advocacy Council on Children and Youth, 1981).]

A Wisconson study observed women for two years after their release from the women's prison at Taycheedah (Wagner 1986). Few of these women had those personal or criminal-history characteristics associated with a high risk of criminal behavior. They were found 44 percent less likely than male releasees to commit further criminal offenses, and they were one-third less likely to commit a serious, person-related offense if they did recidivate. In New York, another study found that women prisoners had a substantially lower rate of being returned to prison (16.9 percent) than male prisoners (37.3 percent) (McDermott 1985).

Most imprisoned women are mired in serious economic, medical, mental health, and social difficulties which are often overlooked and frequently intensified when women are incarcerated (Pollock-Byrne 1990 and Rafter 1990). Generally, prisons have failed to address women's specific needs, and they have failed to provide women with the same level of programs and services available to male prisoners.

Community-based programs are better suited to meet women offenders' diverse needs and these services are more effective than incapacitation in enabling women to lead law-abiding lives in the community (DeJesus and Gibney 1988 and McDonald 1986). In Pennsylvania, for example, the Program for Women Offenders found that its services reduce the recidivism of women who complete its program. In 1981, a random sampling of more than 1,000 clients found an extraordinarily low 3.2 percent rate of recidivism. In 1988, another random sample study found a rate of recidivism—17.7 percent—that was higher but nonetheless far below recidivism rates found in studies of other interventions with male offenders. The appendix to this chapter shows various programs throughout the nation that deal with female offenders.

Steps in the Deincarceration of Women

Recent public opinion polls show that Americans support rehabilitative and nonincarcerative sanctions for nonviolent offenders.[5] Against this backdrop, the deincarceration of large numbers of women prisoners should be an attainable goal. But is this fair? Is focusing so exclusively the need to deincarcerate women unfair to

---

[5]A new generation of public-opinion surveys first informs citizens about various aspects of the topic they are going to express their views on. These studies consistently find that public opinion is flexible and often more supportive of alternative sanctions than legislators and other policy makers believe. See Russ Immarigean, "Surveys Reveal Broad Support for Alternative Sentencing," *The National Prison Project Journal*, 9 (Fall 1986), and John Dable, *Crime and Punishment: The Public's View* (New York: The Public Agenda Foundation, 1987).

male inmates, many of whom could also benefit from community-based programs? There are two ways in which to respond to this question. First, as we have seen, women are especially appropriate for community-based programs, because they are disproportionately incarcerated for nonviolent offenses. Second, despite the fact that female prisoners are clearly the best candidates for alternatives to incarceration, few states faced with overcrowding in their facilities have focused directly on their women inmates. Hence, a specific focus on this neglected population is long overdue and may provide a model for deincarceration that could ultimately benefit male prisoners as well.

Having said this, halting the rush to build new women's prisons will not be easy. Many women's prisons are makeshift and over-crowded, and some are under court order to improve conditions. Those who favor alternatives to women's imprisonment must recognize that careful planning is now an essential ingredient in any systematic effort to reduce the female prison population. Female prisoners are no longer few in number, and, as a consequence, existing community-based resources (for example, drug-treatment programs) will need to be expanded to accommodate larger numbers of women. In addition, states and local communities must develop new nonincarcerative pretrial and sentencing options for women who are otherwise likely to receive a jail or prison term.

A screening process can identify offenders facing a strong likelihood of being imprisoned. Courts and community programs can use standard prison-risk instruments based on such variables as current charges, prior convictions, and length of time spent in jail awaiting trial to identify the women who are probably going to receive prison sentences. In New York, for example, one community-service program combines the use of a research-based profile of jail-bound offenders with the in-court assessments of project staff to identify possible clients (McDonald 1986). In North Carolina, alternative programs use a prison-risk score sheet, based on a cross-sectional study of sentenced felons in the state, to identify offenders who have a strong probability of being convicted and sentenced to an active prison term (Wallace and Clarke 1984).

Advocates—probation officers, community case planners, and others—can then prepare alternative sentencing that make use of community service, individual or group counseling, day-care provisions, educational opportunities, employment, restitution, and/or third-party supervision. Central to the success of these plans is an assessment of these women's needs, monitoring of their progress, and aftercare support services.

Most importantly, states need to reduce the number of imprisoned women as a matter of public policy. Delaware, for instance, is currently providing a good example of what a state might do to reduce its use of imprisonment for women offenders.

The Women's Correctional Institution in Claymont, Delaware has been overcrowded with both pretrial and sentenced women. The prison's capacity was 66 prisoners when it opened in 1975. This number was expanded to 90 several years later. Nonetheless the prison housed an average of 145 women during 1988. The women's prison population increased by 39 percent between 1986 and 1988.

In 1988, the National Center on Institutions and Alternatives (NCIA) developed a profile of women incarcerated in the state and made specific recommendations to reduce the number imprisoned (Hayes 1989 and Roche 1989). The use of empty work-release beds, creation of additional work-release beds, and immediate classification of all female prisoners serving sentences of less than one year could save fifty beds. Increased pretrial staff to supervise women in the community could save 15 beds. More residential drug-treatment space could save sixteen beds. And, a day-reporting program could save up to twenty-five more beds.

Conclusion

The growth in women's prison populations has been dramatic. To date, most correctional leaders have responded to this crisis by attempting to build their way out of it. There is another option. The money currently being allocated to build and house women in cells could instead be diverted to support alternatives to women's incarceration. Overcrowding and overuse of women's prisons can be avoided by planning creatively for reduced reliance on imprisonment for women offenders. Practitioners working with women offenders advance several recommendations which should guide such an approach, including:

- Criminal sanctions for women should be based on the least restrictive alternative consistent with public safety. Women offenders recidivate at a much lower rate than men. Studies indicate that women are more likely to recidivate when support services are lacking in the community. Women can be safely diverted or released from confinement when these services are made available.

- Criminal sanctions should directly address social and economic problems faced by women offenders. Intermediate sanctions such as home confinement and intensive supervision can be useful if they provide direct services to women in need. They are less likely to be successful, however, if they are used primarily as a means of discipline or surveillance. Boot camps and electronic moniotoring, for instance, may not be as constructive for women as other forms of intervention.

- Community resources should be better coordinated and used more routinely in fashioning sanctions for women offenders. While programs that can successfully divert women from dysfunctional behavior often can be established more easily within the community, women frequently must go from agency to agency to have their needs addressed. This can be counterproductive for women trying to rebuild their lives. Recognizing how disruptive this can be, several years ago, the New Jersey Association on Corrections initiated a regular series of meetings for local service providers so that they could coordinate their efforts to help women being released from jail or prison. In many cases, too, programs that can successfully divert women from dysfunctional behavior can be more easily established within the community.

- Jurisdictions need to identify women who will likely be imprisoned so community resources can be marshalled to address their needs. Few jurisdictions use formal methods to target this population.

- Criminal justice officials need to learn more about the characteristics of women who are on probation or parole as well as those who are imprisoned. Are women with similar characteristics treated differently? Are probation and parole agencies doing all they can to divert women from incarceration? Are the services of these agencies specific enough for the different types of interventions women need to lead law-abiding lives?

The dramatic increases in women's imprisonment seen in the last decade are likely to continue unless meaningful alternative programs are used more widely in place of confinement. Although they have grown significantly in recent years, the populations of women's prisons are still sufficiently small that a well-planned and coordinated effort is likely to show meaningful results. In the process, we may also learn more about how to develop cost-effective and humane methods of reducing our reliance on imprisoning men.

REFERENCES

American Correctional Association, *The Female Offender: What Does the Future Hold?* Washington, D.C.: St. Mary's Press, 1990.

Austin, James, and Aaron McVey, *The 1989 Prison Population Forecast: The Impact of the War on Drugs*, San Francisco: NCCD, December 1989.

Avallone, Anthony V., and Richard D. Talisano, *Task Force on Women, Chil-*

dren, and the Criminal Justice System: Executive Summary/Final Report and Recommendations. Hartford: The Permanent Commission on the Status of Women, 1989.

Cahalan, Margaret Werner, *Historical Statistics in the United States*, 1950–1984, (Washington, D.C.: Bureau of Justice Statistics, U.S. Department of Justice, 1986).

Census of Local Jails. Washington, D.C.: Bureau of Justice Statistics, 1990, p. 3.

Chapman, Jane Roberts, *Economic Realities and the Female Offender.* Lexington, Mass.: D. C. Heath, 1980.

Chesney-Lind, Meda, "Women's Prison Reform in Hawaii: Trouble in Paradise," *Jericho*, 43 (Spring 1987), 6–7.

Citizens' Council on Women, *Annual Report 1986* and *Annual Report 1987*. Springfield, Ill.: Citizens' Assembly, 1987 and 1988.

DeConstanzo, Elaine J., and Helen Scholes, "Women Behind Bars: Their Numbers Increase," *Corrections Today*, 50, no. 3 (June 1988), 104–108.

DeJesus, Alma, and William D. Gibney, *The Case for Expanding Work Release for Women* (New York: Prisoners Legal Services of New York, 1988).

Fenster, C., "Differential Dispositions: A Preliminary Study of Male-Female Partners in Crime." Unpublished paper presented to the annual meetings of the American Society of Criminology, 1977.

Gilfus, Mary E., *Seasoned by Violence/Tempered by Law: A Qualitative Study of Women and Crime.* Dissertation presented to the Faculty of the Florence Heller School for Advanced Studies in Social Welfare at Brandeis University, 1988.

Hayes, Lindsay M., and others, *The Female Offender in Delaware: Population Analysis and Assessment.* Alexandria, Va.: National Center on Institutions and Alternatives, 1989.

Herr, Kathleen, and others, *Services for Women Offenders in Massachusetts: A Report of the Advisory Group on Female Offenders.* Boston: Executive Office of Human Services, 1988.

Lindsey, Karen, "When Battered Women Strike Back: Murder or Self Defense?" *Viva*, September 1978, pp. 58–59, 66, 74.

McDermott, M. Joan, *Female Offenders in New York State.* Albany, N.Y.: New York State Division of Criminal Justice Services, 1985.

McDonald, Douglas Corry, *Punishment Without Walls: Community Service Sentences in New York City.* New Brunswick, N.J.: Rutgers University Press, 1986.

Miller, Marsha L., "Perceptions of Available and Needed Programs by Female Offenders in Delaware. Delaware Council on Crime and Justice, 1990.

Pollock-Byrne, Joycelyn, *Women, Prison, and Crime.* Pacific Grove, Calif.: Brooks/Cole, 1990.

Prison and Jail Crowding Commission, *Prison and Jail Overcrowding, A Report to the Governor and Legislature.* Hartford: Office of Policy and Management (Annual Reports), 1981–1989.

Prisoners in 1990. Washington, D.C.: Bureau of Justice Statistics, 1991.

Prisoners in 1989. Washington, D.C.: Bureau of Justice Statistics, 1990.

Profile of State Prison Inmates, 1986. Washington, D.C.: Bureau of Justice Statistics, 1988.

Rafter, Nicole Hahn, *Partial Justice: Women, Prisons and Social Control.* New Brunswick, N.J.: Transaction Books, 1990, p. 181–182.

Roche, Timothy J., *Addendum to NCIA's Report on the Female Offender in Delaware.* Alexandria, Va.: National Center on Institutions and Alternatives, 1989.

Uniform Crime Reports, Washington, D.C.: Federal Bureau of Investigation, June 1990, pp. 177, 179.

Uniform Crime Reports, Washington, D.C.: Federal Bureau of Investigation, June 1989, p. 175.

"U.S. Leads World in Imprisonment," *New York Times,* January 7, 1991, p. 1.

Wagner, Dennis, "Women in Prison: How Much Community Risk?" Madison, Wis.: Wisconsin Department of Health and Social Services, 1986.

Wallace, LeAnn W., and Stevens H. Clarke, *The Institute of Government's Prison Risk Scoresheet: A User's Manual.* Chapel Hill, N.C.: The University of North Carolina at Chapel Hill, 1984.

Ward, David, and others, "Crimes of Violence by Women." In Donald J. Mulvihil and others (eds.), *Crimes of Violence,* vol. 13, a Staff Report to the National Commission on the Causes and Prevention of Violence. Washington, D.C.: U.S. Government Printing Office, 1968.

Women in Crime: The Sentencing of Female Defendants, Sacramento: California Department of Justice, Bureau of Criminal Statistics, 1988.

APPENDIX

Exhibit A

Programs that Reduce Women's Imprisonment

In recent years, a variety of private, non-profit agencies have started community-based programs that are alternatives to incarceration for women offenders. Services offered by these programs uniformly address basic social, economic, and health problems associated with female criminality. Some successful programs include:

> **The Program for Female Offenders,** the country's oldest multiservice centers working with women offenders, started in Pittsburgh in 1974 and has now expanded to Allentown, Harrisburg, and Philadelphia, Pennsylvania. It stresses job-readiness and placement services and has

developed antishoplifting, child-care, parenting, and child-abuse-prevention programs. The program operates three work-release centers. Ms. Charlotte S. Arnold, Executive Director, The Program for Female Offenders, 1520 Penn Avenue, Pittsburgh, PA 15222; (412) 642-7380.

Community Services for Women, managed by Social Justice for Women in Boston, Massachusetts, prepares alternative sentencing plans for women convicted of misdemeanor and felony offenses. Alternative sentencing plans address addiction, employment, family, and health problems. Plans consist of community service or restitution matched with the offenders' specific skills and special support services to meet their needs. The program monitors these plans and reports on each offender's progress. Ms. Betsey Smith, Executive Director, Social Justice for Women, 108 Lincoln Street, 6th Floor, Boston, MA 02111; (617) 482-0747.

The Neil J. Houston House, also operated by Social Justice for Women, is a residential treatment program for pregnant women. Pregnant prisoners are released early from prison to finish their sentences while receiving substance-abuse treatment and perinatal infant care. Women in the program attend parenting classes and family-support groups that address underlying health problems such as malnutrition and HIV infection. They also receive early intervention services for newly born babies for thirty-six months after birth and a resettlement program helps program graduates with mandatory well-baby checkups, detoxification screening, and additional counseling. Ruth Smith, Program Director, Neil J. Houston House, 9 Notre Dame Street, Roxbury, MA 02119; (617) 445-3066.

The Elizabeth Fry Center, located near Golden Gate Park in San Francisco, is one of five residential centers in the state for low-risk women prisoners who have children under six years of age. In the mid-1980s, the state legislature authorized an early-release program whereby the California Department of Corrections contracts with public or private agencies for community correctional centers that accept inmate mothers. These centers offer shelter, meals, child care, job workshops, parenting classes, money-management training, employment workshops, substance-abuse counseling, recreational opportunities, and religious programs. The Rev. Deborah Haffner, Executive Director, The Elizabeth Fry Center, 1251 Second Avenue, San Francisco, CA 94122; (415) 681-0430.

Our New Beginnings, conceived by seven female prisoners serving time in Oregon's Women's Correctional Center in 1980, provides a broad array of transitional services to female offenders. Today, ex-offenders as well as trained social workers provide emergency housing, mental-health counseling, job placement, literacy tutoring, self-esteem building, acupuncture, anger counseling, and other services. Women in the program assess their own needs with help from case managers. A Moms and Addicted Babies Program gives residential support for women breaking away from drug abuse. Ms. Carole Pope, Executive Director,

Our New Beginnings, Inc., 1814 N.W. Hoyt, Portland, OR 97209; (503) 222-3733.

Summit House, in Greensboro, North Carolina, is an alternative to prison for prisoners who are pregnant or have children under seven years of age. The program offers nonviolent misdemeanor and felony offenders direct services that include individual and group counseling, financial management and employment training, and workships on parenting and women's health issues. Women at Summit House gradually move through a program of decreasing restrictiveness and increasing privileges to gain work-release opportunities. Money earned from this option is used for spending money and to pay for victim restitution and program costs. Ms. Marilyn R. Mink, Executive Director, Summit House, 608 Summit Avenue, Suite 103, Greensboro, NC 27405; (919) 275-9366.

The Helen B. Ratcliff House, in Seattle, Washington is a transitional program for female felons released on work release from the state prison system. The program's priority is to gain employment for each offender. A cottage-industry program is available for women who have not yet obtained outside employment. The program addresses past physical and sexual abuse, dependent and abusive relationships, and mother-child reunification issues and offers self-esteem and empowerment classes. Ms. Diane DeLapp, Director, The Helen B. Ratcliff House, Pioneer Human Services, 1531 13th Avenue South, Seattle, WA 98144; (206) 587-4806.

The Women at Risk Program, developed by a citizen's reform group located in Asheville, North Carolina, is a treatment program for victims of physical or sexual abuse who have been charged with or convicted of criminal charges. Fifteen-member groups meet in four twelve-week treatment cycles, during which participants are taught parenting skills and problem-solving techniques that do not rely on violence or other self-destructive behavior. An outreach worker helps women stay in treatment for the full program. The worker meets with women before the program starts, when they miss meetings, and as other emergencies arise. Ms. Ellen Clarke-Sayer, Executive Director, Women at Risk Program, Western Carolinians for Criminal Justice, P.O. Box 7472, Asheville, NC 28807; (704) 252-2485.

Genesis II for Women, in Minneapolis, Minnesota, assists women in conflict with the law to develop self-sufficient and law-abiding behavior. Women and their children attend day treatment including individual and group therapy, independent living skills, adult education, sex-offender treatment, and parenting education. Children are cared for in an on-site licensed day-care center. Ms. Janet Johnson, Executive Director, Genesis II for Women, Inc., 3036 University Avenue, S.E., Minneapolis, MN 55414; (612) 348-2762.

15

Tenuous Connections: The Significance of Telephone Communication between Prisoners and Their Wives

Laura T. Fishman

This chapter examines how wives' continuing relationships with their incarcerated husbands are shaped by prison policies concerning telephone calls. A combination of data sources are used to construct an ethnographic account of the experiences of thirty women married to men incarcerated in two prisons. Findings show that within the constraints of telephone calls, relationships can be strengthened or undermined as prisoners and their wives attempt to resume remnants of their preprison marital ties and participate in household decisions. Difficulties of separations were, for the most part, eased by frequent telephone contacts. Telephone conversations also can lead to attempts made by husbands to place restrictions on their wives and to retain their dominance and authority. Long-distance telephone calls can further strain wives' limited financial resources. It is concluded that certain prison policies believed functional for the prison treatment programs can have dysfunctional consequences for prisoner-wife interaction.

Imprisonment usually interrupts, rather than ends, the relationship between a prisoner and his wife. Although such an interruption is critically important, the partners are usually not cut off from one another as much as is commonly supposed. To the extent that prison

The original version of this chapter appeared under the title, *Women at the Wall: A Study of Prisoners' Wives Doing Time on the Outside*, by Laura T. Fishman (State University of New York Press, 1990). This material appeared in condensed form in the *International Journal of Offender Therapy and Comparative Criminology*, 32, no. 1 (April 1988), pp. 55–60.

systems permit inmates access to the telephone, incarcerated husbands continue to participate in their households and to influence the ways in which their wives structure their lives and organize their homes.

This chapter examines the extent of incarcerated husbands' influence, as perceived by their wives and elucidates some ways in which the prison system affects both the everyday lives of such women and the quality of their relationships with their incarcerated partners. To do this, the nature of telephone visits from the perspective of prisoners' wives is examined by analyzing their account of how through phone calls couples preserve their commitments to one another and maintain a thread of continuity through the most traumatic and disruptive episode of their lives. Attention is given to how telephone contacts affect the quality of marital relationships as well as the quality of life of these prisoners' wives.

The traditional concept of prison is that of a "closed system" or what Goffman (1961) terms a "total institution." Closed prison systems are those with policies and practices that, in effect, sever most ties between prisoners and their families, friends, and communities. The thick walls that surround such prisons are thought not only to keep prisoners in, but to keep the rest of the world out. In recent years, however, prisons have begun to allow, and often to encourage, contacts with the outside world. This trend has arisen in part from the finding that prisoners with strong family or community ties are less likely to return to prison (for example, Adams and Fischer 1976; Holt and Miller 1972; and Homer 1979) and from the observation that inmates with family ties are more tractable. Thus, many prisons have introduced family programs that allow prisoners greater communication with their families and friends through visitation, letters, and telephone and home visits (Dickinson 1984, Schafer 1978).[1] Accordingly, such reports have begun to break down the monolithic image of prisons as "total" institutions and to document the effects of such contacts on prisoners' adjustment to prison and parole.

Since in-prison visitation has traditionally been the major form of contact between prisoners and their wives, it has received the most attention. For instance, it has been observed that in-prison visitation can encourage couples to revert to patterns of communication reminiscent of courtship and thereby reaffirm marital ties (Holt and Miller 1972; and Schwartz and Weintraub 1974). Several investigators (Burstein 1977; Fishman 1988; and Koenig and Gariepy 1985)

---

[1]Survey data indicate that prison visiting opportunities in general have expanded in the last two decades: the number of prisons permitting prisoners more than four visits per month as well as lengthened time for each visit has increased (Dickinson 1984, and Schafer 1978).

have explored the topics of conversation in which prisoners and their wives engage and report that a frequent topic is concern about the future, including hopes, dreams, and aspirations. Such conversations provide relief from daily stress for both partners. Several writers have noted that prisoner-wife contacts can undermine, rather than strengthen, marital relations (Fishman 1988; Freedman and Rice 1977; and Holt and Miller 1972), and that the inherent limitations of allowed forms of communication may negatively effect the course of a marital relationship during the period of incarceration.

A small but growing literature has begun to examine the impact of imprisonment, as perceived by the wives, on their marital relationships. One pervasive finding is that many wives believe their husbands' punishments have been imposed on the family (Morris 1965, Schneller 1978, and Swan 1981). Swan (1981) suggest that the form and extent of this perceived punishment is closely related to the kinds of hardships the wives experience during involuntary separation. such hardships typically include financial deprivation, sexual-emotional effects (for example, loneliness and depression), and child-care or discipline problems.[2]

Much of the literature to date assumes that prisoners' wives experience the effects of involuntary separation in complete isolation from their husbands, with the exception of occasional in-prison visits. However, it is clear that ongoing communication between husbands and wives colors the daily lives of those both inside and outside the prison walls, affecting the quality of marital relationships, as well as the texture of social and domestic life. Thus, a thorough understanding of wives' adjustments to their partners' incarceration requires consideration of the nature of their continuing contacts. The major hardships perceived by these women to have resulted from their husbands' incarcerations are explored in depth and the effects of interactions on the structure and quality of domestic life are discussed.

The present chapter, based on extensive interviews with prisoners' wives, examines the nature and content of prisoner-wife interactions through telephone contact.

Methodology

The research reported here is based on a case-history approach, focusing on prisoners' wives' experiences with enforced separation. It is based on material gathered from thirty Vermont women (1) who

---

[2]Similar kinds of difficulties have been reported by the following research studies: Daniel and Barrett (1981); Koenig and Gariepy (1985); Morris (1965); and Schneller (1978).

were legally married to or had lived in common-law arrangements with their men for at least six months prior to arrest, and (2) whose husbands had served at least six months in either of two Vermont correctional facilities (Londonderry Correctional Facility, a traditional medium-security prison, and Newport Community Correctional Facility, a community-based prison). All records of both facilities were reviewed in order to define a population of "married" (legally or common-law) men currently incarcerated. Sixty-nine men who were "married" at the time of conviction and sentencing were identified. All sixty-nine were interviewed; sixty-five agreed to participate in the study and provided the names and addresses of their wives. Fifty of these sixty-five wives were contacted by telephone (fourteen could not be located) and, of these, thirty agreed to participate in the study.

The final study population consisted of thirty white women who agreed to be interviewed. While four lived in more rural areas, twenty-six resided in urban or suburban areas. The majority appeared to be working class and lower class in socioeconomic status; five were classified as middle class since they had at least some college education and/or held white-collar jobs and pursued a middle-class round of activities. The wives' spouses were generally serving short sentences (on average, between six months and two years),[3] primarily for alcohol-related property crimes. Few men had been convicted of crimes of violence, possession of heroin, or other more serious offenses.[4]

In-depth interviews were administered to these women, a minimum of two times over a twenty-four-month period.[5] The interviews ranged in length from three hours to ten hours and sought to elicit wives' perceptions and assessments of their experiences with the crisis of enforced separation.[6] In addition to these interviews, data

---

[3]According to the wives, fifteen men were to serve two years or less, six men were to serve three years, and eight were to serve four years or more.

[4]Many men had been charged with more than one offense. Nineteen women said that their men had been arrested for such crimes against property as concealment and/or receiving stolen property or breaking and entering. Eleven named such crimes against a person as aggravated and simple assault, armed robbery, and kidnapping. Five reported charges of forgery and counterfeiting. Three women said that their men had been charged with sexual offenses such as attempted rape and lewd and lascivious conduct. Four said their husbands had been arrested for escaping from prison. Only two wives reported that their husbands had been charged with sale or possession of drugs.

[5]There was considerable variation in the number of sessions. Thirteen women were interviewed from three to seven times; twelve wives were interviewed twice, and five only once. Three factors determine the frequency and duration of interviews: the willingness of wives to share information, their proximity to the research base, and whether or not they were hospitalized during the research period.

[6]Most interviews were conducted in wives' homes. During each interview, notes could be taken without apparently disturbing the wives. Since a voice print can be a

sources include prison records, summaries of meetings with small groups of wives, and notes on telephone conversations with the wives.

The study process was guided by the principles of grounded theory articulated by Glaser and Straus (1967) and elaborated by Charmaz (1983). The analysis to follow was generated directly from the data gathered from the interviews and the other sources of data.

Employment, Unemployment, and Struggles with Poverty

Most of the women in the study population married men with whom they shared some elements of personal history. These common elements made it easier for wives to accept the notion that they ought to continue to maintain ties with their spouses, rather than sever them and to continue to sustain their marital ties in the face of persistent poverty.

Most women and men came from families which shared a common struggle with poverty. These women reported that they and their husbands came from families in which periods of employment alternated with extended periods of unemployment and/or receipt of public assistance. Nine women did not report such difficulties while they were being raised; this was true of only seven men. All of their families were relatively stable; the work ethic and their roots in the community were highly valued.

Upon marriage, poverty was the norm for the majority of the couples. Even when the men were working, twenty-two wives reported that they could not supply basic family needs out of the money available to them. Only four wives described their economic situation as "comfortable."

What was most worrisome for most women was their husbands' unemployed status. According to the wives, eighteen men were unemployed prior to their imprisonment; nine men were employed.[7] Of these, six worked as unskilled, semiskilled, or industrial and service workers. The majority of jobs were seasonal. Only three women were married to men employed in white-collar occupations that provided their families with a "comfortable" income. Three men were getting money by stealing or drug dealing.

---

valid source of identification, a tape recorder was not used. The decision to hand-record was based on the assessment that the wives were likely to be more candid than if a tape recorder was used.

[7]Researchers have uniformly been struck by the high number of unemployed married prisoners. A disproportionate number of married prisoners in penal institutions of the United States are recruited from the unemployed. The findings reported here are no exception to earlier research: for example, see Blackwell 1959; Morris 1965; Swan 1981.

Not all the women, however, attempted to rely on their husbands' incomes. Nine women worked outside the home. Three women worked as waitresses or kitchen workers in hospitals. One woman did semiskilled factory work. Five kept jobs as clerks, administrative assistants, and so on. Two women attended college. Either at their husbands' insistence and/or their own personal preference, the remaining wives were homemakers. Most of these women received some form of public assistance to supplement their husbands' earnings; in some cases they were entirely dependent on it.[8]

For most wives, the imprisonment of their husbands meant a continuation of poverty with some kind of governmental assistance or income from low-paying jobs. The everyday lives of the women, whether they were working or at home, centered around absent husbands, household concerns, and children.

General Problems of Separation

In many respects, the experiences these prisoners' wives encountered during involuntary separation parallel those of single mothers who live at the edge of subsistence. Prisoners' wives share many experiences with women whose husbands are absent due to separation, desertion, divorce, and so forth.[9] The women interviewed also recounted numerous problems centered around finances, loneliness, anxiety and stress, and child management. An additional difficulty mentioned by these wives, but scarcely noted in previous reports, was that of "waiting" or psychological adjustment to the prospective duration of their husbands' incarceration and absence. Rather than feeling "liberated," they were emotionally and socially isolated, as well as overloaded with demands on their time and energy.

Loneliness and Deprivation

Twenty-five prisoners' wives mentioned deprivation of their husbands, and the attendant loneliness, as an important hardship they experienced. They missed their husbands as companions, fathers, bill payers or income providers, and as handymen around their homes.

---

[8]Some wives did not report the fact that their husbands were employed so that they could combine public assistance with income from their husbands' jobs. This is illegal. Women were willing to risk detection, since there was no way they could depend on their husbands' incomes.

[9]For an extensive discussion of the kinds of hardships divorced wives experience, see Arendell (1986); Wallerstein and Kelly (1980); and Weiss (1979). Some research also has documented the problems encountered by military wives when temporarily separated from their husbands; refer to Macintosh (1968); McCubbin and Dahl (1976); McCubbin and others (1980); and Montalvo (1976).

This form of felt deprivation primarily stems from their husbands' physical absence, rather than from their criminal behavior or convictions and could result from any type of involuntary separation.[10] Loneliness and disorientation were often compounded with sexual frustration resulting from their husbands' prolonged confinement. Two wives, determined to remain faithful to their husbands, talked about how they dealt with sexual deprivation:

> The time is getting closer to his release. But where is my sex life? I do know that I must have done it once because I have Lilly to show for it. I feel that the first few months is when you feel the horniest. Then you get used to it.

> When Rudi comes home, that's when he loses weight. I just wear him out. But when the men are in, the women just try to shut off their sexual feelings. You can use Rosemary and her five sisters— that means masturbating.

Waiting

Twenty-six women reported that, after their husbands' imprisonment, their most difficult problem was that of coming to terms with the lengths of their husbands' sentences. A recurrent theme that emerges from wives' accounts is that they felt as though they, themselves, were "doing time." They would not be able to resume active, meaningful roles as wives until their husbands returned. What made waiting particularly difficult was the suspension of their identities as wives. In many cases, they were estranged from their families and sometimes avoided or were shunned by neighbors. It is not surprising, then, that these wives often felt themselves to be living "one day at a time." They frequently remarked that they, themselves, were imprisoned, particularly by their homes and suffered from isolation, lack of stimulation, continuous pressure from others, boredom and monotony. As one wife said:

> When the men are in jail, you only have yourself to lean on. When you have kids, you have to worry about them alone. It's like a prison. You can't say that you're fed up and that you won't worry and you can't walk out. In jail you don't have to worry about anything. They tell you what to do every minute. Outside it's

---

[10]Here is at least one important difference between the effects of enforced separation on prisoners' wives and those reported in studies of wartime separation or service couples. In the social environments in which prisoners' wives lived in Vermont, they were often the only wives in their particular predicament. In wartime or on military bases, a number of women in the wives' immediate circles shared the same situation.

harder because I have to do it. I'd wake up and I didn't want to clean the house but I had to clean because I didn't want it to be dirty. If you have a dirty house, then you don't respect yourself. When Spike was in jail, I was in jail in my own home. I could go as I wanted but I had to come back all the time.

Child Care and Discipline

Child-management problems can be viewed within the larger context of problems experienced by single mothers. Of the twenty-one wives with children, seventeen reported having full responsibility for raising their children. An important source of problems for wives was the restrictions placed on their freedom as a result of having sole care of their children. Nine wives reported that their tolerance was reduced. When their energies were absorbed by their own concerns or daily tasks, children's demands seemed to drain already reduced reserves. They often reacted by yelling at, shoving, shaking, or slapping their children. When stress became overwhelming, children became targets of wives' anger and frustration. One mother of two preschool children described her experiences:

> I yelled at the kids, hit them too much and I felt like killing them. One time, instead of killing them, I broke a popcorn bag and threw it all over the house. Instead of killing them, I threw pictures of them all over and broke the pictures. While I threw these pictures all over, they never moved an inch. After that, Randy called and I was crying. That was all I could do on the phone. He kept asking me if I can handle them. I said that I wanted to go somewhere and do something besides be with them. I just wanted them to stop doing disastrous things.

Whether or not prisoners' wives worked outside their homes, sixteen women with children complained about the task overload. Unrelieved responsibilities can be especially depleting if there is no one to attend to the wives' needs; that is, no one with whom to talk, share household responsibilities, and so on, and many wives reported that this often led them to despair.

Finances

Twenty wives experienced extreme financial pressures. Even when finances had not been a major concern before their husbands' imprisonment, it became one later.[11] Women whose husbands had been

---

[11]For a discussion of the financial burdens placed upon wives during their husbands' imprisonment, see Bakker and others (1978); Daniel and Barrett (1981); Koenig and Gariepy (1985); Morris (1965); Schneller (1978); and Swan (1981).

steadily employed indicated that the problems arising from loss of income far outweighed any benefits from increased control:

> I chain smoke now. That's new since October. I have been eating badly and sleeping badly. I feel there's no time to do anything but exist. I have to find out if I'm eligible for Medicaid and food stamps. I have to make out on a very small amount of money and I keep saying to myself there's no way I can do it. I have to find a way to make extra money. I know I can make $200 a month extra. I don't want to work nights and do this to Sara. His parents will help me. It's hard to say to them that I need $200 a month for three months. But I'm going to have to. It's easier for me to ask them for a hug and some support, but not for money.

These women reported that they were "just scraping by," living at or below the poverty level. The majority collected welfare before their husbands' imprisonment. One new source of financial strain, however, was that before imprisonment they had been accustomed to having their husbands provide some cash for "extras." After imprisonment, these extras were no longer affordable.

Four wives who received welfare claimed that their financial situation had improved. These women increased their incomes by combining a number of sources, including part-time work, welfare assistance, help from relatives, and rent from boarders. A few wives also reported that they acquired additional income from occasional participation in such illegal activities as shoplifting, passing "bad" checks, welfare fraud, and drug distribution. While these income packages were better, in some sense, than those they had before their husbands were imprisoned, they were frequently still insufficient.

Only six women reported that the family income had not changed significantly as a result of the enforced separation. In most of these families, the husband had not held a regular job, while the wife was gainfully employed and had been the primary breadwinner before enforced separation. After their husbands' incarceration, these women continued working and providing for their families. A few women reported that, since their husbands were unemployed prior to imprisonment, they qualified for welfare assistance and continued receiving their welfare grants after their husbands' imprisonment.

In addition to the financial adjustments wives make with a reduced income, imprisonment of their husbands usually carries some additional economic implications for the wives. According to the wives, any money their incarcerated husbands earn is minimal— usually just enough to cover some of their personal incidentals. And so the financial burden of supplying prisoners with approved material goods often falls on the limited financial resources of wives. For most of the wives, monetary problems existed without dealing with husbands' needs as a source of added worry. The additional costs attached to the maintenance of contacts with their husbands contributed to the economic hardships borne by the wives. Long-distance telephone contacts between couples could become expensive for many wives.

A common response to the harsh economic conditions prisoners' wives face was expressions of anger and resentment. Many wives reported that they sometimes experienced anger and resentment when they believed that their men's lives in prison were better than theirs on the outside. Looked at from the outside, the prison system sometimes seemed preferable to being overloaded with stresses and strains. These wives came to believe that their men were both well cared for and free from responsibility:

> He's up there and he gets three good meals a day. He's eating food like steak and roast beef and I'm eating hot dogs and hamburgers. What worries does he have up there? I used to tell him that I would like to trade places with him. I'll go up there for five days and he comes here and he would have all the burdens. And I'd have a much needed rest. He can pinch the pennies and worry about the kids and wonder if the bills are being paid. Those guys have the best of everything. They have their own rooms, color TV and wall-to-wall carpets. I get very hostile. I don't have these things. Let me take a vacation. . . . Then I hear their gripes. But none of the men have any worries. They don't have to face the bill collectors, wonder where the food is coming from, go to the hospital and really face the responsibilities of their families.

In many cases, these wives reached the conclusion that prison was a more positive experience than it is. When their husbands participated in prison programs—such as group counseling, education, Bible study, and arts and crafts—their anger and resentment intensified. These contrasted markedly with what they perceived to be a dearth of services upon which they could draw.

Marital Relationships on the Outside

In order to adjust successfully to the physical absence of their husbands, wives of prisoners must be willing to assume many of their husbands' former responsibilities. They must often also maintain their husbands' sense of a place in the family circle through correspondence, telephone calls, and visiting. According to wives' accounts, the Vermont correctional system does not conform to the conventional notion of a prison as a "closed system." All Vermont prisons make at least minimal arrangements for visitation, correspondence and telephone conversations between prisoners and their families. Arrangements vary, but some facilities allow extensive contacts with the outside and promote prisoners' interactions with families. All inmates have access to public pay phones for receiving unlimited calls at specified times of the day. Calls are rarely monitored, but, when they are, prisoners are informed in advance.

Telephone contacts were frequent when husbands were incarcerated in facilities close to their homes. Nineteen women reported that they spoke with their husbands at least once per week and sometimes three or more times per day. Women whose husbands were incarcerated far from home reported unpredictable and infrequent telephone contact. Long-distance calls were generally not maintained on a daily, or even biweekly, basis.

Use of Telephone and Marital Relationships

In general, marital ties were reinforced and reaffirmed through telephone conversations, even among those couples who had relatively fewer telephone contacts. Although conversations included such topics as child-care and discipline matters and prison life in general, wives reported telephone calls were used primarily to communicate about intimate matters—emotions and sex—that are difficult to put into writing.

Telephone conversations therefore helped couples to gain or rekindle elements of their relationships. Also, through their conversations spouses restated their plans for the future, provided information about their lives and shared their concerns about their children and homes. One wife recalled that her telephone calls with her husband were about:

> Oh, stupid things: how much we missed each other, how lonely we were. We pulled each other's hearts out! We'd listen to each other breathe. It was sort of a continuation of the talk during the visit: what the kids were doing; what did he do that day; how we both were trying to change. It was the same old shit constantly.

On the telephone, men made promises similar to those they had made before marriage, assuring their wives that they were ready to settle down. All of these men promised to become steadily and gainfully employed, to provide a satisfying standard of living, and to stay out of trouble. Most of the women believed that the exchange of intimacies and promises enabled them to sustain their commitments to their husbands and marriages.

Through communicating with their husbands, "waiting" became worthwhile for many wives and most came to believe that marital ties had been strengthened by it—a belief probably arising from their husbands' renewed interest in family well-being and plans for a conventional life. In effect, use of the telephone allowed wives to place their men in the role of understanding-but-distant observers in their lives. This helped them to sustain their beliefs that their relationships were worthwhile and that their husbands were worth waiting for. Regardless of the type of prison, none of the wives reported having sufficient opportunity to interact with her husband in a realistic way. This meant that wives had to form judgments about the likelihood that their spouses were prepared for conventional life after release on the basis of very little—and often distorted—information.

In most instances, wives reported that telephone calls were like visits; they were planned for, looked forward to during the day, and thought about after they were over. These conversations, therefore, created a diversion from wives' domestic and work-related chores and the tedium of prisoners' lives inside.

It is also clear from wives' reports that telephone communication enabled the men to retain remnants of their former roles as husbands and fathers. In exile, they could continue to shape their children's lives. As one wife related, husbands could continually remind their wives of their presence within their households:

> The phone calls help. He wakes me in the morning. He is the first person I talk to in the morning and the last person I talk to at night.

Fourteen of the nineteen wives who had regular telephone contact with their husbands said that their husbands used these opportunities to maintain some aspect of their positions as heads of the household. For instance, some demanded that their wives stay more or less confined to their homes, thereby demonstrating love, loyalty, and faithfulness. Working-class men were most likely to want their wives at home minding the children; they also frequently demanded that their wives have minimal interaction with friends and relatives and report, by telephone, the minute details of their lives. If these wives left the house for any reason, accusations of infidelity and arguments would invariably follow. To ensure that their wives stayed at home, some husbands called as frequently as possible to check up on them. One woman described how her husband controlled her life:

> He was very bossy. I couldn't go to the movies or to concerts. When I would get my welfare checks, I had to go somewhere to cash the checks and pay bills. I had to do this. He more or less had to know where I was. When I went to my mother's house, I called to tell him where I was. Whenever he called, I was usually here. If I went shopping and took longer than I thought, I'd call to tell him where I was. This way, there would be no arguments that I was away longer than I was supposed to be. I have had him yell at me for not being there when he called. . . .

He was worried about what I was doing. He asked what I did and at times he didn't believe it. He wasn't in the house and he didn't know. It was kinda hard to reassure him. It was hard because he'd say, "I'm here and you're not here with me."

Most wives were aware that they were their husbands' major contacts with the outside world. They also were mindful of their husbands' fears about the possibilities for illicit sexual affairs or commitments to other men. Some husbands became suspicious of social activities that might provide wives with opportunities to meet other men. For instance, one wife recounted how she had to check in by telephone with her husband after attending a dance:

He won't let me go to dances. I can't even go with his sister or the guy who lives upstairs with his girlfriend. Once I did go to a dance and I had to call him when I got back. And he told me what time I was to be back. I did call him and I told him what I did at the dance. I told him exactly. I'm very honest with him. He doesn't want me to go out because he feels that I would look at other men. I don't drink and he felt that I did drink and that when I went to that dance, I danced with men. I told him that I didn't do either. He didn't believe me. After that, I decided not to go to any more dances.

On the surface, prisoners' wives generally seemed to accept their husbands' authority in these matters. But the cost of compliance is high. By muting their own needs, they were left dissatisfied and socially isolated. A great deal of ambivalence about this issue is also evident. Fifteen wives reported that their husbands' attitudes contributed to their own sense of being in prison. The more "open" a prison system, of course, the better men were able to control—or attempt to control—wives' lives. By using the telephone as frequently as possible, men could assume roles as prison guards constantly alert to any possible infraction of "the rules." Ten men used the technique of calling at "unpredictable" times—in effect, the prison strategy of spot-checking. As one wife elaborates:

I never phoned him. He phoned me. He phoned maybe once or twice a week. If I wasn't home when he called, the next time he'd ask me where I had been and whom I saw. If he knew I'd planned to go somewhere and I wasn't there, he'd call later. Sometimes he reacted so violently if I wasn't home but if there was a legitimate reason, like I had to go to the doctor, then he was fine. He wanted me to do the things I had to do.

Another wife recalled:

We usually talked once a day. He usually called me at work. Otis was checking up on me. He did that even when he wasn't in jail.

He had nothing to do and he had to have something to relieve the pressure. He was wondering what would happen to me. Was I getting involved with another man worried him.

Of the nineteen women in frequent telephone contact with their husbands, only four reported that husbands seldom or never appeared to be checking up on their activities or whereabouts. All these wives were expected to act in the same manner as they had always done, that is, to pursue a middle-class lifestyle, have their own interests, to be active in the community, and to pursue their own recreational interests. In effect, these husbands continued to be more egalitarian and less obsessively jealous in their relationships with their wives. According to two women, their spouses insisted that they "get out and have some fun."

Effects of Telephone Contacts on Marital and Family Roles

The extent to which wives were able to assume their absent husbands' duties and responsibilities varied with the frequency of telephone contacts, since more frequent contacts enabled husbands to exercise more control over their households. Most women reported their husbands continued to make major household decisions; in particular, those regarding household finances, child-related issues, and major household purchases. Wives frequently deferred to their husbands in these matters. One wife, for example, discussed the kinds of decisions that she referred to her husband:

> I call him everyday. I have a wicked phone bill. I get $525 a month from welfare. I usually can pay my bill from that. I let him know what goes on here everyday. I tell him little things about what we're doing. This brings us closer. Our oldest one wants to quit school. She really wants to quit. I told him that. He's thinking about it now. I just bought this dryer and I called him and asked if that was OK. He still makes the decisions. He's supposed to be the head of the family and he should be making the decisions even though he's in jail. I feel that our separation has brought us closer together.

Wives frequently deferred to their husbands in these matters thus relieving themselves of the burden of responsibility while allowing the husbands to preserve a sense of being the heads of their households.

Eleven wives said that their husbands reasserted their dominance by demanding that they reorganize their lives and households around their husbands' own needs—both material and emotional: relaying messages, handling legal affairs, running errands and filling their "grocery lists," which might include snack foods, beverages, cigarettes, books, clothes, and personal care items.[12] One woman made this clear: "He'd ask me for things every time he'd call. I'd say to myself, 'What am I, a grocery store?' " However, most of these wives maintained that they derived satisfaction from nurturing their husbands in this way and that, even with limited financial resources, they sought to fulfill their husbands' requests. By accepting these orders, wives reported, they were able to legitimate further their husbands' roles as heads of their households.

Since telephones promote communication, they can also undermine or weaken marital ties. When couples regularly conversed over the phone, marital conflicts sometimes erupted about exactly the same issues which, in other cases, strengthened marital ties. Wives' accounts indicate that disagreements and verbal clashes generally centered around husbands' attempts to retain their dominance and authority and wives' resistance to this. For instance, twelve wives reported that, as they developed greater confidence in their own abilities, judgments, and decisions, they became less likely to seek their husbands' "permission" to do things, defer to them, or rely upon their judgments in handling household decisions. This led to clashes over household budgets—how far to go into debt, kinds of appliances to buy, and so on—child rearing, wives' work, and the scheduling of visits to prison.

In the course of these disagreements, many of these twelve wives began to adopt the position that they, too, were qualified to make decisions and should share equally in doing so. Recognizing that this was extremely threatening to their husbands, most wives compromised by establishing some areas of personal autonomy for themselves, while deferring to their husbands on other issues; for example, the children. It is interesting that, whether or not couples were in frequent and regular contact by telephone, the lowest rate of marital stress was found among those whose decision making was jointly shared. In all cases, this was a continuation of a marital pattern established before imprisonment.

Marital conflicts sometimes erupted about the length of the grocery list which also strengthened marital ties. Wives indicated that disagreements and verbal clashes generally centered around their husbands' increasing demands for material goods. Usually wives were exhausted and worried about finding enough money on which to live

---

[12]Following the precepts of community corrections, Vermont correctional centers permit prisoners to acquire all of the following goods depending on their security classification: their own clothes, items for body care, reading material, certain electrical appliances (stereos, radios, televisions, and so on) and other items for recreational purposes, arts and crafts, decorative items for their rooms, coffee, tea, cigarettes, snack foods that do not require cooking, and cigarettes.

and to finance their visits to the prison, much less to support their husbands. Only a few flatly refused to exceed their already tightly stretched budgets. For instance, one of the women, who resisted her husband's demands for her to deliver what she considered an excessive amount of material goods, describes how their arguments affected her:

> I'd get hurt and I knew he was getting at me. His hollering upsets me and he'd say to me that he was the boss. I don't let it bother me as much now. I tell him that I'm a person and I have a life to lead, too. I've smartened up. In the past, when he hung up, I'd cry and be very mad and then I'd try to get back to him on the phone. And then I couldn't because the line would be busy and then I'd become madder. I'd get madder and madder the longer I waited to get through and then I'd cry even more. Then I'd be even madder when I finally got to talk to him. I felt used all the time by him and he got angry because I felt this way. I felt used because he kept wanting things. If I couldn't get hold of him on the phone that night, I'd wait until morning and then I wouldn't be mad by then.

Another wife recalled her reactions to her husband's demands for money:

> We'd argue about whether I was spending too much money or I couldn't give him as much as he wanted. He was afraid I'd be running the road. I kept it a secret the one time that I did run on him but then I told him on the phone. We argued for four and a half hours. Then the time went out on him.

Some wives reported that they and their husbands also argued over wives' needs to limit the number of long-distance telephone calls which severely strained their limited financial resources. For these women, paying long-distance telephone bills simply meant that the rest of the family had to go without. Such arguments frequently escalated over the course of a series of telephone calls. Differences were usually resolved in the wives' favor since the men were only "symbolic heads of household." It was up to the wives whether or not to follow their men's decisions and demands. Most wives realized that they actually had the "final" say in these matters and acted accordingly.

The nature of relationships between couples varied substantially depending on frequency of telephone contact. Among those with infrequent contact, fifteen wives reported that they were unable to predict when, and to what extent, they could depend on their husbands' companionship and support. Husbands were often not well-informed about important household events and decisions, or the stresses experienced by their wives and were less able to assess their wives' loyalty and fidelity. The wives, in turn, experienced considerable uncertainty regarding when their husbands might call (and thus, when they might leave the house) and which decisions should be referred to their husbands. In general, they were likely to consult with their husbands on broad policy issues, while making their own decisions on more trivial day-to-day matters. Wives in this position were less likely than the others to refer household decisions to their husbands and to consider them active heads of their families. They were more likely to busy themselves with child-rearing and domestic activities. Social and emotional support from their husbands, while evident to some degree, was clearly limited and these wives learned not to depend on it.

Conclusions

While most women in this study experienced problems typical of those faced with enforced separation (social, emotional and sexual deprivation, financial difficulties, and child management), a significant number reported difficulty coming to terms with the prospective duration of the separation and a feeling of being themselves imprisoned. It is likely that some of the wives created their own prisons by putting their lives "on hold" until their husbands returned.

Most wives did not experience a drop into poverty upon their husbands' removal from their households, although this phenomenon was reported by some wives whose husbands were steadily employed prior to imprisonment. Rather, most of the wives lived on the edge of subsistence during their married years, and imprisonment simply meant a continuation of persistent financial hardships. Within this segment of the population of poor single mothers, transition in family status (that is, their husbands' enforced separation from their households) appeared to have little impact on their continuing impoverishment. The observation that a fundamental cause of poverty among female-headed households is due to familial changes (for example, divorce, widowhood, and so on) perhaps is more relevant for middle-income white women than for lower-income white women.[13]

The current literature indicates that the imprisonment of husbands results in their wives bearing a greater economic responsibility for themselves and their children. The results reported here suggest

---

[13]The literature on the poverty of women offers a related and important factor to explain the "feminization of poverty": the male flight from responsibility. Specifically, Ehrenrich (1983) claims that the majority of men who are not living with their wives and children have abdicated their familial responsibilities. She further reports that most divorced men neither financially support nor directly care for their children after separation or divorce. There is little doubt that this analysis of women and poverty is valid, but, as shown here, it is not the whole story.

that their incarcerated husbands' needs place a severe financial burden on wives' already sagging budgets. Not only do wives wonder where food, clothing, rent and utilities will come from, but they acquire some additional worries: for example, how to pay the additional costs to the maintenance of contact with their husbands as well as how to supply material goods for their husbands.

The wives in this group have considerable contact with their husbands through telephone conversations, a mode of communication that substantially alleviated some of the difficulties associated with separation. From the wives' accounts, it is clear that telephone calls helped to strengthen marital ties. Telephone contacts improved family morale by adding intensely pleasurable events to the couples' memories about their relationship and helping them weather the difficulties involved in "waiting" for the men's release. Finally, communication with their husbands, through the telephone, served another function for the wives: that of providing temporary release from the feeling that they, too, were imprisoned or being punished. Such interactions further allowed the wives to reaffirm their commitments to waiting for their husbands' release.

Despite the obvious benefits of such communication, it should not be overlooked that, more often than not, men used telephone contacts to place restrictions on their wives, to make demands and to maintain their authority and dominance. Also, a significant proportion of these men used the telephone to check up, periodically and unpredictably, on their wives' activities. In response, the wives reported that they had no lives of their own and were forced to create "prisons" for themselves.

Telephone conversations could produce some additional stresses and strains. With frequent long-distance telephone calls, many wives confronted their husbands' increasing demands for material goods which, in turn, only made the financial burdens carried by wives even heavier. Arguments could erupt around the wives' decisions to limit the supply of goods they delivered to the prison and/or to limit the number of long-distance telephone calls. Such contacts therefore did not always strengthen the relationships between them.

The wives' accounts also suggest that telephone conversations serve to exacerbate the sense of unreality associated with marital relations during a husband's incarceration. The conversations allowed wives to sustain idealized notions of their husbands' abilities to assume roles as conventional husbands and fathers. Telephone conversations also seemed somehow separate from the realm of real-life issues and concerns. Wives selected issues to be discussed with their husbands and, since they were imprisoned, husbands were unable to engage in the sorts of "fast-living" activities which were the source of many previous domestic conflicts.

It is concluded that prison policies believed beneficial for the institution can have dysfunctional consequences for prisoners' wives. Prison policies can set the wives up for experiences that they find to be extremely stressful. For instance, the policy permitting prisoners to telephone their wives can provide incentives for men to "do time" and not stir up trouble. This policy also can lead to another set of consequences: wives' financial packages seldom can cover their husbands' long-distance telephone calls without depriving other members of their households of some of the basic necessities; and telephone conversations can also become the vehicles for empty promises, marital discord, and discontent.

Finally and most importantly, the present conclusions suggest that, in the future, correctional programs and policies be analyzed in terms of their impact not only on the prisoners but also in terms of their potential impact on their wives and families. Correctional planning and policy making should not only encourage prisoners to maintain relationships with their families but also mitigate the "pains of imprisonment" without penalizing the wives. The findings presented here provide some insight into these issues, but a great deal remains to be done.

REFERENCES

Adams, D., and J. Fischer, "The Effects of Prison Residents' Community Contacts on Recidivism Rates," *Corrective and Social Psychiatry*, 22 (1976), 21–27.

Arendell, T., *Mothers and Divorce: Legal, Economic, and Social Dilemmas*. Berkeley: University of California Press, 1986.

Bakker, L. J., B. A. Morris, and L. M. Janus, "Hidden Victims of Crime," *Social Work*, 23 (1978), 143–148.

Charmaz, K., "The Grounded Theory Method: An Explication and Interpretation." In R. M. Emerson (ed.), *Contemporary Field Research: A Collection of Readings*. Boston: Little, Brown, 1983, pp. 109–126.

Daniel, S. W., and C. J. Barrett, "Needs of Prisoners' Wives: A Challenge for the Mental Health Profession," *Community Mental Health Journal*, 17 (1981), 310–322.

Dickinson, G. E., "Changes in Communication Policies," *Corrections Today*, 46 (1984), 58–60.

Ehrenreich, B., *The Hearts of Men: American Dreams and the Flight from Commitment*, Garden City, N.Y.: Anchor Press, 1983.

Fishman, L. T., *Women at The Wall: A Study of Prisoners' Wives Doing Time on the Outside*. Albany, N.Y.: State University of New York Press, 1990.

Fishman, L. T., "Visiting at the Prison: Renewed Courtship and the Prisoner's Wife," *Free Inquiry in Creative Sociology*, 16 (1988), 115–121.

Fishman, L. T., "Prisoners and Their Wives: Marital and Domestic Effects of Telephone Contacts and Home Visits." *International Journal of Offender Therapy and Comparative Criminology*, 32 (1988), 55–66.

Fishman, S. H., and A. S. Alissi, "Strengthening Families as Natural Support Systems for Offenders," *Federal Probation*, 43 (1979), 16–21.

Fishman, S. H., and C. J. M. Cassin, *Services for Families of Offenders: An Overview*. Washington, D.C.: U.S. Department of Justice, National Institute of Corrections, 1981.

Freedman, B. J., and D. G. Rice, "Marital Therapy in Prison: One-Partner 'Couple Therapy,'" *Psychiatry*, 40 (1977), 175–183.

Glaser, B. G., and A. L. Strauss, *The Discovery of Grounded Theory: Strategies for Qualitative Research*. Chicago: Aldine, 1967.

Goffman, E., *Asylums: Essays on the Social Situation of Mental Patients and Other Inmates*. Garden City, N.Y.: Doubleday, 1961.

Handler, E., "Family Surrogates as Correctional Strategy," *The Social Service Review*, 48 (1974), 539–549.

Holt, N., and D. Miller, *Explorations in Inmate-Family Relations*. Sacramento: Department of Corrections Research Division, 1972.

Homer, E. L., "Inmate-Families Ties—Desirable But Difficult," *Federal Probation*, 43 (1979), 47–52.

Koenig, C., and L. Gariepy, *Life on the Outside: A Report on the Experiences of the Families of Offenders from the Perspective of the Wives of Offenders*. Chilliwack, British Columbia: Chilliwack Community Services, 1985.

Kotarba, J., "The Accomplishment of Intimacy in the Jail Waiting Room." *Qualitative Sociology*, 2 (1979), 80–103.

Levy, H., and D. Miller, *Going to Jail: The Political Prisoner*. New York: Grove Press, 1971.

MacIntosh, H., "Separation Problems in Military Wives," *American Journal of Psychiatry*, 125 (1968), 260–265.

McCubbin, H. I., and B. B. Dahl, "Prolonged Family Separation in the Military: A Longitudinal Study." In H. I. McCubbin and others (eds.), *Families in the Military System*. Beverly Hills: Sage Publications, 1976, pp. 112–144.

McCubbin, H. I., C. B. Joy, J. K. Cauble, J. M. Comeau, J. M. Patterson, and R. H. Needle, "Family Stress and Coping: A Decade of Review," *Journal of Marriage and the Family*, 42 (1980), 855–871.

Montalvo, F. F., "Family Separation in the Army: Study of Problems Encountered and the Caretaking Resources used by Career Army Families Undergoing Military Separation." In H. I. McCubbin and others (eds.), *Families in the Military System*. Beverly Hills: Sage Publications, 1976, pp. 147–173.

Morris, P., *Prisoners and Their Families*. New York: Hart, 1965.

Schafer, N. E., "Prison Visiting—A Background for Change," *Federal Probation*, 42 (1978), 47–50.

Schneller, D. P., *The Prisoner's Family: A Study of the Effects of Imprisonment on the Families of Prisoners.* San Francisco: R and E Research Associates, 1978.

Schwartz, M. C., and J. F. Weintraub, "The Prisoner's Wife: A Study in Crisis," *Federal Probation,* 38 (1974), 20–26.

Swan, L. A., *Families of Black Prisoners: Survival and Progress.* Boston: G. K. Hall, 1981.

Walker, N., "Side-Effects of Incarceration," *The British Journal of Criminology,* 23 (1983), 61–71.

Wallerstein, J., and J. Kelly, *Surviving the Breakup: How Parents and Children Cope with Divorce.* New York: Basic Books, 1980.

Weiss, R. S., *Going It Alone: The Family Life and Social Situation of the Single Parent.* New York: Basic Books, 1979.

Zemans, E., and R. Cavan, "Marital Relationships of Prisoners in the United States," *Journal of Criminal Law, Criminology and Police Science,* 49 (1958), 50–57.

DISCUSSION QUESTIONS
SECTION 5: WOMEN AND PRISONS

1. What kind of architecture do many prisons for women take on? Why do you think prisons for women are constructed the way they are? Explain how the physical appearance of women's prisons may be deceptive of the treatment of female prisoners?

2. What is the profile of a woman prisoner? What are the major problems facing incarcerated women? How successful has litigation been used in eliminating discriminatory treatment of female prisoners? What is implied by the statement that litigation is but a catalyst for change?

3. What programs have tried to cope with the problems associated with incarcerated mothers and their children? Is it correct to assume that women criminals make poor mothers? Do women who commit crime give up their right to be mothers? Should children be allowed to live with their mothers inside of correctional facilities? From your point of view, what programs or practices should exist concerning incarcerated mothers and their children?

4. A trend has existed since the late 1970s of incarcerating more and more criminals. Do you agree or disagree with this approach to dealing with crime? What alternatives exist? Specifically, is incarceration an effective crime-control measure for female criminals?

5. What kinds of problems do the wives and lovers of incarcerated men face? What are the social ramifications of imprisonment, not for the male prisoner, but for all of those who know or depend on him? What social functions do telephone conversations play in the lives of prisoners and their dependents? If you were the warden, how would you structure the use of the telephone by prisoners?

6. What are the arguments for and against training women prisoners primarily in traditional feminine social roles?

7. In what ways have male and female prisoners been treated differently? Do good reasons exist as to why male and female prisoners might be treated differently?

8. Which Constitutional amendments have been applied to the treatment of women prisoners and how have they been applied? In general, how have the courts ruled in terms of the disparate treatment of male and female prisoners? Provide five examples of conditions that have been remedied by the courts.

9. The position of correctional officers is one in which guards are

expected to maintain authority and control over the actions of prisoners. In your opinion, are female guards able to maintain authority and control over male prisoners? What light does research shed on this issue? In general, what are the opinions of male guards and inmates concerning the employment of women guards in all-male prisons?

Section 6

Abortion—A Right to Privacy?

Is the freedom for women to decide when and under what conditions they become mothers the most precious of all freedoms—or is it? Is abortion an issue that affects only women? Is it an issue of privacy? Can the states intrude into the affairs and personal decisions of their citizens?

The issue is abortion, and this section discusses the readiness of the legal system to uphold others' rights to tell pregnant women what they may or may not ingest, where they may or may not work, whether they may or may not terminate their pregnancies, and how they may or may not give birth. Indicated in the first article is that this is an egregious assault on women's sense of self and bodily integrity. In an attempt to protect the health of the woman and her fetus, the Courts may be doing serious damage to the woman's mental health. The inability to protect one's bodily integrity leads to helplessness and an acute sense of powerlessness. Chrisler favors safer workplaces for both women and men, widely available prenatal care, and better drug and alcohol abuse prevention and treatment programs.

Muraskin reviews the arguments set forth in *Roe* v *Wade*. Here the Court did not accept the argument that a woman has a constitutional right to have an abortion whenever she wants one. Does the state have the right to interfere with the decision of childbearing? What the Court did in *Roe* was to establish a sliding scale that balanced the right of the woman against the right of the state at various times during her pregnancy.

What are the issues that the Court deals with regarding abortion? There are significant constitutional issues at stake in the judicial bias against women. The first issue deals with privacy, the other with the Fourteenth Amendment rights to due process and equal treatment. Is this a question of a woman's right to autonomy over her body, or does the issue go further? What compelling reason is there for the Supreme Court of the United States to continue to listen to arguments regarding a women's right to privacy? A review of all cases since *Roe* is included. The decision is still in the hands of the Court.

16

Whose Body Is It Anyway? Psychological Effects of Fetal-Protection Policies

Joan C. Chrisler

This chapter examines the possible effects of fetal-protection policies on women's mental health. Research on personal control, learned helplessness, and self-esteem/self-worth is reviewed and findings applied to pregnant women who are threatened by fetal-protection policies.

To consider pregnancy a conflict of maternal and fetal rights is even more negative and detrimental to women than to consider it a disease (Hubbard 1990). Yet, there is an alarming trend in the U.S. legal system to do just that. In recent years, pregnant women have been ordered to undergo Caesarean sections, have been barred from high-paying blue-collar jobs, have been temporarily prevented from having abortions (Gallagher 1984), and have been arrested for drinking alcohol (Stellman and Bertin 1990) and taking drugs (Roberts 1990). Although the physicians, employers, police officers, attorneys, and judges involved in these cases would argue that they were only trying to do what was best for the health of the woman and her fetus, these policies are a form of social control; the end result is the clear suggestion that "a pregnant woman is not a competent person" (Hubbard 1990, p. 174).

Psychological research has shown that people need a sense of personal control—that is, the feeling that they can make decisions and take actions that result in desirable consequences (Rodin 1986). Adler (cited in Rodin 1986, p. 140) has argued that the need to exercise control is "a basic feature of human behavior." Those who have a strong sense of personal control are able to reduce the negative impact of stressors and, thus, tend to have better physical and mental health than those with a weak sense of personal control (Elliot, Trief, and Stein 1986; Matheny and Cupp 1983; and Sals and Mullen 1981).

The sense of personal control develops over the course of life and fluctuates in response to environmental events as one experiences stressors, success and failure, and how much control one actually has in different situations (Rodin 1986). Thus, the sense of personal control emerges as people develop theories of physical and social causality (Rodin 1986) and estimate their own levels of competence in effecting change. It is not surprising that poor women of color would have fewer opportunities to experience the kind of personal control and success that leads to self-efficacy. These are also the women who make up the majority (about 70 percent) of the defendants charged with "prenatal crimes" (Roberts 1990).

One's self-concept is multidetermined, but the sense of mastery, of being in control of one's environment, especially one's own body, is considered crucial (Ashurst and Hall 1989). Everyone fears "being out of control" and "losing control" (Ashurst and Hall 1989; Chrisler, 1991), and people have been known to take extraordinary measures in order to regain a sense of control over themselves, including self-destructive behaviors such as anorexia nervosa and suicide. "Stress can be reduced through five basic types of control (Sarafino 1990): (1) behavioral control—the ability to take action; (2) cognitive control—the ability to think of possible strategies; (3) decisional control—the ability to choose between alternative responses; (4) informational control—the ability to obtain knowledge about events; and (5) retrospective control—the ability to understand the causes of events that have already occurred." The readiness of the legal system to uphold others' right to tell pregnant women what they may or may not ingest, where they may or may not work, whether they may or may not terminate their pregnancies, and how they may or may not give birth is an egregious assault on women's sense of self and bodily integrity. It strips women's ability to exercise behavioral, cognitive, and decisional control. It happens most often to women who lack informational control and often leaves women without retrospective control. In an attempt to protect the health of the woman and her fetus, the courts may be doing serious damage to the woman's mental health.

"According to learned helplessness theory, depression occurs when few rewarding, pleasurable experiences are available and/or people lack the ability to reduce or avoid unpleasant stressful experiences." Walker (1979) suggested that learned helplessness explains why battered wives stay with their husbands. These women have become depressed because every attempt they have made to avoid battering or escape from the situation has met with failure. Lack of personal and financial resources, the shortage of shelters, and well-meaning relatives and friends who urge them to give him another chance or to be a better wife have contributed to a sense of helplessness and to their resignation to an inescapable fate, which traps them in a cycle of violence.

Imagine a drug-addicted woman who discovers that she is pregnant. Her pregnancy is probably unplanned, perhaps a result of contraceptive failure or drug-induced lack of motivation to use the contraceptives regularly or properly. Perhaps she cannot afford contraceptives or is uninformed about where to obtain them. Because some drugs (for example, heroin and methadone) disrupt the normal menstrual cycle, addicted women are accustomed to irregular cycles and missed periods (Al-Issa 1980). She may not realize that she is pregnant until several months have passed. An abortion may not be possible because of cost, availability, religious values, or pregnancy stage. Drug-treatment programs have long waiting lists, few emergency beds available for pregnant women, and poor reputations for meeting the needs of women addicts (Cuskey, Berger, and Densen-Gerber 1981). If she has heard about women who have been arrested for fetal abuse, she may be afraid to seek prenatal care, for fear of being arrested. She will undoubtedly feel anxious, frightened, depressed, and helpless—a poor prognosis for both the woman and her fetus.

Self-esteem and perceptions of self-worth are crucial components in the etiology, maintenance, and remission of depression (Kuiper and Olinger 1989). Fetal-protection policies contribute to women's low self-esteem and low self-worth in several ways. First, they affect women's judgments of their own virtue. The very fact that the policies exist suggests that women have inadequate morals and ethics or are incapable of living up to social standards. Left to their own devices, women will be neglectful, "bad" mothers who willingly subject their future children to toxic or unsafe conditions or frivolously obtain abortions for "convenience."

Second, these policies affect women's evaluation of their acceptance. It is difficult to maintain a sense of self-worth while knowing that society values a fetus more than a woman and while running the risk of being labeled a child abuser because one is addicted or attempting to earn a living by working in a dangerous environment. Society has extremely negative attitudes toward women alcoholics and drug users. The stigma of addiction is unquestionably greater for women than for men, particularly if those women are mothers, and leads to social rejection (Gomberg 1979).

Third, these policies suggest that a pregnant woman cannot be a competent person (Hubbard 1990). Denying women the right to control their own bodies and make decisions about their health and occupational status promotes an external locus of control. The inability to protect one's bodily integrity leads to helplessness and an acute sense of powerlessness.

Low self-esteem and self-worth are components of many psychological problems, including depression, addiction, eating disorders, and social anxieties and contribute to the continued oppression of women (Sanford and Donovan 1984). It is ironic that policies intended to discourage women from taking health risks may actually have the effect of promoting that same risky behavior.

Conclusion

The very existence of fetal-protection policies leads to anxiety in women of childbearing age, affects the development of self-esteem and personal control in girls who grow up knowing that their ability to control their own bodies and make decisions about their own health is limited, and causes depression, helplessness, and powerlessness in women charged with fetal abuse. Commenting on the effects of these policies, Stellman and Bertin (1990) wrote that at best, women "will suffer the anxiety that even moderate normal activity can damage their real or potential offspring. At worst, women will be treated as walking wombs, perpetually pregnant until proven otherwise, with pregnancy police peeping in at every door and restricting every activity" (p. A23).

Making poor women into criminals is obviously easier than revamping the health-care system (Roberts 1990) to better serve everyone's needs. However, if government agencies, health-care providers, and legislators are serious about improving the physical and mental health of women and children, they will do the following:

- increase funding for research and training aimed at improving women's health
- expand drug- and alcohol-treatment programs and make them more sensitive to the particular needs of women
- develop and publicize health-education and drug-abuse-prevention programs
- increase family-planning services which must be allowed to provide abortion information and referrals
- make prenatal care available to all women and ensure the confidentiality of physician/patient communication
- make certain that prenatal screening and fetal monitoring are available (but not mandated)

- develop occupational health and safety standards to make the workplace safer for everyone and impose stiff penalties on employers who violate those standards, and
- enact legislation to protect women against unnecessary surgery, including Caesarean section, hysterectomy, and tubal ligation.

The best way to improve women's mental health is to empower women to make their own decisions and to take control of their lives and to provide them with the resources they need to do so. When this occurs, there will be no further need for "pregnancy police" and fetal-protection policies.

REFERENCES

Al-Issa, I., *The Psychopathology of Women*. Englewood Cliffs, N.J.: Prentice-Hall, 1980.

Ashurst, P., and Z. Hall, *Understanding Women in Distress*. London: Tavistock/Routledge, 1989.

Chrisler, J. C., "Out of Control and Eating Disordered." In N. Van Den Bergh (ed.), *Feminist Perspectives on the Treatment of Addictions*. New York: Springer, 1991.

Cuskey, W. R., L. H. Berger, and J. Densen-Garber, "Issues in the Treatment of Female Addiction: A Review and Critique of the Literature." In E. Howell and M. Bayen (eds.), *Women and Mental Health*. New York: Basic Books, 1981, pp. 269–295.

Elliott, D. J., P. M. Trief, and N. Stein, "Mastery, Stress, and Coping in Marriage among Chronic Pain Patients," *Journal of Behavioral Medicine*, 9 (1986), 549–558.

Gallagher, J., "The Fetus and the Law: Whose Life Is It Anyway?" *Ms.*, 13 (September 1984), 62–66, 134–135.

Gomberg, E. S., "Problems with Alcohol and Other Drugs." In E. S. Gomberg and V. Franks (eds.), *Gender and Disordered Behavior: Sex Differences in Psychopathology*. New York: Brunner/Mazel, 1979, pp. 204–240.

Hubbard, R., *The Politics of Women's Biology*. New Brunswick, N.J.: Rutgers University Press, 1990.

Kuiper, N. A., and L. J. Olinger, "Stress and Cognitive Vulnerability for Depression: A Self-Worth Contingency Model." In R. W. Neufeld (ed.), *Advances in the Investigation of Psychological Stress*. New York: Wiley, 1989, pp. 367–391.

Matheny, R. B., and P. Cupp, "Control, Desirability, and Anticipation As Moderating Variables between Life Changes and Illness," *Journal of Human Stress*, 9 (1983), 14–23.

Roberts, D., "The Bias in Drug Arrests of Pregnant Women," *New York Times*, August 11, 1990, p. A25.

Rodin, J., "Health, Control, and Aging." In M. M. Baltes and P. B. Baltes (eds.), *The Psychology of Control and Aging.* Hillsdale, N.J.: Erlbaum, 1986, pp. 139–165.

Sanford, L. T., and M. E. Donovan, *Women and Self-Esteem.* New York: Penguin, 1984.

Sarafino, E. P., *Health Psychology: Biopsychosocial Interactions.* New York: John Wiley & Sons, 1990.

Stellman, J. M., and J. E. Bertin, "Science's Anti-Female Bias," *New York Times*, June 4, 1990, p. A23.

Suls, J., and B. Mullen, "Life Change and Psychological Distress: The Role of Perceived Control and Desirability," *Journal of Applied Social Psychology*, 11 (1981), 379–389.

Walker, L. E., *The Battered Woman.* New York: Harper and Row, 1979.

17

Abortion: Is It Abortion or Compulsory Childbearing?

Roslyn Muraskin

As this work goes into print, controversy over abortion remains central to the question of women's rights. The Supreme Court is faced with cases further restricting the rights of females to have an abortion. There continues to be public debate in state courts and legislatures as well as in the Supreme Court regarding women's rights to privacy. This article reviews the cases, the issues, and the holdings. We have not heard the end of this issue. Reproductive rights are the focus for recognition of the Constitutional right to privcy. The cases we have seen and the cases yet to be decided are good examples of how the courts "protect" the rights of women. Or, viewed from a different perspective, is the unborn fetus a person, and a person with rights? The article points out that the case of Roe v. Wade *did not give all women the right to an abortion. Rather, it applied a sliding scale. The future? Time will tell.*

Reproductive freedom has been joined with such accepted rights as freedom of speech or assembly. There are those women who have come to the conclusion out of simple personal concern that if they do not control their bodies from the skin in, they can never control their lives from the skin out. There are those who feel that women's role as the most basic means of production will remain the source of their second-class status, if outside forces continue to either restrict or compel that production.

The freedom for women to decide when to become a mother and under what conditions is an issue of great concern in today's world.

Is abortion an issue that affects women only, and is it an exmple of sex discrimination? Are we to think primarily of the fetus and thus conclude that abortion is murder? Is abortion to be viewed from a religious perspective, thinking of how the legal codes of Western religions treat the subject? Is abortion a question of privacy? Should states be prevented from intruding into the affairs and personal decisions of their citizens? If a woman is a victim of rape or sexual abuse, is she entitled to an abortion without interference from the state? Is it an issue of discrimination against the poor, who may need to subsidize abortions, or even racial discrimination because of the high proportion of minorities who choose to abort? The question that comes to mind is not, "how can we justify abortion," but "can we justify compulsory childbearing?"

What are the issues that the Court talks about when we talk about abortion? There are two significant Constitutional issues at stake in judicial bias against women. The first issue has to do with the right to privacy, which is implied in the Constitution. The other issue concerns the Fourteenth Amendment right to due process and equal treatment. Is the issue simply one of female autonomy over her body? The conflict continues. It is an issue that keeps coming back to haunt the courts. The Supreme Court held that laws prohibiting abortion are unconstitutional. In *Roe* v. *Wade* (1973) the Court held that "No state shall impose criminal penalties on the obtaining of a safe abortion in the first trimester of pregnancy." As of this writing, women cannot be charged criminally with obtaining an abortion, but there are administrative regulations and legal penalties that prevent it.

Abortion is an emotional, legal, religious, and highly volatile issue. In December 1971, the Supreme Court heard a case (*Roe* v. *Wade*) brought to it by an unmarried pregnant woman from Texas, who complained that the Texas statute permitting abortions only when necessary to save the life of the mother was unconstitutional.

What was held in *Roe* was that a state may not during the first trimester of pregnancy, interfere with or regulate the decision of a woman and her doctor to terminate the pregnancy by abortion; that from the end of the first trimester until the fetus became viable (usually about twenty-four to twenty-eight weeks), a state may regulate abortions only to the extent that the regulation relates to the protection of the mother's health; and, that only after the point of viability may a state prohibit abortion, except when necessary to save the mother's life. The Court further permitted the state to prohibit anyone but a licensed physician from performing an abortion.

The Court did not accept the argument that a woman has a Constitutional right to have an abortion whenever she wants one, and that the state has no business at all interfering in her decision. Rather, the Court established a sliding scale that balanced the right of the woman against the right of the state to interfere with the decision, it would have to prove that it had a compelling interest in doing so. During the first three months of pregnancy, when continuing the pregnancy is more dangerous than ending it, the Court found that no such compelling state interest existed for overriding the *private* decision of a woman and her doctor. When abortion becomes a more serious procedure, the Court found that the state's interest in the matter increases enough to justify its imposition of regulations necessary to ensure that the mother's health will be safeguarded. In the last trimester of the pregnancy, the Court found that the state's interest in the health and well-being of the mother as well as in the potential life of the fetus is sufficient to outweigh the mother's right of privacy except where her life was at stake.

In the language of the Court:

> This right of privacy . . . is broad enough to encompass a woman's decision whether or not to terminate her pregnancy. The detriment that the State would impose upon the pregnant woman is apparent. Specific and direct harm medically diagnosable even in early pregnancy may be involved. Maternity, or additional offspring, may force upon the woman a distressful life and future. Psychological harm may be imminent. Mental and physical health may be taxed by child care. There is also the distress, for all concerned, associated with the unwanted child, and there is the problem of bringing a child into a family already unable, psychologically and otherwise to care for it. In other cases as in this one, the additional difficulties and continuing stigma of unwed motherhood may be involved. All these are factors the woman and her responsible physician will consider in consultation.

The Court continued by indicating in *Roe* that the right to terminate her pregnancy at whatever time was not acceptable by the Court. They indicated further that the right to privacy was not absolute.

With regard to the argument presented that the fetus is a person, the Court went on to comment:

> . . . in nearly all . . . instances [in which the word 'person' is used in the Constitution] the use of the word is such that it has application only postnatally. None indicates, with any assurance, that it has any possible prenatal application. All this together with our observation . . . that through the major portion of the nineteenth century prevailing legal abortion practices were far freer than they are today, persuades us that the word *person* as used in the fourteenth amendment, does *not* include the unborn. . . .

In answering the question when life begins, the Court further stated;

> It should be sufficient to note . . . the wide divergence of thinking on this most sensitive and difficult question.

> In areas other than criminal abortion, the law has been reluctant to endorse any theory that life as we recognize it, begins before live birth or to accord legal rights to the unborn except in narrowly defined situations and except when the rights are contingent upon live birth. In short the unborn have never been recognized in the law as persons in the whole sense.

> We repeat . . . that the State does have an important and legitimate interest in preserving and protecting the health of the pregnant woman . . . And that it has still another important and legitimate interest in protecting the potentiality of human life.

The Court had decided to allow the mother to abort at the end of the first trimester and then to allow her physician to decide medically if the patient's pregnancy was to be terminated after this period. The judgment was to be effectuated by a decision free from the interference of the state.

At the same time that the Supreme Court had decided the *Roe* case, it decided a second case—that of *Doe* v. *Bolton*, which involved a Georgia abortion statute that set forth several conditions that were to be fulfilled prior to a woman obtaining an abortion. These included a statement by the attending physician that an abortion was justified with the concurrence of at least two other Georgia licensed physicians; the abortion was to be performed in a hospital licensed by the State Board of Health as well as accredited by the Joint Commission on Accreditation of Hospitals; there was to be advance approval by an abortion committee of not less than three members of the hospital staff; and, the woman had to reside in the state of Georgia.

The Court, then, held that these provisions were overly restrictive, treating abortion differently from other comparable medical procedures thereby violating the constitutional rights of a woman to have an abortion. Since *Roe*, several states have passed laws that require the husband of a pregnant woman, or the parents of a single mother to give their consent prior to having an abortion. Both of these requirements were struck down by the Supreme Court (*Planned Parenthood of Central Missouri* v. *Danforth*). The Court had declared these provisions unconstitutional on the grounds that if the state has no right to prohibit abortions before the fetus becomes viable, it also has no right to authorize other—that is, husband or parents—to prevent a woman from obtaining an abortion.

What then is to happen when husband and wife cannot agree? Who is to prevail? The Courts have argued that the woman should. Since it is the woman who physically bears the child and who is the more directly and immediately affected by the pregnancy, as between the two, the balance would seem to weigh in her favor.

The state until this point did not appear to have the Constitutional authority to give a third party an absolute and possible arbitrary veto over the decision of the physician and his/her patient. There has developed the question of the authority a parent has over a child. It has been well understood that Constitutional rights do not mature and come into being magically when one attains the state-defined age of majority. Minors as well as adults are protected by the Constitution and possess Constitutional rights.

There does exist a suggested interest in the safeguarding of the family unit and of parental authority. The idea that to provide a parent with absolute power over a child and its physical well-being is not likely to strengthen the family unit. Neither is it likely that such veto power will enhance parental authority or control where the minor and the nonconsenting parent are so fundamentally in conflict and the very existence of the pregnancy already has fractured the family structure. The Court continues to review cases whereby the parent of the female will make the decision for her regardless of her wishes.

Two other important issues bearing on the ability of women to obtain abortions are the right of hospitals to refuse to perform abortions and the right of Medicaid to refuse to pay for nontherapeutic abortions. In one case, *Nyberg* v. *City of Virginia*, a federal court of appeals concluded that a public hospital may not refuse to perform abortions.

> It would be a nonsequitur to say that the abortion decision is an election to be made by the physician and his patient without interference by the State and then allow the State, through its public hospitals, to effectively bar the physician from using State facilities to perform the operation.

Theoretically, private hospitals may refuse to perform abortions, but it is not always easy to determine when a hospital is private. One needs to review whether it leases its facilities from the local government; whether it receives tax advantages; whether it is extensively regulated by the state; whether it has received tax advantages, whether it has received public monies for hospital construction; and, whether it is part of a general state plan for providing hospital services. Litigation continues.

Under the decision in *Roe* v. *Norton* (1973), the Court concluded that federal Medicaid provisions prohibit federal reimbursement for abortion expenses unless a determination has been made that the abortion was medically necessary. The Court held that the government is not required by the Constitution to pay for any medical service, but once it does decide to do so, it must not unduly disadvantage those who exercise a Constitutional right. Of late, laws have been passed that no birth-control clinic that receives funding from the federal government may give information dealing with abortion.

There continues to be discussion of what rights a woman has as a person. Is having an abortion murder? Murder, as defined by the law, is killing that is unjustified, willful, and malicious. We live in a society that defines childrearing as the mother's job. There is no way that a pregnant woman can passively let the fetus live. She must create and nurture it with her own body in a symbiosis that is often difficult, sometimes dangerous, always uniquely intimate. Pregnancy is most gratifying, but for those who are the unwilling "victims" it becomes an invasion.

Those who are against abortion would tell you that when a woman chooses to have sex, she must be willing to accept all consequences. Those who are against abortion will defend the rights of the fetus to develop, to be given life, and to grow. Those who are against abortion state that whatever the costs, even to those who are victims of rape, there is a life growing, and it is murder to do anything but carry it to full term. Better that any number of women should ruin their health or even die than one woman should get away with not having a child merely because she does not want one.

There have been cases in Idaho that attempt to make doctors criminally liable for performing abortions rather than the mother. For example, under the Idaho proposal, a man who had committed "date rape," a term describing sexual assault by an acquaintance, could conceivably force the woman to carry the child.

Further decisions have been made affecting the woman's right to choose. For example, in *Bellotti* v. *Baird* (1979), the Court voted 8–1 that a state may require a pregnant unmarried minor to obtain parental consent for an abortion if it also offers an alternate procedure. In *Harris* v. *McRae* (1980), the Court upheld 5–4 the Hyde Amendment, which denies federal reimbursement for Medicaid abortions. And, in *City of Akron* v. *Akron Center for Reproductive Health* (1983), the Court voted 6–3 that states cannot mandate what doctors tell abortion patients nor require that abortions for women more than three months pregnant be performed in a hospital. In *Thornburgh* v. *American College of Obstetricians and Gynecologists* (1986), the Court voted 5–4 that states may not require doctors to tell women about risks of abortion and possible alternatives nor dictate procedures to third-trimester abortions.

In the case of Ohio upholding a law that required a minor to notify one parent before obtaining an abortion, Justice Kennedy wrote that:

it is both rational and fair for the State to conclude that, in most instances, the family will strive to give a lonely or even terrified minor advice that is both compassionate and mature.

However, Justice Blackmun, who was the senior author of *Roe*, wrote in what is described as a stinging dissent that Kennedy and his adherents were guilty of "selective blindness" to the reality that "not all children in our country are fortunate enough to be members of loving families. For too many young pregnant women parental involvement in this most intimate decision threatens harm, rather than promises comfort." He ended by stating that:

> . . . a minor needs no statute to seek the support of loving parents. . . . If that compassionate support is lacking, an unwanted pregnancy is a poor way to generate it.

And, in *Webster* v. *Reproductive Health Services* (1989), the Court upheld 5–4 Missouri's law barring the use of public facilities or public employees in performing abortions and requiring physicians to test for the viability of any fetus believed to be more than twenty weeks old.

> Debate over these and other issues has spawned extensive litigation and put the Court in the position of reviewing medical and operational practices beyond its competence. We therefore believe that the time has come for the court to abandon its efforts to impose a comprehensive solution to the abortion question. Under the constitution, legislative bodies cannot impose irrational constraints on a woman's procreative choice. But, within those broad confines, the appropriate scope of abortion regulation "should be left with the people and to the political processes the people have devised to govern their affairs."

The Court stated that Missouri had placed no obstacles in the path of those women seeking abortions. Rather, the state simply chose not to encourage or assist abortions in any respect.

Abortion remains as newsworthy and important a subject today, as we approach the twenty-first century, as it was when *Roe* was decided in 1973. Perceptions of the abortion law differ. For the Courts, it has become a Constitutional issue. The focus is on the Fourteenth Amendment and whether a woman who is denied an abortion is denied due process. The issue is difficult because most people do not see it as a clear issue of law. Is the issue one that concerns only women? And, if so, is it then a case of sex discrimination? Or, are we to look at the issue from the view of the fetus and then view it as an issue of murder? Should abortion be viewed from a religious perspective, thinking of how the legal codes of Western religions treat the subject? Is it simply an issue of privacy and telling the states they cannot intrude into the private affairs of its citizens? Or, do we view abortion as a matter of health, of preventing injuries and death to women who undergo abortions? The answer lies in the fact that all of the above are the issues with no easy solution.

One of the most recent cases was *Rust* v. *Sullivan* (1991), in which the Court upheld 5–4 the federal government's ban on abortion counseling in federally funded family-planning clinics. And, as of this writing, the Court has heard argument in the case of *Planned Parenthood* v. *Casey* (1992). It will rule on the constitutionality of a law passed in the state of Pennsylvania as follows:

Informed Consent:

At least 24 hours before the abortion, except in emergencies, the physician must tell the woman:

- The nature of the proposed procedure or treatment and the risks and alternatives.
- The probable gestational age of the unborn child.
- The medical risks associated with carrying her child to term.
- That government materials are available that list agencies offering alternatives to abortion.
- That medical assistant benefits may be available for pre-natal care, childbirth and neonatal care.

Parental Consent:

If the woman is under 18 and not supporting herself, her parents must be informed of the impending procedure. If both parents or guardians refuse to consent, or if the woman elects not to seek the consent, judicial authorities where the applicant resides or where the abortion is sought shall . . . authorize . . . the abortion if the court determines that the pregnant woman is mature and capable of giving informed consent.

Spousal Notice:

No physician shall perform an abortion of a married woman . . . without a signed statement . . . that the woman has notified her spouse.

Exceptions:

- Her spouse is not the father of the child.
- Her spouse, after diligent effort, could not be located.

- The pregnancy is the result of spousal sexual assault ... that has been reported to a law enforcement agency.
- The woman has reason to believe that notifying her spouse is likely to result in bodily injury.

Reporting:

Each abortion must be reported to the state on forms that do not identify the woman but do include, among other items:

- The number of the woman's prior pregnancies and prior abortions.
- Whether the abortion was performed upon a married woman and if spouse was notified.

The Constitution has been interpreted in many cases to protect the woman from arbitrary, gender-based discrimination by the government, yet the struggle continues. Cases continue to be heard by the Court. In no instance is reference made to women's rights. Rather, the cases are based on the constitutional theory of the right to privacy. Of the Supreme Court Justices, Harry Blackmun was the only Justice who was part of the original 7–2 majority in *Roe;* Justice John Paul Stevens has supported abortion rights since his appointment in 1975; Justice William Rehnquist dissented in *Roe;* Justice Byron White dissented in *Roe;* Justice Antonin Scalia looks to overturn *Roe;* Justice Anthony Kennedy looks to overturn *Roe;* Justice Sandra Day O'Connor has signaled her unhappiness with *Roe;* Justice David Souter has voted to uphold the ban on abortion counseling.

As of this writing the Supreme Court has refused to overrule the *Roe* v. *Wade* decision. The Court has, however, upheld state restraints on a woman's right to choose an abortion freely. In the June 1992 decision of the Court [*Planned Parenthood of Southeastern Pennsylvania* v. *Casey*, 51 Crim. L. Rep. 2253 (June 26, 1992)] by a 5–4 decision, the Court refused to turn the constitutional clock back to 1973, a time when states could make abortion a crime and punish both a woman and her physician. But the Court through this latest decision does allow states to impose conditions on the woman seeking an abortion—an "informed consent" provision that includes a lecture to women in an effort to "educate" them about alternative choices to abortion, as well as a twenty-four-hour waiting period.

The decision of the Court gives the states considerable leeway that can make abortions costlier and more difficult to obtain. Such requirements by the state could prove to be particularly difficult for the poor woman who lives and works far from the abortion clinic.

Even a waiting period as short as twenty-four hours will force some women who cannot afford to stay overnight to make two trips to the clinic. The issue of whether such a procedure will pose an undue unconstitutional burden to choose has been left open.

Before Congress during the Summer of 1992 is a bill that forbids states to restrict a woman's right to choose before the fetus is viable, or even later if the operation is needed to protect the life or health of the woman. The theories behind the proposed legislation "are that Congress has a right to make secure the liberties protected by the fourteenth amendment, and that Congress has the duty to regulate interstate commerce, which would be burdened if women had to travel from state to state in search of safe abortions" (Clymer, 1992: A-11). The current President, George Bush, has promised to veto any such bill passed by the Congress. This will not help women who wish to exercise their right to choose.

According to Ellen Chester (*The New York Times*, 1992), "It has been seventy years since Margaret Sanger claimed that science would make woman 'the owner, the mistress of her self.'" But the spirit of her words lives on. Following the Court's decision in the Pennsylvania case, a case was decided by the Court on July 17, 1992, with regard to the French abortion pill, RU-486. This case was first presented to Justice Clarence Thomas, but he asked the full Court to render a decision, which was to support the government's seizure of the drug, thus raising the stakes in the battle over women's bodies. The decision rendered by the Justices by a 7–2 vote upheld an appellate-court ruling that bars return of the drug to Leona Benten, who brought the drug into the country. RU-486 holds the promise of allowing women to end pregnancy early without undergoing complicated abortion procedures later on. The Court and the present administration still believe that they can play politics with a woman's body.

The struggle is not over yet.* The final decision is not in. But for those who enjoy a safe bet, it is that women will be limited in years to come to choose for themselves whether to have an abortion. Battles already won are still being fought.

CASES CITED

Bellotti v. Baird, 443 U.S. 622, 99 S. Ct. 3035, 61 L.Ed. 2d 797 (1979).

City of Akron v. Akron Center for Reproductive Health, Inc., 462 U.S. 416, 103 S. Ct. 2481, 76 L.Ed. 2d 687 (1983).

---

*There is in place, Fall 1992, a gag order passed by Congress, which states that only physicians can advise women regarding abortions in health clinics that receive federal monies. Workers in the clinics are forbidden to disseminate such information.

Doe v. Bolton, 410 U.S. 179, 93 S.Ct. 739, 35 L.Ed. 2d 201 (1973).

Harris v. McRae, 448 U.S. 297, 100 S.Ct. 2671, 65 L.Ed. 2d 784 (1980).

Nyberg v. City of Virginia, 667 F. 2d 754 (CA 8 1982), dsmd 462 U.S. 1125 (1983).

Planned Parenthood of Southeastern Pennsylvania v. Casey, 00 U.S. 00, 51 Crim L. Rep. 2253 (1992).

Planned Parenthood of Central Missouri v. Danforth, 428 U.S. 52, 96 S.Ct. 2831, 49 L.Ed. 2d 788 (1976).

Roe v. Norton, 408 F. Supp. 660 (1973).

Roe v. Wade, 410 U.S. 113, 93 S. Ct. 705, 35 L.Ed. 2d 147 (1973).

Rust v. Sullivan, 500 U.S. 00, 114 L.Ed 2d 233 (1991).

Thornburgh v. American College of Obstetricians and Gynecologists, 476 U.S. 747, 106 S. Ct. 2169, 90 L.Ed. 2d 779 (1986).

Webster v. Reproductive Health Services, 492 U.S. 490, 109 S. Ct. 3040, 106 L.Ed. 2d 410 (1989).

REFERENCES

Chesler, Ellen. "RU-486: We Need Prudence, Not Politics." *New York Times*, August 2, 1992. Op Ed page.

Clymer, Adam. "Lawmakers Fear Amendments on Abortion Rights." *New York Times*, July 31, 1992, p. A-11.

DISCUSSION QUESTIONS
SECTION 6: ABORTION–A RIGHT TO PRIVACY?

1. Make the argument for a woman's right to privacy when it comes to controlling her own body.

2. Make an argument for the necessity of being in control? What is it about fetal-protection policies that contribute to women's low self-esteem and low self-worth?

3. How can government revamp the health-care system so that everyone's needs can best be served?

4. If *Roe* v. *Wade* were to be overturned, how quickly would the legislators pass laws making the right to choose the right of every woman?

Section 7

Women: Victims of Violence

The amount of violence aimed at women is staggering and horrific. All women are affected by this violence, and women's behavior is controlled and limited by it. Over one-third of all women who cohabit with men are battered by those men in their own homes. In many instances, the most dangerous place for a woman is her own home.

The traditional stance of the criminal justice system toward incidents of domestic violence was to look the other way. The battering of women was perceived by police officers to be the outgrowth of a domestic dispute that was really none of their business. Domestic violence had to be redefined as assault before new tactics and procedures emerged for dealing with offenders.

The civil-rights movement of the 1960s and the women's rights movement a decade later sought to challenge existing stereotypes that ignored the problems of women. For example, pro-arrest procedures were adopted by many police departments. And, in the beginning, further acts of family violence appeared to be quelled by arrest and jail actions. But, more recently, findings from replication studies and other policy-evaluation research offer little support for these early deterrence claims and raise questions about the efficacy of pro-arrest policies. Additionally, it has also been found that arrest policies may be more detrimental to battered women from minority groups and women with fewer resources and opportunities. Continued efforts to develop effective criminal justice policies clearly depend upon studying domestic violence using a variety of perspectives and methodologies.

Fear of crime affects all of us. Research shows it is particularly an issue for women. For most, safety concerns directly influence women's behavior. Many women avoid or, worse, do not even consider activities that are innocuous in and of themselves. The fear of crime has made risky going to a laundromat at night, walking alone in a city park, or taking public transportation. Fear of crime has become part of the lives of women.

A great deal of what we know about fear of crime is curiously flat. We know the demographic characteristics of the fearful, but beyond our personal experiences we know little about the nature of fear and its consequences. This understanding seems a logical first step toward designing interventions to reduce fear. And we have to do that. Fear of crime stands to further erode the quality of women's lives.

An underlying theme of the articles in this section is the pervasive violence and fear that is so much a part of many women's lives. These articles are an effort to reconsider in preliminary fashion how we measure fear of abuse, a beating, a crime, and the implications fear has for all women. And then, and only then, will women be better able to defend themselves from the ugly consequences of physical and psychological abuse and thereby construct a better world in which to live.

18

The Issue Is Rape

Florence Horne

Rape is, and has always been, a topic of relevance for women. By defi-nition, rape is a crime perpetrated by men against women. In spite of increased knowledge and awareness on the subject, this crime seems to be on the increase. Is this because women are reporting the crime in record numbers? Has the increase in drug abuse added to the number of sexual crimes and violence in general? The answers are not clear.

We do know that changes in legislation have helped crime victims in general. Training for medical and criminal justice personnel is now required in some states and is routine in others. Schools and universities throughout the country have begun to provide awareness and infor-mational seminars on the subject, and women are signing up for self-defense classes in record numbers. Rape is no longer a taboo subject.

Progress has been made, but it is only a beginning. Underlying problems that create hate and perpetrate violence need to be solved. Until that time comes, rape will continue to be a relevant topic for men and women alike.

Rape has existed from the beginnings of time in nearly all societies and cultures and with people of all races and backgrounds. In spite of this long history, very little was written on the subject until the early 1970s. In Susan Brownmiller's book, *Against Our Will: Men, Women and Rape* (1975), the author mixes historical fact with per-sonal opinion. She argues that men have always had more power and status than females and that from prehistoric times to the present rape has served the function of intimidating women. Brownmiller concluded, "When men discovered that they could rape, they proceeded to do it. . . . Rape is man's basic weapon of force against women, the principal agent of his will and her fear" (p. 14).

Even though many people believe these views to be extreme, the book is considered a landmark since it was the first in-depth attempt to deal with this complicated and emotionally charged subject. The book is filled with fascinating and well-documented research that helps the reader understand the origins of myths about rape that are still evident in contemporary society. Brownmiller traces the use and meaning of rape in war from Biblical times to the 1960s. She unravels the origins of American rape laws and explains how, why, and under what circumstances rape first came to be considered a crime. She also shows how medieval rape codes, written in an age when women had few legal rights, continue to influence both societal attitudes and institutional response to women rape victims today.

History of Rape Laws

The rape laws in America are rooted in English common law and ancient male concepts of property. Historically, women and children were considered the property of their husbands and fathers (*Rape, Sexual Assault* 1990). The law of rape, in fact, had evolved to protect the theft of female sexual property, not to protect women themselves. But rape was also punished by death because it was akin to murder, for a woman's chastity defined her worth as a person; without it, she herself was worthless. From this principle derived the expression that rape was worse than death; it was a kind of death (Clark 1987).

This posed a paradox for English legal practice. On the one hand, the rapist deserved to be punished because he had attacked female chastity, a valuable possession. On the other hand, the violated woman had lost her credibility as a prosecutrix along with her chastity. It was this paradox that accounted for the low conviction rate for rape; juries hesitated to hang a man for rape on the testimony of a woman who admitted publicly that she was unchaste and therefore unworthy (Clark 1987).

Traditional rape law evolved through case-by-case judicial determination of what acts constituted the crime. This process of lawmaking, the common-law system, defined rape as the "carnal knowledge of a woman by force against her will." The common law instituted a resistance standard for the victim as a means to distinguish forcible carnal knowledge (rape) from consensual carnal knowledge (fornication or adultery). Both forms of carnal knowledge were crimes, but if the act were forcible, the victim escaped punishment for fornication of adultery (Battelle 1977).

Traditional common law did not require corroborative evidence of each element of the crime to support a criminal conviction for rape. Courts simply relied upon juries to weigh the evidence, which might consist of nothing more than the victim's testimony, and render a verdict. It was assumed that a false complaint would be exposed in the adversary process, with the presumption of innocence serving to protect the defendant. Some courts departed from this tradition and established special corroboration requirements to confirm the victim's testimony. In addition, failure of the victim to file a "prompt report" with the police would also make conviction impossible. The victim's consent could be implied from her sexual history and reputation for chastity, proof of which was admissible and a matter of course (Battelle 1977). Lord Chief Justice Matthew Hale, the seventeenth-century English jurist, assured himself a place in history when he wrote: "It is true that rape is a most detestable crime and, therefore, ought to be severely and impartially punished with death; but it must be remembered that it is an accusation easily to be made and hard to be proved, and harder to be defended by the accused, though never so innocent" (Hale 1847, p. 634). The practical effect of this commentary was to focus on the victim's behavior and to question her testimony. Rape corroboration rules and the myth that women falsely report rape are clearly the result of this belief system. Hale can also be credited with the legal concept and societal belief that a woman cannot be raped by her husband. "The husband cannot be guilty of a rape committed by himself upon his lawful wife, for by their mutual matrimonial consent and contract the wife hath given up herself in this kind unto her husband, which she cannot retract" (p. 628).

Although codification of common-law offenses occurred in the American colonies and some of the new states as early as the late seventeenth and early eighteenth centuries, it was not until the 1950s that the codification process was complete in all states. During the process, rape retained its common-law definition, but force was perceived as proof of "nonconsent" rather than a separate element of the offense. Some states required resistance to the "utmost," while other states tried to impose a reasonableness standard. Faced with this confusion, an attempt was made in 1962, in the Model Penal Code, to effect a significant change in the common-law definition of rape and especially in the resistance standard. Although there was less emphasis on resistance in the Model Penal Code formulation of rape than in more traditional carnal knowledge statutes, resistance remained an important factor (Battelle 1977). It was not until the early 1970s, with the advent of the rape reform movement, that any significant changes in the law or the institutional response to victims occurred.

The Rape Reform Movement

During the latter part of the 1960s, informal groups of women began to meet to discuss the problems of being female in modern society. These consciousness-raising groups were a major new organizing tool of the women's rights movement. Within the intimate and supportive environment of "CR" groups, women found the courage to share experiences they had never shared before, such as childhood incest and adolescent and adult rape (Largen 1985). With such disclosures came a growing awareness of the oppressive role sexual assault plays in the lives of all women—victims and potential victims alike. It was recognized how the fear of sexual assault affects all women and how the policies and practices of both the "helping" professions and the criminal justice system did not really assist the victim. This new found awareness, and the outrage generated by it, was the beginning of the "anti-rape" or rape reform movement. A collective conscious-raising had taken place, and victims began to tell their stories publicly at "speak outs" for the first time. Taboos against mentioning rape disappeared, and the media was there to spread the word.

Early in the 1970s, rape crisis centers began springing up in a few large cities and university centers where sexual assaults were widespread. Many of these centers were started by victims themselves but were soon joined by other women activists from all walks of life. These early centers represented a rejection of public institutions as being unresponsive to victims' needs. Their goal was to provide emotional support through hotline counseling or escort services to hospitals, police stations, or courts. Counseling services were based on the premise that the rape victim had undergone a life crisis. But it was not until the 1974 publication of *Rape: Victims of Crisis* (Burgess and Holmstrom) that any systemic documentation and analysis of the rape trauma syndrome existed.[1] This publication not only made crisis center theories and practices more credible, but also contributed to the willingness of some medical and mental-health professionals to provide services to victims of sexual assaults (Largen 1985).

These early centers received little or no support from community social-service or criminal justice agencies. But with the surge of pop-

---

[1]Rape trauma syndrome was defined as the cluster of symptoms that all victims experience.

ular interest in rape and the demand for counseling services, rape crisis centers were forced to compete with public institutions for the limited funds available. Many of the centers began working from within the system and became more mainstream. As research on the subject proliferated, the first large national study (Brodyaga, Gates, Singer, Tucker, and White 1975) resulted in the publication by the Law Enforcement Assistance Administration of a prescriptive package intended to provide guidelines for police, medical personnel, and service groups working with victims. But it was not until 1981 that Congress approved a small amount of federal funds to assist rape crisis centers, many of which had been struggling for survival. Perhaps more significant than the money was the acknowledgment by government policy makers that rape victims were worthy of public support (Largen 1987). Today rape crisis centers exist in every state in various stages of activity. Most are small, nonprofit organizations that receive small amounts of state and/or federal funding. One continuing function of these centers is to train medical and criminal justice personnel in rape awareness. Many hospitals now have a close working relationship with rape crisis centers. Even though most centers continue to rely heavily on the use of volunteers, the rape reform movement has finally become accepted by the establishment.

Perhaps the most significant outcome of the rape reform movement was the progress made on the legal front. Coalitions of groups concerned with both women's rights and victim's rights were able to work together for social as well as legal change that was both symbolic and practical. The rape law reform movement represented the first organized attempt to deter crime through more effective laws and to create recognition within the criminal justice system that it has an obligation to protect victims of crime in addition to preserving the rights of the accused (Largen 1987).

By creating criminal law through the legislative, rather than the common-law process, victim advocates hoped to influence decision makers at different levels of the criminal justice system. Another objective of the reform movement was to make legal standards for rape cases consistent with those used in other violent crimes. Some advocates believed that changes would produce higher conviction rates, and the law, therefore, would become a deterrent to crime. Perhaps most important, advocates sought to change social and legal perceptions of the crime by eliminating common-law concepts that reflected institutional sexism and centuries-old myths (Largen 1987).

Michigan was the first state to restructure its rape law through legislation and is still considered to have the most progressive approach. In an effort to place emphasis on the objective circumstances of the crime rather than on the victim, Michigan redefined rape by establishing four degrees of criminal sexual conduct based on the seriousness of the offense, the amount of force or coercion used, the degree of injury inflicted, and the age and incapacitation of the victim. By the end of 1984, all fifty states had followed Michigan's lead in adopting some measure of rape-law reform. The major accomplishments have been the institution of rape shield laws to limit admissibility of evidence on a victim's prior sexual history and the elimination of both corroborative and "earnest resistance" requirements (Doudna 1990). In addition, many states have made the crime of rape sex-neutral, thereby eliminating the presumption of female victims and male offenders. Some rape statutes now contain provisions that prevent the publication of the victim's name, limit the admissibility of certain kinds of evidence, and either require or prohibit the use of certain jury instruction.

Along with other rape-law reform, the concept of marital rape has finally gained some recognition. In 1976, Nebraska struck down its marital exemption in rape, and this was followed by twenty states over the next several years. Most other states have partially abolished the marital exemption or have created a special category for marital sexual assault. Unfortunately, there are still a few states in which husbands have total immunity, especially if they live under the same roof (Finkelhor and Yllo 1985).

Incidence of Rape

Most legal experts, academic scholars, women, and victim's-rights activists will agree that much progress has been made in the field of rape reform during the last twenty years. Why is it, then, that we continue to hear shocking statistics? The Federal Bureau of Investigation (FBI) estimates that a reported rape occurs every six minutes and that one woman in ten can expect to be raped during her lifetime. The FBI *Uniform Crime Reports* (UCR) gather information on crimes reported to the police throughout the United States. This system first began in 1930. These reports continue to use the common-law definition of rape even though assaults or attempts to commit rape by force or threat of force are also included. However, statutory rape (without force) and many other sex offenses are excluded (UCR 1990). If a case is considered "unfounded" by the police, it is also not counted in these reports. Critics believe that UCR estimates on rape are extremely low.

In an effort to get around the FBI's method of tabulating rape and other crimes (Bart and O'Brien 1985), the Law Enforcement Assistance Administration (LEAA) began to collect its own information in 1972. These victimization surveys report crimes as they are perceived by the people who are subjected to them, not as they are perceived by the police. The LEAA's National Crime Surveys (NCS) interview thousands of people each year, obtaining valuable information about the nature and scope of crime in this country. Based on a sampling of households, this survey gathers information regardless of whether or not the crime was reported. It also includes information on male victims (UCR reports do not) and children twelve and over. While NCS surveys clearly show that only a fraction of rapes and sexual assaults are reported to the police, other studies have suggested that even these figures are low. Just as victims are reluctant to report to the police, they may also choose not to respond to household surveys. In the sexual experience survey administered to 6,000 college men and women (Koss, Gidyez, and Wisniewski 1987), the authors concluded that 27 percent of the female students surveyed reported having been a victim of rape or attempted rape at least once since the age of fourteen. In addition, the authors found that 50 percent of these students did not consider what had happened to them a crime, one of the reasons given for not reporting. Sexual assault is least likely to be reported when the male is known to the female victim. Other common reasons for not reporting are that it is too private or personal an experience and the belief that nothing can be done about it. Many victims are also afraid of reprisal.

The Criminal Justice System Response

Before the rape reform movement, women rarely reported the crime to the authorities, and when they did, they were treated badly. Women talked of being victimized twice: once by the rapist and then by the criminal justice system. Past practices on the part of law enforcement included blaming the victim, asking endless questions about the victim's past sexual history and/or trying to persuade the victim that the attack was not actually a crime, particularly when she knew or had a previous relationship with the attacker. Often the victim was required to take a polygraph exam before the police would initiate an investigation (Chambers 1989). In 1977, Gerald Robin wrote that

> forcible rape is unique among crimes in the way its victims are dealt with by the criminal justice system. Raped women are subjected to an institutionalized sexism that begins with their treatment by the police, continues through a male-dominated criminal justice system influenced by pseudoscientific notions of victim precipitation, and ends with the systematic acquittal of many de facto guilty rapists (p. 136).

Many other studies have also documented this negative view. In a 1980 study (Feldman-Summers and Palmer), it was found that the criminal justice personnel that participated (judges, prosecutors, and police) had beliefs about the causes of rape and how rape can be prevented that tend to put the responsibility on the victim.

Certainly the public's perception of police attitudes is one factor in a woman's decision not to report the crime. According to LeDoux and Hazelwood (1987), most anecdotal literature has perpetuated the idea that police are insensitive to rape victims. Empirical literature, however, presents a more balanced view. To test this, LeDoux and Hazelwood conducted a nationwide study (1985) of 2,170 county and municipal law-enforcement officers to examine their attitudes concerning rape. Analysis of the data revealed that officers are not typically insensitive to the plight of rape victims, even though they are often suspicious of victims who meet certain criteria, such as previous and willing sex with the assailant, or those who provoke rape through their appearance or behavior. Further, a small group of officers agree with the myths that "nice women do not get raped" and "most charges of rape are unfounded." In contrast to earlier studies, the results of this 1985 study indicated that most officers do view rape as a serious crime that deserves severe punishment. The respondents also believe that prosecutors, victims, and potential jurors are not properly prepared to play their assigned roles in a trial. The most encouraging aspect of the study concerned the impact of training. The majority of respondents had recently received training and believed that this had helped to change previously held attitudes. The authors concluded that continued training, which in many jurisdictions is now required, will improve investigative capabilities in the future.

The picture that emerges, therefore, is mixed and somewhat confusing. The reform movement and changes in the law have certainly brought access to justice where there was none before. In addition to the women's and victim's advocates previously discussed, a greater number of women have entered the legal profession and can work from inside the system to bring about change. Over the years, there has been a great increase in the number of sexual crimes reported, but the FBI continues to list rape as the most underreported violent crime in America. In spite of the progress, beliefs based on mythology still affect the way society in general and the criminal justice system in particular treat victims of rape and sexual assault. Progressive laws can be passed, but attitudes are harder to change. The consequences of cultural biases can be read in the statistics; fewer than one-third of all rapes result in arrest, and a much smaller fraction result in conviction (Douda 1990). Rape continues to be a difficult crime to prove.

The 1990s and Beyond

As we enter the twenty-first century, one ponders the questions: Will women ever be free of rape and sexual assault? What can be done to prevent this crime that all women fear and whose victims suffer physical and psychological scars that can last a lifetime? We have discussed the accomplishments, the public concern, the services that are now available, and the changes in the law. Rape should never again be "unspeakable." But prevention is another thing.

One of the goals of the early reform movement was to change a society that both permitted and sometimes encouraged sexual violence. This has clearly not been accomplished. Reform efforts to date have targeted symptoms rather than underlying causes. Permanently altering violence against women requires fundamental social change. According to Chapman (1990),

> Violence against women is a world wide phenomenon accompanied by a high degree of official and social tolerance. . . . The Nineties will see new issues emerging in global violence against women, but new opportunities for remedies as well. These remedies point toward the empowerment of women to seek equity in their personal as well as public lives. (p. 2)

In 1886, Sir James F. Stephen wrote the following:

> I pass over many sections punishing particular acts of violence. . . . In particular the whole series of offenses relating to the abduction of women, rape, and other crimes. Their history possesses no special interest and does not illustrate either our political or social history. (pp. 117–118)

Stephen's dismissal of the importance of these crimes reflects the attitude that prevailed at that time. In retrospect, we have come a long way, even though traces of this attitude remain. That a woman means "yes" when screaming "no" still remains an integral part of our rape laws. Perhaps, by the twenty-first century, rape laws will be such as to secure, to make safe, equal rights and justice under the law.

REFERENCES

Bart, P., and P. O'Brien, *Stopping Rape.* New York: Pergamon Press, 1985.

Battelle Law and Justice Study Center Report, *Forcible Rape: An Analysis of*

Legal Issues. Washington, D.C.: National Institute of Law Enforcement and Criminal Justice, 1977.

Brodyaga, L., M. Gates, S. Singer, M. Tucker, and R. White, *Rape and Its Victims: A Report for Citizens, Health Facilities, and Criminal Justice Agencies.* Washington, D.C.: U.S. Government Printing Office, 1975.

Brownmiller, S., *Against Our Will: Men, Women, and Rape.* New York: Simon and Schuster, 1975.

Burgess, A., and L. Holmstrom, *Rape: Victims of Crisis.* Bowie, Md.: Brady, 1974.

Chambers, A. M., *Rape: Issues in Focus.* Albany, N.Y.: Senate Research Series, 1989.

Chapman, J. R., *Violence and Human Rights: New Directions for the 90s.* New York; Guilford Press, *Response,* 13, no. 2 (1990).

Clark, A., *Women's Silence, Men's Violence: Sexual Assault in England 1700–1845.* London: Pandora Press, 1987.

"Crime in the U.S.," *Uniform Crime Reports.* Washington, D.C.: Federal Bureau of Investigation, U.S. Department of Justice, 1989.

The Crime of Rape. Washington, D.C.: U.S. Department of Justice, Bureau of Justice Statistics, 1985.

Doudna, C., "Ending the Rape of our Liberty," *McCalls,* May 1990.

Feldman-Summers, S., and G. C. Palmer, "Rape As Viewed by Judges, Prosecutors, and Police Officers," *Criminal Justice and Behavior,* 7, no. 1 (March 1980).

Finkelhor, D., and Yllo, *License to Rape: Sexual Abuse of Wives.* New York: Holt, Rinehart & Winston, 1985.

Hale, M., *History of the Pleas of the Crown,* vol. 1. Philadelphia: R. H. Small, 1847.

Koss, M. P., C. A. Gidycz, and N. Wisniewski, "The Scope of Rape: Incidence and Prevention of Sexual Aggression and Victimization on a National Sample of Higher Educational Students," *Journal of Consulting and Clinical Psychology,* 55(2), 162–170. 1987.

Largen, M. A., "The Anti-Rape Movement Past and Present." In A. W. Burgess (ed.), *Rape and Sexual Assault: A Research Handbook.* New York: Garland, 1985.

Largen, M. A., "A Decade of Change in the Rape Reform Movement." New York: Guilford Press, *Response,* 10, no. 2 (1987).

Ledoux, J. C., and R. R. Hazelwood, "Police Attitudes Toward Rape," *Journal of Police Science and Administration,* 1985.

Ledoux, J. C., and R. R. Hazelwood, "Police Attitudes and Beliefs Concerning Rape." In A. W. Burgess and R. R. Hazelwood (eds.), *Practical Aspects of Rape Investigation: A Multidisciplinary Approach.* New York: Elsevier, 1987.

Rape, Sexual Assault, and Child Sexual Abuse: Working towards a More Responsive Society. Albany, N.Y.: Governor's Task Force on Rape and Sexual Assault, 1990.

Robin, G. O., "Forcible Rape: Institutionalized Sexism in the Criminal Justice System," *Crime and Delinquency*, April 1977.

Russell, D., "The Prevalence and Incidence of Forcible Rape and Attempted Rape of Females," *Victimology: An International Journal*, 7, no. 1–4 (1982).

Schram, D., "Rape." in J. Chapman and M. Gates (eds.), *The Victimization of Women*. Beverly Hills, Calif.: Sage, 1985.

Sutherland, S., and D. Scherl, "Crisis Intervention with Victims of Rape," *Social Work* 17 (1972), 37–42.

19

Battered Women Who Kill Their Abusers: Their Courtroom Battles

Shelley A. Bannister

Over one-third of women who live with male lovers or husbands are beaten by those men during the course of the relationship. Men are rarely arrested for these crimes; when arrested and prosecuted, they are rarely convicted. Those men convicted of battering their wives receive minimal sentences. Men who kill their wives often receive lenient sentences. Women who kill their male abusers, however, rarely receive any leniency from the courts. Their claims of self-defense are refused, they are silenced in the court system, and they are sentenced to lengthy prison sentences. The treatment of women in the criminal justice system mirrors the degree of respect that women receive from men in the remainder of society: women are raped in staggering proportions, girl children are sexually assaulted by male family members, and women are harassed on the streets and on the job. This article explains the level of violence and legal consequences of women's acts of self-defense against men who batter them.

People charged with criminal offenses in the United States enter a world regulated by rules that appear illogical and often nonsensical. They hear words used in sentence patterns that make no sense, even though the words used may sound familiar. For women who are battered by their husbands or male partners, the sense of unreality that exists in the court system mirrors that which they experience in the battering relationship: the batterer has total control over the woman just as the judge does in the court system. The batterer's behavior is illogical, irrational, and not understandable. This chapter will discuss what happens to battered women when they enter the criminal justice system after killing their male abusers in acts of self-defense.

When we consider the fate of battered women in court, we must remember that "[f]or centuries, beating women has been the norm for societies around the world and has rarely been viewed as criminal activity" (Paterson 1979, p. 80). Annually, more than one-third of the women who live with men are beaten and/or tortured by those men (Crites and Hepperle 1987, p. 36). The abuse of women in the home ". . . is part of contemporary family life" (Bograd 1988, p. 11). The FBI estimates that wife abuse is "probably the most frequently occurring crime in the United States today" (Crites 1987, p. 39).

Wife abuse must be looked at in the context of the other forms of violence that men use against women: at least one out of every three girls will be sexually assaulted by either a family member or a stranger by the time she is eighteen years old; women have an almost one-in-two chance of being raped or being the victim of an attempted rape during their lives; and women who leave abusive males "will typically experience a 74 percent drop in income, sending them and their children below the poverty level." (Crites and Hepperle 1987, p. 36). In short, "[w]omen live in an environment of violence" (Spencer 1987, p. 54).

As will be discussed later in this chapter, judges tend to impose lenient sentences on men who are convicted of beating their wives or partners. They do not show the same leniency to women who act in self-defense against their batterers, however (Crites 1987, p. 45, and Edwards 1987, p. 165). "[A] large group of judges are influenced, if not controlled, by their traditional, sexist beliefs" (Crites 1987, p. 51).

Sexist beliefs of this type lead to massive amounts of violence against women in their own homes. Over one and one-half million women are physically battered by their male partners each year (Browne 1987, p. 5). Men do not stop with beatings; two-thirds of all intraspousal killings are of wives by husbands (Browne 1987, p. 10).

The Battering Cycle

Male violence against women in the home often follows a cycle of battering. This cycle became apparent to and was reported by Lenore Walker in 1979 following a series of interviews with battered women. "The battering cycle appears to have three distinct phases, which vary in both time and intensity for the same couple and between different couples. These are: the tension-building phase; the explosion or acute battering incident; and the calm, loving respite" (Walker 1979, p. 55).

In the first phase, the tension builds between the spouses (or partners). "[M]inor battering incidents occur." The woman attempts to keep the man as calm as possible, doing what seems to have worked in the past, either granting his every whim or staying out of his way. "She lets the batterer know that she accepts his abusiveness as legitimately directed toward her." This is not because she truly believes that he has the right to beat her, but she hopes that she can keep him from beating her more severely. She enters a stage of denial as she attempts to prevent him from seriously hurting her: she denies her anger at him and at herself for remaining; she rationalizes that maybe he is right and she does deserve what he does to her. She looks for ways to explain his violent behavior, blaming it on herself, on others, or on his work. She is generally happy when a minor incident remains minor and does not escalate into a full-blown attack, even when she realizes that the attack is inevitable (Walker 1979, pp. 56–57).

As the tension builds, the man becomes more and more fearful that his wife will leave him because of his abusive behavior; this fear is played out in increased anger, jealousy, and hostility. The woman tries to control her own behavior as well as that of other family members to minimize the tension. Nevertheless, the tension does build to a breaking point; minor battering incidents increase in frequency and in severity. The woman withdraws in fear; the man feels her distance, he moves in on her, and the tension becomes unbearable (Walker 1979, p. 59).

The second phase is the acute battering incident, "characterized by the uncontrollable discharge of tensions that have built up during phase one" (Walker 1979, p. 59). It is the uncontrolled nature of the beating that distinguishes the phase from the first phase. The batterer initially justifies his behavior to himself as an attempt to teach the woman a lesson. He "stops when he feels she has learned her lesson. By this time, however, she has generally been very severely beaten." Phase two is usually triggered by an outside event or some internal condition in the man; it usually is not triggered by something the woman does. There are exceptions to this, however. Sometimes the woman will deliberately bring on the beating as a means of controlling when it occurs, since his violence is inevitable and since it is followed by a period of calm. The tension of waiting for this extreme brutality can cause a woman to want to get it over with rather than just wait for him to act. This is not to say, of course, that the woman wants to be beaten; she simply wants to have *some* control over when it occurs. This is the briefest of phases, usually lasting between two and twenty-four hours, again with some exceptions.

Women suffer from many physical ailments as they wait for the beatings to occur: sleeplessness, high blood pressure, skin reactions, stomach ailments, heart palpitations, anxiousness, depression, and other psychophysiological ailments. Acts of self-defense by the women may result in more serious injuries: "women have had their arms twisted and broken when they raise them to ward off blows . . . The violence has an element of overkill to it, and the man cannot stop even if the woman is severely injured." Her "screaming and moaning may excite him further" (Walker 1979, pp. 59–62).

The women appear to remain constantly alert and conscious during the attack, remembering every word they screamed at them and every blow they inflicted on them. They know that resistance will bring more violence and that escape is impossible; they feel trapped. "There is also a sense of distance from the actual attack. Some women say that it was as though they could stand back and watch their disembodied selves being thrown against a wall or down a flight of stairs. The dissociation is coupled with a sense of disbelief that the incident is really happening to them" (Walker 1979, p. 62).

Often after an attack, both the man and the woman will minimize and rationalize the brutality, the woman, glad to be alive, the man incredulous that he did it. Battered women, Walker found, respond like other disaster victims, not feeling the emotional stress of the brutality until twenty-four to forty-eight hours after the occurrence (Walker 1979, p. 63).

The third phase of calm is "welcomed by both parties" (Walker 1979, p. 65). The man "knows he has gone too far, and he tries to make it up to her. It is during this phase that the battered woman's victimization becomes complete." The man apologizes, says he'll never do it again; he seems to believe that he will not hit her again. He begs for her forgiveness. "He also believes that he has taught her such a lesson that she will never again behave in such a manner, and so he will not be tempted to beat her" (Walker 1979, pp. 65–66).

This is when a battered woman is most likely to leave, at the beginning of this phase. She has been badly beaten, has been humiliated, and is angry and incredulous of his new promises. As time passes and his pleas for forgiveness become more intense, she begins to falter in her determination to leave. All of his ploys "worked on her guilt: she was his only hope; without her, he would be destroyed. What would happen to the children if she took their father away from them?" (Walker 1979, p. 66). Women have been socialized to believe that they are responsible for their husbands' behavior and that marriage is for life. He and his family and friends make her believe that he will only seek help if she is there to support him.

Walker found, however, that batterers usually seek help only *after* the women leave and then only as a ploy to get their wives or partners back. The men attempt to convince their wives that they will commit suicide if the women do not return. "Battered women sense their men's desperation, loneliness, and alienation from the rest of society. They see themselves as the bridge to their men's emotional well-being" (Walker 1979, p. 68). The two are in a symbiotic relationship which becomes almost impossible for the woman to leave (Walker 1979, p. 68). Even when the women are able to get away from the men, the batterers almost always follow them, continuing to terrorize and threaten the women's lives (Walker 1989, p. 267).

The Legal Arena

The law, that "set of formalized and codified rules that govern people's behavior and carry negative sanctions for violation," serves as the foundation for the procedures and the substance of the criminal justice system (Sokoloff and Price 1982, p. 10). United States law derives from the English common law and has been written by generally white, male legislatures (Sokoloff and Price 1982, pp. 12–13; Chambliss 1988, p. 101).

These laws governing the procedures used in the criminal justice system appear to grant a number of rights to people charged with criminal offenses. Only when one becomes involved in the system as a criminal defendant does one realize that the rights that appear on paper to be so protective in reality do not protect the defendant from injustice within the system.

Criminal defendants have the right to an attorney if they are charged with crimes that may result in their incarceration, whether for a misdemeanor or a felony. A defendant's relationship with that attorney is crucial to what will happen to him or her in the criminal justice system. A defendant, especially when poor, has little control over who his or her lawyer will be and whether the lawyer will listen to his or her preferred account of the events in question.

Often, people's accounts of "what happened" in the commission of a crime are obscured, and even changed, when the story is told in a courtroom. This occurs for a number of reasons: the court has no interest in the defendant's economic and/or social background (these factors are not deemed legally relevant to the proceedings), the system has no time to deal with people on an individual basis, and/or the truth will not help the parties secure the most advantageous resolution of the conflict. What is presented in court, then, is a construction of reality that differs from that experienced by the defendant.

This courtroom reconstruction of reality occurs regularly in the cases of battered women who have killed their abusers. These women have experienced specific oppression at the hands of their abusers in addition to the societal oppression that women experience in the

United States. This often leads to an inability to express clearly their account of what happened to their lawyers and/or to the court. It can lead to a partial telling of the battering story with omissions that affect the verdict and obscure the truth. Generally, it leads to a vast disparity between what has happened in the women's lives and how those lives are depicted in male-dominated courts. The failure to explain fully battered women's stories results in the incarceration of a large number of women for crimes of which, if fully explicated, they would have been exonerated.

The criminal defendant usually has her or his first contact with the legal arena at the point of arrest. The arrest occurs either after the issuance of an arrest warrant or by an officer who possesses probable cause to believe that the arrestee has committed a crime (McLauchlan 1977, p. 106). The arrest of a battered woman who has just killed her abuser in a desperate act of self-defense can take place at the scene of the final fight or at the police station where she has gone to turn herself into the authorities. If arrested at the scene, she will be taken to a police station for processing. Processing includes being fingerprinted, photographed, searched, and usually questioned. Before she can be questioned by law-enforcement officials, she must be read her rights as required by the United States Supreme Court: she has the right to remain silent; anything that she says can and will be used against her in a court of law; she is entitled to an attorney and, if she cannot afford an attorney, one will be appointed to represent her; and she can stop the questioning process at any time (*Miranda* v. *Arizona*, 1964).

During questioning, the defendant is encouraged by the police to cooperate. This is particularly true and particularly effective with battered women who have just been involved in a life-threatening situation which they were forced to end with violence. The women are often "severely disoriented and unable to give a clear accounting of events" (Browne 1987, p. 159). In some instances, police attempt to assist the women in their recollection of what happened, prompting the women with the police reconstructions of the killing (Browne 1987, p. 159).

During the questioning process, the investigative stage of the case, the police are framing their own construction of reality; the police are creating the "facts" that will later be re-created in court as the true picture of what happened between the woman and the man who battered her (Ericson and Baranek 1982, p. 20). Often, the defendant's confession supports the police version of the truth. The confession has been crafted, not by the woman with help from her attorney, but by her adversary in the criminal justice system, the law-enforcement officer who represents an arm of the state. During the police construction of reality, much hinges on the statements made in the confession. This confession later will hamper the defense attorney's attempts to successfully defend her or his client (Ericson and Baranek 1982, p. 21).

The defendant plays a very small role, if any, in this construction of reality. In the eyes of the state, the defendant occupies the lowest possible position in terms of credibility. The very fact that she or he committed the crime (especially in cases where a battered woman defends herself forcibly) renders her less believable (Ericson and Baranek 1982, p. 22). Additionally, the police and the state possess a great deal of discretion in the facts they choose to accentuate and the rules they wish to follow for the particular case (Ericson and Baranek 1982, p. 21).

For example, the prosecuting attorney decides which charges to bring against any defendant. His or her discretion here is limited only by the number of possible charges that fit the alleged fact situation. In a killing, the prosecutor may seek a charge of first-degree murder, which is typically defined as an intentional act committed with the knowledge that the action is likely to cause death or great bodily harm to the victim. This usually requires proof of premeditation, even if only planned moments before the act. The prosecutor may choose to charge the offender with second-degree murder or voluntary manslaughter, which require a showing that the defendant intended her or his behavior, but there is a mitigating factor present, such as provocation or that she or he unreasonably believed that he or she had a right to kill the person. The sentences attached to these two offenses range from death to natural life; from a number of years in prison to probation. Or, the prosecutor can charge the defendant with involuntary manslaughter, which involves an unintentional killing that results from a reckless act. This is usually a probational offense (Ewing 1987, pp. 43–44).

Every criminal defendant has the right to be represented in court by an attorney (Sixth Amendment, U.S. Constitution). The attorney will be appointed by the court if the defendant is indigent [*Gideon* v. *Wainwright* (1963) and *Argersinger* v. *Hamlin* (1972)]. Indigents must turn to public defenders or to pro bono attorneys. Often, the lawyers assigned to represent indigents are just starting out in their legal practice (Champion 1990) and may lack the experience necessary to successfully defend their clients. Even defense lawyers who have been in practice longer may not have the same amount of experience in the criminal justice system as the other participants: the prosecutors practice in these courts on a daily basis, often remaining assigned to the same judge and courtroom for years; the law-enforcement officers make regular appearances in the courts as part of their jobs. Defense lawyers, on the other hand, may do criminal defense work part-time, spending the rest of their time in the civil courts (Ericson and Baranek 1982, p. 25).

The defendant's right to counsel is considered the cornerstone of our legal system in providing fundamental fairness to the accused (*Gideon* v. *Wainwright*, 1963). Yet, with the problems placed upon the defense lawyer through the defendant's confession, the provision of an attorney at trial is often too late. Additionally, while professional ethics require the defense attorney to do her or his best to defend the client, the attorney also has her or his professional reputation and reputation for cooperation to protect. The defense lawyer may be subject to extreme pressure from other court personnel to protect her or his relationships with influential parties and may not fight for the client as much as he or she could (Ericson and Baranek 1982, pp. 24–26).

Despite pressure on the defense attorney that is adverse to the interests of the client, the criminal defendant is forced by her or his circumstances to have faith in the attorney. It is difficult for a defendant to test whether or not the attorney is working to the best of her or his ability for the client. Battered women frequently encounter defense attorneys who have the same biases against them as do the police, the prosecutors, and the judges. Just as the police and the state create their construction of reality of the case, the defense attorney attempts to create her or his own. In cases in which the defense attorney fails to understand the reasonableness of the woman's actions, he or she may not raise self-defense issues at all and will accept a conviction on a lesser charge as a victory (Gillespie 1989, p. 25).

The defense attorney's efforts to create a successful defense also are stymied by circumstances out of the attorney's control, such as a signed confession. The defense lawyer may very well be forced to accept the police construction of reality (Ericson and Baranek 1982, pp. 26–27). "Once the mould is set by law-enforcement agents there are few resources available to the accused to shape his destiny within the criminal process" (Ericson and Baranek 1982, p. 28).

Logically, the court process should focus on the criminal defendant. "Yet the typical felony defendant is largely powerless to control his fate—more object to be acted on than the key to what happens" (Neubauer 1988, p. 180). Uneducated and often times poor, criminal defendants are "ill-equipped to deal with the technical abstractions of the criminal court process. . . . Many are too inarticulate to aid their attorney in preparing a defense. Many hold unfavorable attitudes toward the law and the criminal justice system and thus regard the judge and all other court personnel, including their defense attorneys, with hostility and distrust" (Neubauer 1988, p. 180). In such a foreign environment, these beliefs are understandable. "In the courtroom [the defendant] experiences formality, rules of interaction, unavailability and inaccessibility of information . . ." (Ericson and Baranek 1982, p. 179).

When the defendant appears in court for the preliminary stages of the case as well as for the trial, he or she must be led to his or her proper place before the bench; the other participants all know their rightful places. All eyes are on the judge, although all participants are talking about the defendant, "treating [the defendant] like a dependent child who is to be seen and not heard" (Ericson and Baranek 1982, p. 181). The spacing and placing of a criminal defendant who is being held in custody awaiting disposition of her or his case is even more carefully delineated. The accused is brought from the holding cell, often at the back of the courtroom, by a uniformed deputy. The deputy remains in close proximity to the defendant, sometimes physically holding the defendant. Communication between the defendant and her or his attorney is thus compromised; these are supposed to be privileged, private communications. The defendant encounters the same degree of depersonalization and powerlessness of being discussed while standing mute as well as the additional pressure of being a prisoner and thus being assumed to be guilty (Ericson and Baranek 1982, pp. 181–182).

Criminal defendants often stand out in the courtrooms because of their apparel; they rarely are as well-dressed as the other participants, especially those defendants in custody. The defendant enters a courtroom that is surrounded by an "aura of respect and camaraderie" and he or she, frankly, does not fit in (Ericson and Baranek 1982, p. 182). Often, lawyers keep suits and dresses for defendants to wear in court, hoping that the defendants will look like the jurors themselves as much as possible (Bennett and Feldman 1981, p. 15). The aim here is to lessen the social distance between the accused and the finder of fact. This is a good defense strategy (Walker 1989, p. 237).

By the time the defendant gets to the trial court, she or he "confronts a reality constructed by criminal control agents which she or he cannot effectively counter, or indeed, 'wish away' " (Ericson and Baranek 1982, p. 22). In fact, the court "partly functions to legitimate the reality constructed by these agents of criminal control" (Ericson and Baranek 1982, p. 23). In a perfect example of reverse logic, the reality construction created by these law-enforcement officers becomes *the* court-recognized theory; this serves to legitimate and justify everything that the court personnel including the prosecutor and the police have done already in the case.

Up to 90 percent of all criminal defendants plead guilty to the original charges brought against them or to reduced charges (Cole 1989, p. 125). Without this large number of negotiated pleas, the criminal justice system in the United States would collapse, as there are not enough courtrooms, judges, prosecutors, defense attorneys, nor other personnel to adjudicate all of the cases brought to court. The defendant does not negotiate her or his own plea agreement. This is done by the defense attorney with the prosecutor. Generally speaking, the defendant is "manipulated and coerced" into taking the deal by the defense lawyer. Because the lawyer has obligations to other criminal defendants as well as relationships with the prosecutor, the police, and possibly the judge, the defendant's ability to ensure that he or she is getting the best possible outcome is limited. The plea negotiation is not done in open court; the defendant, therefore, has no way to monitor the process and what is said (Ericson and Baranek 1982, p. 24).

If the defendant does not accept the plea agreement, the case proceeds to trial which may be by jury or by judge. At trial, the prosecution has the burden of proving the defendant's guilt beyond a reasonable doubt. This is done through the presentation of the story of the case, a story that recounts and proves the charged criminal behavior (Bennett and Feldman 1981, p. 18). The prosecutor presents this story in the opening statement, where she or he explains the case against the defendant in a narrative form. Then she or he presents witnesses who are subject to cross-examination by the defense. Physical evidence is also introduced during the prosecutor's case-in-chief (McLauchlan 1977, pp. 114–115).

In the trial of a battered woman who has killed her abuser, the primary witnesses for the prosecution include any eye-witnesses to the killing, which might include neighbors who heard the fight. The prosecution may also call as witnesses police officers who arrived at and viewed the scene and recovered the body. The prosecutor may introduce the defendant's statement through the police officers and others who witnessed the taking of the statement/confession. During the investigation, the police officers make notes and written reports of what they say the defendant said, as well as notes of interviews with other witnesses and what they observed at the scene of the crime. At the trial, the police witnesses' testimony seems more credible than the defendant's testimony because of the presence of the notes. Most defendants do not testify from notes but from their memories. Their questionable ability to remember events clearly without the assistance of notes, coupled with their self-interest in achieving a not-guilty verdict, renders their testimony less credible (Ericson and Baranek 1987, p. 23). If the defendant's testimony contradicts the state's construction of reality, this can be viewed as "tantamount to deviance," yet another deviant act to be held against the accused (Ericson and Baranek 1987, p. 21).

The defendant is not required to take the stand in her or his own defense. Because the burden of proof is on the prosecutor, the defense may sit back and remain silent. Usually, however, "the defense will present evidence . . . [T]his will be done largely to present, to the jury, whatever counterevidence is available since the subtleties of the burden of proof may escape most juries" (McLauchlan 1977, p. 118). Most judges will instruct the jury at the conclusion of the case that the defendant is not required by law to testify and that the jury cannot hold the defendant's failure to testify against her or him. Most jurors, however, do think that if a person is not guilty and has nothing to hide, that she or he should testify. As a result, failure to testify serves as further "evidence" against the defendant.

Once the defendant is on the stand, her or his everyday style of talking can be used against her or him (Ericson and Baranek 1987, p. 196). A criminal defendant who answers a question about whether he or she had been drinking prior to the time of the offense, "yeah, I guess a little," appears to be hiding the real truth or trying to downplay the amount of alcohol consumed. In fact, the defendant may just think and speak in those imprecise terms.

Difficulties abound when a defendant chooses to take the stand in her or his own defense. A defendant's prior criminal record is inadmissible against her or him unless she or he testifies, and then only as to credibility (Lilly 1978, pp. 288–289). She or he may be impeached with prior inconsistent statements given to law-enforcement personnel or made to others regarding the offense (Lilly 1978, pp. 298–299). And, obviously, a criminal defendant's testimony is always subject to the claim that she or he is lying to save herself or himself from prison. The lawyer's job is made easier if the defendant chooses to remain silent; the lawyer can rely on the state's inability to prove the defendant guilty beyond a reasonable doubt and the defendant does not take the risk of seeming unbelievable (Ericson and Baranek 1987, p. 198).

Battered Women in Court

A small percentage of battered women end their abuse by ending the lives of their abusers (Ewing 1987, p. 5). Women who kill their batterers generally are not acquitted of homicide charges, in spite of what the popular press would have us believe. In fact, many of these women plead guilty or are convicted of some form of homicide charges and are usually sentenced to long terms in prison (Ewing 1987, p. 41). This fact stands in stark contrast to the opposite reality that men who are prosecuted by their wives or partners for battering them usually receive extremely lenient sentences when convicted. In fact, the chance that a male batterer will be convicted at all is minimal (Buzawa and Buzawa 1990, p. 87).

Some judges have recognized that an attack in the home is no different in terms of harm than an attack that occurs in the street between strangers. Too many judges, however, appear to be "unready and unwilling to implement new legislation protecting battered women or to respond to growing social pressure that assault on a wife or lover within the home is no less assault than is the same behavior on the street against a stranger" (Crites 1987, pp. 41–42).

Offenses against women in the home by their male lovers or husbands are not seen by judges, especially male judges, as serious. Crites (1987) cites a number of examples: the usual sentence for a batterer in Denver in 1982 was a $25 fine even when injuries such as brain damage, attempted strangulation, and harm to limbs, the eyes, ears, and nose were suffered by the woman. In a 1982 New York case, a man received unsupervised probation after cutting his wife's face (Crites 1987, p. 44).

In some instances, judges refuse to follow the law, even laws that require them to impose particular sentences on batterers. A Hawaii law requires that a convicted batterer must serve forty-eight hours in jail and should be ordered to receive counseling. During a five-month period in Honolulu, in 1987, only 1 out of 111 convicted batterers was sent to jail and only 8 were sent to counseling (Crites 1987, p. 44).

Men who kill their wives often are excused of their crimes or treated leniently because of judges' perceptions that the woman goaded the husband into the act of killing her. There seems to be a "clear gender bias" in what constitutes provocation and mitigation of sentences when one considers the differences in outcomes and sentences between killings of women by men and killings of men by women (Edwards 1987, p. 165). For example, in a 1984 Denver case, a man was sentenced to two years of work-release for killing his wife by shooting her in the face five times. The judge justified the sentence by referring to the woman's provoking acts: she left the man without warning and filed for an order of protection without telling him where she was. The judge stated that her actions provoked her husband into a state of passion "as it would any reasonable person under the circumstances" (Crites 1987, pp. 44–45).

Battered women who kill their abusers in self-defense rarely receive such levels of compassion from their courts. "There is nothing necessarily wise or enlightened about judges. They share the same prejudices and stereotyped beliefs as the rest of the population; to the extent that state court judges tend to be white males past middle age, their attitudes about women may be more traditional than most" (Gillespie 1989, p. 27).

The women often raise the affirmative defense of self-defense to murder/manslaughter charges brought against them. "While results vary, many of these defendants are convicted, despite their claims of self-defense and the abundant evidence that they were severely abused by the men they killed" (Ewing 1987, p. 5). The results of four studies of battered women who killed or attempted to kill their abusers illustrates this.

1. Lenore Walker reported the criminal case dispositions of twenty-eight women: the charges against one woman were dropped; seven women pled guilty to reduced homicide charges, four of the seven were sentenced to probation, and the other three were incarcerated from one to eight years in prison; fifteen of the twenty-eight went to trial: eight were convicted and seven were acquitted; the sentences for the convicted ranged from ten years probation to twenty-five years in prison (Ewing 1987, p. 41).

2. Angela Browne's study involved the legal dispositions of forty-one women: 33 had been charged with murder, six with attempted murder, and three with conspiracy to commit murder; of these 41, 9 were acquitted, thirty-one were convicted and one woman's case was dismissed prior to trial. Of the 31 convicted, 11 received probation; the other twenty received prison sentences, ranging from 6 months to fifty years (Ewing 1987, pp. 41–42).

3. Ann Jones' study involved thirty-three women: eight were acquitted, the charges for three of them were dropped, one was found not guilty by reason of insanity, and twenty-one pled guilty or were convicted of homicide charges; two of the latter group got life sentences, and ten received other prison sentences from five to twenty-five years (Jones 1980, pp. 281–321).

4. Charles Ewing reviewed the cases of 100 battered women who had killed their abusers: 9 pled guilty to homicide charges and were sentenced to probation to up to twenty years in prison; 3 were found not guilty by reason of insanity; the charges were dropped against 3; 85 went to trial relying on self-defense—22 were found not guilty. Sixty-three were convicted as follows: 1st degree murder—7; second-degree murder—15; third-degree murder—1; unspecified murder—12; voluntary manslaughter—11; involuntary manslaughter—5; unspecified manslaughter—8; manslaughter with firearm—1; reckless homicide—3. Twelve convicted of murder received sentences of life in prison, one without parole for fifty years. The others got from four years probation to twenty-five years in prison (Ewing 1987, pp. 31–40).

One may reasonably ask, why so many convictions when so many of the women were acting in self-defense? We are not discussing women who just decided one day to kill their male partners. The doctrine of self-defense, however, was created by men to be applied to fights between men, and it has been interpreted by men to exclude women's actions to defend themselves against men in the home (Gillespie 1989, p. 50). The definition of self-defense has been limited statutorily and by case law; women's cases often do not fit within these narrow boundaries (Ewing 1987, p. 47).

The law of self-defense generally states that a person may use reasonable force against another person when the person reasonably believes that the other person is threatening her or him with imminent and unlawful bodily harm and that her or his force is necessary to prevent the threatened harm (Samaha 1990, p. 196). One may only use such force likely to cause death or great bodily harm when that is the threat against one (Samaha 1990, p. 202). Self-defense acts as a justification for the act; the defense of insanity, also posed by some battered women who kill their abusers, serves as an excuse for the behavior (Ewing 1987, p. 47). When one is found to be insane, the judge or jury is stating that a person is unable to form the criminal intent to commit the offense (Samaha 1990, p. 259).

In the self-defense cases, a woman must show that she reasonably believed that she was in imminent danger and that it was necessary for her to use deadly force against that danger (Ewing 1987, p. 47). If a battered woman kills her abuser while he sleeps, the judge or jury may and usually does find that the requirement of imminence has not been met, even if she reasonably believed that he would kill her when he awoke (Ewing 1987, pp. 47–48). Similarly, if a woman kills following a beating and not actually during it, a judge or jury may find that there was no imminent threat of danger (Edwards 1987, p. 164). Women who kill during a fight often are still convicted because the man had no weapon except his hands, even though he had inflicted severe injury with those hands during an earlier beating (Ewing 1987, p. 48).

Battering men, without the aid of any additional weapons, have inflicted severe damage on or killed their women partners. Women's arms have been "twisted and broken, [women] were thrown across rooms and down stairs, and choked until they passed out. They were hurled against objects and had objects hurled against them. When they raised their arms to defend themselves, their arms and ribs were broken. . . . [Battered women] reported broken necks and backs, concussions, severe internal injuries, and bleeding. . . . Rape and sexual sadism are a common element of wife abuse" (Gillespie 1989, pp. 51–52). Pregnant women were beaten in the stomach; most women report being sexually abused as well as physically abused (Gillespie 1989, p. 52).

Additionally, if the man uses an ordinary object which is not usually seen as a dangerous weapon, juries have difficulty seeing the danger the woman was in. Many women are convicted of murder after defending themselves against such attacks as being beaten with a chair or being subjected to a terrifying automobile ride with a drunken man who is threatening to kill them both (Gillespie 1989, pp. 58–59). As Gillespie states about the woman who was attacked with a chair, "[t]rapped in the tiny house trailer and unable to fend off the blows with her bare hands, her only legal course of action was to submit to the beating and pray, one supposes, that he would stop before he maimed or killed her" (Gillespie 1989, p. 58). Women, generally, have not been taught to fight; women do not learn the necessary skills nor develop the strength that men have in such fights (Edwards 1987, p. 164). Yet, the law of self-defense expects women to use only that force equal to the force used by the man (Ewing 1987, p. 50).

Frequently, the woman is punished with a guilty verdict precisely because of all the beatings in the past that did not result in her death. How can a woman convincingly explain that this time was different—that this time she reasonably believed her abuser would kill her? Judges or jurors question whether her perception that this time he meant to kill her was reasonable (Ewing 1987, pp. 48–49). "[O]nce a man has established himself as a nonlethal wife beater, some judges and juries will presume that he will always be a nonlethal wife beater" (Gillespie 1989, p. 60). However, research consistently disproves this theory: "[w]here battering is chronic, the most common pattern is for the beatings to get progressively more violent" (Gillespie 1989, p. 60).

Women whose aggressive acts fit the standard established by men for men in self-defense cases are generally more likely to succeed in court, as the above discussion makes evident. Battered women, however, have developed a modified form of the law of self-defense to explain why their violent reactions to men's violence are reasonable. This is a defense based on the "battered woman syndrome," a term used to describe the psychological condition that results from experiencing violence in the cycle described by Walker (Browne 1987, p. 177, Ewing 1987, pp. 51–52). Women who are beaten by their husbands experience "high levels of anxiety, panic attacks, and waves of depression" (Buzawa and Buzawa 1990, pp. 86–87). Testimony about the syndrome assists jurors in understanding why women act as they do, especially since the response to battering can be confusing to outsiders (Crites and Hepperle 1987, p. 36).

A battered woman defendant relying on this defense presents

the testimony of an expert witness whose task is to explain to the judge and/or jury that "the psychological reality of these women justifies their actions" (Walker 1989, p. 267). The history of the abuse leads the woman to reasonably believe that killing the abuser is her only possible means of escape from her life-threatening situation (Walker 1989, p. 267). The law of self-defense is a subjective test requiring the judge and/or jury to decide what was *reasonable* for the defendant at the time of the killing. The expert testifying about the battered women's syndrome explains that a battered woman who was faced with the very real probability of death at the hands of her husband or partner did act reasonably in killing him. In fact, the jury or judge should understand that this response was a *healthy* one and normal (Walker 1989, p. 169).

The bias against battered women who kill their abusers is not restricted to the formal law. "It is also common, although never admitted as official policy, for an attorney to measure the probable amount of 'prosecutable' injury a battered woman has sustained by counting the number of stitches required to close her wounds. And if battered women who kill can demonstrate serious bodily injuries (and a crime scene that backs up their story of imminent danger according to a male standard), they are most likely to be believed by the authorities; if the injuries are bad enough or permanent enough, they may be 'lucky' and escape being charged with a crime" (Walker 1989, pp. 236–237).

Conclusion

Women in the United States occupy a marginal position (Walker 1989, p. 237, and Edwards 1987, p. 154). The marginality of women is illustrated by the vast amount of violence against women. Whenever marginal people strike back against their abusers or oppressors, they are judged harshly (Walker 1989, p. 237). Women who kill men are punished severely to reinforce society's view of women's inferiority and subordination to men and to remind other women that this type of behavior will not be condoned by the ruling patriarchy (Bannister 1989, p. 4).

The court system fails battered women because it is based on a male model of how to determine fact. "In the male model, events are seen as factual entities, taken separately from the context in which they occurred; intellectual understanding is separate, too, from process analysis. . . . Men, therefore, can more easily tell their stories using the rules of the legal system." (Walker 1989, p. 257) Women include their prior knowledge of how a person has acted as well as nonverbal behavior in their analyses of the circumstances that led to their acts of self-defense. This analysis of process often appears as "opinion" testimony in court, which is generally only allowable from an expert witness (Walker 1989, pp. 256–257). Women do not operate well in this system, in which the rules of evidence render background material and information irrelevant and extraneous (Walker 1989, p. 257). Women often have trouble "separating discrete factual events from the general patterns of their lives" (Walker 1989, p. 258). Additionally, the stark courtroom atmosphere, the neutrality that appears as hostility, with its absence of smiles and lightness and the barking of the judge, all intimidate the women as they testify. A battered woman, who already feels unsafe in this world, who was violated and silenced by her abuser, may be silenced by this atmosphere forever (Walker 1989, pp. 12, 258).

REFERENCES

Bannister, Shelley, "Another View of Political Prisoners," *The Critical Criminologist* (Newsletter of the American Society of Criminology), 1, no. 4 (Winter 1989).

Bennett, W. Lance, and Martha S. Feldman, *Reconstructing Reality in the Courtroom*. New Brunswick, N.J.: Rutgers University Press, 1981.

Bograd, Michele, "Feminist Perspectives on Wife Abuse: An Introduction." In Kersti Yllo and Michele Bograd (eds.), *Feminist Perspectives on Wife Abuse*. Newbury Park, Calif.: Sage Publications, 1988.

Browne, Angela, *When Battered Women Kill*. New York: The Free Press, 1987.

Buzawa, Eve S., and Carl G. Buzawa, *Domestic Violence: The Criminal Justice Response*. Newbury Park, Calif.: Sage Publications, 1990.

Chambliss, William J., *Exploring Criminology*. New York: Macmillan, 1988.

Champion, Dean J., *Criminal Justice in the United States*. Columbus, Ohio: Merrill, 1990.

Cole, George, *The American System of Criminal Justice*. Pacific Grove, Calif.: Brooks/Cole, 1989.

Crites, Laura L., "Wife Abuse: The Judicial Record." In *Women, the Courts, and Equality*. Laura L. Crites and Winifred L. Hepperle (eds.), Newbury Park, Calif.: Sage Publications, 1987.

Crites, Laura L. and Winifred L. Hepperle, *Women, The Courts, and Equality*. Newbury Park, Calif.: Sage Publications, 1987.

Edwards, Susan S. M., " 'Provoking Her Own Demise': From Common Assault to Homicide." In *Women, Violence and Social Control*. Atlantic Highlands, N.J.: Humanities Press International, 1987.

Ericson, Richard V. and Patricia M. Baranek, *The Ordering of Justice: A Study of Accused Persons as Dependents in the Criminal Process*. Toronto, Canada: University of Toronto Press, 1982.

Ewing, Charles Patrick, *Battered Women Who Kill: Psychological Self-Defense as Legal Justification.* Lexington, Mass.: Lexington Books, D.C. Heath, 1987.

Gillespie, Cynthia K., *Justifiable Homicide: Battered Women, Self-Defense, and the Law.* Columbus, Ohio: Ohio State University Press, 1989.

Jones, Ann, *Women Who Kill.* New York: Holt, Rinehart and Winston, 1980.

Lilly, Graham C., *An Introduction to the Law of Evidence.* St. Paul, Minn.: West Publishing, 1978.

McLauchlan, William P., *American Legal Processes.* New York: Wiley, 1977.

Neubauer, David W., *America's Courts and the Criminal Justice System.* Pacific Grove, Calif.: Brooks/Cole, 1988.

Paterson, Eva Jefferson, "How the Legal System Responds to Battered Women." In Donna M. Moore (ed.), *Battered Women.* Beverly Hills, Calif.: Sage Publications, 1979.

Samaha, Joel, *Criminal Law.* St. Paul, Minn.: West Publishing, 1990.

Sokoloff, Natalie J. and Barbara Raffel Price, "The Criminal Law and Women." In Sokoloff and Price (eds.), *The Criminal Justice System and Women.* New York: Clark Boardman, 1982.

Spencer, Cassie C., "Sexual Assault: The Second Victimization." In Laura L. Crites and Winifred L. Hepperle (eds.), *Women, the Courts, and Equality.* Newbury Park, Calif.: Sage Publications, 1987.

Walker, Lenore E., *The Battered Woman.* New York: Harper Colophon Books, 1979.

Walker, Lenore E., *Terrifying Love: Why Battered Women Kill and How Society Responds.* New York: Harper and Row, 1989.

CASES CITED

Argersinger v. Hamlin, (1972) 407 U.S. 25, 92 S. Ct. 2006, 32 L. Ed. 2d 530.

Gideon v. Wainwright, (1963) 327 U.S. 335, 83 S. Ct. 792, 9 L. Ed. 2d 799.

Miranda v. Arizona, (1964) 384 U.S. 436, 86 S. Ct. 1602, 16 L. Ed. 2d 694.

20

Arrest Policies for Domestic Violence and Their Implications for Battered Women

Susan L. Miller

Historically, the criminal justice system has failed to adquately respond to woman battering. In response to criticisms, the system has moved toward emphasizing pro-arrest policies. Much of this redirection resulted from outcry from feminist groups and the findings from the Minneapolis Domestic Violence Experiment, which indicated that arrest deters offenders at higher rates than separation or mediation. Consequently, in the past five years, many police departments have restructured their policies and procedures; replication efforts have begun to test the deterrence hypothesis using different samples and geographic sites. Two particular concerns have been raised as a result of these shifts in policy: first, the replication studies have failed to demonstrate convincingly that arrest of batterers deters repeat offenses from occurring in sites other than Minneapolis; arrest may in fact make the situation worse. And, second, pro-arrest policies may introduce disproportionately negative ramifications for women of lower socioeconomic classes and minority women.

This chapter will explore the changes in how the criminal justice system responds to woman batterers, beginning with a review of the policy changes since the 1980s. Next, the replication efforts of pro-arrest studies will be evaluated. These implications for victims will be assessed in terms of the replication studies and the differential impact these policies may have for lower-class and minority women. Finally, a brief review of alternatives and supplements to arrest will be conducted. This chapter provides a comprehensive review of the current status of policies of the criminal justice system in its attempt to combat woman battering.

Historically, the crime of intimate violence has been shrouded in secrecy, viewed as a private matter and not as a social problem. Both legal and social institutions have reinforced the "hands-off approach" that has characterized responses to woman battering.[1] However, since the 1970s, efforts initiated by the battered women's movement have successfully propelled the issue of intimate violence into the national spotlight (see Schechter 1982).[2] Much of the research and political activism has focused on identifying the correlates of abuse, providing services for victims, creating or strengthening domestic violence legislation, and improving the criminal justice system's responses to woman battering. One of the most compelling criticisms concerning the handling of woman battering has been leveled against police officers' failure to arrest woman batterers and adequately protect victims. Consequently, in the 1980s, innovative laws were introduced and policy efforts were designed to improve the criminal justice system's treatment of domestic disputes. Included was the move toward pro-arrest policies. This chapter will focus on the problems that facilitated these policy innovations, the pro-arrest strategies themselves, and will review the current status of pro-arrest strategies. Special attention will be paid to the different impact these policies may have for lower-class and minority battered women. It will conclude with a brief review of alternative dispositions (other than arrest) and their value to battered women.[3]

------

[1]Special thanks to Bruce Kubu for his research assistance and Cynthia Burack for her helpful comments regarding an earlier draft of this chapter.

[2]Although methodologies vary, incidence rates of woman battering range from 16 percent using nationally representative household surveys (Straus and others 1980) to 50 percent based on victimization surveys and interviews (Walker 1979, Freize and others 1980, Russell 1982). According to national household survey data, these percentages suggest that over 1.5 million women are battered each year (Straus and others 1980; and Straus and Gelles 1986) while victimization data from the National Crime Survey provides estimates that 2.1 million women are battered annually, with violence recurring in 32 percent of the cases within six months of reporting (Langan and Innes 1986).

[3]Although this chapter's emphasis is explicitly focused on heterosexual violence perpetrated by men against women, there are other studies that explore similar issues for different samples [see Lobel (1986) and Renzetti (1987) for research on battered lesbians; see McLeod (1984) for a discussion about battered men]. Samples of battered lesbians or battered men, though different, share some commonalities, such as reasons that would inhibit victims' disclosure of violence. Both battered men and battered lesbians may fear social stigmatization; this fear compounds disclosure issues and isolation. For battered lesbians, reporting may be particularly risky, especially if their relationships are not socially desirable or institutionally sanctioned. Additionally,

Criminal Justice System's Responses to Woman Battering

The handling of domestic disputes has evoked deep feelings of frustration from both police officers responding to these calls *and* from battered women responding to police officers' inaction.[4] Since mediation or separation were the common modes of police response, batterers were not punished for their actions, and victims of their violence were not adequately protected (Stanko 1985). These official responses were justified by cultural norms and gender role expectations, despite the accumulated evidence showing that unchecked intimate violence escalates in frequency and intensity, with some episodes resulting in the death of the victim (Walker and others 1982).[5]

For years, battered women faced police officers who routinely supported the offender's position, challenged the credibility of the victim—often blaming her for her own victimization—and trivialized her fears (Karmen 1982, and Gil 1986). Police officer training manuals reinforced officer behavior, stressing the use of family-crisis intervention or separation tactics (IACP 1967, and Parnas 1967). This policy emphasis sanctioned the discretion of police officers; it thus also sanctioned their reluctance to initiate criminal justice proceedings when officers thought that a reconciliation might occur and make arrest actions futile (Field and Field 1973; and Lerman 1986). Not only did the police fail to formally respond to battering by invoking arrest; other components in the system responded similarly (for example, prosecutors and judges).[6] Taken together, the failure of the system to appropriately respond to woman battering perpetuated the silence surrounding intimate violence.

Statistics indicate that when police *do* retain the discretion to

---

traditional sources of help that are available for victims, such as shelters and laws, have been designed primarily to benefit women engaged in heterosexual relationships.

[4]More thorough reviews of police responses to woman battering are available elsewhere [see Elliott (1989); Buzawa and Buzawa (1990a,b); and Hamner and others (1989)].

[5]For instance, a study in Kansas City (Missouri) revealed that in 85 percent of the domestic assault or homicide incidents, police had been called in at least *five* times before in 50 percent of these cases (Police Foundation 1977).

[6]For instance, see Parnas 1970; Truninger 1971; Field and Field 1973; Vera Institute of Justice 1977; Laszlo and McKean 1978; Paterson 1979; Klein 1981; Lerman 1981; Stanko 1982; Lerman and Livingston 1983; Bowker 1983; Ellis 1984; and Kuhl and Saltzman 1985.

arrest in domestic-assault incidents, officers largely do *not* arrest.[7] For example, three different studies indicate that for domestic-violence incidents, police arrest rates were 10 percent, 7 percent, and 3 percent (see Buel 1988). In Milwaukee, although 82 percent of battered women desired arrest of their abusers, police arrested only 14 percent of these offenders (Bowker 1982). Similarly, in Ohio, police arrested only in 14 percent of the cases, even though in 38 percent of these incidents, victims were either injured or killed (Bell 1984).

As a result of police departments' inadequate responses to treat battering as a serious offense, class-action suits were introduced against police departments by victims (Martin 1978, and Paterson 1979). In fact, battered women who felt unprotected by police have received some satisfaction from this kind of court action, arguing successfully that the equal protection clause of the Fourteenth Amendment is violated when police treat women who are assaulted by an intimate partner differently from people assaulted by strangers.[8] Class-action suits, political activism by feminists, and victims' advocacy groups proved instrumental in challenging the efficacy and unresponsiveness of police departments (Schechter 1982). The stage was set for researchers to explore new and different responses by police to battering, including advocating pro-arrest or mandatory arrest policies.

Mandatory Arrest Policies

Movement away from discretionary arrest policies and toward mandatory or pro-arrest policies is attractive for a variety of reasons. First, the psychological benefit to battered women cannot be overstated: arrest demonstrates a willingness to officially assert that battering will not be tolerated. Second, some police officers believe mandatory-arrest laws assist in clarifying police roles by providing more guidance and training (Loving 1980). Third, evaluations of jurisdictions that enact mandatory-arrest laws indicate that rather than making police officers more vulnerable, police injuries decrease (National Criminal Justice Association 1985); this decrease may be due to the advance notice or warning about the consequences of abusive

---

[7]However, see Smith's (1987) analysis of interpersonal violence that found particular extralegal factors, such as race, gender, victim's preference, economic status of neighborhood, and demeanor of combatants toward officer, influenced police arrest decisions.

[8]For more details on litigation by battered women, see Moore 1985 and Eppler 1986.

behavior once mandatory-arrest policies are in effect. Fourth, the onus of responsibility is transferred to police and does not remain solely on the battered woman's shoulders. Thus, many believe that officer-initiated arrest empowers the victim (Buel 1988):

> Arrest can kindle the battered woman's perception that society values her and penalizes violence against her. This perception counteracts her experience of abuse . . . When a battered woman calls the police and they arrest the man who beats her, her actions, along with the officer's actions, do something to stop her beating . . . Now her actions empower her. The woman may begin to believe in herself enough to endeavor to protect herself. (Pastoor 1984)[9]

A fifth advantage of mandatory arrest policies is the feeling that more equitable law enforcement will result than with a discretionary-based arrest system. Buel (1988, p. 224) argues that mandatory arrest that is conducted whenever specific, objective conditions are met, will "ensure that race and class distinctions are not the basis for determining how police intervene in family violence situations."[10] Sixth, strong police action can contribute to purposeful follow-through by the other components of the criminal justice system.

And finally, some early research findings indicate that recidivism of batterers dramatically decreases after instituting mandatory-arrest policies. For instance, homicides decreased from twelve or thirteen annually to one in the initial six months of 1986 in Newport News, Virginia (Lang 1986); in Hartford County, Connecticut, the number of calls for police service for domestic violence incidents decreased by 28 percent (Olivero 1987). Perhaps the most conclusive research findings are attributed to the Minneapolis Domestic Violence Experiment, conducted by Sherman and Berk (1984).

The Minneapolis field experiment manipulated types of police response to misdemeanant domestic assault.[11] The research findings

---

[9]However, an alternative interpretation challenging Pastoor's empowerment hypothesis has been raised by MacKinnon (1983). Essentially, she argues that police intervention increases dependency on the state by battered women. Additionally, MacKinnon argues that manipulating police responses fails to "address . . . the conditions that produce men who systematically express themselves violently toward women, women whose resistance is disabled, and the role of the state in this dynamic (MacKinnon 1983, p. 643). See also Rifkin (1980) for a discussion of the limitations of what the law can accomplish since it remains embedded in patriarchal foundations which do not challenge sexual stratification in society.

[10]Buel (1988, p. 224) contends that officers disproportionately arrest batterers who are men of color and/or from the lower socioeconomic classes; mandatory arrest would restructure this traditional police response.

[11]The Minneapolis Domestic Violence Experiment randomly assigned police officers to deliver one of three possible responses to misdemeanant domestic assaults—mediation, separation, or arrest. Using a six-month follow-up period, both victim

reveal that arrest is twice as effective a deterrent for batterers than the more traditional police strategies of separation or meditation (Sherman and Berk 1984).[12] A subsequent national survey of police departments indicates that jurisdictions supporting arrest for minor domestic assault are increasing in numbers (from 10 percent in 1984 to 31 percent in 1986); eleven states attribute these policy changes to the publicized results of the Minneapolis experiment's success (Cohn and Sherman 1986).[13]

New Concerns about Mandatory Arrest Policies

Ostensibly, mandatory arrest policies appear to solve the dilemmas faced by battered women. In fact, it is difficult not to wholeheartedly embrace such a transformation of police procedure in dealing with woman battering. However, there are at least *three* considerations that limit unconditional acceptance of the interpretation that arrest deters battering, or that mandatory arrest eliminates disparity in arrest practices. First, there are methodological problems associated with the original (first-wave) research, the Minneapolis Domestic Violence Experiment (Sherman and Berk 1984), which was instrumental in generating additional evaluations of mandatory-arrest policies. Second, there are problems identified with the NIJ-funded replication studies and contrary results reported from other (second-wave) studies. And, third, there may be unintended negative consequences of mandatory arrest for battered women themselves, particularly for women of color or women from lower socioeconomic groups (Miller 1989). These concerns raise hesitations about fully accepting the conclusion that arrest of woman batterers deters subsequent acts of intimate violence.

Methodological Problems

Methodological problems associated with Sherman and Berk's (1984) seminal study are now legion (for instance, see Lempert 1984; Binder and Meeker 1988; and Fagan 1989). The most salient problem con-

---

reports and police reports indicate that arrest deterred offenders significantly more than the alternative interventions (Sherman and Berk 1984).

[12]At least one effort to replicate this finding in a nonexperimental setting has been successful (see Berk and Newton 1985).

[13]However, a reexamination of the mandatory arrest policy enacted in Minneapolis revealed that despite the policy, out of 24,948 domestic assault calls in 1986, less than 3,645 resulted in arrest; instead of arrest, officers used mediation techniques to dispense with cases (Balos and Trotzky 1988).

cerns the sample. The deterrent effect attributed to mandatory arrest was based on a small number of follow-up interviews completed by the battered women: Sherman and Berk (1984, p. 265) report a 62 percent completion rate for the initial face-to-face interviews, and a 49 percent completion rate for the biweekly follow-ups for six subsequent months (161 respondents from a sample of 330 victims). Sherman and Berk (1984) contend that the experimental design of the research had no effect on the victim's participation decisions during the follow-up phase. It may be likely that further violence occurred, but is undisclosed in follow-up interviews, or simply lost due to case attrition. If these problems escape detection, a research artifact may be created during the follow-up stage, or, the observed deterrent effect may only be temporary, contingent on pending charges (Jaffe and others, 1986).

Victims may display reluctance in requesting police service after experiencing the consequences of official intervention once a mandatory-arrest policy becomes effective (Sherman and Berk 1984, p. 269). This dynamic would mask continued violence in follow-up interviews and in official records, demonstrating a deterrent effect in reporting practices, but not actual battering incidences (Berk and Newton 1985). In fact, Buzawa (1982) contends that once a woman loses control over the outcome of a domestic dispute, she may be deterred from calling the police.[14] Battered women who call the police for help may only desire the cessation of the immediate abuse; in these cases, arrest may be acknowledged by the woman as a possible alternative, but one that is *not* desirable. An unintended consequence may be that battering *escalates* as a result of an arrest, with increased intimidation, threats, or retaliation from the abuser, causing the victim to be silent (Goolkasian 1986, p. 35).[15]

Findings of a deterrent effect may really be a result of displacement in which the original violent relationship has terminated, but the batterer simply moves into a new violent relationship with a new partner (Reiss 1985, and Fagan 1989). This displacement effect is related to selective attrition problems identified by Elliott (1989, p.

---

[14]Buzawa's (1982) position stems from an examination of aggregate domestic-assault arrest data from Detroit after an aggressive arrest policy went into effect. Considerably *fewer* calls for police assistance were made by victims *after* the policy was in place. This effect of victim deterrence may be more magnified in jurisdictions that have mandatory-arrest policies because victims would have even less power to state their preference (Buzawa 1982).

[15]One way of assessing this hypothesis is to keep track of calls to domestic violence hot lines or shelters to see if these more informal responses increase after mandatory-arrest policies go into effect. This would seem to indicate that battered women still desire help, but not in terms of official intervention. This issue might be even more complicated for some battered women (for example, women of color or from lower socioeconomic groups). This will be addressed in the next part of the text.

453). These may occur if arrest affects the termination of the relationship, thereby limiting the deterrent interpretation of lower recidivism rates after a pro-arrest policy goes into effect. Ford (1984) offers support for this hypothesis with evidence that arrest may be correlated with breaking up, which is one successful way of stopping further violence. A displacement effect could also exist under the guise of a deterrent effect if the violence shifts its focus to other family members. If a relationship remains intact but the couple moves away from the area, their absence in official records may be misleading if it is interpreted as a deterrent effect (Lempert 1984).

Given the plausibility of alternative explanations, some researchers have suggested caution in adopting such dramatic policy shifts based on the "success" of the Minneapolis experiment, fearing that the changes are not well-thought-out, not well-grounded in empirical support, and are generated from research that is methodologically problematic (Lempert 1984; Gelles and Mederer 1985; Binder and Meeker 1988; and Elliott 1989)."[16]

Failures and Problems with Replication Studies and Other Pro-Arrest Evaluations

Based on the questions and concerns generated by Sherman and Berk's Minneapolis experiment, the National Institute of Justice[17] has funded six different replication studies to facilitate further exploration of the deterrent effects of police response to battering (U.S. Department of Justice 1985). It is hoped that these new studies will address and correct some of the important issues and problems raised by the Minneapolis experiment, although the evaluations are not yet near completion.[18] At the date of this writing, only one NIJ funded replication study, in Omaha, Nebraska, has published results of research (see Dunford and others 1990). However, other research has been published that evaluates policy impacts of mandatory or presumptive arrest in other jurisdictions.[19] This section will explore the

---

[16]However, it is not always feasible to stall policy decisions while awaiting for results of replication studies, in light of public sentiment and political pressures (see Sherman and Cohn 1989).

[17]The National Institute of Justice was the original funding source for the Minneapolis Domestic Violence Experiment (Sherman and Berk 1984).

[18]The six sites where replication projects are in progress are Dade County, Florida; Atlanta, Georgia; Charlotte, North Carolina; Milwaukee, Wisconsin; and Colorado Springs, Colorado.

[19]Mandatory arrest limits police officer discretion while dictating arrest action; presumptive arrest is designed to strongly guide police officer discretion in the direction of arrest.

findings of four such studies: London, Ontario; Phoenix, Arizona; the District of Columbia; and Omaha, Nebraska.[20]

Researchers examining the impact of a proarrest policy change in London, Ontario, found that the numbers of cases in which the police initiated criminal charges of woman abuse increased dramatically (2.7 percent in 1979 to 67.3 percent in 1983), the numbers of cases dismissed or withdrawn decreased substantially, and victim self-reports revealed a decrease in subsequent violence for the year following the policy change and police intervention (Jaffe and others 1986). However, results from a police officer survey indicated that only 21 percent of the police surveyed believed the new policy was effective in stopping intimate violence, and 32 percent thought women stopped calling the police after the policy was enacted (Jaffe and others 1986). Elliott (1989) addresses this contradiction, maintaining that the study is plagued by serious methodological problems that question the success of the new arrest policy, such as the absence of control groups to use for comparisons, and the unrepresentativeness of the sample of victims used. In light of these problems, it is difficult to conclude with any confidence that pro-arrest policies in Ontario facilitated victim reporting, or that the deterrent effects indicated were really *true* ones.

Buzawa and Buzawa (1990b) contend that police officers are generally distrustful of police-policy directives designed by outside political leaders or nonpolice personnel. This distrust is manifested in officer circumvention of laws or policies, which "extends to ignoring or subverting recognized rules of criminal procedure or explicit organizational goals and directives" (Buzawa and Buzawa 1990b, p. 100). Research that evaluates the impact of a presumptive arrest policy adopted by the Phoenix, Arizona police supports the idea that police circumvent policy (Ferraro 1989b); despite the change in law and department policies, arrests were made in only 18 percent of the domestic assault cases. Ferraro (1989b) suggests that most of the noncompliance by the police was related to legal, ideological, and political considerations, which led them to ignore the policy change. In this analysis, Ferraro was able to gather detailed qualitative data through interviews with victims. These provided explanations as to why some battered women, particularly those from lower-class positions, would be less inclined to call the police if it meant their

---

[20]As of 1990, thirteen states have enacted mandatory arrest policies for domestic violence offenders (the application of arrest varies, dependent on if the offense is a felony or misdemeanor, whether or not crime is a first offense, for violation of restraining order, if victim is in danger, and for primary aggressor only) (Buzawa and Buzawa 1989b).

partners would be arrested, creating financial hardship for the family, including possible job loss.

In 1987, the District of Columbia's police department enacted new legislation that directed officers to arrest batterers. However, an evaluation conducted two years after its imposition found that police had failed to enforce the guideline, continuing to resort to mediating domestic disputes and keeping arrests at a minimum (Baker and others, 1989). These findings are based on interviews with almost 300 victims who sought protection at either the Superior Court or the Citizens Complaint Center. Similar to other pro-arrest policy implementation evaluations, police circumvented the policy. In the D.C. study, only 5 percent of the cases resulted in arrest; this rate remained low even when the complainant was seriously injured (requiring medical treatment) or had been threatened with knives, guns, or other weapons.[21] The most commonly cited reasons offered by police to explain their failure to arrest were they believed nothing could be done (23.7 percent), the police thought the case was "domestic" or the couple lived together (22.6 percent) (and, thus, the police did not want to get involved), or the victim was instructed to go to the Citizens Complaint Center (20.1 percent) to explore civil remedies.

In its replication, the Omaha Police Experiment followed the design of the Minneapolis Domestic Violence experiment by randomly assigning cases to one of three police interventions: separation, mediation, or arrest. They developed two types of outcome measures: official recidivism (measured by new arrests or complaints noted in police records) and victim reports of repeat acts of violence (fear of injury, pushing-hitting, and physical injury) (Dunford and others 1990, p. 188). Victims were interviewed twice over a six month period, with the overall completion rate being 73 percent (n = 242).[22]

Several comparisons between the two experiments concerning the victim interview data are important to highlight: the proportion of initial interviews completed in Minneapolis was 62 percent, and in Omaha, the proportion was 80 percent; the proportion completing

---

[21]In fact, the police filed a report in only 16.4 percent of the incidents, arrests were never made if the victim had broken bones or was taken to the hospital for her injuries, and only 27.2 percent of the abusers were arrested when they had threatened or attacked their partner with weapons (for example, knives or guns), even if the weapon was visible to the police. "When the incident included an attack on a child, arrests were made only 11 percent of the time. However, when the incident included damage to the victim's car, the police made arrests in 25 percent of the cases . . . The single factor most highly correlated with whether an arrest is made is *whether the abuser insulted the police officer.* The arrest rate for such incidents was 32 percent." (Baker and others 1989, pp. 2–3; emphasis in original).

[22]Follow-up interviews were also conducted after twelve months, but these findings are not reported in their 1990 article.

the six-month follow-up interview for Minneapolis was 49 percent, while in Omaha, the proportion was 73 percent. Additionally, only in the Omaha experiment were face-to-face interviews the only type conducted.

Dunford and others (1990) conclude there are virtually no differences in the prevalence and frequency of repeat offending regardless of the police intervention assigned to the case. Thus, the Omaha experiment was unable to replicate the Minneapolis findings. Omaha researchers also sought to determine if one of the interventions (separation, mediation, or arrest) could delay a repeat of violence for a longer period of time than the other interventions. After conducting time-to-failure analyses, Dunford and others (1990, p. 202) present that "[a]fter six months at risk, no one treatment group could be described as requiring more time to fail than any other treatment group."

The conclusion reached in the Omaha Police Experiment provides ample caution for mandatory or presumptory arrest policies to be adopted in other jurisdictions:

> [A]rrest in Omaha, by itself, did not appear to deter subsequent domestic conflict any more than did separating or mediating those in conflict. Arrest, and the immediate period of custody associated with arrest, was not the deterrent to continued domestic conflict that was expected. If the Omaha findings should be replicated in the other five sites conducting experiments on this issue, policy based on the presumptory arrest recommendation coming out of the Minneapolis experiment may have to be reconsidered. (Dunford and others 1990, p. 204).[23]

The last line in their article offers an admonition to both researchers and practitioners interested in the reduction of woman battering to begin considering new or additional strategies to cope with this problem.

These studies reviewed indicate that, for a variety of reasons, mandatory (or presumptive) arrest polices *do not* provide the anticipated panacea to the woman-battering problem. Additionally, Buzawa and Buzawa (1990b, pp. 102–105) cite several reasons for not supporting mandatory arrest policies: first, they argue that the benefits do not outweigh the costs because convictions will not dramatically increase. A victim may refuse to comply with prosecutorial

---

[23]Moreover, Dunford and others (1990, p. 204) also report that victim-based measures of repeat violence indicated that victims who called the police were not placed in greater danger of being recipient of subsequent violence: "what the police did in Omaha after responding to cases of misdemeanor domestic assault (arrest, separate, mediate), neither helped not hurt victims in terms of subsequent conflict."

efforts voluntarily; or, if forced to testify, her recall ability may be deliberately vague or too incomplete to warrant further prosecutorial efforts (Ferraro 1989b). Second, police may engage in arrest-avoidance techniques that would limit assistance to victims: "the net result may therefore be to shift help from some victims who receive no police assistance to another group who obtain the degree and type of help that a paternalistic system believes is appropriate, whether desired or not" (Buzawa and Buzawa 1990b, p. 103). Third, in cases in which a victim is not desirous of an arrest, mandatory policies perpetuate the belief that police disregard victims' preferences.[24] Buzawa and Buzawa suggest that victim preferences must be elicited out of earshot from the offender, and that police should be trained in other victim-sensitive skills. Fourth, these policies entrust too much power to police departments; "dual arrests" (of both the victim and offender) or threats of such an outcome might result.[25]

The last two reservations involve the potential for police to misuse their arrest powers; critics point out that police may make more trivial arrests of victims if they are repeatedly called to the same house. Policies may as well encourage judges not to treat the cases seriously. To support this last claim, the researchers refer to Ferraro's (1989a) finding that policies "created great uncertainty both for the judiciary and the department and tended to trivialize cases clearly warranting arrest" (Buzawa and Buzawa 1990b, p. 105).

Race and Class Implications

Another potential problem with mandatory arrest policies is that they may produce unanticipated and negative consequences for some women. Due to limited opportunities, resources and alternatives, men who abuse women from minority or low socioeconomic groups may be disproportionately arrested in jurisdictions favoring pro-arrest policies, creating added problems for battered women.[26] However, a

---

[24]On this point, Buzawa and Buzawa (1990, p. 103) suggest "a mandatory-arrest policy merely appears to make victims and assailants pawns to larger policy goals formulated by administrators and well-meaning 'victim advocates,' whose goals may not be shared. Despite her emotional involvement and trauma, the victim is usually in a better position than patrol officers to determine the likely impact of an offender's arrest." It is likely that this consideration is magnified for certain groups of battered women, discussed under the next heading.

[25]Buzawa and Buzawa (1990b) acknowledge that adding "primary aggressor" clarifications to the statutes may eliminate this problem, but in doing so, police discretion would increase.

[26]Supplemental approaches to exploring the ramifications of new policies have been suggested, entailing renewal of the dialogue between practitioners, battered women, and academics, and expanding present research designs and methodologies (see Miller 1989 for a more complete discussion).

discussion acknowledging the differential concerns of battered women from minority and low-income groups is absent from the domestic-violence literature.[27] The responses of women from different racial, ethnic, class, and religious groups may indicate that policies designed to assist them may prove to be inadequate or inappropriate based on their cultural or community needs. Lockhart (1985) contends that any mainstream research on battering suffers from major short-comings in design:

> . . . racial comparisons made by these researchers were based on an implicit assumption that all groups in this country are ho-mogeneous, regardless of their political, socio-historical, and eco-nomic experiences. *Researchers who ignore the fundamentally different realities of racial groups commit serious methodological and theoretical errors.* (Lockhart 1985, p. 40, emphasis added)

Hagan and Albonetti (1982) report that blacks and lower-socioeconomic-status individuals are more likely than whites and higher-socioeconomic-status individuals to perceive injustice oper-ating against them by police, juries, and court personnel. Minority groups indeed have a long history of uneasy relations with police (see Overby 1971 and Rossi and others 1974). If a legacy of distrust exists between the minority community and law enforcement agents, mi-nority women may not embrace the new arrest polices. Some mi-nority group women may object ". . . to mandatory arrest laws because they are viewed as providing police with yet another means of harassing minority group men rather than as protection for bat-tered women" (Goolkasian 1986, p. 37). Many black women them-selves may be ambivalent about seeking relief from the criminal justice system:

> The effects of racism and sexism seem too great to tackle in the face of having been victimized by a loved one. The woman often times feels powerless to change her situation, tending to feel she is being forced to tolerate the situation longer because the very system which has historically served to subjugate and oppress her is the only system which can save her from the immediate abusive system (Hearing on Violence Prevention Act, Formal Tes-timony, 1978, p. 521).[28]

---

[27]There are some exceptions in the research on battered women where differences in culture and their relationship to battering have been addressed: see Lockhart (1985, 1987), Asbury (1987), and Coley and Beckett (1988) for research concerning black women, Scarf (1983) on battered Jewish women, and Carroll (1980) for a comparison of battered Mexican-American and Jewish families; Lobel (1986) and Renzetti (1987) on battered lesbians; Feinman (1987) on battered Latino women; and *Response* (1985) on battered women in New Zealand.

[28]In the same vein, Tong (1984) contends that black women especially may

This testimony echoes informal conclusions regarding black women's reluctance to involve police in their personal lives:

> All (abusive) men, regardless of race, should be dealt with, but black men are going to be dealt with more severely. Naturally, this troubles [black] victims. Black women know they don't want him (the abuser) in jail—all they want is for the abuse to stop . . . There's a lot of guilt involved when you're talking about reporting a man. There's a fear that it's not supporting black and other minority men and that they shouldn't be punished (Williams 1981, p. 22).

McLeod (1984) discusses two competing hypotheses concerning disproportionate representation of minority citizens and calls to the police: first is the differential participation hypothesis, which states that statistics accurately reflect that minorities are more involved in domestic violence incidents; and second is the differential notification hypothesis, which suggests that these statistics are misleading in that they only reflect *reporting* rates, and *not* participation rates.

Research conducted by Block (1974) found that black victims have higher reporting rates than whites with assault-and-battery incidents and so are overrepresented in official police statistics. Similarly, Hindelang (1976) claims the statistics are misleading; they reflect assaults known to police only. National Crime Survey (NCS) data also seem to support the differential notification hypothesis: the data show overrepresentation of minorities in abuse victimizations (11.3 percent of population are black; 17 percent of male victims are black) (McLeod 1984).

With any assessment of pro-arrest policies, it is necessary to discern whether or not there are class differences in victims' reporting of intimate violence to the police. Schwartz (1988) tackles the issue of differential representation of minority and lower-class citizens reflected in victimization surveys. Essentially, he argues that there is evidence suggesting that the NCS is more likely to be biased in favor of showing more *middle- and upper-class* women's victimizations, rather than overrepresenting lower classes, citing Sparks' (1981) research: "[he] argues that black and lower-class persons systematically underreport assaults in NCS interviews, and that any findings which show a greater incidence of victimization of lower-class persons are in fact stronger than would be indicated by these data" (Schwartz 1988, p. 378).

Additionally, Schwartz challenges the pervasive protestation

---

question arrest policies, with regard to the treatment of black men, based on other experiences with the law; for example, black rapists historically have received harsher treatment than white rapists (Davis 1981; Wolfgang and Riedel 1975).

that there are *not* class differences in intimate violence vulnerability. He argues that this issue is largely ignored by feminists conducting research on battered women because they do not want to advance the myth that battered women are primarily located in the lower end of the economic spectrum. Schwartz contends that since feminist ideology embraces framing the issue within a context that insists all women are equally oppressed and vulnerable to victimization in a patriarchal society, they refuse to investigate class distinctions. Feminists (and other researchers) are able to effectively criticize the methodology of studies that do find greater incidence rates among lower class women. Schwartz contends that this is very easy to do (for example, reporting artifacts—data sources—oversample poorer persons, who are more likely to use services such as the police, courts, shelters, or other social service agencies; see Okum 1986, p. 48).[29]

Conspicuously absent in the District of Columbia's mandatory arrest policy evaluation is any mention of the racial breakdowns of victims and offenders.[30] However, the study does offer some relevant economic information: 55.5 percent of the battering victims earned $15,000 or less; 79 percent earned less than $20,000. The authors assert that "[c]ontributions from other household members do not significantly increase these victims' financial security: Even with other family member's income, 63 percent of the victims lived in households whose income was $20,000 or less per year" (Baker and others 1989, pp. 29–30). Even more important is the finding that the victims whose abusers were arrested were even poorer.

> These results reflect the fact that victims who have lower incomes do not have resources, other than the police and the Citizens Complaint Center, to escape domestic violence. They do not have lawyers to commence legal action; they do not have the option of moving their families to separate homes; they do not have the income to enter family counseling designed to stem the violence. The police response to their plight is possibly their only protection. (Baker and others 1989, p. 30).

---

[29]There exists even more of a split in the discourse between feminist analysis and more mainstream analysis regarding the issue of class differences in intimate-violence victimizations. Several researchers refuse to even raise the issue, positing that the question is inherently sexist and a form of victim blaming because of its assumption that victimization can be avoided if only one changed the victim's personal characteristics (see Wardell and others 1983; Klein 1982; Davis 1987; Dobash and Dobash 1979; and Stark and others 1979). However, see Breines and Gordon 1983 for an opposing—and more courageous—position.

[30]According to 1990 Census population counts for the District of Columbia, the racial distribution is 26.6% white, 65.8% black, and 4.6% other (American Indian, Eskimo or Aleut, Asian or Pacific Islander, and combined other races). (U.S. Department of Commerce, Bureau of the Census, 1991).

Both minority and lower-class women have traditionally placed greater reliance on the police intervention to resolve conflicts within their intimate relationships. Social class may be inextricably linked to race in the study of intimate violence; this is because nonwhites are overrepresented in the lower socioeconomic groups, and socioeconomic status affects options (Lockhart 1985, 1987). Women with more income have greater access to resources to assist them in keeping their abuse private; they have the ability to afford private physicians and safe shelters, which results in their being able to escape detection from law enforcement, hospital emergency rooms, or social service agencies (Prescott and Letko 1977; Stark and others 1979; Washburn and Frieze 1981; and Asbury 1987).

Findings from the National Commission on the Causes and Prevention of Violence suggest that "... lower-class people are denied privacy for their quarrels: neighborhood bars, sidewalks, and crowded, thin-walled apartments afford little isolation" (Eisenberg and Micklow 1977, p. 142). Therefore, it is entirely plausible that mandatory and pro-arrest policies may disproportionately affect minority women and women from lower socioeconomic statuses who may have fewer opportunities and alternatives available for settling disputes privately (Stanko 1985). The economic consequences of arrest may be more devastating for lower-socioeconomic households. If the batterer is jailed, income may be lost, thus increasing the probability that a woman may not call the police if arrest would be imminent. Thus, it seems clear that limited alternatives exist for economically disadvantaged battered women, especially women from minority groups, who are faced with the dilemma of being dependent on the police for assistance whenever their partners engage in violence against them.

Brief Review of Alternatives and Supplements to Arrest

Early efforts of the battered women's movement were designed to assist the *victims* of domestic violence by establishing shelters and crisis lines. Not all of these programs received unanimous support; shelters have been viewed (mostly by pro-family groups) as instrumental to the destruction of the family. Empirical assessments refute these contentions (Stone 1984).[31] By the early 1980s, domestic-

---

[31]Stone (1984) conducted interviews of shelter residents to determine if shelters can be blamed for dissolving marriages. This research is important, given the recent pro-family criticisms that shelters persuade battered women to leave their spouse and family. Stone (1984) found that the women who had made the decision to file for a divorce had decided *prior* to going to the shelter. Overwhelmingly, the battered women

violence legislation was enacted in most states (Morash 1986). Included were a variety of programs or remedies: civil protection orders were established to provide effective procedures to insure victim safety;[32] legal advocacy and job-training programs designed to empower women became readily accessible in shelters. However, not all of these options have been successful. Grau and others (1984) report that restraining orders designed to provide civil court alternatives to formal sanctions are largely ineffective. Based on 270 victim interviews in four states, they argue that civil protection orders do little to prevent or reduce future violence, and the potential helpfulness of these orders is limited by implementation problems (for example, long waiting periods and little or no protection offered to cohabitators or unmarried individuals), circumvention by police officers who fail to enforce the orders, and an overall lack of coordination and integration of civil and criminal remedies (Grau and others 1984).

More recently, attention has shifted toward exploring the relationship dynamics of battering, concentrating on providing treatment for offenders.[33] Many of these intervention or treatment efforts apply a feminist, antisexist, psychotherapeutic approach that challenges male batterers to examine traditional gender role socialization, responses, and practices (for example, see Adams 1989). Evaluations of counseling programs indicate much variability in recidivism rates, often as low as 2 percent in programs in which batterers were eager to participate (Dutton 1987) to as high as 39 percent (Gondolf 1984). Some of this variability is attributed to small sample sizes and different measures of recidivism. Deterrence may be most effective when both social *and* legal penalties are utilized (Fagan 1989). For instance, one study that followed batterers who were arrested and participated in court-mandated counseling demonstrated low recidivism rates (as measured by wives' reports) after thirty months (Dutton 1986b).

Police-policy changes can not exist in a vacuum. Arrest is only the initial step in the criminal justice system continuum and can easily be circumvented by unresponsiveness from other key players in the system (Elliott 1989). There has been some demonstrated success in reducing battering through innovative programming that provides a combination of services, including policies that involve the

---

interviewed indicated that the shelter provided an opportunity to feel safe and protected while recovering from physical and emotional trauma, and a place where they could think and make rational decisions about their futures.

[32]Since 1976, thirty-one states have enacted some form of civil protection order for battered women (Grau 1982).

[33]See Saunders and Azar (1989) for a review of treatment programs for family violence in general.

prosecutor taking responsibility for initiating prosecution and not the victim (see Lerman 1981 and 1986 for a comprehensive review of these types of programs). Fostering links between the criminal justice system and social service agencies might be helpful, especially for women with limited opportunities to explore other alternatives. Mandated counseling programs may provide this link; they would add another official component, besides the arrest itself, to the increasing societal and institutional recognition that woman battering is an act of criminal proportions. It has been suggested that a collaboration of legal sanctions and social services, such as court-mandated counseling, generally tend to complement each other and correct power imbalances between victims and offenders, rather than being coercive (Dutton 1986a).[34] Third-party mediation programs are also being used as a method to formally mediate interpersonal disputes with the assistance of a trained mediator who strives to develop a way to solve disputes nonviolently.[35] Prosecutor's offices have introduced pre-trial mediation programs as an alternative to formal criminal processing. The idea behind mediation is to informally educate both the victim and the offender about more effective methods for resolving conflict and to inform both parties about their legal rights. Some preliminary evaluations of mediation programs indicate they offer similar reductions in recidivism as more formal case processing (Bethel and Singer 1981–1982). However, mediation programs have been criticized for their failure to assign blame, and for allowing violence to be seen as part of a dysfunctional family, rather than as violence directed against women (Lerman 1984).

Despite training, it is still very rare for police to refer battered women to outside agencies (Loving 1980; Donlon and others 1986). Consistent police training for handling domestic violence cases, proper control over training course content, and funding support for this training are virtually nonexistent (Buzawa and Buzawa 1990b). Other research indicates that policy changes exert little influence over officer beliefs and practices: Ferraro (1989a) found that most of the male officers disliked the presumptive arrest policy enacted in Phoenix, Arizona, with most of the female officers feeling similarly. For women who perceive the consequences of arrest to represent a greater

---

[34]Similar to the research concerns raised by pro-arrest policies, research would need to be conducted with mandated counseling programs to discern any inherent class or race biases (see, generally, Marsella and Pedersen 1981). Self-help style books that employ a multicultural perspective and are written by women from similar backgrounds which are designed to assist minority battered women may also benefit practitioners and policy makers who may not understand the role that racism and racist stereotypes may play, or the value of support systems within different cultural communities (for good examples of this, see White 1985 and Zambrano 1985).

[35]See Ray (1982) for a thorough review of such mediation programs.

hardship than the actual physical battering itself, some intermediate interventions will be necessary. Otherwise, the possibility exists of women being left without effective remedies after the failure of official ones.

Conclusion

Mandatory arrest policies or laws may exacerbate an already difficult problem, despite good intentions or conventional wisdom. Given the inconsistent research findings and the negligible deterrence effects found in the policy evaluation research, it appears that many battered women will not benefit from mandatory-arrest policies, and that these policies might be particularly detrimental for battered women of color and/or women from lower socioeconomic groups. Given these findings, expansion of state authority to intrude into peoples' lives seems unwarranted in the area of domestic violence, unless a victim specifically requests such action. Efforts to improve police responses must be embedded within the context of emerging knowledge of the range of intimate violence remedies and the entire criminal justice system. Otherwise, operational changes that dictate police response to battering incidents will remain largely fractured, rhetorical, and ineffective.

REFERENCES

Adams, D., "Stages of Anti-Sexist Awareness and Change for Men Who Batter." In L. J. Dickstein and C. C. Nadelson (eds.), *Family Violence: Emerging Issues of a National Crisis*. Washington, D.C.: American Psychiatric Press, 1989, pp. 63–97.

Asbury, J., "African-American Women in Violent Relationships: An Exploration of Cultural Difference." In Robert L. Hampton (ed.), *Violence in the Black Family*. Lexington, Mass.: Lexington Books, 1987.

Baker, K., N. Cahn, and S. J. Sands, *Report on District of Columbia Police Response to Domestic Violence*. Washington, D.C.: D.C. Coalition Against Domestic Violence and the Women's Law and Public Policy Fellowship, Georgetown University Law Center, 1989.

Balos, B., and I. Trotzky, "Enforcement of the Domestic Abuse Act in Minnesota: A Preliminary Study," *Law and Inequality*, 6 (1988), 83–125.

Bell, D. J., "The Police Response to Domestic Violence: An Exploratory Study," *Police Studies*, (1984), 23–30.

Berk, R. A., and P. J. Newton, "Does Arrest Really Deter Wife Battery? An Effort to Replicate the Findings of the Minneapolis Spouse Abuse Experiment," *American Sociological Review*, 50 (1985), 253–262.

Bethel, C. A., and L. R. Singer, "Mediation: A New Remedy for Causes of

Domestic Violence," *Vermont Law Review*, (6)2 and (7)1, 1981–1982.

Binder, A., and J. W. Meeker, "Experiments as Reforms," *Journal of Criminal Justice*, 16 (1988), 347–358.

Block, R., "Why Notify the Police: The Victim's Decision to Notify the Police of an Assault," *Criminology*, 11 (1974), 555–569.

Bowker, L. H., "Police Service to Battered Women: Bad or Not So Bad?" *Criminal Justice and Behavior*, 9 (1982), 476–486.

Breines W. and L. Gordon, "The New Scholarship on Family Violence," *Signs: Journal of Women in Culture and Society*, 8, no. 3 (1983), 490–531.

Buel, S. M., "Recent Developments: Mandatory Arrest for Domestic Violence," *Harvard Women's Law Journal*, 11 (1988), 213–226.

Buzawa, E. S., "Police Officer Response to Domestic Violence Legislation in Michigan," *Journal of Police Science and Administration*, 10, no. 4 (1982), 415–424.

Buzawa, E. S., and C. G. Buzawa (eds.), *Domestic Violence: The Criminal Justice Response*. Westport, Conn.: Greenwood Press, 1990a.

Buzawa, E. S., an C. G. Buzawa, *Domestic Violence: The Criminal Justice Response*. Newbury Park, Calif.: Sage Publications, 1990b.

Carroll, J. C., "A Cultural-Consistency Theory of Family Violence in Mexican-American and Jewish-Ethnic Groups." In M. A. Straus and G. T. Hotaling (eds.), *The Social Causes of Husband-Wife Violence*. Minneapolis: University of Minnesota Press, 1980, pp. 68–81.

Cohn, E. G., and L. W. Sherman, "Police Policy on Domestic Violence, 1986: A National Survey," *Crime Control Reports*, no. 5 (1986). Washington, D.C.: Crime Control Institute.

Coley, S. M., and J. O. Beckett, "Black Battered Women: A Review of Empirical Literature," *Journal of Counseling and Development*, 66 (1988), 266–270.

Davis, A. Y., *Women, Race and Class*. New York: Random House, 1981.

Davis, N. J., A. J. Hatch, C. Griffin, and K. Thompson, "Violence Against Women in the Home: A Continued Mandate of Control," *Violence, Aggression and Terrorism*, 1, no. 3 (1987), 241–276.

Dobash, R. E., and R. P. Dobash, "Love, Honor and Obey: Institutional Ideologies and the Struggle for Battered Women," *Contemporary Crises*, 1 (1977), 403–415.

Dobash, R. E., and R. P. Dobash, *Violence Against Wives: A Case Against the Patriarchy*. New York: Free Press, 1979.

Donlon, R., J. Hendricks, and M. S. Meagher, "Police Practices and Attitudes toward Domestic Violence," *Journal of Police Science and Administration*, 14 (1986), 187–192.

Dunford, F. W., D. Huizinga, and D. S. Elliott, "The Role of Arrest in Domestic Assault: The Omaha Police Experiment," *Criminology*, 28, no. 2 (1990), 183–206.

Dutton, D., "The Prediction of Recidivism in a Population of Wife Assaulters."

Paper presented at the Third International Family Violence Conference, Durham, N.H., 1987.

Dutton, D., "The Outcome of Court-mandated Treatment for Wife Assault: A Quasi-experimental Evaluation," *Violence and Victims*, 1 (1986a), 163–176.

Dutton, D., "Wife Assaulters' Explanations for Assault: The Neturalization of Self-Punishment," *Canadian Journal of Behavioral Science*, 8, no. 4 (1986b), 381–390.

Eisenberg, S. E., and P. L. Micklow, "The Assaulted Wife: 'Catch 22' Revisited," *Women's Rights Law Reporter*, 3 (1977), 142.

Elliot, D. S., "Criminal Justice Procedures in Family Violence Crimes." In L. Ohlin and M. Tonry (eds.), *Family Violence*. Chicago: University of Chicago Press, 1989, pp. 427–480.

Ellis, J. W., "Prosecutorial Discretion to Charge in Cases of Spousal Assault: A Dialogue," *Journal of Criminal Law and Criminology*, 75, no. 1 (1984), 56–102.

Eppler, A., "Battered Women and the Equal Protection Clause: Will the Constitution Help Them When the Police Won't?" *The Yale Law Journal*, (1986), 788–809.

Fagan, J., "Cessation of Family Violence: Deterrence and Dissuasion." In L. Ohlin and M. Tonry (eds.), *Family Violence*. Chicago: University of Chicago Press, 1989, pp. 377–425.

Feinman, C., "Domestic Violence in Australia." Paper presented at the Annual Meeting of the American Society of Criminology, Montreal, 1987.

Ferraro, K., "The Legal Response to Women Battering in the United States." In J. Hamner, J. Radford and E. Stanko (eds.), *Women, Policing, and Male Violence*. London: Routeledge & Keegan Paul, 1989a, pp. 155–184.

Ferraro, K., "Policing Women Battering," *Social Problems*, 36, no. 1 (1989b), 61–74.

Field, M. H., and H. F. Field, "Marital Violence and the Criminal Process: Neither Justice Nor Peace," *Social Service Review*, 47 (1973), 221–240.

Ford, D. A., "Prosecution as a Victim Power Resource for Managing Conjugal Violence." Paper presented at the annual meeting of the Society for the Study of Social Problems, San Antonio, Texas, August 1984.

Frieze, I. H., J. Knoble, C. Washburn, and G. Zomnir, "Types of Battered Women." Paper presented at the annual research conference of the Association for Women in Psychology, Santa Monica, Calif., 1980.

Gelles, R. and H. Mederer, "Comparison or Control: Intervention in the Cases of Wife Abuse." Paper presented at the annual meeting of the National Council on Family Relations, Dallas, 1985.

Gil, D. G., "Sociocultural Aspects of Domestic Violence." In M. Lystad (ed.), *Violence in the Home: Interdisciplinary Perspectives*. New York: Brunner/Mazel, 1986, pp. 124–149.

Gondolf, E. W., *Men Who Batter: An Integrated Approach Stopping Wife Abuse*. Homes Beach, Fla.: Learning Publications, 1984.

Goolkasian, G. A., *Confronting Domestic Violence: A Guide for Criminal Justice Agencies*. Washington, D.C.: U.S. Government Printing Office, 1986.

Grau, J. L., "Restraining Order Legislation for Battered Women: A Reassessment," *University of San Francisco Law Review*, 16 (1982), 703–741.

Grau, J., J. Fagan, and S. Wexler. "Restraining Orders for Battered Women: Issues of Access and Efficacy," *Women and Politics*, 4, no. 3 (1984), 13–28.

Hagan, J., and C. Albonetti, "Race, Class, and the Perception of Criminal Injustice in America," *American Journal of Sociology*, 88, no. 2 (1982), 329–355.

Hamner, J., J. Radford, and E. Stanko, *Women, Policing and Male Violence: International Perspectives*. London: Routledge, Keegan & Paul, 1989.

Hearing on Violence Prevention Act, Formal Testimony, Harriet Tubman Woman's Shelter presented by Kenyari Bellfield in U.S. Congress, House Subcommittee on Select Education of the Committee on Education and Labor, *Domestic Violence: Hearing on H.R. 7297 and H.R. 8498*, 95th Congress, 2nd session, March 17, 1978; 1985.

Hindelang M. J., *Criminal Victimization in Eight American Cities: A Descriptive Analysis of Common Theft and Assault*. Cambridge, Mass.: Ballinger, 1976.

International Association of Chiefs of Police, *Training Key 16: Handling Disturbance Calls*. Gaithersberg, Md.: International Association of Chiefs of Police, 1967.

Jaffe, P., D. A. Wolfe, A. Telford, and G. Austin, "The Impact of Police Charges in Incidents of Wife Abuse," *Journal of Family Violence*, 1 (1986), 37–49.

Karmen, A., "Women as Crime Victims: Problems and Solutions." In B. R. Price and N. J. Sokoloff (eds.), *The Criminal Justice System and Women*. New York: Clark Boardman, 1982, pp. 185–201.

Klein, D., "Violence Against Women: Some Considerations Regarding its Causes and its Elimination," *Crime and Delinquency*, 27, no. 1 (1981), 64–80.

Kuhl, A., and L. E. Saltzman, "Battered Women and the Criminal Justice System." In I. L. Moyer (ed.), *The Changing Role of Women in the Criminal Justice System*. Prospect Heights, Ill.: Waveland Press, 1985, pp. 180–196.

Lang, "How to Stop Crime the Brainy Way," *U.S. News and World Report*, July 21, 1986, pp. 55–56.

Langan, P. A., and C. A. Innes, *Preventing Domestic Violence against Women*, Special Report. Washington, D.C.: U.S. Department of Justice, Bureau of Justice Statistics, 1986.

Laszlo, A. T., and T. McKean, "Court Decision: An Alternative for Spousal Abuse Cases." In *Battered Women: Issues of Public Policy*. Washington, D.C.: U.S. Commission for Civil Rights, 1978, pp. 327–356.

Lempert, R., "From the Editor," *Law and Society Review,* 18, no. 4 (1984), 505–513.

Lerman, L., "Criminal Prosecution of Wife Beaters," *Response,* 4, no. 3 (1981), 1–19. Washington, D.C.: Center for Women's Policy Studies.

Lerman, L., "Court Decisions on Wife Abuse Laws: Recent Developments," *Response.* (May/June 1982). Washington, D.C.: Center for Women's Policy Studies.

Lerman, L., "Mediation of Wife Abuse Cases: The Adverse Impact of Informal Dispute Resolution of Women," *Harvard Women's Law Journal,* 7 (1984), 65–67.

Lerman, L., "Prosecution of Wife Beaters: Institutional Obstacles and Innovations." In M. Lystad (ed.), *Violence in the Home: Interdisciplinary Perspectives.* New York: Brunner/Mazel, 1986, pp. 250–295.

Lerman, L., and F. Livingston, "State Legislation on Domestic Violence," *Response,* 6 (1983), 1–28. Washington, D.C.: Center for Women's Policy Studies.

Lobel, K., *Naming the Violence: Speaking Out Against Lesbian Battering.* Seattle: Seal Press, 1986.

Lockhart, L. L., "Methodological Issues in Comparative Racial Analyses: The Case of Wife Abuse," *Social Work and Abstracts,* 21 (1985), 35–41.

Lockhart, L. L., "A Reexamination of the Effects of Race and Social Class on the Incidence of Marital Violence: A Search for Reliable Differences," *Journal of Marriage and the Family,* 49, no. 3 (1987), 603–610.

Loving, N., *Responding to Spouse Abuse and Wife Beating: A Guide for Police.* Washington, D.C.: Police Executive Research Forum, 1980.

MacKinnon, C., "Feminism, Marxism, Method, and the State: Toward a Feminist Jurisprudence," *Signs,* 8 (1983), 635.

Marsella, A., and P. Pedersen, *Cross Cultural Counseling and Psychotherapy: Foundations, Evolutions and Cultural Considerations.* Elmsford, N.Y.: Pergamon Press, 1981.

Martin, D., "Overview—Scope of the Problem." In *Battered Women: Issues of Public Policy.* Washington, D.C.: U.S. Commission for Civil Rights, 1978.

McLeod, M., "Women Against Men: An Examination of Domestic Violence Based on an Analysis of Official Data and National Victimization Data," *Justice Quarterly,* 1984, pp. 171–193.

Miller, S. L., "Unintended Side Effects of Pro-Arrest Policies and Their Race and Class Implications for Battered Women: A Cautionary Note," *Criminal Justice Policy Review,* 3, no. 3 (1989), 299–316.

Moore, "Landmark Court Decisions for Battered Women," *Response,* 8, no. 5 (1985).

Morash, M., "Wife Battering," *Criminal Justice Abstracts,* June 1986, pp. 252–271.

National Criminal Justice Association, "Domestic Violence Arrests Deter Batterers," Police Agencies Report, *Justice Bulletin,* 5, no. 3 (1985).

Okum, L., *Women Abuse: Facts Replacing Myths*. Albany: State University of New York Press, 1986.

Olivero, "Connecticut's New Family Violence May Be One of the Toughest—But Is It Tough Enough?" *Hartford Advocate*, November 16, 1987, p. 6.

Overby, A., "Discrimination Against Minority Groups." In Leon Radzinowicz and Marvin E. Wolfgang (eds.), *The Criminal in the Arms of the Law*. New York: Basic Books, 1971, pp. 569–581.

Parnas, R. E., "The Police Response to the Domestic Disturbance," *Wisconsin Law Review*, 31 (1967), 914–960.

Parnas, R. E., "The Judicial Response to Intra-Family Violence," *Minnesota Law Review*, 54 (1970), 585–645.

Pastoor, M. K., "Police Training and the Effectiveness of Minnesota 'Domestic Abuse' Laws," *Law and Inequality*, 2 (1984), 557–607.

Paterson, E. J., "How the Legal System Responds to Battered Women." In D. M. Moore (ed.), *Battered Women*. Beverly Hills, Calif.: Sage Publications, 1979, pp. 79–100.

Police Foundation, *Domestic Violence and the Police, Studies in Detroit and Kansas City*, 1977, p. 9.

Prescott, S., and C. Letko, "Battered: A Social Psychological Perspective." In M. M. Roy (ed.), *Battered Women: A Psychosociological Study of Domestic Violence*. New York: Von Nostrand Reinhold, 1977, pp. 72–96.

Ray, L., *Alternative Means of Family Dispute Resolution*. Washington, D.C.: n.p., 1982.

Reiss, A. J., Jr., "Some Failures in Designing Data Collection That Distort Results." In L. Burstein, H. E. Freeman, and P. H. Rossi (eds.), *Collecting Evaluation Data: Problems and Solutions*. Beverly Hills, Calif.: Sage Publications, 1985.

Renzetti, C., "Building a Second Closet: Official Responses to Victims of Lesbian Battering." Paper presented at the Annual Meeting of the Academy of Criminal Justice Sciences, San Francisco, Calif., 1987.

"Response to Wife Abuse in Four Western Countries," *Response to Violence in the Family and Sexual Assault*, 8, no. 2 (1985) 15–18. Washington, D.C.: Center for Women's Policy Studies.

Rifkin, J., "Toward a Theory of Law and Patriarchy," *Harvard Women's Law Journal*, 3 (1980), 83.

Rossi, P., R. A. Berk, and B. Edison, *The Roots of Urban Discontent*, New York: Wiley, 1974.

Russell, D. E. H., *Rape in Marriage*. New York: MacMillan, 1982.

Saunders, D. G., and S. T. Azar, "Treatment Programs for Family Violence." In L. Ohlin and M. Tonry (eds.), *Family Violence*. Chicago: University of Chicago Press, 1989, pp. 481–546.

Scarf, M., "Marriages Made in Heaven? Battered Jewish Wives." In Susannah Heschel (ed.), *On Being a Jewish Feminist*. New York: Schocken Books, 1983.

Schechter, S., *Women and Male Violence: The Visions and Struggles of the Battered Women's Movement*. Boston: South End Press, 1982.

Schwartz, M. D., "Ain't Got No Class: Universal Risk Theories of Battering," *Contemporary Crises*, 12 (1988), 373–392.

Sherman, L., and R. Berk, "The Specific Deterrent Effects of Arrest for Domestic Assault," *American Sociological Review*, 49 (1984), 261–272.

Sherman, L., and E. G. Cohn, "The Impact of Research on Legal Policy: The Minneapolis Domestic Violence Experiment," *Law and Society Review*, 23, no. 1. (1989), 117–144.

Smith, D. A., "Police Responses to Interpersonal Violence: Defining the Paramenters of Legal Control," *Social Forces*," 65, no. 3 (1987), 767–782.

Sparks, R., "Surveys of Victimization—An Optimistic Assessment." In M. Tonry and N. Morris (eds.), *Crime and Justice: An Annual Review of Research*, vol. 3. Chicago: University of Chicago Press, 1981, pp. 1–60.

Stanko, E. A., "Would You Believe this Woman: Prosecutorial Screening for 'Credible' Witnesses and a Problem of Justice." In N. H. Rafter and E. A. Stanko (eds.), *Judge, Lawyer, Victim, Thief: Women, Gender Roles and Criminal Justice*. Boston: Northeastern University Press, 1982, pp. 63–82.

Stanko, E. A., *Intimate Intrusions: Women's Experience of Male Violence*. London: Routledge & Kegan Paul, 1985.

Stark, E., A. Flitcraft, and W. Frazier, "Medicine and Patriarchal Violence: The Social Construction of a 'Private' Event," *International Journal of Health Services*, 9 (1979), 461–493.

Stone, L. H., "Shelters for Battered Women: A Temporary Escape from Danger Or the First Step Toward Divorce?" *Victimology*, 9, no. 2 (1984), 284–289.

Straus, M. A., R. Gelles, and S. K. Steinmetz, *Behind Closed Doors: Violence in the American Family*. New York: Anchor Press, 1980.

Straus, M. A., and R. Gelles, "Societal Change and Change in Family Violence from 1975 to 1985 as Revealed by Two National Surveys," *Journal of Marriage and the Family*, 48 (1986), 465–479.

Tong, R., *Women, Sex, and the Law*. Totowa, N.J.: Rowman and Allanheld, 1984.

Truninger, E., "Marital Violence: The Legal Solution," *Hastings Law Journal*, 23 (1971), 259–273.

U.S. Department of Justice, *Replicating an Experiment in Specific Deterrence: Alternative Police Responses to Spouse Assault: A Research Solicitation*. Washington, D.C.: U.S. Department of Justice, National Institute of Justice, 1985.

Vera Institute of Justice, *Felony Arrests: Their Prosecution and Disposition in New York City's Court*. New York: Vera Institute of Justice, 1977.

Walker, L., "Battered Women and Learned Helplessness," *Victimology*, 2 (1977), 528–531.

Walker, L., *The Battered Woman*. New York: Harper and Row, 1979.

Walker, L., Thyfault, and Browne, "Beyond the Juror's Ken: Battered Women," *Vermont Law Review*, 7 (1982).

Wardell, L., D. Gillespie, and A. Leffler, "Science and Violence Against Wives." In *The Dark Side of Families: Current Family Violence Research.* D. Finkelhor, R. Gelles, G. Hotaling, and M. Straus (eds.), Beverly Hills, Calif.: Sage Publications, 1983, pp. 69–84.

Warrior, B., *Working on Wife Abuse*. Cambridge, Mass.: Author, 1980.

Washburn, C., and I. H. Frieze, "Methodological Issues in Studying Battered Women." Paper presented at the First National Conference for Family Violence Researchers, University of New Hampshire, Durham, N.H., July 1981.

White, E. C., *Chain Chain Change: For Black Women Dealing with Physical and Emotional Abuse*. Seattle: Seal Press, 1985.

Williams, L., "Violence Against Women," *The Black Scholar*, January-February 1981, pp. 18–24.

Wolfgang, M. E., and M. Riedel, "Rape, Race and the Death Penalty in Georgia," *American Journal of Orthopsychiatry*, 45 (1975), 658–668.

Zambrano, M. M., *Mejor Sola Que Mal Acompanada: For the Latino in an Abusive Relationship*. Seattle: Seal Press, 1985.

21

Women: Victims of Sexual Assault and Violence

Albert R. Roberts

The present chapter examines criminal justice agency responses to women victims of sexual assault. The focus includes the following: the increased prevalence of sexual assault throughout the United States; review of the traumatic and debilitating effect of sexual assault upon its victims; the passage of federal legislation and national activities in support of the development of rape crisis centers, battered women's shelters, prosecutor-based victim/witness assistance progress, and victim compensation programs. In addition, two major sections of this chapter focus on both positive and negative responses from the police and courts toward victims of sexual assault and domestic violence. The final section includes discussion related to the fear of AIDS among victims of sexual assault and the debate among legislators and criminal justice authorities regarding voluntary vs. mandatory testing of sex offenders for HIV.

After many decades of neglect, victims of sexual assault have become the focus of increased empirical research, reporting, legislation, and prevention and recovery services. The women's movement, federal and state legislation, rape-law reforms, and media attention to the sexual victimization of women have provided the main impetus for changes during the past decade.

Rape! This word brings forth images of a young woman being dragged into a dark alley by a crazed stranger who holds a knife to her throat. In reality, college-aged women are more likely to be in danger of being raped by a fellow student while on a date rather than by a stranger. The traditional definition of rape was "unlawful sexual intercourse with a female, by force or without legal or factual consent" (*Uniform Crime Reports* 1981). However, this definition does not take into account men who are victims of sexual assault. In recent years, a number of states have extensively revised their statutes on rape to address issues of sexual assault, criminal sexual penetration, criminal sexual conduct, and intercourse without consent. The purpose of these reform statutes was to focus on the violence committed by the assailant rather than the suffering of the victim. These new sex-neutrality statutes recognize that the rape victim may be a woman or a man. Language in the revised statutes now refers to the victims as "persons" rather than as "women." In this chapter, the following definition of rape will be used:

> Rape is defined as nonconsensual sexual penetration of an adolescent or adult obtained by physical force, by threat of bodily harm, or when the victim is incapable of giving consent by virtue of mental illness, mental retardation, or intoxication (Searles and Berger 1987).

A number of the reform statutes further expand the definition of rape beyond penile-vaginal intercourse to include fellatio or cunnilingus, or anal sodomy by physical force.

Criminologists estimate that only one out of every four forcible rapes are reported to the police (Schmalleger 1990, p. 43). According to the *Uniform Crime Reports* (1990) of the Federal Bureau of Investigation, there were close to 100,000 reported rapes during 1989. Because of the large number of rapes that are never reported to the police, a more accurate figure may be two to four times the number reported by the FBI. While precise prevalence rates on sexual assault are debatable, there is general agreement that rape is one of the most traumatic and debilitating of crimes.

The present chapter sheds light on criminal justice agencies responses to women victims of sexual assault by examining the following: scope of the problem; federal legislation and national activities; police responses; courts and prosecutorial responses; and the high risk of being exposed to HIV as a result of being raped by an ex-offender.

Scope of the Problem

Victimization of women and children has become recognized as one of the most formidable problems of our times. The *Uniform Crime Reports* (1989) of the Federal Bureau of Investigation indicates that there were 92,489 reported rapes during 1988. Based on recent random surveys, the lifetime likelihood of becoming a victim of sexual assault has been estimated at from 13.5 percent to 44 percent of all women. (Kilpatrick and others 1985; Koss and others 1987; Russell 1982).

Sexual assault is recognized as one of the most traumatic and debilitating crimes for adults as well as children. Several of the short-term physical and psychological reactions to rape include anxiety, fear, depressive symptoms, loss of self-confidence, sleep difficulties and nightmares, headaches, and stomachaches and/or backaches (Atkeson and others 1982; Calhoun and others 1982; Ellis and others 1980; Kilpatrick and Veronen 1983, and Kilpatrick 1984). The above studies found that at three months post-crime, most of the women studied had greatly diminished depressive symptoms, sleep disorders, and psychosomatic problems.

A small group of the rape victims in the latter-cited studies continued to have anxiety attacks, fears and phobic reactions, sexual dysfunction, and low self-esteem two years after the assault (Kilpatrick 1984; Murphy and others 1988; Becker and Skinner 1983; Becker and others 1984; and Becker and others 1986). A significant number of rape victims have exhibited suicide ideation and suicide attempts after the rape. Kilpatrick and associates studied a representative sample of 2,004 adult women and found that nearly one out of every five rape victims (19.2 percent) had attempted suicide. Forty-four percent of the women who had been raped exhibited suicidal ideation and 14 percent of the group had a postassault nervous breakdown (Kilpatrick and others 1985).

In addition to psychiatric and mental-health disorders, every victim of a completed rape faces the possibility of becoming exposed to human immunodeficiency virus (HIV). The lethal disease, Acquired Immune Deficiency Syndrome (AIDS) is transmissible through the transfer of body fluids and has no known cure. In testimony before the Presidential Commission on the HIV Epidemic (1988), witnesses expressed considerable concern about the high risk among rape victims of exposure to sexually transmitted diseases (STDs) including HIV as a result of the sexual assault.

Police Responses to Victims of Sexual Assault and Domestic Violence

For decades, women victims of sexual assault were confronted with insensitive, callous, and cynical court personnel and police. All too often, a victim of sexual assault who reported the crime to the police would encounter a judgmental and blaming attitude, with police officers making statements such as: "no wonder you got raped with that short skirt;" or, "going out alone in that neighborhood at night was asking for it!" Similarly, witnesses who agreed to testify against the perpetrator encountered many difficulties when dealing with deputy prosecutors and their staff. Witnesses would report how frustrating it was for them to come to court again and again only to learn that their case was postponed or, as a result of a continuance, was rescheduled for a different court date. Added to the frustration of continuances and long waits in overbooked courts, witnesses reported numerous instances of serious threats against them and/or members of their immediate families by defendants.

During the decade of the 1980s, a growing number of police officers and prosecutors began to be responsive to the needs of victims of sexual assault and domestic violence. Increasingly, police academies are providing specialized training for new police recruits (lasting between two and twenty hours) on rape victims and domestic violence. By the early 1980s, the International Association of Chiefs of Police, Inc., (I.A.C.P.) had developed training guidelines on investigating forcible rape as well as woman battering and had distributed them to a number of large city police departments throughout the United States. These specialized training programs helped to increase police awareness and sensitivity to victims of sexual assault and domestic violence.

A highly publicized Supreme Court case led to mandated police training on intervening in domestic-violence incidents. The suit was brought by Tracey Thurman against the Torrington Police Department in 1986. Ms. Thurman of Torrington, Connecticut had been beaten repeatedly by her husband, and Ms. Thurman's injuries included multiple stab wounds to the chest, neck and face; fractured cervical vertabrae and damage to her spinal cord; permanent paralysis/below the neck; lacerations to the cheeks and mouth; loss of blood; shock; scarring; severe pain; and mental anguish. Tracey Thurman was awarded $2.3 million in compensatory damages against twenty-four police officers. The jury found that the Torrington, Connecticut police had deprived Tracey Thurman of her constitutional right to equal protection of the law (Fourteenth Amendment of the U.S. Constitution). The jury further concluded that the Torrington police officers were guilty of gross negligence in failing to protect Tracey Thurman and her son Charles, Jr. from the violent acts of Charles Thurman, Sr.

As a result of the court decision in the Thurman case, police departments and state legislators throughout the country began mandating increased police training on domestic violence. Therefore, during the last half of the 1980s, there was a proliferation of police-training courses on how best to handle domestic violence calls.

Professor Dennis P. Rosenbaum, in his study of Detroit's sixteen-week police-training program, documents the need for police training programs to prepare new recruits to:

a. be immediately sensitive and responsive to victims' emotional crisis;

b. encourage victims to engage in a healthy ventilation and expression of the full range of their emotions;

c. make interventions that result in a reduction in the victim's injured pride, feelings of self-blame, and likelihood of self-destructive reactions;

d. identify victims who may require subsequent assessment and treatment by mental-health professionals;

e. empower troubled victims to take remedial actions that will reduce feeling of helplessness and impotent rage;

f. make well-informed and appropriate referrals to adjunctive service agencies (Rosenbaum 1987, p. 505).

In recognition of the extensive amount of time needed to respond to victims of domestic violence and sexual assault, large urban police departments have developed civilian crisis-intervention units. Police-based crisis intervenors and victim advocates are on-call twenty-four hours per day, and are usually quick to respond to a victim of violent crime. These crisis intervenors and victim advocates provide immediate crisis counseling, advocacy, transportation to and from hospital-based rape crisis centers or battered womens' shelters, and referrals to the local prosecutor's office and social-service agencies. The coordinator of the victim-assistance or crisis-intervention unit usually is the trainer for the domestic-violence and victim-assistance courses at the police academy. In addition, the police chief or captain to whom the unit coordinator reports makes every effort to encourage patrolmen to radio the victim assistance unit whenever they believe a victim of sexual assault or battering can be aided by the victim advocate (Roberts 1990).

Courts and Sexual Assault

Formal decision making at the early stages of the criminal justice process determines which criminal incidents will be viewed as legitimate and which victims will receive the full benefits of the criminal law. In the past, many police officers would treat female rape victims' complaints as either unfounded or they would view her as seductive and untrustworthy. In addition, some prosecutors would reject the officers judgment that the victim was raped and refuse to initiate formal proceedings. Only in the cases in which the rape victim was married or still living in her parent's home would prosecutors consistently view the rape as a more serious and a legitimate criminal case (Myers and LaFree 1982; Berger, Searles, and Neuman 1988; and Kerstetter 1990).

Feminist conflict theory has resulted in the reform of rape laws. Conflict theorists argue that the legal system protects only "valuable" women—those women who conform to traditional sex-role stereotypes and are young virgins or married women. In the past, criminal justice officials tended to dismiss cases when the rape victims had a bad reputation, were hitchhiking, were drinking directly prior to the offense, or had sexual intercourse with the defendant prior to the sexual assault. In general, when a woman did not seem to fulfill traditional sex-role stereotypes and she was raped, she did not receive the full protection of the criminal justice system.

During the past decade, most state legislatures have modified or reformed their rape statutes in several ways to include:

- mandating increased services to victims of sexual assault, particularly counseling and hotline services;
- laws that protect the confidentiality of communications between sexual assault victims and their counselors;
- rape shield laws to protect rape complainants from having to reveal publicly any past sexual history;
- reforms that removed the spousal exemption that gave husbands immunity from prosecution for forcing their wives to have sexual intercourse;
- laws designed to preserve medical evidence for the prosecution and that pay for or reimburse rape victims for medical examinations and or ambulance costs (Anderson and Woodard 1985; Berger, Searles, and Neuman 1988; Field 1983, Estrich 1987, and Finkelhor and Yllo 1985).

By June 1990, important studies had taken place to attend to the criminal justice and psychological needs of sexual assault victims, while also protecting victim's rights.

Thirty-seven states have enacted legislation to cover the costs of medical examinations for rape victims. In addition, these costs are sometimes covered by VOCA funds, through either victims assistance or victim compensation. In most communities it is no longer routine for victims to bear this cost. Twenty-four states have provided state funds for sexual assault services. All 50 states have some type of protection to shield rape complainants from having to disclose publicly their past sexual activities. The majority have accomplished this goal through legislation, but a few states have relied upon judicial opinions or court rules. Generally, laws have been successful in limiting the type of inquiry in rape cases, thus improving the treatment of rape victims and increasing the number of rape reports and prosecutions. (Burnley 1990)

Sexual assault victims deserve sensitive and fair treatment by police, prosecutors, hospital emergency-room physicians and nurses, social workers and psychologists, defense attorneys, judges, jurors, newspaper reporters, and the community. Not only is fair, sensitive, courteous, and humane treatment the right thing to do, it is absolutely necessary in order to reduce secondary trauma to rape victims and improve their cooperation in criminal court proceedings. Despite the significant progress during the past 15 years in improving the criminal justice system's responsiveness to victims of sexual assault, rape remains one of the two most underreported crimes. Many women still do not officially report rape because they feel it is too personal an incident to talk about to a stranger; they also fear that if the perpetrator is apprehended and the case goes to trial, the woman will be forced to relive the traumatic event—in effect, being raped a second time by an insensitive defense attorney.

Sexual assault legislation has had a significant impact on the criminal justice processing of sexual assault complaints and cases. Rape reform legislation has heightened awareness in most communities across the United States and has increased the responsiveness of criminal justice leaders to rape victims. It is important to note that, while criminal law reforms and new revised sexual assault statutes have led to changed attitudes and behavior among criminal justice agency staff, the full impact of these reforms has not yet been realized.

Model Prosecutor-Based Victim/Witness Assistance Program

The Victim/Witness Division of the Greene County Prosecutor's Office (Xenia, Ohio) was created in January 1982 to serve victims of sexual crime involved in the criminal justice system. A portion of the prosecuting attorney's budget, allocated by the Board of County Commissioners, was the original source of funding. The division soon expanded its services to victims of other crimes as a result of numerous referrals. In December 1982, the Victim/Witness Division received a grant from the Ohio Department of Public Welfare, Bureau of Children Services, to add Project PAAR (Prevent Abuse/Assist Recovery), "a comprehensive program designed to help prevent sexual abuse of children and to assist in the recovery of the child in cases where abuse has occurred."

Today a full range of support services is provided to all victims of violent crime. The division specializes in sexual assault, child sexual abuse, and domestic violence. Sources of funding are the Prosecutor's Office and a series of grants from the State of Ohio. The division's 1985 budget was $92,500, 40 percent of which came from county general revenue and 60 percent from grants from the Ohio Department of Human Services and the Ohio Department of Health.

The Victim/Witness Division provides services to all victims of crime from the time the crime is reported through the entire investigation and prosecution process. Division staff and trained volunteers provide 24-hour crisis intervention assistance to all victims. Response to a request for assistance is made within one hour. The Victim/Witness Division representative's primary roles are as advocate and source of information for the victim. In addition, the worker acts as liaison between the victim (and the victim's family) and the hospital, law enforcement personnel, and the prosecutor.

Witness assistance services are provided to those who pursue prosecution. Any time a victim is required to participate in a segment of the criminal justice process, a Victim/Witness Division worker is available to assist the victim and the victim's family. Court-related services offered include witness notification, information about criminal justice system procedures, transportation services, employer intervention, court escort, and court support at all stages of prosecution. The division's good relationship with other county service agencies and various police departments enables it to employ a "team approach" to working with crime victims. Victims receive direct services from division staff as well as referrals to other appropriate agencies. Another important area of activity is the division's education program. Public awareness/prevention educational presentations are provided on request, to any public or private group or organization, on a variety of topics such as sexual assault, child sexual abuse, and domestic violence.

As a result of funding for Project PAAR, Victim/Witness Division staff are able to respond on a 24-hour basis (contacting victims within one hour after the abuse is reported to the police, a hospital, or other agency) to requests for assistance in cases of child sexual abuse. All appropriate Victim/Witness Division services are provided to victims of child sexual abuse and supportive family members. Project PAAR works in close cooperation with the Greene County Bureau of Children's Services, Greene County Children's Mental Health, the Domestic Violence Project, Inc., Greene Memorial Hospital, police agencies in Greene County, and the staff of the Greene County Prosecutor's Office. Objectives of the project are to prevent child sexual abuse through a comprehensive, effective education-outreach program and to increase the likelihood of child sexual abuse reporting by making the services of the Victim/Witness Division and Project

PAAR known to potential victims. To these ends, the division presents educational programs to public and private groups. Age-appropriate educational presentations concerning child sexual abuse prevention are provided at all elementary, junior high, and high schools. Students also receive printed materials (Roberts, 1990).

The Risk of AIDS among Rape Victims

The fear of AIDS among victims of sexual assault is a new issue that significantly magnifies the trauma experienced by these victims. Rape now carries the additional long-term threat of a time-bomb ticking away, with the victims not knowing whether they will become HIV-positive at some time in the future as a result of being raped. Although the risk of contracting AIDS from a sexual assault is not known, the AIDS epidemic poses a threat to all rape victims.

The physical and psychological trauma that results from rape is compounded many times by the intense fear of contracting AIDS as a direct result of the crime. "Sexual assault and child sexual abuse victims must now fear that they not only may have contracted a sexually transmitted disease like gonorrhea, but also a life threatening disease for which there is no known cure. AIDS furthers the trauma and the post-traumatic stress of the victim (Burnley 1990).

Defense attorneys and victim-rights advocates have called for protecting the rights of rape victims rather than allowing them to be exploited further by the perpetrator.

Sally F. Goldfarb, a senior staff attorney at the National Organization for Women (NOW) Legal Defense and Education Fund stated: "The AIDS epidemic has turned the crime of rape, which is a horrifying and damaging crime under any circumstances, into one that is potentially fatal" (Goldfarb 1990). Dr. Jane Nady Burnley, Director of the U.S. Department of Justice's Office for Crime Victims, advocates that "sexual offenders should be tested at the earliest possible juncture in the criminal justice process (Hoffman 1989, p. 36).

Several magistrates call for protecting the privacy rights of people charged as well as those convicted of rape regardless of the rights and potentially life-threatening danger to the victim. Judge Richard Andrias, a New York State Supreme Court Justice wrote: "Any testing prior to conviction takes the presumption of innocence . . . and turns it on its head" (Hoffman 1989, p. 36).

Whose rights should be protected, the victim's or the defendant's? Some state legislators have passed laws that protect suspects and convicted rapists' rights to privacy and confidentiality, while other laws compel high-risk sex offenders to be tested for the AIDS virus and the test results immediately given to the victim.

Most Americans are supportive of rape-reform statutes that define rape as forcing another person to have sexual intercourse against their will. There is general agreement that rape is a crime of violence that is best categorized as a felony rather than a misdemeanor. However, when it comes to legislation and state criminal codes, there are differing views among the states with regard to the following: (1) Should testing of accused or convicted sex offenders for human immunodeficiency virus (HIV) be mandatory or voluntary? When a person knowingly exposes another person to HIV, AIDS, ARC, or an STD, should that act be statutorily defined as a felony? (3) Under what conditions should HIV test results be given to the victim of sexual assault?

There is now a penalty for knowingly exposing another person to AIDS or other sexually transmitted diseases. Fifteen states have now passed legislation which attempts to protect individuals from sexual partners who willfully expose another person to HIV, AIDS, and other sexually transmitted diseases (STDs). Eleven of the fifteen states have made it a felony to knowingly expose another person to HIV or AIDS.

For example, in Oklahoma it is a felony for a person who knows he or she is infected with HIV to expose his or her sexual partner either by not "first informing the person," or by not taking prophylactic precautions (Hoffman 1989, p. 40). A few other states, like Maryland, prohibit all individuals with the human immunodeficiency virus (HIV) from knowingly transferring or attempting to transfer the virus to another person. However, in Maryland, violating the provisions in the statute is a misdemeanor offense (Maryland Code Annotated Health–General 1990, p. 421).

As of May 1991, twenty-six states across the nation had passed legislation regarding HIV testing of convicted sex offenders, but only a few of these states also require that a person accused of rape or other sex crimes be tested for HIV or other sexually transmitted diseases (STDs). Requiring alleged sex offenders to be tested after arrest is a violation of the right to privacy of the individuals who are falsely identified and are eventually found not guilty. For example, the state of Nevada requires that after a person has been arrested for sexual assault, and the victim or a witness alleges that forced sexual penetration has taken place, "the health authority shall test a specimen submitted from the arrested person for exposure to the human immunodeficiency virus and syphilis" (Nevada 1989).

Several of the progressive states require testing sex offenders for HIV as soon as possible after the probable cause is found that the accused committed the offense and the defendent has been charged and the victim believes that infected blood or semen has been transferred from the accused into her body. In 1988, California was the first state to enact this type of AIDS testing statute, with the primary purpose of benefiting the victims of sexual assault by informing them when the defendant is infected with the AIDS virus thereby enabling the victim to receive treatment at the earliest possible time.

Thirteen of the twenty-six states with legislation related to the testing of sex offenders and the disclosure of test results allow for the voluntary testing of convicted sex offenders, and, in many of these states, the victim may only have access to the test results with a court order, and/or demonstrating a compelling need. Several of these states require varying degrees of consent (informed consent or written informed consent) from the offender as well as pre- and/or post-testing counseling. New York not only requires written informed consent of the offender prior to testing, but also guarantees the defendent's right to privacy by requiring that the victim must demonstrate "compelling need for the disclosure," before the test results will be revealed (New York Public Health Laws, 1991). In addition, in the case where the offender has been previously tested, the New York statutes will not allow the victims to receive the test results unless the prosecutor can demonstrate that there is a "clear and imminent danger to an individual whose life or health may unkonwingly be at significant risk as a result of contact with the accused (New York Public Health Laws, 1991).

Conclusion

During the past decade, sexual-assault-reform legislation has resulted in several long-overdue improvements in the criminal-justice processing of sexual-assault cases, for example, passage of rape shield laws, confidentiality laws to protect communications between the victims and their counselors, and laws designed to preserve medical evidence. Many states and counties have also made major strides in developing victim assistance programs. Most noteworthy are the following:

- police training on domestic violence throughout the country;
- hospital-based rape-crisis programs at large hospitals;
- hundreds of prosecutor-based victim/witness-assistance programs; and
- over 1,200 shelters for battered women developed in rural, urban, and surburban areas.

Recent legislation on the testing of sex offenders for HIV, AIDS, and other sexually transmitted diseases (STDs) has the potential of protecting the rights of victims of sexual assault. During the three-year period from 1989 to 1991, over half of our nation's states passed timely legislation to guide the intervention of police, prosecutors, forensic specialists, public-health officers, prison officials, and magistrates. Unfortunately, some of the states have ignored the rights of the innocent victim of rape and, instead, have focused their efforts on protecting the privacy rights of violent and chronic rapists. The statutes in most states need to be liberalized so that early testing of sex offenders and disclosure of HIV test results to the victim becomes required. A major commitment to protecting the human rights of victims from further abuse and exploitation by offenders, legislators and the criminal justice system is necessary in a humane society. No state, in good conscience, should claim to provide equitable, fair, and just treatment to all of its citizens, if it places the rights of a sex offender above those of the innocent victim. This is particularly true if the innocent victim may die as a result of being sexually assaulted and may also unknowingly pass a life-threatening disease on to those close to him or her.

REFERENCES

Anderson, J. R., and P. L. Woodard, "Victim and Witness Assistance: New State Laws and the System's Response," *Judicature*, 68, no. 6 (1985), 221–244.

Atkeson, B. M., K. S. Calhoun, P. A. Resick, and E. Ellis. "Victims of Rape: Repeated Assessment of Depressive Symptoms," *Journal of Consulting and Clinical Psychology*, 50 (1982), 96–102.

Becker, J. V., and L. J. Skinner, "Assessment and Treatment of Rape-Related Sexual Dysfunctions," *The Clinical Psychologist*, 36, no. 1 (1983), 102–105.

Becker, J. V., and L. J. Skinner, "Behavioral Treatment of Sexual Dysfunctions in Sexual Assault Survivors." In I. Stuart and J. Greer (eds.), *Victims of Sexual Aggression*. New York: Van Nostrand Reinhold, 1984, pp. 211–234.

Becker, J. V., L. J. Skinner, G. G. Abel, and J. Cichon. "Level of Post Assault Sexual Functioning in Rape & Incest Victims," *Archives of Sexual Behavior*, 15 (1986), 37–49.

Berger, R. J., P. Searles, and W. L. Neuman, "The Dimensions of Rape Reform Legislation," *Law and Society Review*, 22, no. 2 (1988), 329–357.

Burgess, A., and L. Holmstrom, "Rape Trauma Syndrome," *American Journal of Psychiatry*, 131 (1974), 981–986.

Burgess, A., and L. Holmstrom, "Rape: Sexual Disruption & Recovery," *American Journal of Orthopsychiatry*, 49 (1979), 648–657.

Burnley, J., Testimony before the Senate U.S. Select Committee on Children, Youth, and Families, 1990.

Calhoun, K. S., B. M. Atkeson, and P. Resick, "A Longitudinal Examination of Fear Reactions in Victims of Rape," *Journal of Counseling Psychology*, 29 (1982), 655–661.

Criminal Victimization in the United States. Washington, D.C.: U.S. Department of Justice, Bureau of Justice Statistics, 1989.

Estrich, S., *Real Rape.* Cambridge, Mass.: Harvard University Press, 1987.

Ellis, E. M., K. S. Calhoun, and B. M. Atkeson, "Sexual Dysfunctions in Victims of Rape," *Women and Health*, 5 (1980), 39–47.

Field, M. A., "Rape: Legal Aspects." In S. Kadish (ed.), *Encyclopedia of Crime and Justice*, vol. 4. New York: Free Press, 1983.

Finkelhor, D., and K. Yllo. *License to Rape: Sexual Abuse of Wives.* New York: Holt, Rinehart and Winston, 1985.

Harlow, C. W., *Female Victims of Violent Crimes.* Washington, D.C.: U.S. Department of Justice, January 1991.

Hoffman, J., "AIDS and Rape: Should New York Test Sex Offenders?" *The Village Voice*, 34, no. 37 (1989), 35–41.

Kerstetter, W. A., "Gateway to Justice: Police and Prosecutorial Response to Sexual Assaults Against Women," *The Journal of Criminal Law and Criminal Law and Criminology*, 81, no. 2.1 (1990), 267–312.

Kilpatrick, D., *Treatment of Fear and Anxiety in Victims of Rape.* Final Report of NIMH Grant #MH29602, 1984.

Kilpatrick, D., and L. J. Veronen, "Treatment of Rape-Related Problems." In L. H. Cohen, W. L. Claiborn, and G. A. Spector (eds.), *Crisis Intervention.* New York: Human Sciences Press, 1983, pp. 165–185.

Kilpatrick, D., C. L. Best, L. J. Veronen, A. E. Amick, L. A. Villeponteaus, and G. A. Ruff, "Mental Health Correlates of Criminal Victimization: A Random Community Survey," *Journal of Consulting and Clinical Psychology*, 53 (1985), 866–873.

Koss, M. P., C. A. Gidycz, and N. Wisniewski, "The Scope of Rape: Incidence and Prevalence of Sexual Aggression and Victimization in a National Sample of Higher Education Students," *Journal of Consulting and Clinical Psychology*, 55 (1987), 162–170.

Maryland Code Annotated, Health–General, SS 18-505, 18-601.1, (1990), pp. 420–421.

Murphy, S. M., S. Amic-McMullan, D. Kilpatrick, M. E. Haskett, L. J. Veronen, C. L. Best, and B. E. Saunders, "Rape Victims' Self-Esteem: A Longitudinal Analysis." *Journal of Interpersonal Violence*, 3 (1988), 355–370.

Myers, J., and G. D. LaFree, "The Uniqueness of Sexual Assault. A Comparison With Other Crimes," *Journal of Criminal Law and Criminology*, 73 (1982), 1282–1290.

Nevada Revised Statutes Annotated, Vol. 12, S 441A.220 (Michie Supp., 1989) p. 77.

New York Public Health Laws Annotated, Book 44, SS 2781. 2782, 2785 (West Supp., 1991), pp. 47–55.

Presidential Commission on the HIV Epidemic, *Final Report.* Washington, D.C.: Author, 1988.

Resick, P., *Reactions of Female and Male Victims of Rape and Robbery*. Final Report of N.I.J. Grant #85-IJ-CX-0042, 1988.

Roberts, A. R., *Helping Crime Victims: Research, Policy and Practice*, Newbury Park, Calif.: Sage Publications, 1990.

Rosenbaum, D. P., "Coping With Victimization," *Crime and Delinquency*, 33, no. 4 (1987), 502–519.

Russell, D., "The Prevalence and Incidence of Forcible Rape and Attempted Rape of Females," *Victimology: An International Journal*, 7 (1982).

Schmalleger, F., *Criminal Justice Today*. Englewood Cliffs, N.J.: Prentice-Hall, 1991.

Uniform Crime Reports. Washington, D.C.: U.S. Department of Justice, FBI, 1981.

Uniform Crime Reports. Washington, D.C.: U.S. Department of Justice, FBI, 1989.

Uniform Crime Reports. Washington, D.C.: U.S. Department of Justice, FBI, 1990.

Violent Crime in the United States, Washington, D.C.: U.S. Department of Justice, Office of Justice Programs, Bureau of Justice Statistics, 1991.

22

Fear of Crime among Elderly Urban Women

Kathleen J. Hanrahan

Fear of crime apparently is an enduring feature of modern life. The study of this phenomenon has engaged criminologists for over twenty years. We find, consistently, that the elderly, women, minorities, and residents of urban areas are the most fearful. What we have lacked is a clear notion of what is feared and how fear of crime affects the lives of those in its grip. This chapter reports on a study that asked elderly women living in Newark, New Jersey to talk about the problems they face, what crime means in their lives, and how they negotiate their world.

The chapter begins by introducing the student, briefly, to the literature on fear of crime. It will then turn to the findings of this study. The emphasis is on the more descriptive findings about fear of crime, related in the words of the respondents. The chapter will conclude with the implications for studying (measuring) fear of crime and the implications of fear of crime in our lives.

Fear of crime is a prominent feature of modern life. It was not always that way, of course. Crime rates and fear of crime increased dramatically in the 1960s. With that increase came a new way of living. It is sometimes surprising to realize that it was not always neces-

This research was supported by a Graduate Research Fellowship (grant number 88-IJ-CX0027) from the National Institute of Justice. The points of view are those of the author and do not necessarily reflect those of the National Institute of Justice.

sary to lock doors, to watch, and to be so careful. What we have come to accept is, in fact, a reduction in the scope and quality of our lives.

This chapter focuses on the group in our society that has been shown by many years of prior research to be particularly fearful: elderly women. The chapter begins with a review of some of what we know about fear of crime and then illustrates that reality in the words of one group of elderly women.

Prior Research on Fear of Crime

Research conducted over the past two decades has created a considerable body of knowledge about fear of crime. While not unequivocal, the bulk of the evidence shows that (1) the elderly, (2) women, (3) minorities, and (4) urban residents are most fearful of crime. (See, for example, Skogan 1987; Skogan and Maxfield 1981; Baumer 1985 and 1978; Yin 1980; Warr 1984; and Lewis and Salem 1986).

In recent years, research on fear of crime has advanced beyond a simple search for correlates. Sophisticated models have been proposed to explain fear of crime. Two broad categories of explanation are typically encountered:

1. The indirect victimization perspective, which suggests both that the key demographic correlates of fear of crime—age, sex, ethnicity, urban location—reflect vulnerability to crime and that knowlege of others' victimization leads to increased fear (Taylor and Hale 1986, citing Skogan and Maxfield 1981); and,

2. The social disorder perspective, which holds that fear of crime is related to perceptions of a breakdown of social control in the community. This breakdown in control is indicated or symbolized by various social and physical "incivilities," such as public drunkenness or abandoned buildings. These incivilities suggest to residents that traditional social control mechanisms are no longer effective and that traditional values and standards of behavior are no longer in force. Fear of crime is a reaction to this weakening social control (Taylor and Hale 1986, citing Hunter 1978; Garofalo and Laub 1978; and Lewis and Maxfield 1980).

There is a striking consistency in the way that fear of crime has been studied in the published literature. The tradition has been to use a survey approach and to measure fear by a single item. In a review of studies of fear of crime, Ferraro and LaGrange (1987) found the following to be the most frequently used measure: "Is there any area right around here—that is, within a mile—where you would be afraid to walk alone at night?" Another very common item is that developed for the National Crime Survey: "How safe do you feel or would you feel walking alone at night in your neighborhood?"

Increasingly, the traditional approach to studying fear of crime is being criticized (see, for example, Williams and Akers 1987; Ferraro and LaGrange 1987; Gibbs, Coyle, and Hanrahan 1987; and Gibbs and Hanrahan 1990). In addition to the obvious limitations of trying to capture with a single item a phenomenon as complex as fear of crime, researchers have argued that fear of crime needs to be studied in the context of other fears and concerns. That is, the relative salience of fear of crime, compared with other life concerns, needs to be determined (see, for example, Harris 1975 and 1981; Yin 1980 and 1982; and Stein, Linn, and Slater 1984).

The research reported here is based on an exploratory study that was designed to increase our understanding of fear of crime. The primary source of information is interviews with elderly women, many of them minorities, living in an urban setting. In addition, the most commonly used single-item measures of fear of crime were asked during the interviews. The research questions addressed in this study—stated at their most basic level—can be divided into three interrelated questions: (1) what does fear of crime look like—how is it experienced? (2) what are its consequences for the lives of the women studied? and (3) how best can we measure fear of crime?

Methods

The data reported here were gathered during semistructured, intensive interviews with elderly (sixty-five and older), female residents of Newark, New Jersey. Respondents were selected from participants at three of the twenty-two senior-citizen centers operated by the city of Newark.

The sample consists of women who attend the senior centers fairly regularly. As a group, the women interviewed range in age from sixty-five to eighty-five, with an average age of 74.6 years. The majority, 63.2 percent, are black. Most (71.9 percent) are widowed and live alone (70.2 percent) in rented property (57.9 percent). Most are long-term residents of Newark; the mean number of years at the current address is 20.6, and nearly 60 percent of the sample have lived at their current address for more than ten years. Monthly income ranged from a low of $242 to a high of $1,600; the mean is $621 per month. In terms of education, the mean grade attended was just over eighth grade.

Daily Life

All respondents were asked to describe a typical day in their lives. The purpose was to see to what extent crime or fear of crime shapes activities. The large picture shows women who are uniformly busy over the course of the day. While very few work for pay, all maintain households, 76.8 percent reported some chores or housework as part of the average day, and 75 percent mentioned shopping, usually for food. Entertainment such as watching television or sewing or reading was reported by 75 percent of the women, while about one-third mentioned visiting friends or family, and about 27 percent mentioned church activities.

The way that respondents get around—to the senior centers or to shop or visit—gives some indication of feelings of personal safety. It is true that health matters influence local travel arrangements, but crime is at least equally important in the selection. A fair proportion of women walk to their destinations—just over 44 percent walk to the center, in spite of readily available center-provided transportation; a similar proportion walk to shop, and over half of those who visit walk to their friends' or relatives' homes. It should be noted, however, that the women who walk are typically not walking great distances. In many cases, they are walking around the block or across the street to church, for example.

Almost all of the reported activity takes place during daylight hours. The women in the sample make a sharp distinction between daytime and nighttime activities. Most of the women go out at night only infrequently; nearly 10 percent (8.9 percent) never go out, and 67.9 percent seldom do. The "seldom" category is just that; these women go out at night only rarely.

IR#9: . . . [but] the night, you can't get out.

I: You don't go out at night?

IR#9: No, because it's dangerous today, going outside. So many, they steal the pocketbook . . . They are crazy people, so I stay home . . . Some days [my children] are taking me out. Once or twice a month I go to the restaurant with my children.

I: They come and pick you up?

IR#9: Oh, yes.

Combining the response categories for "sometimes" and "often walk alone" totals just under one-fourth of the sample (23.3 percent). Only 11.1 percent walk alone at night, and no one takes public transportation after dark. The most typical arrangement is to be picked up at the door and brought home by someone with a car.

The finding that just over 10 percent of the women walk alone at night is somewhat misleading. Again, these women are often talking about walking across the street or next door to church or a neighbor's house. The following description of nighttime walking gives a fair impression of how it is accomplished. The speaker is seventy-six years old and is describing the last time she walked home from a meeting at 10:00 p.m.:

> *IR#19:* I was scared. When I think cars are coming, I would stop by a house, make out I live there. If I saw a car slowing down I'd make out I was going in this alley way and then I would look [to make sure] he's gone. And that way I'm protecting myself. If a car's coming and I feel that something's coming or something's up then I go up a step. Then let the car pass by, then when I get to the corner and I have to cross over this corner, then I run. Run here, then run there, then to a house.

Even for women who at least occasionally walk at night with others, the nature of the experience typically is not carefree. The following speaker, an 81-year-old woman, describes a group of four friends walking each other home:

> *IR#20:* We walk around the block, we take one girl home first. Then now, we're three. Then we take the other girl home. She runs, you know, we take her to the corner. We wait till she goes into her gate. Now we're two. [The other woman] lives across the way from me, like across, like she lives on this corner, and I live not on that corner but the next corner. A half block in. She waits up there till I go into my gate and then she goes into her house.

Fear of crime clearly shapes both daytime and nighttime activities. Instances in which respondents spontaneously mentioned crime or fear of crime as determining either whether they would take part in an activity or how they would participate were coded for daytime activities for 58.2 percent of the respondents and for nighttime activities for 76 percent of the respondents. For example, the respondent quoted below has reduced her nighttime activities at the church because of fear:

> *GW#1:* When I was a member of the choir, I used to go to choir rehearsal. But, a lot of things when I say used to do, I don't do anymore now because of the risk you take when you go out at night. And all of those rehearsals were at night. A lot of things

that I would probably do, I don't do, because I just don't feel safe out in the streets.

Fear of Crime and Primary Life Concerns and Problems

One of the areas of interest for this study is whether and where fear of crime ranks in the larger context of life concerns. Content analysis revealed seven broad areas of concern for this group of respondents: physical well-being, emotional support, social activity, autonomy, tangible assistance (primarily financial) religious/philosophical lifestyle, and personal safety.

The distribution of concerns is shown in Table 1. The table shows the percentage of cases in which each concern was ranked as the primary concern and the percentage in which the concern was mentioned at all. Not surprisingly, the two leading concerns are emotional support and physical well-being. The majority of women at least mentioned these concerns and they were of primary importance to over one-third and one-quarter of the sample, respectively.

Table 1:   Prevalence of Concerns

CONCERN	PRIMARY % (n)	ALL RANKS[1] % (n)
Physical Well-Being	26.8 (15)	56.6 (30)
Emotional Support	33.9 (19)	58.9 (33)
Social Activity	10.7 (6)	21.4 (12)
Religious/Philosophical Lifestyle	17.9 (10)	25.0 (14)
Autonomy	5.4 (3)	5.4 (3)
Tangible Assistance	1.8 (1)	10.7 (6)
Personal Safety	3.6 (2)	7.1 (4)

[1]Percent of respondents.

Personal safety—a concern with safety from crime or a concern with fear of crime—was mentioned spontaneously by a total of four of the fifty-seven respondents and was the primary concern of two of them. For example, one respondent said:

IR#11: I wish I had a life like when I first got married. I had a nice life. . . . I wouldn't mind that life again, but this one I can't take. I don't care for this life. Because you're always in fear. And there's something around, you're always in fear and then, I don't know, like I said, the people are not like they used to be, you know.

The relatively low salience of fear of crime among this group of respondents—as suggested by this measure—was anticipated by Yin (1982). One part of the explanation is undoubtedly a reflection of the actual importance of fear of crime as it stacks up against matters like physical well-being. As discussed in more detail later, another part of the explanation seems to be that accommodations to crime are taken for granted and simply are not, or are no longer, remarkable.

The core concerns that emerged from the interviews are hardly unanticipated. One concern does deserve mention, however. A fair proportion of respondents, one-fourth in fact, reported a concern with religious or philosophical matters. This concern involved an effort to live right, to incorporate God's word and will in everyday life. As explained by one respondent:

SW#9: I know God and He watches over me. So that's the way I feel. I feel happy, and I feel at peace with myself most of the time. And that, I think, is very important. Because that's why a lot of people, I guess, do a lot of things, like they, in their lifestyle, because they have no God caring in them. And they don't care about anything. But if you got—if you can pray inside of you— and you know Him, then you have guidance for you. . . . I read the Bible a lot . . . This spiritual side, I enjoy it. And it's like I say, I know there's a God and I know He watches over me.

Race is related to the primacy of this concern. Black respondents were far more likely to present this concern than were white respondents—36.1 percent vs. 4.8 percent.

In addition to discussing important life concerns, each woman we interviewed was asked about problems or worries she faces on a day-to-day basis. The purpose, again, was to see where fear of crime ranked in the eyes of these women. Respondents were first asked entirely open-ended questions about problems and worries, following Yin's (1982) approach. Then, respondents were asked if a series of issues, such as health and financial matters, were problems in their lives.

Again, we found that structured questioning yielded more reports of problems or worries particularly for fear of crime. Fully 60.7 percent of respondents to the structured item consider fear of crime a problem or worry, and 35 percent said it is the biggest problem they face. The proportion of respondents who mentioned fear of crime without prompting was just over 10 percent and only two respondents (5.9 percent) considered it the biggest problem they face.

Common Themes in Fear of Crime

We approached understanding what fear of crime means to these women from a variety of angles. As noted, the general pattern we found was that when presented with a question dealing more or less directly with fear of crime, respondents were quite likely to agree that fear is present in their lives. For example, over 90 percent of the women agreed that there is an area within a mile of their homes where they would be afraid to walk at night. In response to the National Crime Survey (NCS) item, 80 percent reported they would feel either "very afraid" or "somewhat afraid" to walk alone at night in their neighborhood. However, when merely offered opportunities to mention fear of crime, or crime generally, respondents were far less likely to make that connection. As noted above, only four of the women mentioned fear of crime as a concern.

There is one major exception to this pattern: the majority of women we interviewed spontaneously mentioned crime and fear as in some way shaping their daily round of activities. Significantly, accommodations to crime and the potential for victimization were not always appreciated or recognized by respondents as fear—but fully 58.2 percent of the respondents report changing their daytime activities in response to crime and 76 percent spontaneously reported the impact of crime on their nighttime activities.

The types of crime feared and the situations that elicit fear show some common patterns:

Types of Crime Feared

By far the most commonly feared crimes are purse-snatching and mugging. In the minds of the respondents, these are not separate crimes. Purse-snatching always involves the potential for violence— even if it is inadvertent in the sense of being thrown off balance as the purse is yanked away.

> *SW#4:* Well I'd just be afraid that somebody . . . you never know what they're gonna do. Cause if they going to snatch your purse and you don't give it up they probably hurt you otherwise and take it, they will think there is money or something in there. So if you don't give up the pocketbook, quite naturally, they gonna do something to you to get the pocketbook.

Most of the respondents, 90.5 percent, believe the elderly, especially elderly women, are preferred targets for purse-snatching and mugging for the obvious reasons:

> *SW#10:* I guess they figure you can't help yourself. You can't run, you know. Mostly every time somebody wanted to take my bag, it was a young person. They run, I couldn't run to catch them. That's why I think they pick on the elderly people. They look at you and figure you're afraid, and they know you can't do anything. They know you're not gonna do nothing.

Assault is feared by a little less than one-third (31.6 percent) of the respondents. In general, this is a fear of random violence happening on the street. Burglary is feared by fewer than 20 percent of the sample. In part this reflects the nature of the crime—property versus violent—but it also reflects the general feeling of security in their homes that is enjoyed by these women. The majority of the women—76.5 percent—are not fearful at home.

Rape was mentioned by 17.5 percent, or ten, of the women. In most cases, this was not volunteered; we asked directly if rape was a concern. The question was based on the infrequent spontaneous mention of rape given the suggestion by Warr (1984) and Gordon and Riger (1988), among others, that female fear of crime is at base fear of rape. There is a small group of women in this study who do fear rape. As suggested by Warr, and Gordon and Riger, these women fear rape as the outcome of a mugging gone very wrong: "If they want to rob me, let them rob me, but don't rape me or anything like that"*(IR#11).* Or, "You never know what the kids got, in their minds, to do. Whether they just pull you in or they just want your pocketbook or, who knows, maybe rape you, who knows" *(IR#19).*

Most respondents feel secure in the belief that rape happens to younger women, not seniors. Even one who knows better is not fearful:

> *SW#21:* You know, I don't worry about [rape] too much. I don't know, I guess I just, well there was a time that you didn't ever hear of older women getting raped, you know? . . . It was always a young woman. If they were going to rape, they would rape a young woman, a child, you know? But this has started happening in the last some years, that they started raping older women. So I guess it just didn't soak in.

This finding, as noted, was unexpected. Whether ignorance or denial is at work seems irrelevant. These women do not fear rape. As discussed below however, they do fear men—at least young men who are not known to them.

Over the course of talking with the women, it became clear that there are some people or situations that trigger fear or that elicit at least wariness on the part of the women. The most common fear stimulus is youth—teenagers and young adults. Over half the respondents (52.6 percent) reported feeling uneasy or fearful if confronted by youth on the street.

GW#14: If I see young boy coming, I'm afraid of him. Them young fellas, I'm afraid of them. All of them are not bad, but I don't know that. And they're strangers I don't know, so I'm just wary of them.

Men were more feared than women, but several respondents noted that girls were also known to snatch purses these days and can no longer be assumed to be safe.

Drug addicts and gangs of people, again, primarily younger adults or teenagers but also adult males hanging out on street corners, were mentioned by over 35 percent of the sample.

A large proportion of respondents (42.1 percent) offered specific places where they were afraid. For the majority of women, the street is the place they are most uneasy.

GW#10: I tell you where I feel most unsafe. Out there in them streets. Maybe they wouldn't, maybe I'd be lucky enough for them not to even think to bother me. But they have mugged and robbed older people and like that, and you don't know whether they going to attack you or not.

Other commonly mentioned locations are banks, elevators and hallways in apartment buildings, public areas like parks, or the commercial area in Newark. In the excerpt below, one woman describes her fears at the bank:

SW#21: . . . like when I'm going to cash my check at the bank. And although it's right across the street, you never know, you might see a suspicious looking person standing on the corner or something. . . .

I: Suppose . . . you see somebody who doesn't look like he belongs in the neighborhood.

SW#21: You would get frightened. You would be frightened. But you would try not to look frightened. You know because sometimes that encourages it. They say, "Oh, she must have something, she must have money." So you just go on, just like you're not paying any attention, but then you are looking. You're looking this way, you know, if somebody's walking behind. I won't just keep looking back at them, but I will just look to the sides and look to this side and just like if I'm looking at something over there, you know.

It is apparent that what was elicited here are basically explanations of crime. Crime is caused by the drug problem, by youth—either alone or in gangs—and to a lesser extent by strangers. Common locations for crime are the streets, banks, and unprotected public areas like elevators and parks. When confronted by any of these kinds of people or locations, the women become fearful. Their strategy for avoiding fear is to avoid the situations.

Self-Protective Measures

The women we interviewed take a fair number of precautions to protect themselves from crime. We asked both completely open-ended and structured questions about precautions.

The findings on self-protective measures lend support to the notion that fear of crime or accommodations to crime shape everyday activities without much notice from respondents. When asked what kinds of things they do to protect themselves either at home or on the street, most respondents could offer only one or two measures—many could think of nothing. The average number of measures reported is .75.

The small number of protective measures reported in response to the open-ended questions is a fairly typical pattern of response (see, for example, Greenberg 1987). In contrast, the conversation preceding that question often contained self-protective measures like not carrying a pocketbook, or keeping cash separate from the purse, or staying alert, or staying home.

When we read a lengthy list of possible protections, the average number reported 7.8. The most common precautions are locking doors and windows (83.6 percent); never going out alone at night (78.9 percent); being more cautious on the street (75.4 percent); using a peephole (or window) to see who is at the door before opening it (71.9 percent); and no longer going out at night (66.7 percent). Over half the respondents (56.1 percent) report that they have attended a crime prevention meeting; this is not surprising since the senior centers often invite local police officials to address the seniors about crime and crime prevention.

The precautions taken reflect a mixture of avoidance and self-protection (Gordon and Riger 1988), but avoidance behaviors clearly carry the day. These women tend to avoid situations likely to be risky and to be careful when the situation cannot be entirely avoided—such as going out during the daytime.

The Nature of Fear

Part of the study involved an attempt to gather richly detailed, first-hand accounts of fear and worry about crime. This effort was notably unsuccessful. There seem to be a few interrelated reasons for the respondents' inability to provide the descriptions. In the first place, articulating emotion is very difficult for anyone. This particular respondent group is not well-suited either by temperament or experience for the task. They are, as a group, relatively inarticulate. Much of the fear of crime intensity—such as there was—was conveyed by tone or loudness of voice with body language or facial expression for emphasis. Moreover, these experiences are presumed to be shared—everyone knows about fear of crime. Respondents would occasionally express surprise at the questions, or ask whether we looked at the neighborhood as we came into the center. More commonly, they would say "you know how it is" instead of providing the rich accounts that were expected. These women are, by and large, apt to act rather than analyze. In the following excerpt, a respondent is relating her reaction to an actual victimization experience:

> *GW#1:* I was getting in my car and this fellow came from behind hedges. . . . And he had a knife that long. He was about to stab my sister and he pulled her bag and threw her down. Fortunately, when he knocked her down he didn't cut her, because she let him have the bag. But if she hadn't a given it up, he was going to stab her. . . .
>
> *I:* How did you feel after that happened?
>
> *GW#1:* How did I feel? I felt like getting out of that neighborhood. Which is exactly what we did.

In addition to talking with women not much interested in analyzing feelings or emotional reactions to events, we were also asking respondents to report experiences in categories that did not map very well their experience of the phenomenon. Marjorie DeVault (1990) has suggested that women often have difficulty articulating their positions because the language we use does not fully reflect the female reality. Certainly this seems to be the case for these respondents. It is doubtful, however, that male respondents would have had a much easier time of it. Much of the literature—and questions drawn from it—simply does not reflect the reality of fear of crime for either gender (see also Wilson 1989).

Stanko (1987) reached a similar conclusion in her earlier study. Based on interviews with both women and men, she suggests that "fear of crime" is not as useful a concept as has commonly been assumed. She suggests "fear of crime, framed as an aberrant part of civilized life, may not be a useful concept to us at all" (p. 12). Instead, Stanko prefers what she calls "the routines of safekeeping"—"a dynamic process of negotiating danger and the potential of violence in everyday life" (p.12).

This study supports the idea that fear of crime as it has been implicitly conceptualized does not match the reality—at least not for this group of women. One final example: Following suggestions in the literature, the interview guide made a distinction between fear of crime and worry about it. Respondents were asked to describe in as much detail as possible one incident of each type that occurred in the preceding six months.

The women understood the difference between fear and worry but they did not see the relevance. Dealing with crime is all of one piece in their lives. Most do not experience fear—the emotion—in relation to crime. Or if they do, it is a rare event. This is because they structure their lives to avoid fear-provoking situations, and they do so, at this point, with little explicit attention to the accommodation. For example, the following respondent has trouble calling her reaction "fear":

> *SW#7:* How often would you say you feel afraid?
>
> *R:* I don't know if I can answer that. . . . I don't know whether you would call it just being careful, or you know, not to go certain places. Just stay at home.
>
> *I:* Would you call it being afraid or would you call it something else?
>
> *SW#7:* Being careful.

Another respondent, when asked as part of the structured list of precautions, whether she is more cautious on the street, reports:

> *SW#3:* No. [I'm not more cautious.] Well, I look back every once in a while to see if anybody is following me, or something like that. Otherwise, I'm all right.

Still another respondent explains why she is not fearful:

> *GW#3:* I feel safe everywhere I go. I feel safe anywhere that I go, beause I try not to go anyplace that I don't think is gonna be safe.

Finally, some respondents are reminiscent of Gordon and Riger's "invincibles." These are women who claim they are not fearful, but who "engage in many precautionary behaviors and in other ways indicate that crime and avoidance of victimization are important factors shaping their lives" (1988, p. 116). Here is an example:

I: ... what about times when you're worried about your safety?

GW#4: I don't worry about it.

I: But you take a lot of precautions.

GW#4: But I just take precautions. That's why I don't worry about it. I just take precautions. When the lady that lives two floors up—she told me some of the things that she does to her door at night. So I do that. Get into bed and sleep like a top.

I: ... What does she do?

GW#4: Well, the chain. I fixed it so that a person can't cut it with a saw. I fold it this-a-way, and fold it up at the bottom, and then I take a string and tie it around this, and. ...

I: The door and the lock.

GW#4: And I put a chair [behind the door]. Because if you push that chair, I can hear you.

Measuring Fear of Crime

As should be apparent by the foregoing, fear of crime as it is experienced by this group of respondents is not adequately captured by traditional approaches to measuring fear of crime. This is more than an academic issue. Fear of crime is the only quality of life measure we have that is related to the activities of the criminal justice system. Reducing fear of crime is the ultimate goal in a large proportion of criminal justice programs and interventions intended to affect the lives of citizens. In the absence of solid measures of fear of crime—which in turn depend on clear understanding of fear and its implications—it is not possible to measure "what works." Accurate and stable measures of fear of crime are needed to design the interventions and then to determine whether or not they succeed.

Traditional measures of fear of crime do not fare well when examined in the light of our respondents' experience of fear of crime. Responses to the NCS item, for example, suggest a high level of fear of crime, at least as this item measures it: 80 percent of the respondents said they would feel either "very unsafe" or "somewhat unsafe" walking alone in the neighborhood at night. Fully 64 percent of the respondents said they would feel "very unsafe."

This finding needs to be set in context however. About half of the respondents (48.2 percent) could not answer the question without offering some qualifications; a few (N = 6) could not answer at all. The general thrust of the qualifications was that the behavior in question—walking alone at night—was so unlikely to take place that respondents could not simply answer the question. As described by one respondent:

SW#18: There's nothing I need to go out there for . . . because I arrange it that way, you know. It would have to be some emergency, which I can't think of what the emergency would be for me to go, but I mean you get where you live where you arrange so you won't be going out at night . . . I just don't have any need to go for nothing. Anything I need can wait.

The rarity of the behavior even caused a few women to misinterpret the response categories:

I: How safe do you feel, or would you feel, walking alone at night in your neighborhood?

SW#13: Well, in the first place, I don't walk to things. I'm a senior citizen—I should do what I have to do in the daytime. Should do it then. I should. So if I go out, I don't go by myself.

I: Let's say for some reason you did. Would you feel very safe, reasonably safe, somewhat unsafe, or very unsafe?

SW#13: Well, I might, I might say reasonably. I might, yes, I might take a chance. I might take a chance. Because I said, . . . I believe in God, that He'll take care of me. Not to run all around—in emergencies. You wouldn't run out there any old, any night . . . But like in emergencies, you have to do things sometimes—you just have to do it. And that's what you'd call reasonable. I would say reasonably I would feel safe. I just feel like nothing's going to happen to me, because it's—I'm doing it for some good.

While the problem of the rarity of the behavior in question has been mentioned before (see, for example, Garofalo 1979), the difficulty we encountered in getting respondents to answer the question has not been reported. It is likely that embedding a structured response question in an otherwise largely unstructured interview guide contributed to the problem. However, the responses suggest that there is more to the problem than that. In fact, this is such an alien activity for most of the respondents that it is a wonder and probably a tribute to fairly aggressive probing that more women did not refuse to answer at all. In any event, the "fear" reported is all extremely hypothetical.

Most respondents were also asked the item found by Ferraro and LaGrange (1987) to be the most commonly used measure of fear of crime: "Is there any area right around here—that is, within a mile—where you would be afraid to walk alone at night?" Over 90 percent (93.5 percent) of the respondents claimed there was such an area.

We were concerned that this item would strike respondents as a repetition of the NCS item (which always came first). That did not happen. Perhaps because the NCS item drew the fire of so many of those who never go out at night, this item was simply answered by nearly all respondents. Further, their answers suggest that they heard a different question, and the inter-item correlation between the NCS item and this one (.32) suggests that while there is some overlap, they do not measure exactly the same thing.

In response to the question, many women immediately said, "Yes, there is such an area," and then described a place by Newark's main train station, or by the train tracks, or where drugs are sold, or some similar specific location.

> *SW#8:* I can't think of the name of that street . . . The street looks good and all, but they, it's just the boys on the corner with the dope and all. . . .

> *GW#14:* Yeah, that's Livingston Street. I wouldn't walk that corner block. I wouldn't walk it alone never.

Many of the areas had a "no-one-would-go-there" quality and as such represent even more unlikely behavior than does the NCS item.

The point is that both these items and related measures rely on the researcher providing the framework for understanding the role of fear of crime in respondents' lives. That framework does a poor job of reflecting fear as it is actually experienced by these women. Left to their own devices, respondents sketch a somewhat different picture of fear.

It became apparent over the course of the study that the impact of crime on the lives of these women is not incident-specific. Crime and fear of it are more a subcontext of their lives. Asking respondents to tell us about the incident in the past six months in which they were most afraid yielded answers like the following:

> *SW#18:* I don't know of any special incidents, you know. I think it's just general, not anything special. Just have crime on my mind . . . out there at night. But I don't know of anything special. . . . I don't do much walking around. But do I feel afraid then? I think it's always some, I don't say fear, but you [have to be] cautious. That's not fear, I guess, to be cautious. . . daytime I'm not as afraid but not 100 percent [safe], you still [feel] a little fear there, you say "let's try to be careful."

> *SW#4:* I tell you the truth, I think of crime everyday, mostly. At home—because I leave my little foyer light on, even today, to go out. When I unlock my door to go in and I can't see around, before I lock my door I usually just put the latch on the screen door and I look around in the house. If I see somebody had been there, then I would run out.

> *I:* Is this every time you go in the house?

> *R:* Oh, I look every time I go in the house.

Improving Our Measures of Fear

It is clear from all that has gone before that fear of crime as it is experienced in the lives of this group of women does not lend itself well to measurement by either the NCS item or items of this type. The experience described by these women is not incident-specific. It is largely unemotional. Actual fear is likely to be experienced only if the restrictions and precautions the women accept fail for some reason. The reality of fear of crime is diffuse, hard to recognize and articulate, and has become under most circumstances an accepted fact of life. Basically, fear of crime limits or constrains activities, requires vigilance that is nearly second-nature under some circumstances, and, above all, it has been normalized.

It is not possible in a single chapter to do more than sketch ways to improve measuring fear of crime. Stanko (1987) and others (for example, Gibbs and Hanrahan 1990; and Wilson 1989) suggest taking a broader, contextual approach to fear of crime. We need to measure not what people fear when they are alone on the streets at night, but the type of accommodation to crime or negotiation with safety that never being out alone at night entails. Safety or safekeeping, not fear of crime, seems the more useful concept.

Gibbs has proposed a transactional approach to measuring safety. He suggests adapting a model proposed by Lazarus (1975) to measure need for safety and the extent to which the environment can meet that need. His proposal is outlined elsewhere (see, for example, Gibbs and Hanrahan 1990). Taking a demand-supply approach to safety would measure safety relative to other concerns; this would help determine the magnitude of the problem. This type of measurement would also provide program-relevant information about the source and shape of the problem—is it due to relatively high need or to relatively low environmental supply?

Implications

Leaving for the moment the measurement issues raised by the fear described by the women in this study, what are the implications of this fear? We have seen, repeatedly, that one characteristic of fear of crime is its impact on daily life in the form of restrictions and avoidance behavior. Most of the women are not actively suffering in the sense of living with gnawing fear, but most have changed routines and activities in order to insure that their level of fear stays manageable.

Clearly it is too high a price to pay for feeling safe when women forgo simple pastimes like going to visit at church in the evening or going to play bingo once a week because they fear being mugged on the street. The cost is more striking when we consider that most of the respondents have accepted the cost.

We should not be willing to accept too much and to understand too much about the tradeoffs these elderly women make in order to survive with a measure of peace of mind. It is tempting to see the elderly as "other"—survivors of earlier and different generations. The truth is, of course, that these women are no different from the rest of us—older perhaps, but not different. And they have responded to fear of crime by sharply curtailing activities and the scope of their lives.

Beyond letting us glimpse our own futures, the women in this study also provide a look at the past. They have lived through interesting times. They remembered, among other events, world wars, share-cropping in the south, raising children during the depression, taking part in civil rights bus boycotts, the riots in Newark. They remembered other things as well—things less spectacular except in the cumulative impact of their absence.

The women remember when Newark was a nice city. They remember a time when Springfield Avenue, the site of some of Newark's most extensive riot damage and still quite uninviting, was a wonderful place to shop. They remember a time when people could take their children to a park in the evening, when a woman could visit a friend and walk home alone after dark, when friends routinely shopped downtown, or even when homeowners could leave their doors and windows not just unlocked but open to the summer breeze. The women in the study remember these times. They are gone for the rest of us and we stand to lose more unless we find a way to deal with fear of crime.

We asked the women if they had any suggestions for reducing fear for themselves or others like them. As is often the case (see, for example, Eagleton Institute of Politics 1988), the respondents had few suggestions. Some even recommended avoidance behavior:

> *IR#10:* Walk in groups. . . . and don't go where you're not supposed to go. And don't go out at night unless you have to.

The most usual responses were to look for increased police protection—more police, or a return to foot patrol, for example. Many feel that the police should be more responsive. One particularly disgruntled respondent reported:

> *SW#1:* The police—you call them, they don't come. They don't try to help you. They have meetings and stuff here [speakers at the senior center] about the police and all that stuff, but I sit and listen at them and that's all. . . . they talk about the crime

and what they'll do and what they won't do. And what they say they gonna do, they don't do it, the police don't.

I: What are some of the things that they don't do?

SW#1: Like I said, Sunday morning. I told you I called them. They was parked cross my driveway and the [tenant] couldn't get her car out my driveway. I called them eight o'clock in the morning, and they ain't showed up yet.

That respondents do not know what to do to increase feelings of safety, and that many do not seem to consider that something should be done, illustrates the need for new thinking about interventions. Perhaps, as suggested earlier, studying the problem using a technique that explicitly recognizes tradeoffs in needs and resources will be illuminating.

We need also to be realistic about what role the criminal justice system can play in fear-reducing strategies. Much of what ails the neighborhoods in Newark and impinges on the lives of the women living in them requires resources and commitments that exceed those given to criminal justice agencies. The criminal justice system is obligated to attempt to respond to fear of crime, but we will need a community-wide base of commitment to respond adequately.

REFERENCES

Baumer, T. L., "Testing a General Model of Fear of Crime: Data from a National Sample," *Journal of Research in Crime and Delinquency*, 22 (1985), 239–255.

Baumer, T. L., "Research on Fear of Crime in the United States," *Victimology*, 3, no. 3–4 (1978), 254–264.

DeVault, M. L., "Talking and Listening from a Woman's Standpoint: Feminist Strategies for Interviewing and Analysis," *Social Problems*, 37 (1990), 96–116.

Eagleton Institute of Politics, Center for Public Interest Polling, Rutgers University, *A Survey of New Jersey's Senior Citizens: Crime Safety, Housing and Transportation*. Trenton, N.J.: New Jersey Department of Community Affairs, Division on Aging, 1988.

Ferraro, K. F., and R. LaGrange, "The Measurement of Fear of Crime," *Sociological Inquiry*, 57, no. 1 (1987), 70–101.

Garofalo, J., "Victimization and the Fear of Crime," *Journal of Research in Crime and Delinquency*, 16, no. 1 (1979), 80–97.

Garofalo, J., and J. Laub, "The Fear of Crime: Broadening Our Perspective," *Victimology*, 3 (1978), 242–253.

Gibbs, J. J., and K. J. Hanrahan, "Is Fear of Crime a Meaningful Measure?" Paper presented at the American Society of Criminology, Baltimore, Md.: November 1990.

Gibbs, J. J., E. Coyle, and K. J. Hanrahan, "Fear of Crime: A Concept in Need of Clarification." Paper presented at the annual meeting of the American Society of Criminology, Montreal, November 1987.

Gordon, M. T., and S. Riger, *The Female Fear*. New York: Free Press, 1989.

Greenberg, S. W., "Why People Take Precautions against Crime: A Review of the Literature on Individual and Collective Responses to Crime." In N. D. Weinstein (ed.), *Taking Care: Understanding and Encouraging Self-Protective Behavior*, 1987, pp. 231–253.

Harris, Louis, and Associates, *The Myth and Reality of Aging in America*. Washington, D.C.: National Council on the Aging, 1975.

Harris, Louis, and Associates, *Aging in the Eighties: America in Transition*. Washington, D.C.: National Council on the Aging, 1981.

Lazarus, R. S., "The Self-Regulation of Emotion," In L. Levi (ed.), *Emotions: Their Parameters and Measurement*. New York: Raven Press, 1975, pp. 47–67.

Lewis, D. A., and G. Salem, *Fear of Crime: Incivility and the Production of a Social Problem*. New Brunswick, N.J.: Transaction Books, 1986.

Skogan, W. G., "The Impact of Victimization on Fear," *Crime and Delinquency*, 33 (1987), 135–154.

Skogan, W., and M. Maxfield, *Coping with Crime: Individual and Neighborhood Reactions*. Beverly Hills, Calif.: Sage Publications, 1981.

Stanko, E. A., "Fear of Crime and Concepts of Personal Safety." Paper presented to the British Criminology Conference, July 1987.

Stein, S., M. Linn, and E. Slater, "Future Concerns and Recent Life Events of Elderly Community Residents," *Journal of the American Geriatrics Society*, 32, no. 6 (1984), 431–434.

Taylor, R. B., and M. Hale, "Testing Alternative Models of Fear of Crime," *Journal of Criminal Law and Criminology*, 77 (1986), 151–189.

Warr, M., "Fear of Victimization: Why are Women and the Elderly More Afraid?" *Social Science Quarterly*, 65 (1984), 681–702.

Williams, F. P., and R. L. Akers, "Fear of Crime: A Comparison of Measurement Approaches." Paper presented at the Academy of Criminal Justice Sciences, St. Louis, Mo., March 1987.

Wilson, N. K., "Violence, Fear and Gender: Some Phenomenological Considerations." Paper presented at the annual meeting of the Western Society of Criminology, February 1989.

Yin, P., "Fear of Crime among the Elderly: Some Issues and Suggestions." *Social Problems*, 27, no. 4 (1980), 492–504.

Yin, P., "Fear of Crime As a Problem for the Elderly." *Social Problems*, 30, no. 2 (1982), 240–245.

DISCUSSION QUESTIONS
SECTION 7: WOMEN: VICTIMS OF VIOLENCE

1. What is it about the feminist movement that has spurred a growth in rape-counseling centers? What progress has been made by the legal system in its handling of rape cases?

2. What is it about the crime of rape that has made it such a taboo subject? Is rape a crime of sex or of power? Explain what Justice Matthew Hale meant when he stated that rape "... is an accusation easily to be made and hard to be proved, and harder to be defended by the accused though never so innocent." Does this hold true today?

3. What are the arguments for and against mandatory-arrest policies for cases involving domestic violence? Do mandatory-arrest policies affect all social classes equally? In instances of domestic violence, what should the police do? Which police tactics appear to be ineffective? Which police tactics work? Are there instances when the police should look the other way? Are there instances when the police should always make an arrest? Specifically, how should abusive husbands be treated? What alternatives to the jailing of offenders exist? What factors enter into determining reasonable police responses to cases involving domestic disputes? If you were chief of police, what policy would you have patrol officers follow?

4. What is the battering cycle? Why do you think the battering of women by men is such a common occurrence? By applying your knowledge of the battering cycle, why do so many women who are physically assaulted by their husbands or boyfriends stay with them? Where can a battered woman seek help? What are her alternatives?

5. What does knowledge of the origins of the laws of rape tell us of the social status of women in society? What are the major sources of statistics on rape and sexual violence? Which method of data collection is best? What are the relative advantages and disadvantages of each method of data collection? How accurate do official statistics appear to be concerning the actual incidence of sexual violence? How have rape laws been modified over the years? How has the possibility of contracting AIDS influenced legislation concerning rape and the victims of rape?

6. What is meant when it is said that the facts of a court case are socially constructed? How does the social construction of events in court impact women who have been raped or abused? In what ways do some defense attorneys compromise the rights of the defendant in

exchange for their own participation and status in the legal system? Generally, how are women who are victims of domestic violence treated by the courts?

7. Generally, what problems do women accused of killing men who have assaulted them face in the courts?

Section 8

The Family

The family has traditionally been idealized as the bedrock of society. The home is most often depicted as a place that nurtures, fosters, encourages, teaches, and reinforces "good" behavior. Home is the seat of personal success and accomplishment. Home is where children grow to become responsible and caring adults. Well, sometimes.

Jill Rosenbaum, in this concluding chapter, points out that the home is also a breeding ground for juvenile delinquency. Criminals are not born, they are made. And, apparently, the home environment is just as central to the production of deviancy as it is for the fostering of conformity.

The importance of family in the causation of delinquency has been well documented since the Gluecks' initial work over fifty years ago. Although their work has received much criticism, especially with respect to the methodology they utilized, it sets forth a series of variables that have been examined by numerous scholars. The myriad of studies since the Gluecks which have included various family variables have consistently shown a relationship between delinquency and dysfunctional families.

While the degree of its importance does vary, the family is an integral part of the major theoretical framework which we employ to understand delinquency. This is especially true of the social control and social learning theories.

We know that a relationship does exist between various family variables and delinquency. It is important to remember that most of the research that has been done has only studied men. Of the other research that exists on the topic, a significant amount of it focuses on the differential impact these family variables have on the behavior of men and women. Very little has centered on the female delinquent per se.

This section allows us to take a closer look at what happens to girls who, when young, lived in homes with an abundance of family problems. Furthermore, it permits us to examine how our cultural values, with regard to the family, have influenced the way in which the criminal justice system treats youth from dysfunctional homes. In looking (over time) at the impact of both the family and the system's response, we may be able to learn from past mistakes and make recommendations for future treatment of delinquent girls.

23

The Female Delinquent: Another Look at the Role of the Family

Jill L. Rosenbaum

This chapter examines the family backgrounds of a group of women who, as adolescents in the early 1960s, were committed to the California Youth Authority predominantly for status offenses. As adults, however, these women were involved in numerous serious offenses. Paricular attention is paid to various measures of family dysfunction, including family violence, parent-child conflict, family size, structure, and stability. Little variation existed with respect to the various measures examined; all of the women came from dysfunctional homes. The Youth Authority's handling of these young women is also explored within the context of the cultural attitudes which existed at the time.

In the early 1960s, a group of delinquent girls participated in an experimental California Youth Authority program. As an alternative to institutionalization, this program sought to return these delinquents to their families, where it was hoped that appropriate adjustment to society's expectations would occur. But their families may have been the cause rather than the solution to their problems. Thus, despite all good intentions, most of these delinquent girls later became serious adult offenders. This chapter focuses on the role of the family in the causation of both the juvenile-delinquent behavior and the adult criminality of this population of girls.

Partial support for this research came from a CSU Summer Stipend. My thanks to Allan Axelrad and Leila Zenderland for comments on an earlier draft of this chapter.

During the 1950s and into the 1960s, the American family was placed on a pedestal and unrealistically idealized. At a time when adjustment and conformity were key words in the culture's vocabulary, sociologists believed that the family's most important function was the socialization of children. The prevailing assumption was that such socialization would produce positive results and society would be the beneficiary. From this uncritical perspective, the family should prevent delinquency; it would never be the cause.

Since this time, however, various aspects of family life and relationships have been viewed by criminologists as the source of delinquency, including parental absence, family size, birth order, and quality of parent-child interaction. The first indication of a problem came from Glueck and Glueck (1950), who found that paternal discipline, maternal supervision, affection of both parents, and family cohesiveness were the most important family correlates of delinquency.

While there are numerous criticisms of their research, the Gluecks established the importance of the effect of family process variables (supervision, attachment, and discipline) on delinquent behavior. Recent research has indicated that there is a good deal of support for the Gluecks' findings. Laub and Sampson's (1988) research found in their reanalysis of the Gluecks' data that "family process variables are directly related to serious delinquency in the predicted theoretical direction." Loeber and Southamer-Loeber's (1986) meta-analysis established further that the most powerful predictors of delinquent behavior are those aspects of family functioning involving direct parent-child contacts.

The Gluecks (1968) studied a matched sample of 500 delinquent and 500 nondelinquent boys from the Boston area. The boys were matched on age, race, ethnicity, intelligence, and neighborhood. These boys were followed up to age thirty-one. The follow-up data indicated that the delinquent group tended to marry at earlier ages, have more illegitimate children, and have lower marital satisfaction. As adults, they seemed to be following the same patterns of home life that they had experienced as youth.

Aside from the Gluecks' early longitudinal research, three other longitudinal studies examined the influence of the family on adult criminality. McCord, McCord, and Zola (1969) found in their follow-up study of boys who had participated in the Cambridge-Somerville delinquency prevention project that the home atmosphere of the youth played a major role in their delinquency. Boys from quarrelsome homes, those who received lax discipline or erratic punitive discipline, and those who suffered from parental absence, cruelty, or neglect were more likely to be delinquent. However, the mother appeared to have the greatest effect in the production of a delinquent child. Maternal passivity, cruelty, absence, and neglect all were highly related to their child's commission of crimes at an early age, the commission of a wide variety of crimes, and the persistence of criminality into adulthood. They argued that the Cambridge-Somerville project "failed primarily because it did not affect the basic psychological and familial causes of crime" (McCord, McCord, and Zola 1969, p. xii). In her later follow-up, Joan McCord (1979) demonstrated the impact on adult criminality of these childhood family dimensions.

Robins (1966) also found family variables to be an important factor in later adult behavior in her follow-up of youth referred to a child-guidance clinic between 1922 and 1932. Her study further indicated that ". . . girls' outcome appears to be somewhat more dependent on problem behavior in the parent than does boys' " (Robins 1966, p. 165). Robins's research further indicated that there are some factors in the family operating that enable delinquency to be passed from one generation to the next.

A great deal of attention has been paid to the absence of at least one parent. Nye (1958) attempted to understand the causal impact of the broken home. He classified broken and unbroken homes in terms of the happiness of the parents and children. From his analysis, Nye argued that the degree of happiness in the home was more important than the presence of both parents. However, Nye (1958) notes that a broken home may, in fact, add strains that can further promote delinquency. At best, however, there is a weak association between broken homes and delinquent behavior (for example, Gove and Crutchfield 1982; Rosen and Neilson 1982; and Wilkinson 1974). More recently Rosen (1985) suggested, "Although it may be possible to dismiss the broken home as the single major factor in delinquency causation, it still may be significant when combined with other factors."

Some have argued that large families are conducive to delinquent behavior (Nye 1958; Rosen 1985; and Fischer 1984). The Gluecks found large families to be related to delinquency, but also that there is a strong relationship between large families and disorderly homes. The higher rate of delinquent behavior in large families may result from parents having less time and energy per child and thus less attachment to their children than parents with fewer children (Hirschi 1983).

Research consistently has shown that those youth whose bond to their parents is weak are more likely to be delinquent. According to Hirschi (1969), youth who are more attached to their parents have greater direct and indirect controls placed on their behavior. The parental attachment factor explains delinquency better than any other factor (Nye 1958; Gold 1963; Hindelang 1973; Gove and Crutchfield 1982; and Rosenbaum 1987).

Morris (1964) and Gold (1970) have suggested that female delinquency is more likely than male delinquency to reflect problems at home. Therefore, it may be that women who end up in state facilities tend to come from the most troubled families. Indeed, it may be that their homes are more troubled than those of their male counterparts.

In contrast to previous research that has dealt mostly with male delinquents, the study discussed in this chapter examines the impact of the family on a group of delinquent females. Utilizing case files beginning with first arrest and concluding with discharge from the California Youth Authority, delinquent women and potential dysfunction in their families were explored. In doing so, such variables as family size and structure, family criminality, mental-health and alcohol problems, family conflict, and family violence were examined.

Data and Methods

The Sample

In 1980, records were requested on 240 women who had been committed to the California Youth Authority (CYA), the state agency for juvenile offenders. All of these girls had, as juveniles, taken part in a CYA experimental program in the early 1960s, the Community Treatment Project (CTP). This program began in 1961 as a combined experimental and demonstration project to assess the effect of keeping delinquent youth in the community under intensive supervision (Lerman 1975). One of the assumptions behind this program was that troubled youth should remain in the community in order to cope better with both family tensions and community pressures. It was believed that these youth would confront problems and work toward solutions more effectively within the community than within the confines of an institution (Adams and Grant 1961). All of the individuals taking part in this program spent at least thirty days in a state facility, but most spent the majority of their CYA commitment in the community.

The records requested included adult arrest records and CYA files of all women committed to the CYA from San Francisco and the Sacramento Valley areas during the early 1960s. Records were returned from California Identification and Investigation (C.I.&I.) on 159 of these women. In total, 59 of the 240 cases were unavailable because the juvenile records had been purged, and 22 others could not be located. Comparisons of the missing cases with those available indicated minor differences. The only variable showing a significant difference was race (fewer minority women had their records purged). Although we assumed that those with purged records had fewer arrests than those for whom we had complete records, a five-year follow-up by the CYA indicated that most of the purged group had at least one postrelease arrest.

The ethnic makeup of the final sample of 159 was 51 percent white, 30 percent black, 9 percent Latino, and the remaining 10 percent were Asian or Native American. Two-thirds of the girls had been committed to the Youth Authority only for status offenses, mostly for running away.

Method

All C.I.&I. arrest data were coded by two independent coders who were in agreement 92 percent of the time. Upon completion, three independent coders reviewed the Youth Authority records that included home-investigation reports, information gathered at intake reception centers, parole reports, and discharge summaries. The reports consisted of all of the written comments of those individuals who worked with the CYA wards during their commitment to the Youth Authority. These individuals included parole agents, social workers, teachers, and CYA chaplains. From these reports, family background data were coded. The interrater reliability was 88 percent.

In coding arrests, arrest incidents were used rather than charges. Only the most serious charge at each incident was coded regardless of whether the charges were altered at a later date or whether the women were actually convicted of another offense. Thus the data may underestimate the number of criminal acts committed by these women. Blumstein and Cohen (1979) have argued that because of plea bargaining and other reasons for altering or dismissing charges, initial arrest charges probably are better indicators of actual behavior than convictions.

Findings

Preliminary analysis of the adult arrest records indicated that all but 6 of the 159 (96 percent) were arrested as adults. Most of the women (70 percent) had at least four arrests after their release from the CYA, and nearly all (82 percent) had been convicted of at least one moderately serious crime (not included were lesser offenses such as prostitution, possession of any drug, and theft of less than $100; Warren and Rosenbaum 1986). Although women are considered to be less threatening to society than men, only a small percentage of all arrests were the "stereotypic" female crimes of prostitution and drug offenses (Rosenbaum 1988).

Originally we had hypothesized that those with less serious records would have come from the most functional families. However, all of the girls came from extremely troubled homes. Thus, there was very little variation within the numerous family structure and family problem variables included in these data.

It became clear, in fact, that we have no cause to be surprised that these women became serious offenders. Indeed, it would have been surprising had they not. As indicated by the results to be presented, these women came from families where conformity to societal expectations was the exception rather than the rule.

Family Structure

Although there is little consensus on this issue, recent research by Van Voorhis and others (1988) indicates that a relationship between status offenses and broken homes and status offenses and single-parent families does exist. Consistent with these data, very few of these girls came from intact families (7 percent). At the time of their commitment to the CYA, 25 percent were living in two-adult homes; however, some of these were foster homes, while others were the homes of relatives. For example, one girl was living with her grandparents, who were both eighty-one years old. Still others were living with their mother and one of a number of stepfathers or boyfriends. Ten percent of the girls had been deserted by both parents. The remainder of the sample were living in single-parent homes.

By the time these girls were sixteen, their mothers had been married an average of four times. One mother had married three times in the previous seven years. Another had been married five times since the birth of her daughter (four divorces and one death), and was planning to marry for a sixth time. Still another woman had married a number of times with some of the marriages overlapping. This woman was married to a man in northern California, but thought she still might be married to a previous husband who was currently living in Mexico. He had left for Mexico and never returned; the woman thought that this was because he already was married when they had married.

Family Size

Family size has been cited as a factor in delinquency causation (Hirschi 1969). In this study, three girls were only children, while another six had one sibling. The average, however, was 4.3 children per family. Not surprisingly, given the number of multiple marriages, children in a "family" often were fathered by a variety of men. For example, one girl had four siblings, each fathered by a different man. Another ward's mother had nine children with all but two fathered by different men. Still another was one of eight children by at least three different fathers, with the mother unsure who fathered the ward and her younger sister. Yet for this group of girls, the actual size of the family appears to be less important than the way it functioned.

Family Criminality

A minority (24 percent) of the girls came from families where no other criminality was present. Thus, 76 percent of the wards had at least one other family member with a criminal record. Often several family members had records. Similar numbers of the known birth fathers and mothers had served time in state prison (30 percent and 32 percent, respectively). Case files frequently indicated that the girls' brothers and/or sisters were in placement at a Youth Authority facility, while others were in jail or prison.

Parental criminal activity ranged from fairly minor offenses to serious violent crimes. Of the mothers, 51 percent had felony arrest records. Many were for such offenses as narcotics violations and welfare-related offenses. The fathers tended to have difficulty with alcohol, which often led to assaults and other criminal behavior. One father had an arrest record that included sodomy, assault, burglaries, and forgeries. The day after he was released from San Quentin, he was arrested for another burglary and forgery. One of the other wards was not on speaking terms with anyone in her family, except a brother who was serving time in San Quentin.

Family Violence

Farber and Kinast (1984, p. 298) found in their study of runaways that "an astounding amount of violence was directed toward youth who ran away." Although much of the information on the violence in these families was not included in the case files, it is evident that violence was present in many of these homes. Records failed to mention spousal violence unless specific charges were filed. However, a number of the known fathers had spent time in jail for "fighting with wife." One father had been committed to DeWitt State Hospital following a fight with his wife over the presence of the wife's boyfriend. Another beat the mother of one ward numerous times because she had listed her husband as the girl's father even though she knew another man had sired the child. One particular file notes that "the girl had strong memories of watching or hearing her mother being choked by the father and also of being locked in the closet for long periods of time." Still another indicated that the father of a ward had died from stab wounds inflicted by the mother. Although this woman was charged with murder, she was never convicted and continued to have custody of the children.

In total, 37 percent of the mothers had been charged with child abuse and/or neglect. One mother whose new boyfriend did not like children packed their belongings and locked them out of the house. Another left four children between the ages of six and fifteen alone without money for a month while she went to Hawaii to "rejuvenate herself." Some mothers had numerous abuse and/or neglect charges filed during the first six months of the girl's life. One woman was arrested when her daughter was two weeks old for child neglect; and, according to the social worker, "by the time the girl was sent to the CYA, her mother had the longest record of abuse and neglect charges one could imagine." In yet another family, "the ward's parents never cared for the children and were continuously sentenced to the county jail. After the parents' third arrest, the four children were placed in the home of their grandmother, who herself had served time in jail in the past for neglecting her children."

Family Conflict

At least a weak relationship between family conflict and delinquent behavior has been found in a number of studies (see McCord and McCord 1959; Gove and Crutchfield 1982; Canter 1982; and Cernkovich and Giordano 1987). In the two-parent families examined in this study, a great deal of conflict was present. Of these parents, 71 percent fought regularly about the children. Since there were often his, hers, and theirs present, the sources of conflict tended to result from one set of children having a bad influence on the others, the type of punishment invoked, or one particular child receiving too much attention. Conflict in the home was not limited to the children, for conflict over the use of alcohol was present in 81 percent of the homes. Case files indicate that 34 percent of the fathers were known alcoholics, as were 31 percent of the mothers. Furthermore, many of the parents had histories of mental illness. In total, 29 percent of the fathers and 27 percent of the mothers had been diagnosed as neurotic or psychotic. A caseworker described one of these families in the following way: "The father appears to be an ineffectual, highly neurotic person who is maintaining a very sick relationship with an alcoholic woman." The case files indicate that this case was not atypical.

   A poor relationship between parent and child is highly influential in the child's subsequent delinquency (see Patterson 1982; Hirschi 1969; Nye 1958; Gove and Crutchfield 1982; Rosenbaum 1987; and Van Voorhis and others 1988). Not only did these girls probably suffer from their parents' broken marriages and multiple relationships, alcoholism, and mental illness, but they typically lacked the nurturing youth require. Many of the girls received very little positive feedback from parents in the home. From the perspective of the parole officers, 53 percent of the fathers who were in the home rejected their daughters, as did 47 percent of the mothers. Rejection came in many forms. One father was so angry that his child was a girl that he made her dress in boy's clothing and cut her hair extremely short. Another father wanted nothing to do with his daughter until she conformed to his rules; he requested that she be "locked in a room until she conformed to his rules or until she was twenty-one—whichever comes first." One ward said of her parents: "My mother is cruel and has never shown any love for me and my father has always been ashamed of me." That these girls chose to run away from such homes is not surprising.

Research on parental supervision and delinquency has indicated that a relationship between the two exists (Nye 1958; Hirschi 1969; Hindelang 1973; Bahr 1979; and Wells and Rankin 1988). Of the 159 homes studied, consistent supervision of the youth was present in a minority of the homes (22 percent). The mothers appeared to be not only neglectful, but 96 percent were described as passive and 67 percent as irresponsible. One typical mother was described as "an hysterical and frantic women whose supervision and discipline fluctuate from lax to severe."

Generational Cycles

The mothers of the CYA wards tended to marry young, with 44 percent having had the ward by the time she was eighteen, although only 32 percent of the girls were oldest children. The mothers' psychological and financial resources were obviously limited and the added burden of children appeared to increase the strain.

These daughters tended to follow in their mothers' footsteps and begin bearing children at an early age. By the time they were discharged from the Youth Authority, over half (56 percent) of the wards had children. Some had more than one. One girl had two children before the age of sixteen and a third while committed to the CYA. Parents often encouraged this behavior. One mother explained to her daughter's parole officer that she was happy to hear that her fifteen-year-old daughter was pregnant because "that is what women are supposed to do." Another ward wanted to place her as yet unborn child up for adoption, but her parents refused to grant permission.

The men in the wards' lives bore a striking resemblance to the men chosen by their mothers. Many were significantly older than the girls and had criminal records. One sixteen-year-old girl had married her thirty-four-year-old pimp, who had a number of arrests and convictions for drug offenses. Another sixteen-year-old's boyfriend was twenty-two, twice married, with seven children, two by the wives and five by five separate girlfriends. This man also had a record for stabbing his mother and beating one wife. Still others were residing with men who were physically abusive toward both them and their children.

The wards' mothers did not have the supports or resources needed to cope with their environments. They often were socially isolated and distrusted those attempting to help. They tended to believe that welfare workers tried to take away their funds, and social workers tried to take away their children. These attitudes and fears began long before the wards were born. The mothers of the CTP girls did not know how to be mothers, for they were often children themselves when their children were born, and lacked the emotional resources to instill a sense of trust and security necessary for self-esteem and growth. Over time, just trying to survive depleted whatever emotional resources they might once have had.

The mothers were passive by nature and, because their lives consisted of a series of crises, they were inconsistent authority figures. Rules were made one day and forgotten the next because of financial difficulties, conflicts with the men in their life, and problems with other children.

Discussion

The preceding analysis indicated that there was virtually no variability among the various measures of family dysfunction. Although some variation existed with respect to the number of actual arrests, more than 90 percent of the women had arrests after their release from the CYA. Statistical analysis of the various family dysfunction measures and arrest data was relatively useless because of the overwhelming concordance of the dysfunctions and subsequent delinquent behavior.

Homer (1973) categorizes runaways into two types, youth who are "running from" and those that are "running to." The CTP girls who ran generally fit the "running from" category. Individuals who fall into this category are generally weak, not trusting of others, and lack warmth and nurturing during childhood. It is possible that running away and the subsequent delinquent behavior may have been a plea for the love they lacked. Since the records indicate that these girls often returned home on their own accord, it may be that they were hoping that, upon their return, they would find the mothering and protection they so desperately sought. Unfortunately, their mothers were unable to give these girls the nurturing they desired, for they had not been adequately nurtured themselves. Instead these mothers often turned to their daughters for nurturing, thus reversing roles and having the daughter mother her own mother.

As late as the 1960s, there was little scholarly literature on female offenders. However, the literature that did exist focused on the appearance of the girl (Cowie, Cowie, and Slater 1968; and Morris 1964) and its relationshp to lack of love and nurturing. Konopka (1966) argued that the delinquency of girls was rooted in the family and their desparate need for love. Morris (1964) went one step further and argued that delinquents tended to be less attractive and, as a result, received less love.

After close examination of the files, it appears that not only were these women victims, they were double victims: victims of their families and victims of the criminal justice system as well. Most of these girls were sentenced to the CYA for status offenses (mainly running away). That they chose to run away from home is not surprising given the data on their home life. The numerous attempts to run away also may have been futile efforts to break the generational cycle of despair. In this respect it is important to remember that prior to 1978, girls who ran away from home received severe court sanctions. They were more likely to be held in detention than were female delinquents and male runaways (Mann 1979).

It is important to remember that these were the days when "Ozzie and Harriet," "The Cleavers," and "Fathers Knows Best" provided images by which families were judged. Such images were venerated as American icons. Not only did society believe strongly in the family unit, it did so uncritically. This widespread belief may, at least in part, have been responsible for the long-term prognosis of these girls. The notion that teenage girls need their mothers may have been the major contributing forces behind their later, more serious criminal behavior. Not only did the criminal justice system continue to return these girls to their mothers after they ran away, but even after they had been made wards of the court, they were returned home once again. These were often homes like one described by a social worker as "an animal-like environment." One girl was returned to her family, even though they sometimes lived in an abandoned car. Still another was returned home, although her parole officer stated, "both her parents seem to be ineffectual, highly disturbed people, who have as a result damaged all their children."

Despite such instances (which were typical), the CTP believed that youth were better off in their homes and tried to return as many as possible. This was such a high priority that one ward was returned to her home upon the mother's release from prison for throwing lye in her lover's face, because her parole officer believed "the girl had not been too damaged." No doubt, these adolescent girls' attitudes and ideas about the world were largely shaped by their mothers, who averaged four marriages, who were often alcoholic or diagnosed as psychotic/neurotic, and who frequently provided role models for criminal careers. In light of these findings, it is not surprising that these young runaways became serious adult offenders.

The early CYA records indicate that when there was no home to return to, many of these runaways were sent to the Youth Authority for lack of any alternative placements. With fathers whose whereabouts were unknown and mothers who were often in jail, prison, or mental-health facilities, the Youth Authority may have been the only available option. Many of the girls lacked supervision from an early age. When they ran away or were removed from the home due to child abuse or neglect or other charges, the youth often were placed in foster homes. In fact, at one time or another during their CYA commitment, 67 percent were removed from the home and placed in group and foster homes (Turner 1969). In these homes the girls experienced sharp changes, particularly in rules and discipline, for which they were ill-prepared. As a result, there were numerous complaints to officials and/or runaways in the first few months of foster care. This is not surprising since, according to Russell (1981, p. 65), "Family disruptions which necessitate the placing of children away from the home produce many disorganizing emotional conflicts which can render their adjustment in any new living situation problematical and can predispose them to running away." However, many of these adolescents were deemed foster-home failures and thus were sent to the CYA.

It is important that we remember what is missing from the early CYA files. For instance, we know of family violence only when official action was taken. Yet it is evident, if we look closely, that in a number of families there was significant violence and some instances of incest. But in the early 1960s, criminal justice agencies and the community were not as aware of the extent and nature of family violence and child sexual abuse. Thus, while we know that these families were dysfunctional, the full extent of the difficulties faced cannot be known. It may be that the case files only disclose the "tip of the iceberg."

The rationale for the CTP program was to keep many of these girls in the community in order to "work out" difficulties in their homes and the community in the hope that this would further reduce their criminality. The program did not succeed in keeping these women from further involvement in the criminal justice system, as originally hoped (Palmer 1974; Lerman 1975; and Warren and Rosenbaum 1986). The failure of CTP may be due to the fact that the deep-seated nature and long-term implications of their family problems were not understood. This may have been the result of both the cultural attitudes at the time and the fact that the wide array of family therapy available today was not available to the CTP practitioners during the 1960s.

Labeling theorists could easily look only at the arrest data and claim that the system was at fault, that left alone these girls would have matured, and that their criminality was simply childhood excitement. However, when one delves into the backgrounds of these offenders, the picture becomes clouded. While some of these girls may have fared much better had they not become involved with the system, many would have had ongoing difficulties with the criminal justice system if only because of their family socialization; some, perhaps, may have had even more serious records. To argue that the system was at fault would appear to be untenable. It is impossible to disentangle the system effects and the family effects on the adult criminal behavior of these girls. Finally, it is clear that the options available for dealing with runaways were severely limited.

In retrospect, the initial findings of persistence in offending and increased severity no longer appear surprising. Furthermore, family structure, family instability, and family mental health do not explain the difference in the severity of the adult criminal records, in that all of the women came from very dysfunctional homes. Although we were unable to predict types of later criminality as was done in a follow-up of males (McCord 1979), this analysis does give some insight into the families in which these girls were raised and how the CYA commitments came about. As Robins (1966) suggested earlier, it may be that women have more difficulty than men in handling the stress of dysfunctional homes. This may account for their higher runaway rate. It is also possible that young women are more likely to become double victims than young men. The high rate of return to dysfunctional homes reflects society's, and thus the CTP's, belief in the family and that girls are more in need of their mothers than boys, regardless of the mother's stability.

Given our more realistic appraisal of family viability today, perhaps the current counterparts will stand a better chance. Today we still make numerous attempts to work out problems in the families of delinquent youth so that families can be reunited. However, we no longer do so at the youth's expense. We have learned that, perhaps with respect to minor offending, the least intervention is the best. Facilities for youth who are having problems at home are becoming available. These transitional shelters give the youth breathing space. Furthermore, there are now programs that enable the emancipation of youth. These programs enable underage youth to move away from the home into a monitored setting where support is available. If these programs can become separate from the criminal justice system and encourage individual autonomy without the stigmatizing effect of earlier programs, perhaps some of the current generation of female offenders will have a better chance and not repeat the failures of previous generations when they become adults.

REFERENCES

Adams, S., and M. Q. Grant, *A Demonstration Project: An Evaluation of Community Located Treatment for Delinquents.* Sacramento: California Youth Authority, 1961.

Bahr, S., "Family Determinants and Effects of Deviance." In W. Burr, R. Hill, F. Nye, and I. Reiss (eds.), *Contemporary Theories About the Family.* New York: Free Press, 1979.

Blumstein, A., and J. Cohen, "Estimation of Individual Crime Rates from Arrest Records," *Journal of Criminal Law and Criminology,* 70, no. 4 (1979), 561–585.

Canter, R., "Family Correlates of Male and Female Delinquency," *Criminology* 20 (1982), 149–167.

Cernkovich, S., and P. Giordano, "Family Relationships and Delinquency," *Criminology* 25 (1987), 295–319.

Cowie, J., V. Cowie, and E. Slater, *Delinquency in Girls.* London: Heinemann, 1968.

Farber, E., and C. Kinast, "Violence in Families of Adolescent Runaways," *Child Abuse and Neglect* 8 (1984), 295–299.

Fischer, D. G., "Family Size and Delinquency," *Perceptual and Motor Skills* 58 (1984), 527–534.

Glueck, S., and E. Glueck, *Unravelling Juvenile Delinquency.* Cambridge, Mass.: Harvard University Press, 1950.

Glueck, S., and E. Glueck, *Delinquents and Non-delinquents in Perspective.* Cambridge, Mass.: Harvard University Press, 1968.

Gold, Martin, *Status Forces in Delinquent Boys.* Ann Arbor, Mich.: Institute for Social Research, 1963.

Gold, Martin, *Delinquency in an American City.* Monterey, Calif.: Brooks/Cole, 1970.

Gove, W., and R. Crutchfield, "The Family and Juvenile Delinquency," *Sociological Quarterly* 23 (1982), 301–319.

Hindelang, M. J., "Causes of Delinquency: A Partial Explication and Extension," *Social Problems* 20 (1973), 471–487.

Hirschi, T., *Causes of Delinquency.* Berkeley: University of California Press, 1969.

Hirschi, T., "Crime and Family Policy." In R. Weisheit and R. Culbertson (eds.), *Juvenile Delinquency: A Justice Perspective.* Prospect Heights, Ill.: Waveland, 1983.

Homer, L., "Community-Based Resources for Runaway Girls," *Social Casework* 54 (October 1973), 473–479.

Konopka, G., *The Adolescent Girl in Conflict.* Englewood Cliffs, N.J.: Prentice-Hall, 1966.

Laub, J., and R. Sampson, "Unraveling Families and Delinquency," *Criminology* 26 (1988), 355–377.

Lerman, P., *Community Treatment and Social Control: A Critical Analysis of Juvenile Correctional Policy.* Chicago: University of Chicago Press, 1975.

Loeber, R., and M. Southamer-Loeber, "Family Factors as Correlates and Predictors of Juvenile Conduct Problems and Delinquency." In M. Tonry and N. Marris (eds.), *Crime and Justice: An Annual Review of Research,* vol. 7. Chicago: University of Chicago Press, 1986.

Mann, C. R., "The Differential Treatment Between Runaway Boys and Girls in Juvenile Court," *Juvenile and Family Court Journal* 30, no. 2 (1979), 37–48.

McCord, J., "Some Child-Rearing Antecedents of Criminal Behavior in Adult Men," *Journal of Personality and Social Psychology,* 37 (1979), 1477–1486.

McCord, W., and J. McCord, *Origins of Crime.* New York: Columbia University Press, 1959.

Morris, Ruth, "Female Delinquents and Relational Problems," *Social Forces* 43 (1964), 82–89.

Nye, F., *Family Relationships and Delinquent Behavior.* New York: Wiley, 1958.

Osborn, S., and D. West, "The Effectiveness of Various Predictors of Criminal Careers," *Journal of Adolescence* 1 (1978), 101–117.

Palmer, T., *Correctional Intervention and Research.* Lexington, Mass.: D.C. Heath, 1974.

Patterson, G., *Coercive Family Process.* Eugene, Ore.: Castalia, 1982.

Robins, L., *Deviant Children Grown Up.* Baltimore: Williams & Wilkins, 1966.

Rosen, L., "Family and Delinquency: Structure or Function?" *Criminology* 23 (1985), 553–573.

Rosen, L., and K. Neilson, "Broken Homes." In L. Savitz and N. Johnston (eds.), *Contemporary Criminology,* New York: Wiley, 1982.

Rosenbaum, J., "Social Control, Gender and Delinquency: An Analysis of Drug, Property and Violent Offending." *Justice Quarterly* 4, no. 1 (1987), 117–132.

Rosenbaum, J., "Age, Race and Female Offending," *Journal of Contemporary Criminal Justice* 4, no. 3 (1988).

Russell, D., "On Running Away." In C. Wells and I. Stuart (eds.), *Self-Destructive Behavior in Children and Adolescents.* New York: Van Nostrand Reinhold, 1981.

Turner, Estelle, *A Girls' Group Home: An Approach to Treating Delinquent Girls in the Community.* Sacramento: California Youth Authority, 1969.

Van Voorhis, P., P. Cullen, R. Mathers, and C. Garner, "The Impact of Family Structure and Quality on Delinquency: A Comparative Assessment of Structural and Functional Factors," *Criminology* 26, no. 2 (1988), 235–261.

Warren, M. Q. and J. Rosenbaum, "Criminal Careers of Female Offenders," *Criminal Justice and Behavior* 13, no. 4 (1986), 393–418.

Webb, D., "More on Gender and Justice," *Sociology* 18, no. 3 (1984), 367–381.

Wells, E., and J. Rankin, "Direct Parental Controls and Delinquency," *Criminology* 26 (1988), 263–285.

West, D., and D. Farrington, *Who Becomes Delinquent?* London: Heinemann, 1973.

Wilkinson, K., "The Broken Family and Juvenile Delinquency: Scientific Explanation or Ideology?" *Social Problems* 23 (1974), 726–739.

DISCUSSION QUESTIONS
SECTION 8: THE FAMILY

1. Can we always assume that home life is better than institution-alization for the treatment of juvenile delinquents? What kinds of alternative community-based programs might be developed to bridge the gap between an abusive home life and the forced confinement of young people in penal types of facilities?

2. Where and how in our society do people learn how to be good parents? Is it really surprising to learn that mistreated children grow up to be mistreating parents? Being as specific as you can, what kinds of behaviors on the part of parents serve to generate conditions out of which delinquent behavior becomes likely?

3. Just what is a troubled home? What is the connection between troubled homes and the commission of delinquent acts? What particular kinds of troubled family life do girls, in particular, experience? Generally what are the consequences when troubled youth attempt to escape their home life by running to the streets?

4. What are some solutions for dealing with troubled youth? Juvenile institutions are often depicted as schools of crime. Some family environments are clearly criminogenic. What solutions exist? What can be done? In your opinion, what should be done?

Conclusion

Women's issues infuse every aspect of social and political thought. In this text we have focused on the areas of crime and criminal justice because our basic human rights in society are inextricably linked to our treatment by and our participation in the criminal justice system. The text, throughout, encourages the questioning of traditional assumptions concerning men, women, and their relationships. Due to the fact that our persons and our lives are reflections of us and what we do, what we say, and how we treat each other, we, as participating members of the human race, are ultimately responsible for human affairs. If the structure of society is found to be corrupt, we should work to change it. If problems are too big for one person or group to solve, we should come together in cooperation and mutual support. And if we as a social group are consistently trod upon, we, as victims, should be willing to do what is necessary to fight oppression and alleviate repressive conditions wherever they exist.

While focusing on the topics of women and the issues of women in present-day society, the underlying theme of the text is that of discrimination, oppression, estrangement, and alienation. The subject matter revolves around the criminal justice system because few aspects of social life reflect more clearly the status and treatment of women in society. Anyone who has ever been discriminated against and treated as inferior and subservient can identify with the struggles of women in contemporary society. The struggle of women continues.

There is no way to automatically allow both sexes to enjoy the equal protection of the laws unless we are commited to the elimination of all sexual discrimination. Women still struggle. We continue to repeat what Abigail Adams asked so long ago, "Remember the Ladies." This text is but another step in that long and arduous fight for freedom and equality.

Biographies of Editors

Roslyn Muraskin received her Ph.D degree from the Graduate Center of City University of New York in Criminal Justice. She holds an M.A. in Political Science from New York University and a B.A. in Political Science/Speech from Queens College. She is the Associate Dean of the College of Management at the C.W. Post Campus of Long Island University, as well as the Director of the School of Public Service. She holds the rank of Associate Professor of Criminal Justice at the Post Campus. Her publications include *Issues in Justice: Exploring Policy Issues in the Criminal Justice System* (1990); Foreword for *Criminal Justice Today: An Introductory Text for the Twenty-First Century* (1991); is the editor of the refereed Journal, *The Justice Professional;* contributed to *Ethics in Criminal Justice* (1990), "Police Work and Juveniles," in *Juvenile Justice, Policies, Programs and Services* (1989); was the editor of *Ethics, Justice and Fairness* (1988), *The Future of Criminal Justice Education* (1987), *Victims of Crime: Who Cares, A Study of Crime Victims* (1986), and *Women: Victims of Domestic Violence, Rape and Criminal Justice* (1985). Her major interests of research include women inmates in correctional facilities and issues of privacy as they pertain to women. She serves as the Vice-President of the Northeastern Association of Criminal Justice Sciences and Vice-President of the Northeastern Region of Criminal-Justice Educators of New York State.

Ted Alleman has a diverse professional background that includes working as a computer systems analyst, originating a publishing house that specializes in the publication of prisoner literature, administering a state agency, as well as teaching and writing in the social sciences. Ted graduated from the University of Delaware; California State University, Dominquez Hills; and spent three years working on his Ph.D. at Penn State. His interest in the concerns of women and women's issues stems from a personal belief in political libertarianism and a fascination with the study of human behavior in all its multifarious forms. Teaching and writing in the social sciences now serve as Ted's major preoccupations at Penn State University, where he holds a joint appointment in the departments of sociology and the administration of justice.

Biographies of Contributors

Shelley A. Bannister is an Associate Professor of Criminal Justice and Women's Studies at Northeastern Illinois University, a culturally diverse state university located in Chicago, Illinois. She is a criminal defense and civil rights attorney who has practiced in Illinois and federal courts for the last thirteen years. She has represented a number of women charged with criminal offenses, including the murders of their male partners/husbands. Many of her clients have been prisoners in state institutions. She holds an M.A. degree in Criminal Justice and is completing a dissertation towards her Ph.D. in Sociology with a concentration in Women's Studies.

Meda Chesney-Lind is an Associate Professor of Women's Studies at the University of Hawaii at Manoa. She is also Vice-President-elect of the American Society of Criminology. The author of over fifty monographs and papers on the subject of women and crime, she has just finished the first comprehensive book on female delinquency to be published in the United States since the 1950s, *Girls, Delinquency and Juvenile Justice*, written with Randall G. Shelden, is published by Brooks/Cole.

Joan C. Chrisler, Ph.D., is an Assistant Professor of Psychology at Connecticut College. Her research has focused on various aspects of women's physical and mental health, particularly premenstrual syndrome, menopause, and eating disorders. She is co-editor (with Doris Howard) of *New Directions in Feminist Psychology: Practice and Research*.

Laura T. Fishman is an Associate Professor of Sociology at the University of Vermont. She holds an M.A. in Sociology from the University of Chicago and a Ph.D. in Sociology from McGill University. Her major research and teaching interests include crime and corrections, women and crime, and families of prisoners. As a black criminologist, Professor Fishman has worked as a researcher in several low-income areas of Chicago and New York City. Her research activities have culminated in her having a street-wise familiarity with juvenile gangs, prostitution, and both organized and professional crime. Her publications include "Treacherous Trysts, Tender Trace: Prisoners' Wives as Contacts' Contraband Carriers," Spring 1991 in *Women and Criminal Justice;* "Visiting at the Prison: Renewed Courtship and the Prisoner's Wife," in *Free Inquiry in Creative Sociology,* 1988; "Stigmatization and Prisoners' Wives' Feeling of Shame," in *Deviant Behavior,* 1988; "Prisoners and Their Wives: Marital and Domestic Effects of Telephone Contacts and Home Visits," in the *International Journal of Contemporary Ethnography,* 1987.

Sean A. Grennan, Ph.D., is an Associate Professor of Criminal Justice at Long Island University/C.W. Post Campus, a private university located in Brookville, New York. Dr. Grennan received his Ph.D. in Criminal Justice from the Graduate Center of City University of New York. His major areas of research are women in policing, police use of deadly force, and organized crime. He is a former New York City police officer.

Thomas E. Guild, J.D., is an Associate Professor of Business Law at the University of Central Oklahoma. A licensed attorney, he has taught and researched in the areas of criminal law, constitutional law, and privacy rights. He recently co-authored (with Joan Luxenburg) an article on "HIV-Infected Inmate Assaults on Correctional Personnel," in the *Journal of Correctional Training,* September 1990.

Donna C. Hale, Ph.D., is Associate Professor of Criminal Justice at Shippensburg University. She is the co-editor of *What Works in Policing* (1992), as well as the author of several articles regarding police and society. Professor Hale has also served as guest editor for *Crime and Delinquency* and *Criminal Justice Review.*

Kathleen J. Hanrahan is an Assistant Professor in the Department of Criminology at Indiana University of Pennsylvania. She received her doctorate from Rutgers University, School of Criminal Justice. She is the author or co-author of several articles, monographs and books, including *The Question of Parole*, with Andrew von Hirsch; *A Handbook for Parole Board Members;* and "Criminal Code Revision and the Issue of Disparity" with Alex Greer.

Florence Horne is a social worker and family therapist. After receiving her M.S.W. from Adelphi University in 1979, Ms. Horne worked at Planned Parenthood of Nassau County, New York, where she was Director of Education and Counseling. In 1985 Ms. Horne became Director of Nassau County Services to Rape Victims, an organization that maintains a twenty-four-hour hotline and advocacy program and provides both professional training and continuing education. While in this position, Ms. Horne also served on the Executive Boards of the Nassau Coalition on Child Abuse and Neglect, as well as on the Nassau-Suffolk Task Force for Crime Victim Services.

Drew Humphries is an Associate Professor of Sociology at Rutgers University at Camden. She received her Doctorate of Criminology from the School of Criminology at the University of California, Berkeley, in 1973. She has published in the areas of social control, political economy of crime, and ideology. Recent publications focus on sexual assault and crack-addicted mothers. They include "Crack Addicted Mothers," in *Women and Criminal Justice* (Fall 1991); "Sexual Assault: Individual and Community Options in the Wake of Legal Reform" with co-author Susan Caringella-MacDonald, in *Criminology as Peace-Making*, eds. Richard Quinney and Harold Pepinsky, Indiana Press, 1991; and also with Susan Caringella-MacDonald, "Murdered Mothers, Missing Wives: Reconsidering Female Victimization," in 1990 edition of *Social Justice.*

Russ Immarigeon, M.S.W., graduated from the School of Social Welfare at the State University of New York at Stony Brook. He started his career in criminal justice as a sentencing advocate for the Legal Aid Society of New York. He has worked on research projects evaluating the effectiveness and feasibility of bail guidelines, mandatory sentences, sentencing guidelines, and substance abuse treatment. In the early 1980s he served as a state coordinator for the National Council on Crime and Delinquency. Later he worked as a consultant with such organizations as the Center for Effective Public Policy, the Maine Council of Churches, the Massachusetts Council for Public Justice, and the New York State Coalition for Criminal Justice. He has written widely about prison overcrowding, privatization, probation, and alternatives to incarceration for the *National Prison Project Journal, Corrections Compendium*, the *IARCA Journal*, and other publications. For five years he served as associate editor of *Criminal Justice Abstracts*.

Joan Luxenburg, Ed.D., ACSW, is a Professor of Sociology and Criminal Justice at the University of Central Oklahoma. Certified by the Oklahoma State Health Department as an AIDS Educator and a Test Site Counselor, Dr. Luxenburg leads a support group at the Oklahoma City AIDS Support Program. A former chair of the Sexual Behavior Division of the Society for the Study of Social Problems, Dr. Luxenburg has published articles on CB Radio Prostitution and is currently investigating the use of condoms in highway rest area prostitution and truck stop prostitution.

Daniel J. Menniti is Professor of Criminal Justice at Shippensburg University. He is a Ph.D. licensed psychologist as well as an attorney admitted to practice in state and federal courts. He has been a member of the Pennsylvania State Board of Pardons for twelve years and has authored several articles on law and psychology.

Alida Merlo has been a Professor of Criminal Justice at Westfield State College in Westfield, Massachusetts since 1975. It was through an undergraduate course in juvenile delinquency that she first became interested in criminal justice. After graduating from Youngstown State University, she became a Juvenile Court Probation Officer and then the Intake Supervisor for girls residing in Mahoning County in Ohio. She completed her master's degree in Criminal Justice at Northeastern University in Boston, Massachusetts, and was awarded the Doctor of Philosophy in Sociology at Fordham University in New York. Professor Merlo has served as the Trustee for Region One for the Academy of Criminal Justice Sciences, and currently serves as trustee-at-large. She is actively involved in professional organizations on the state, regional, and national levels. Her interests in criminal justice include corrections, women in criminal justice, juvenile justice, and criminology.

Susan L. Miller received her Ph.D. in Criminology from the University of Maryland. She is currently an Assistant Professor in the Sociology Department at Northern Illinois University. Her research interests include theories of punishment, gender and social control, and intimate violence. Her most recent publication is a study of courtship violence and gender implications for deterrence theory in *Law and Society Review* (co-authored with Sally Simpson).

Imogene L. Moyer, Ph.D., is Associate Professor of Criminology and Women's Studies at Indiana University of Pennsylvania. The second edition of her book, *The Changing Roles of Women in the Criminal Justice System*, was published in 1992. She also has published on women and crime in numerous professional journals. In addition to conducting research on child sexual abuse, she has done research on women's prisons, police processing of women offenders, the status of women in academia, and women pioneers in criminology.

Susan O. Reed is Coordinator of the Criminal Justice Program at the University of Wisconsin–Oshkosh. She has administered programs in adult and juvenile corrections, both institutional and community-based in Pennsylvania and New York. She holds an M.S.W. from the University of Pennsylvania and an M.P.A. and Ph.D. in Public Administration from New York University. Dr. Reed has studied the quality of mental health care in jails, programming for street people with AIDS, and programming for women and families with AIDS.

Albert R. Roberts received his doctorate in Social Welfare with a split minor in social work research and criminal justice from the University of Maryland at Baltimore in 1978. He is a fellow of the American Orthopsychiatric Association and a lifetime member of the Academy of Criminal Justice Sciences. He is a Professor and Director of the Administration of Justice Program at the School of Social Work at Rutgers University. His primary areas of teaching specialization include: Juvenile Justice, Justice in American Society, Correctional Systems, Family Violence, and Program Evaluation. He has over seventy-five publications to his credit, including research articles and several books on the topics of juvenile offender treatment and rehabilitation, correctional education, victim and witness assistance programs, wife abuse, and family violence. His most recent books include: *Crisis Intervention Handbook: Assessment, Treatment and Research* (1990); *Helping Crime Victims* (1990); and *Juvenile Justice: Policies, Programs and Services* (1989).

Jill Leslie Rosenbaum is Professor of Criminal Justice at California State University, Fullerton. She received her Ph.D. in 1983 from SUNY, Albany. She is completing a longitudinal study of a group of women who took part in an experimental program for delinquents during the 1960s. Her ongoing research interests include gender differences in delinquent behavior and the impact of popular culture on youth.

Inger J. Sagatun is a Professor in the Administration of Justice Department at San Jose State University, San Jose, California. She received her Ph.D. in Sociology from Stanford University in 1972 and has previously taught at the University of Bergen, Norway, and the University of California, Riverside. Her research is in the areas of juvenile delinquency, family violence, and child abuse and she is currently working on a book entitled *Child Maltreatment and the Law.*

Judith D. Simon holds a J.D. from Washington University Law School (1990) and is currently Assistant General Counsel, Office of General Counsel, Federal Bureau of Prisons, Department of Justice.

Rita J. Simon, a sociologist, is a University Professor in the School of Public Affairs at The American University. She has authored several books and articles in criminal justice, including *The Crimes Women Commit, The Punishment They Receive* (1990); *The Insanity Defense: A Critical Assessment of Law and Police in the Post-Hinckley Era* (1988); *The Jury: Its Role in American Society* (1980).

Nanci Koser Wilson is Associate Professor of Criminology at Indiana University of Pennsylvania, where she is also a member of the Women's Studies faculty. Feminist criminology has been her major focus; she taught one of the first courses on women and crime (in 1973 at Southern Illinois University) and is a co-founder of the American

Society of Criminology's Division on Women and Crime. Recent publications include: entries in the *Women's Studies Encyclopedia;* "Gendered Interaction in Criminal Homicide," in Anna F. Kuhl (ed.), *The Dynamics of the Victim-Offender Interaction* (Anderson Press); and, "Feminist Pedagogy in Criminology," *Journal of Criminal Justice Education,* 2, no. 1.